The Role
of Communication
in Learning to Model

The Role of Communication in Learning to Model

Edited by

Paul Brna
University of Northumbria at Newcastle

Michael Baker
CNRS & Université Lumière Lyon 2

Keith Stenning
University of Edinburgh

Andrée Tiberghien
CNRS & Université Lumière Lyon 2

2002

LAWRENCE ERLBAUM ASSOCIATES, PUBLISHERS
Mahwah, New Jersey   London

Lawrence Erlbaum Associates, Inc., Publishers
10 Industrial Avenue
Mahwah, NJ 07430

Cover design by Kathryn Houghtaling Lacey

Library of Congress Cataloging-in-Publication Data

The role of communication in learning to model / edited by
Paul Brna ... [et al.].
     p.   cm.
Includes bibliographical references and index.
ISBN 0-8058-4064-8 (cloth : alk. paper)
1. Communication in education. 2. Education—Simulation
methods. 3. Models and modelmaking.   I. Brna, Paul.
LB1033.5 .R65   2002
371.102'2—dc21   2001053242
                                                       CIP

Books published by Lawrence Erlbaum Associates are printed
on acid-free paper, and their bindings are chosen for strength
and durability.

Printed in the United States of America
10 9 8 7 6 5 4 3 2 1

Contents

List of Contributors

Keith Stenning: *University of Edinburgh, Scotland*
James G. Greeno: *Stanford University, USA*
Rogers Hall: *University of California at Berkeley, USA*
Melissa Sommerfeld: *Stanford University, USA*
Muffie Wiebe: *Stanford University, USA*
Jacques Vince: *UMR GRIC-COAST, Université Lumière Lyon 2, France*
Andrée Tiberghien: *UMR GRIC-COAST, Université Lumière Lyon 2, France*
John R. Frederiksen: *University of Washington, USA*
Barbara Y. White: *University of California at Berkeley, USA*
Rosemary Luckin: *University of Sussex, England*
Benedict du Boulay: *University of Sussex, England*
Zvia Fund: *Bar-Ilan University, Israel*
Anders Bouwer: *University of Amsterdam, The Netherlands*
Vania Bessa Machado: *University of Amsterdam, The Netherlands*
Bert Bredeweg: *University of Amsterdam, The Netherlands*
Susan Bull: *University of Birmingham, England*
Vania Dimitrova: *Leeds University, England*
Paul Brna: *University of Northumbria at Newcastle, England*
Mark Burton: *ARM, England*
Kristine Lund: *UMR GRIC, CNRS & Université Lumière Lyon 2, France*
Denis Alamargot: *Laboratoire LaCo-CNRS, Université de Poitiers, France*
Jerry Andriessen: *University of Utrecht, The Netherlands*
Michael Baker: *UMR GRIC, CNRS & Université Lumière Lyon 2, France*

Preface

Understanding how students learn to model is a multidisciplinary activity. It can be argued that those working in different disciplines such as physics, maths, economics, and history may generate different views of the process of modeling. These views, in turn, have implications for how learning to model is understood, and how this might be supported pedagogically. Because most pedagogical situations involve communicative interactions between students and teachers, as well as interactions with complex learning resources, such as computers, there is a persuasive argument that experts who study modeling in different disciplines need to work together with experts in linguistics, cognitive psychology, artificial intelligence, as well as various social (and human) sciences.

In this book we see a number of experts from different disciplines taking a look at three different strands in learning to model. They examine the activity of modeling from different theoretical standpoints, taking into account the individual situation of the different individuals involved. First, there is a need for models to be related one to another, sometimes to understand the relationships that hold between putative variants, sometimes to understand different kinds of phenomena and how they relate to each other and to theoretical models that have a perceived bearing on the phenomena. For example, accounts of learning at a symbolic level and at a neurological level may help us understand the interplay between the affective and cognitive aspects of learning (Damasio, 1999). Further, accounts of how learners negotiate the different representational systems themselves need to be analyzed and understood. The process of inspecting the ways in which modeling can be studied may in turn help researchers (cognitive scientists, linguists, narratologists, psychologists, educationalists, etc.) understand the kinds of difficulties faced by learners, and hopefully, move toward new and more insightful models of the processes by which learning to model takes place.

One of the central modeling processes is that of coordination of initially disparate representations into a heterogeneous reasoning system. This coordination can be understood as the development of representational practices that occur in discourse and engage learners in social interaction (chap. 1, this volume). Models built by learners need to be examined carefully by the learners themselves in order that they may understand the relationships that hold between various concepts. Encouraging and supporting the mapping between the relationships that hold between phenomena and theoretical constructs may be needed to help the learner build a model with added confidence (chap. 2, this volume). If coordination is necessary, and we would argue that it is, then so is communication and the ways this might be organized. Communication in interactions can take several forms, each of which may relate in different ways to cooperative modeling and learning. One such form of interaction is argumentative interaction, that may force students to differentiate different types of knowledge that are drawn upon in modeling (chap. 11, this volume). When people work together to learn to model then the different communicative roles that can be adopted can have an important effect (chap. 8, this volume).

The study of communication and coordination in the context of learning to model should illuminate both our understanding of communication and coordination and our understanding of learning to model in its various forms. We can also examine the different ways in which we might seek to "provoke" learners to examine the links between models and to understand the various relationships that hold between different entities involved in the modeling processes. The process of "engineering" productive interactions through the use of ICT technologies needs to be informed by work of this kind.

The ways in which communication supports learning to model raises the issue of the relation of education to communication. The enterprise of education involves a species of communication, even if this has not been the commonest conceptualization of education itself. Educational communication is a particularly hard case for theories of communication. Teaching a student a new concept constitutes an episode of communication, one that has the distinctive property that its parties do not share a language at its outset. They may share all the words they need, at least if no new technical terms are used. They may even implicitly share the concepts which figure in the episode, before it takes place. But they do not share the assignment of concepts to words which the teacher intends that the student should acquire, and which the teacher regards as largely diagnostic of the student having succeeded. For learning to have taken place, this new assignment of concepts to words must make some real difference to what the student can do with the new explicit concept. Usually, the key performance is to make new inferences. And when the student has succeeded, teacher and student do share a new language within which they can communicate about the topic. So a language new to the student is constructed during the communication episode, even though not all learning takes place *during* communication.

Theories of communication need to be able to understand this communication of languages as distinct from communication within languages. Theories of education, as a species of communication, inherit this need. Practices of education have to be aimed at facilitating this difficult kind of communication. Logic is one of the oldest theories of communication. Teaching logic is one of the oldest educational practices. Logic as a theory and as an educational practice can be understood as attempting to make this task of communicating languages easier. Logic is a model of communication, and teaching logic is teaching students to model their own communicative practices.

The chapters in this book seek to bridge the modeling of communication and the modeling of particular scientific domains. In so doing they seek to throw light on the educational communication that goes on in conceptual learning.

In the first part of the book, Stenning, Greeno, Hall, Sommerfield, and Wiebe take as their data recordings of a group of middle school children learning mathematical and scientific concepts about biology—population dynamics—with the aid of computer models of populations. They seek to show that three levels of analysis—logical semantic analysis of the representations involved; discourse analysis of the group dialogue dynamics; and analysis of social role adoption—are all required to understand the conceptual learning that takes place. They see conceptual learning as learning to coordinate materials from the plethora of representations involved (e.g., texts, spoken dialogue, diagrams, interfaces, gestures) into an integrated heterogeneous reasoning system.

Vince and Tiberghien describe a theoretical perspective on the process of modeling which emphasizes the relationships between the world of theory and model, and the world of objects and events. An exploration is provided of the notion of establishing relations between different semiotic registers associated with a concept or relations between concepts with the hypothesis that conceptual understanding requires constructing relations between the different external representations of a given concept or conceptual relation. Taking into account the kinds of difficulties that students have, they demonstrate how to design an environment for learning about the physics of sound including concepts such as vibration, propagation, frequency, and amplitude.

Fredericksen and White take as their data recordings of groups of high school children engaged in learning about electricity. The innovative curriculum links the learning of models of many different levels of analysis of electrical phenomena from the behavior of electrons to the dynamics of circuits, presented again in a rich representational repertoire of diagrams, language, and animation. The authors conceptualize learning as involving the linking of these models together into an integrated understanding.

In the second part of the book, the focus turns to how to provoke students to model. Luckin and de Boulay explore the relationship between interaction and communication in the design of interactive learning systems for middle school and high school students learning the concepts of ecology and evolutionary biology. They compare an individually used system that allows running of population models with a collaboratively used system supporting the production of textual arguments and explanations. In the one the user and computer communicate; in the other it is mainly the intra-group communications that drive learning. Subtle changes in the design of the students' interactions with the computer lead to large changes in the kind of modeling that students engaged in.

Fund describes a study that examines several kinds of support for learning science using a computer-based problem solving environment. The combinations of these kinds of components were then used to construct support programs derived from a study of teaching. Fund finds an important value in the provision of support for the activation and deployment of meta-cognitive skills such as monitoring and control, self-assessment, and self-regulation. Fund is particularly interested in the ways in which students develop and exploit some external representation of their knowledge.

Bouwer, Machado, and Bredeweg describe their approach to the construction of an interactive model building environment that supports scientific investigation by allowing students to build models and experiment with them. The strength of their work is the combination of an environment in which model of scientific phenomena can be built, and an environment within which predictions can be checked.

Bull, Dimitrova, and Brna describe an approach to the design of learning environments that focuses on reflection through a dialogic process which entails the learner externalizing some part of their model of the world which is then used to generate a model of the learner (student model). Then this student model becomes the means by which reflection is stimulated. The externalization process goes hand in hand with transformation because the expression that describes the elements of the model has to be constructed.

In the third part of the book, we focus on communication and language. Brna and Burton draw on Tiberghien's view of learning to model in physics to investigate how several students collaborate in a modeling activity to construct an external representation. They describe an approach based on building a simulation of this interaction where the primary factor is a system of roles that captures notions of linguistic and "physical" activity. The Clarissa system allows for an exploration of the value of how to organize the reallocation of different roles at various points in the discourse, allowing several agents to work together to construct and use a shared external representation of their physics understanding. The activity of building a model of those learning to model inevitably focuses on a small range of issues. In this chapter, the role of shared external representations is considered.

Lund provides an interesting study based on an analysis of a multi-participant interaction involving the ways in which teachers study the dialogue of students, and come to understand how students model. She examines the extent to which teachers actually integrate what they have learned during their training into their professional practice, and how teachers can be helped to learn how students model. This approach has value for those concerned with how to incorporate modeling more effectively into school curricula.

Alamargot and Andriessen take the differences between spoken and written language in learning as their topic and seek to apply theories of writing to the development of insights into learning. Computer mediated collaborative learning disentangles some of the diverse differences. Computer chat has obvious similarities to written text (it is visual, and at least possibly persistent) but shares other aspects with the spoken word—chiefly its synchronicity. The learning of writing is the fundamental formalization of natural language communicative habits that underlies all later formalizations, such as logic and mathematics.

Finally, Baker argues that one particular type of social interaction—argumentative interaction—plays a specific and important role in one aspect of learning science: learning to model. In order to support this claim, he first describes epistemic, cognitive, and linguistic dimensions of modeling in science, and of argumentative interactions, and then proposes general relations between them. These general claims are then illustrated by analysis of three specific interaction sequences, drawn from corpora collected in situations that were designed for learning to model. It is concluded that argumentative interactions embody discursive operations by which different types of concepts and knowledge are dissociated from each other, this being a necessary precursor to establishing complex relations between models and their associated experimental fields, that is, to modeling itself.

The different chapters brought together in this volume illustrate the diversity and vivacity of research on a hitherto relatively neglected, yet crucially important, aspect of education across disciplines: learning to model. Learning to model is crucial if students are to be able to go beyond calculation and formal reasoning to understand the fundamental concepts that underlie many disciplines, in close relation to the world in which they live. A common thread across the research presented here is the view that communication and interaction, as fundamental to most educational practices, as a repository of conceptual understanding and a learning mechanism in itself, is intimately linked to elaborating meaningful, coherent, and valid representations of the world—in other words, to modeling.

Finally, it is hoped that this volume will both contribute to fundamental research in its field and ultimately provide results that can be of practical value in designing new situations for teaching and learning modeling, particularly those involving computers.

ACKNOWLEDGMENTS

The editors wish to thank the European Union who sponsored the C-LEMMAS Conference held at Ajaccio, Corsica in April 1999. The event entitled "Roles of Communicative Interaction in Learning to Model in Mathematics and Science" provided the basic idea for this book, and was supported via EU TMR Contract No ERBFMMACT970285. From a practical point of view, we thank all those that helped to make the C-LEMMAS conference a success—especially Irene Rudling, Vania Dimitrova, and Shelagh Cooper.

REFERENCE

Damasio, A. (1999). *The feeling of what happens: Body and emotion in the making of consciousness*. New York: Harcourt Brace.

I

Coordinating
Representations

Coordinating Mathematical With Biological Multiplication: Conceptual Learning as the Development of Heterogeneous Reasoning Systems

Keith Stenning
University of Edinburgh

James G. Greeno
Stanford University

Rogers Hall
University of California at Berkeley

Melissa Sommerfeld
Stanford University

Muffie Wiebe
Stanford University

INTRODUCTION

The goal of this chapter is to exemplify deep conceptual learning that involves the coordination of initially disparate representations into a heterogeneous reasoning system. This coordination can be understood as the development of representational practices that occur in discourse and engage learners in social interaction. We analyze data from three perspectives with the aim of comparing and integrating approaches that are sometimes considered to be in tension. The three approaches are: a foundational semantic analysis of the heterogeneous representations encountered in the learning situation; an interactional analysis of discourse structures that facilitate group reasoning and understanding; and an interactional analysis of how coordinated representational practices expand and stabilize within a discipline-specific domain of inquiry. Our hope is that by combining these approaches, our analysis will treat equally important aspects of representational content, discourse structure, and changes in conceptual understanding as achievements of talk-in-interaction. The chapter has it origins in a collaborative analysis reported in three separate works (Greeno, Sommerfeld, & Wiebe, 2000; Hall, 2000; Stenning & Sommerfeld, 2000). Here, we collect these analyses together and offer integration.

This chapter adds to a line of work in cognitive studies of mathematics education that examines how learners work at the interface between representing and represented worlds to make inferences, identify and recover from conceptual errors, and manage calculation (Cobb, Yackel, & McClain, 1999; Hall, 1996; Nathan, Kintsch, & Young, 1992; Nemirovsky, in press). The data we analyze are videotaped recordings of incidents of group activity drawn from a longitudinal case study of students working in a project-based, middle school mathematics curriculum unit (Goldman, Moschkovich, & The Middle-school Mathematics through Applications Project [MMAP] Team, 1995). This longitudinal case study was part of a research project comparing the use of mathematics in classrooms and adult workplaces where people work together to design things (Hall, 1999), conducted in public school classrooms and professional firms around the San Francisco Bay area. The students were concurrently learning mathematical and scientific concepts about population dynamics by learning to model populations. The MMAP curriculum was developed as a practical pedagogical response to the theoretical problem about conceptual learning that concerns us here. As psychologists and educators (e.g., Brownell, 1935; Wertheimer, 1959) have long recognized, it is one thing for students to learn the operation of a novel mathematical or scientific formalism. It is quite another for them to understand the meaning of that formalism in terms of general concepts and to master its application to new situations. MMAP's response to this crucial educational problem is to teach mathematical formalisms (e.g., graphs and difference equations for functions) and scientific terminology and representations together in a context of their application, in the belief that this concurrent learning can provide a semantically based grasp of their application to the world. Our theoretical task is to find productive relations between analyses of heterogeneous representation systems, learning in group discourse, and studies of the interactional structure of discipline-specific representational practice to help illuminate the learning processes evidenced in this data.

This is not only a theoretical exercise or a problem that is specific to educational research. A central process in scientific or mathematical thinking involves being able simultaneously to look *at* and *through* the interface between representing and represented worlds (Gravemeijer, 1994; Latour, 1999). This is particularly true of thinking practices in which people construct and then explore models to gain access to situations that do not yet exist or that occur across scales of time and space that prevent direct observation. Although this flexible use of modeling is central to many disciplines, pedagogy has until recently focused primarily on the notational structure of formal systems of representation. This approach can trap learners in the situation of looking at complex representational systems without being able to look through them to construct and explore represented worlds (Greeno & Hall, 1997). The MMAP curriculum seeks to avoid this pitfall of the separation of formalism from its understanding and application by concurrently teaching mathematical formalism and scientific concepts, through the modeling of realistic situations assisted by computers. Mature mastery of a formalism does not simply replace looking at with looking through, but means that students can control the level of their attention appropriately for reasoning.

Heterogeneous Reasoning as Rules of Transformation

Linguistic inference rules turn sentences into other sentences, but in recent years there has been much discussion of heterogeneous reasoning systems that have representations in more than one modality (commonly diagrams and sentences) and so require rules that represent sentential information diagrammatically and diagrammatic information sententially. Theoretical interest in heterogeneous reasoning stems, in part, from the fact that much everyday reasoning is heterogeneous. We encounter information in linguistic form, but we also receive diagrammatic information such as maps, graphs, and diagrams, and even when we only encounter linguistic representations, we commonly encounter them in situations where we also have nonlinguistic perceptual input of spatial information about speakers and about their and our own embedding in the world. People generally succeed rather well in combining these different information sources, for example, by using diagrams, material models, or computer programs to simulate events in ways that support conjectures and test hypotheses (e.g., Clement, 1989; Schwartz & Black, 1996; Schwartz, Yerushalmy, & Wilson, 1993).

With this starting point, we are necessarily concerned with the semantics of formal systems—relations between the formalisms and the things they stand for. But in the kind of deep conceptual learning with which we are concerned here, target concepts are not easily differentiated from alternative interpretations by pointing at objects in the world. The classical physical concepts of weight, volume, density, and mass illustrate this point. Every object we can point to has all of these attributes, but pointing does not help differentiate the concepts. As a result, these concepts can only be differentiated by observing which physical transformations preserve which properties. Compression preserves weight and mass, but alters volume and density. Transport to the moon alters weight but not mass, and so on. These physical operations correspond to informational transformations in the representation systems we use to reason about them—informational transformations that in logic are called *inference rules*. Inference rules allow the transformation of representations into other representations with preservation of truth. Stenning (1999) argued for the central role of transformations in learning abstract scientific and mathematical concepts.

Practical pedagogical interest in heterogeneous reasoning stems from the conviction that students should have access to the semantics of representational systems as they learn them, both to support their understanding of their conceptual meanings and to achieve generalization to new circumstances. Classical studies of learning the area of a parallelogram demonstrated that by having young students attend to transformations that convert parallelograms to rectangles (Wertheimer, 1959) or that slide a stack of cards, keeping area, base, and height invariant while varying the angles and perimeter of the figure (Sayeki, Ueno, & Nagasaka, 1991), the students can abstract the quantitative relation between the base, height, and area of the figure and understand and generalize the formula. Brownell (1935) studied learning of place-value addition and subtraction and showed that use of concrete models can support children's understanding the operations of carrying and borrowing, and Resnick and Omanson (1987) found that students who benefited from experience relating procedures with numerical symbols to analogous operations on place-value blocks in reducing the "bugs" in their test performance (Brown & Burton, 1980) also talked more about the correspondence between the operations in the formal symbolic and material domains.

Barwise and Etchemendy (1994) pioneered the foundational study of heterogeneous reasoning systems through their development of Tarski's World and Hyperproof, multimodal computer environments for learning elementary logic. Stenning and his coworkers studied the cognitive impact of such heterogeneous reasoning systems on students' learning (e.g., Oberlander, Monaghan, Cox, Stenning, & Tobin, 1999; Stenning, Cox, & Oberlander, 1995). The upshot of their studies of undergraduate students is that conceptual learning in Hyperproof can be understood as acquisition of the strategy and tactics of using transformations for moving information between modalities. Students who learn well from the heterogeneous system acquire a deep understanding of when, during problem solving, to move information from sentences into diagrams, and when in the reverse direction. Students who fail to benefit from diagrams fail because they have not mastered these strategies. This strategic learning (in this case about the concepts of logic) can be understood as learning to coordinate the various representations used in Hyperproof into an integrated heterogeneous reasoning system containing inference rules that deal with combinations of sentential and diagrammatic information.

This chapter poses the question whether we can extend the theoretical framework developed for analyzing logic learning in Hyperproof to groups of students learning to model population dynamics. This is a substantial extension. Hyperproof is a fully formalized and implemented heterogeneous representation system with identifiable rules of inference. The system of mathematical and scientific concepts that make up the understanding of population dynamics is both much richer and less circumscribed. Furthermore, the activity we analyzed was crucially group learning, whereas the Hyperproof students' data was largely from individuals learning by interacting with the computer. Nevertheless, there are many parallels between the two situations. The MMAP student groups are certainly engaged in learning and reasoning with many different kinds of representation. They have worksheets, reference texts, graphs, graphical computer interfaces, etc. The concepts being learned (exponential growth of populations, the composition of mathematical functions, etc.) are abstract in comparable ways with the abstract concepts of introductory logic.

Heterogeneous Reasoning as Discourse

Analyses of learning heterogeneous reasoning systems have, so far, ignored group learning. Group learning introduces two further theoretical perspectives: the discourse of learning and the social practices of representational use. Taking the perspective of the discourse of group learning focuses attention on the conditions under which groups succeed or fail in coordinating formalisms and their world of reference. Of particular importance are the conditions of explanation. When is it permissible to request an explanation and what will count as an acceptable explanation? When is a proffered explanation deemed satisfactory so that work can continue along the preexisting trajectory, and when should it be acknowledged as demanding a realignment of that trajectory? These questions implicitly refer to perceived audiences to which the group has responsibilities. That audience may be the group itself, with its own canons of adequacy, or it may implicitly or explicitly be some larger community—perhaps most often represented by the group's class—whose norms for explanation may or may not be the same.

Recently, research studies examined discourse in activities that support growth of students' conceptual understanding. For example, Hall and Rubin (1998) examined the development of a representational practice in a classroom taught by Magdalene Lampert, involving a problem of calculating the distance a car would travel, given its speed and the duration of a trip. In one incident analyzed in Hall and Rubin's study, Lampert asked one student to explain to another why numbers for time and rate should be multiplied in this problem. The student explained by drawing a diagram that Hall and Rubin called a "journey line," inscribing distances above the line and times below so that corresponding durations and distances coincided. Lampert then revoiced this explanation (O'Conner & Michaels, 1996), bringing the representational device into the discourse of the whole class and making the representation and its meaning part of the class's common ground. Hall and Rubin argued from this and other examples that relations between uses of representational resources in private, local, and public discourse settings in the classroom constitute important factors in conceptual learning.

A general feature of discourse that favors students' conceptual learning is that differing views are expressed and efforts are made to reconcile differences (Sfard & Kieren, 2001; Tudge & Rogoff, 1989). In ongoing analyses in our Stanford laboratory we are finding that *problematizing* issues and *authorizing* students in discourse are factors that contribute to students' having productive interactions (Engle & Conant, in preparation; Engle, Conant, Wiebe, Erickson, & Greeno, 2000). By problematizing an issue, we refer to construction of a question or argument for which different participants in a conversation have opinions or understandings that disagree, and they recognize a need to resolve or, at least understand, their disagreement. By authorizing students, we refer to positioning them in participation structures so they are entitled and expected to voice their opinions, to require explanations and justifications of themselves and each other, and to work toward agreement or, at least mutual understanding, of significant problematic issues.

The idea that problematizing issues should facilitate learning and understanding fits with a long tradition of theorizing in the psychology of thinking. Dewey (1910/1985) proposed that occasions for thinking are situations involving some inconsistency or incoherence that is perceived as requiring some resolution, to be achieved by reflective thinking. Wertheimer (1959) discussed conditions fostering productive thinking as gaps that are sensed as requiring closure. Problematized issues, with participants authorized to resolve them, correspond in interaction to the kinds of situations that Dewey, Wertheimer, and many others characterized as being conducive to the generation of meaningful understanding and reasoning.

Heterogeneous Reasoning as an Interactional Achievement

Representational systems provide resources for learners to solve problems and give explanations in stable classroom discourse structures. In our third perspective, we analyze how these resources, in use, come to be organized in ways that resemble discipline-specific forms of mathematical reasoning (i.e., using related functions to model interactions between populations and their habitat). From this perspective, we also analyze some of the ways in which discourse structures involving explanation are actually achieved in ongoing talk-in-interaction. In our analysis, computational media and other resources available through talk and embodied action develop into systems of activity (Goodwin, 1994) that make up conceptual understanding. From this perspective, concepts and their implementation in diverse representational technologies are inseparable.

This aspect of our analysis builds on previous studies of how adult design professionals with different levels of work experience (e.g., senior vs. junior civil engineers) or different disciplinary backgrounds (e.g., entomology vs. biostatistics) engage in "teaching and learning events" around moments of disruptions and repair (Hall & Stevens, 1995, 1996; Hall, Stevens, & Torralba, in press; Stevens & Hall, 1998). These studies were sited within the very disciplinary practices that the MMAP curriculum hopes to render for children, and they show that the same kinds of learning through discourse and interactive coordination continue to occur among school alumni who have entered these domains of instruction as professionals.

Our analyses of discourse and semantics as interactional achievements consider how participation structures in a classroom position students as proposers, explainers, formalists, directors, and other relevant roles within the classroom. Our analysis of discipline-specific representation also considers how children are positioned as biological consultants, farmers, fish (predator or prey), and competent or incompetent middle school mathematics students in the incidents that we analyze. One of the intended functions of the MMAP units is to create a fictive world that positions learners outside their lived experience as children and inside, to a level of approximation that depends on their engagement, an adult professional world. In this sense, MMAP units do not just involve "applications" of mathematical concepts, but they provide "imaginable worlds" (J. Knudsen, personal communication) in which the application of mathematical concepts is motivated. In this sense, we expect to find emergent goals within students' work on classroom design projects that reflect the fictive worlds provided in the unit. Following Leont'ev (1981; see also Saxe, 1991; Saxe & Guberman, 1998), we expect these goals to reflect objectives that are thematically associated with professional communities that use mathematical concepts for discipline-specific purposes. In the longitudinal case we analyze in this chapter, those intended thematic objectives have to do with conservation and species management, most visibly brought forward in a fictive consulting world in which students are asked to act as biological consultants to Venezuelan rice farmers. What is surprising, under our analysis, is that students engage in this extended consulting scenario not only as biological consultants, but also as fish, as farmers, and as concerned owners of a predatory species. These emergent positions complement the intended position of mathematics-using biological consultants in ways that are relevant for quantitative reasoning in the models students build to investigate a stream habitat and later use to make arguments about biological conservation and management.

EMPIRICAL SETTING

Data for this chapter come from studies conducted in middle school mathematics classrooms where students worked on design projects. These projects were supported by curriculum units developed to embed important mathematical concepts in realistic applications (Greeno &

MMAP, 1998). The study reported in this chapter is drawn from a larger investigation that included observations of group modeling efforts in a project-based middle school mathematics classroom (Hall, 1999). Students worked in a curriculum unit called Guppies, in which they created mathematical models of biological population growth and ran simulations on computers. As part of this unit, students were to learn both about how to construct mathematical models of population growth and about the mathematical functions (linear and exponential) that underlie them. Specifically, students were asked to act as biological consultants who would devise a proposal for preserving and then returning a population of guppies to a Venezuelan stream environment.

As adapted for use in this classroom, the project lasted approximately 4 weeks and included the following: task memos directing the activities of student groups, worksheets and supporting case material for the contexts of design problems; a software tool (HabiTech™) that allowed students to model and investigate structures and processes in population biology, and a set of extension scenarios asking students to model hypothetical events within the Venezuelan stream environment (e.g., harvesting by farmers or the introduction of a predatory fish). Our analyses focus on a group of students, Manuel, Lisa, Kera, and Nick (the MLKN group), whose improvement on pre/post assessments place them about midway in learning of the half a dozen focus groups videotaped by Hall and his colleagues (Hall, 1999) during this unit in three different classrooms. Figure 1.1 shows how the MLKN group used HabiTech to build a network model of predation and a graph showing an extinction crisis for guppies during their third year in a Venezuelan pond (discussed later). The network consists of linked nodes defining quantities either for populations or for a variety of functions that influence these populations (i.e., birth rate, death rate, rate of immigration, emigration, and user-defined functions). These networks are dynamically linked to graphs and tables showing the values of user-selected quantities (e.g., the graph to the left in Fig. 1.1). Students can "play" their network models by setting a timeline and controlling the flow of time using an interface that resembles a generic tape player (top of Fig. 1.1).

OBSERVATIONS, ANALYSIS, AND ARGUMENT: CHANGES IN CAPACITY FOR WORKING WITH CONCEPTS OF POPULATION GROWTH AND PREDATION

We report examples of interaction in which students achieved understanding that we interpret in terms of successful heterogeneous reasoning; that is, we argue that their conceptual understanding occurred through the coordination of representational resources. We also report examples in which students' understanding fell short, and we interpret these as examples in which coordination between representational resources did not occur.

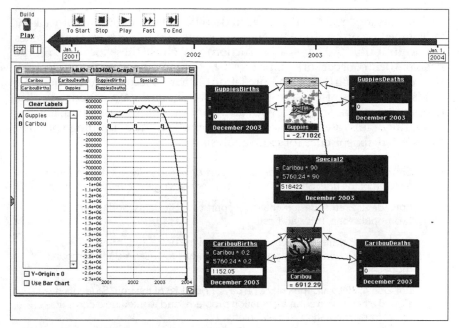

FIG. 1.1. MLKN's network model of predation and a graph showing an extinction crisis for Guppies during their third year in a Venezuelan pond. The predation node is at the center of the network (right), linking together Guppies (top) and Caribou/Wolf Fish (bottom).

In particular, we focus on how a group of students developed an increasingly sophisticated capacity for working with the concept of predation, treated as a functional relation between animal populations (i.e., predator and prey) that can be implemented in particular computational media. An utterance-level comparison of the MLKN group's performance on a pre- and postunit design challenge showed that at the end of the 4-week unit they, like the majority of groups in their classroom (5 of 7 groups), were able to construct and explore a more complete functional model of population growth and predation. In contrast, at the pretest challenge this group failed to mention deaths for either population, they did not link together overlapping timelines for otherwise correct models of mouse and cat births, and they made no mention or use of the concept of predation until questioned about it.

We also focus on episodes in which these same students were required to provide numerical values of a variable referred to as *birthrate*. In one of these episodes they avoided a conceptual error; in others they did not, and we endeavor to explain this.

The learning incidents discussed in this chapter were chosen from a daily videotaped record of the MLKN group's classroom work on the Guppies curriculum unit (20 days of instruction). We chose these incidents on the basis of their conceptual significance (i.e., they involve significant work on the concepts of birthrate and predation); their susceptibility to the three kinds of analysis of concern (i.e., we have detailed data concerning students' talk, action, and work with diverse representational media); and because they illustrate both successful and problematical learning episodes. We selected six episodes for close analysis:

Episode 1: Pretest design challenge, part one. Took place 2 days prior to the start of the unit. Students worked to model a single population of mice.

Episode 2: Pretest design challenge, part two. Students worked to model two populations, mice and cats.

Episode 3: Birthrate. Took place on day 9 of the unit. Students worked on a worksheet to construct a population birthrate for use in their computer model.

Episode 4: Net wall. Took place on days 17 and 18 of the unit. Students designed a net wall to solve a predation problem, and worked on a computational implementation of their solution.

Episode 5: Posttest design challenge, part one. Took place 5 days after the unit. Students again worked to model a single population of mice.

Episode 6: Posttest design challenge, part two. Students again worked with two populations, mice and cats.

Linear Versus Exponential Growth (Episode 1: Pretest, Part 1)

The initial incident from the pretest phase of the Guppies unit sees the students make at least part of one of the fundamental conceptual discoveries of this field: that population models have a recursive characteristic that leads to exponential growth if unchecked—Malthus' equation.

This episode took place prior to the beginning of the unit. Although the students had been in class together all year (the unit began in May), this was the first time this group of students worked together. The assignment the students were given involved projecting how large a population of mice would be in 2 years, given that the mice population starts off at 20 mice and that the mice reproduce every year. The researcher (who was videotaping the interactions) read the problem aloud to the students (the students also had the written problem in front of them), and told them that they had 20 minutes to complete the problem.

The students began to solve the problem using a population model that corresponds to linear growth: They figured out how many seasons the mice would reproduce (8), how many babies the mice would have each season (4, for each of 10 mouse couples), and then came up with a figure that represented the final size of the mouse population (340; 20

originals plus 320 babies). As the students started to graph their answer, however, one of the students noted that the group forgot a crucial fact when calculating their answer: The babies who are born in one season will in turn have babies the next season. That is, the group discovered the recursive nature of population growth in this pretest designed to elicit their conceptual starting points before teaching interventions.

We use two conventions for presenting transcripts. In the first, we compress turns at talk by leaving out material that does not relate directly to our analysis, as reflected in the line numbering. The speaker is indicated by first initial (M, L, K, or N).

60	M	so there's ... equals 40 babies each season
65	M	it's three hundred and twenty
66	K	(inaudible) is that including adults?
67	M	no, three hundred and twenty plus twenty
69	M	by the end of the winter
70	M	three hundred and forty mouse ... mice ... mices. OK.
73	M	Now we need to make a graph of it .

Using a second transcript convention, we show continuous turns at talk to enable an analysis of the sequential organization of students' contributions to ongoing work on modeling animal populations. Again, speakers are indicated by first initial, descriptions of relevant actions (e.g., gesture, gaze, or work with inscriptions) are shown in double parentheses, and the onset/termination of overlapping talk is shown with left and right square brackets (i.e., [onset ... termination]). As the group turns to making a graph, students are attending to different representations, and we need to examine more of the details of interaction.

171	L	Ok um, I don't get why you got sixty. ((leans back, soft laugh, and looks at K))
172	K	That's what I'm think[ing, I was like, where does this come from? ((eyebrows raised and furrowed))
173	M	[Because, OK, ((points up with pencil)) in the first season came out ((pencil beats on table)) forty babies ((looking at L; L and K looking at M))
174	L	Uh huh ((stands, leans against table))
175	M	And then but there's that, ((pen circles on table)) twenty original.
176	K	Oh, so [there's sixty mice altogether, ok. ((looks up, nodding))
177	L	[Oh yeah, ok.
178	M	So there's sixty. ((returns to graph and ruler))
179	K	Ok. ((nodding, glances at camera and returns gaze to L))
180	M	[((marking graph)) See now the first season is over here:::
181	L	[And the second season, that's (an) increase, so then its::: [forty and (3 sec) Wait a minute!

182	K	[Sixty::: that's equal ((inaudible, looks at L then M)) is that a hundred and forty?
183	M	And then sixty plus::: ((looks at K)) [It's gonna be a hundred.
184	L	[(((leans in over M's graph, looking directly at K)) WAIT a minute! It's forty ((kneels down)), and then it's like... ((hands up, form triangle over table surface, fingertips touching)) like forty, right? ((looks at K))
185	K	((leans forward, looking at L)) Mm hm.
186	L	And then you have to pair those up ((brings palms together)) and then they have kids ((hands flatten and spread apart over table surface))
187	M	((looks up at L, mouth drops open))
188	K	Pair the f-
189	M	((looks at camera, eyes widen)) OH, yeah, huh? ((smiles and looks over at L))
190	L	((looking at M, laughing, hands still spread open on table top))
191	K	So [that means
192	M	[We were doing it- ((looks at K with wide smile))
193	K	Ok, ok. ((nodding, R hand beats down on table)) [That goes (back)
194	L	((laughing)) That's a lot of mice ((sits back on heels; looks up at camera, smiling))
195	K	OK, back up.
196	M	((rips the graph sheet off pad))
197	K	Gosh, they'd be repro- Oh my gosh, [that's a lot of nasty mice. OK
198	L	[No no no ((leans in))

Heterogeneous Reasoning in Episode 1

In this incident, the students struggled to coordinate multiple representations. We examine some of the coordinations in detail, seeking to relate features of the incident to successes and failures to learn. The incident began with the group calculating what the population will be after eight breeding seasons. The group initially adopted a linear model implicit in multiplication of a fixed birthrate. Only when they turned to graphing their results did they begin to think of the process that the calculation was intended to reflect.

The interchange on lines 65/66 is an example of the frequent need to coordinate numbers with their semantics—adults still have to be included in the population, and "three hundred and twenty" is the number of babies in eight seasons just calculated. Similarly line 69 is a further reiteration of the semantics of the number "three hundred and twenty plus twenty"—the number represents a population at a time. Line 73 turns to graphing as a different representational modality, and it

1. CONCEPTUAL LEARNING   15

may also reflect an appeal to evaluation by an authority outside the group (e.g., a teacher or the researchers) concerning what should be done next.

What is interesting about this introduction of a new representation (the graph) is that it appears to be what triggers the new thinking that reveals the error (adopting the linear model) that they have all made. M marked a point on the graph to show a value of 60 animals after the first season (line 180). But L realized that something was wrong (lines 181 and 184). M continued calculating the next graph point, but L persisted. She started by reiterating the number and asking for acknowledgment of it (line 184). The number is the number of first-season babies. She then stated that these have to be paired up and themselves reproduce (line 186). L's gesture was intuitively an important part of her communication that she had a new insight, both for herself and for the group. M fairly rapidly saw their mistake, too (lines 187 and 189). They all realized that this was going to make the growth of the population much more rapid, although they did not have any number for it yet. They immediately referred back to the experiential world of "nasty mice" (K at line 197). Perhaps the reality of reproduction lies behind the affective tone of the incident. It was not just a mathematical mistake, but a failure to apply the "facts of life?"

The original adoption of the linear model arose within the "mathematical world." It is, in some sense, the obvious calculation to do—40 babies a season for eight seasons is going to give 320 babies. M drove the group's work forward, and he saw the business of the group very much in terms of calculation. Within this mathematical framing of the task, multiplication was a very natural thing to do. After all, multiplication is something we learn so as to avoid having to do multiple additions. Multiplication is the kind of labor-saving shortcut that mathematics enables, and we see later that labor-saving shortcuts are both a source of creative discovery and also of confusions in learning.

It is hard to say from the evidence at hand whether the group multiplied because it adopted a linear model of population growth, or whether it only implicitly adopted a linear model of population growth because it multiplied. We lean to the latter interpretation. We hypothesize that it was the choice of mathematical operation that drove the processes along, and the choice was driven by superficial features of the words in the problem (e.g., the design challenge says, "We want you to estimate how many mice will be living in the barn (and eating grain) as time goes on"). In fact, the "linear model" is our theorists' imposition onto the conceptual system of the students, who had not yet differentiated between linear and exponential (and other) models of growth. One support for this contention—that the adoption of the model is driven by the formalism—is the prominent affective grounding that happened next when the mistake was discovered. In some sense, mice were the last thing they were thinking about as they multiplied the numbers.

It is likely that the shift in representational modality that the graphing activity entailed played a critical role in the discovery of the group's mistake. Graphing made them break the multiplication down into a series of additions that could be represented in a direct way by the rising line on the graph and successive times along the X-axis. In fact, viewing the videotape, it appears that preparing mentally for this shift in representational activity precipitated L's insight, even before the graph was actually drawn. Preparing for the routine of drawing a graph was sufficient to bring at least L to thinking in terms of process and the mice involved. She thought about what happens in the world of mice—about the semantics: babies grow up and have babies. L's graphical spreading gesture might have had a direct semantics representing an exponentially expanding "family tree." Or its dramatic nature may have less specifically indicated the excitement of her realization. On either account, the gesture itself was another shift of communicative modality.

L's insight was adopted rather rapidly. The affective grounding spread immediately—"gosh that's a lot of nasty mice." The group dynamics reflected in this discourse is the topic of the next analysis. Before passing on to that, it is worth noting the partial nature of the correspondence between model and world, and that this abstraction is reflected in the partialness of insight. The sudden affective grounding did not force the introduction of all the relevant features of mice into the model. For example, the students did not, at this point, raise the issue of death. Yet they may have known that eight seasons (24 months) is more than the life span of a typical field mouse. Much later in the unit, we see them get to grips with this additional complication. At this point, the grounding only corrected some of the inadequacies of their model.

To summarize, this incident illustrates how learning involves the coordination of knowledge about formalism and intuitive knowledge about the world. The incident started with the group's activity being in formal mode, and then exhibited an insight into correspondence between the formalism and its semantics. This shift appears to have been precipitated by preparation for a change in representational modality, which then precipitated a vivid affective grounding.

Discourse Dynamics in Episode 1

Situative analyses of activity focus on activity systems (Engestrom, 1996; Greeno & MMAP, 1998) that usually include two or more individuals interacting with each other and with material and informational systems. A central problem in such analyses is to identify principles of coordination that can explain how the various components of the system interact so that the system functions as it does.

We argue that a central factor in this process is whether and how the group is able to open a discussion when someone in the group recognizes that a mistake has been made, and whether the group is then able to correct the mistake. This requires analyzing properties of the interaction and analyzing how the content of objections that are raised can help the group see that an error has been made. We find that what is at issue in such learning events is how well the objection enables the group to rethink the alignment between their understanding of the context of the problem (their situation model) and their understanding of the formal representation of the problem (their problem model).

Our analyses are framed by two general assumptions pertaining to the coordination of activity. First, we assume that when a group is working on a task, we can consider their activity as movement in a problem space (Newell & Simon, 1972). Second, we assume that contributions to progress on the task are joint actions (Clark & Schaefer, 1989) that achieve a common ground of understanding among the group members. In tying together these two assumptions, we seek to strengthen our position that such cognitive work is both informational and interpersonal, and that coordinations between these aspects need to be better understood.

Taking the view of progress on task work as movement in a problem space allows us to adapt the metaphors of trajectory and momentum to describe the group's activity. We define *trajectory* as the direction the students seem to take themselves to be working on. It is an analytical construct, informed both by the sequence of immediately preceding actions and those that immediately follow, and by using it we attempt to characterize the students' understanding of their work within the problem space. Correcting a mistake would lead the group to establish a new trajectory in its problem solving. Not all trajectories of work are equivalent, of course, and a second metaphor we use is the *momentum* of a trajectory, which depends on the informational and interpersonal force with which the participants are moving. This hypothetical factor is significant for the issue of opening questions, because it influences whether it is relatively easy or hard for a participant to enter a question or challenge and get the group to open it for consideration. Although the assumption that task work is movement within a problem space initially focuses attention on informational aspects of the interaction, it can also be seen that interactions are by no means free from interpersonal aspects.

Attending to interpersonal aspects of interaction focuses our attention on how students are positioned to take part in participation structures that shape their interaction. Positioning expresses how the group members react and relate to one another: who gets to say what, to whom, about which topics. For example, at any moment in the interaction, one of the members may be understood to be (i.e., positioned as) providing direction to the activity with the others following along. The group's practice regarding such situations affects whether the presenter is required to check for mutual understanding in the group before proceeding, and whether such checks require relatively weaker or stronger expressions from the other members. Group practice may allow frequent interruptions, or it could allow presenters to continue uninterrupted unless another member has a strong reason to question or disagree with the information being presented. In such cases when a question or objection is raised and considered, the group's practice may be that members have equal authority in the negotiation, or one of them may be understood to have more authority than the others. These patterns are likely to vary between groups and even within groups across time and across contexts of the working situation.

How Is an Objection Raised and a Discussion Opened?   Episode 1 (Pretest, Part 1) is an example of an objection being made that serves to open a new idea in the group, resulting in a change in the trajectory the group was working on. What about this objection resulted in changing the trajectory?

The main objection that we take to be the cause of the change in the trajectory was a proposal that instead of assuming 40 babies are born every season, the group needed to account for the babies subsequently having babies. This objection arose after a considerable amount of work on the part of the group to negotiate the details of the scenario and, based on those details, to formulate a model of mouse population growth over 2 years. There were also objections throughout the episode made by the same student (L) to different aspects of the details that the students worked out. These objections came in multiple forms, as alternative statements and questions such as "why." The series of objections leading up to the final objection are important to consider, because they contributed to the momentum that built up behind the current trajectory.

L made four objections throughout the episode, and these gained in intensity. The first objection began with a comment made quietly to the group that was not acknowledged. Her second objection was louder and more direct and was acknowledged by another member (lines 171 and 172). The intensity behind L's contributions to the trajectory built, ending with a suggestion that was accompanied by expressive gestures. Throughout the episode, L's objections were acknowledged and "taken up," impacting the elements of the solution the group created. This positioned L as a member who had been paying attention, understanding, and contributing to the solution, so that when she finally made a big objection at the end of the episode, the group acknowledged her suggestion, and changed their solution (and therefore their trajectory).

Although analysis of interaction can reveal a significant amount about how a trajectory changes, it is important not to forget that there is another part to problem solving: cognition. We believe that part of the reason that L's objection in the pretest resulted in a change to the trajectory had to do with what her objection did informationally. Essentially, the students were working on a mathematical solution (problem model) that they had derived from their understanding of the constraints of the problem (situation model). However, as the students began to form their problem model, they did not make significant attempts to connect their math back to the situation to see if their solution was accurate. Although their problem model was informed by their understanding of the situation, they did not attempt to see if their problem model was an accurate representation of the actual situation. At the end of the episode, L suddenly made this connection and noted that after the babies are born they have to pair all the mice up (a reference to the problem model they had constructed), and then all of the mice would have babies. This objection serves to reconnect the problem model with the situation model, and reveals what the previous problem model was missing.

What Is the Trajectory and How Do We Know?

The group initially began to solve the problem using a linear model of population growth, assuming the same numbers of babies were born every season. There are a number of levels that could be the trajectory the students are on. Throughout the episode, while the students were creating their linear model, they spent a lot of time discussing the components of the model (e.g., how many seasons the mice reproduce). These small discussions are trajectories of their own, but for this analysis we take those conversations to be a part of a larger trajectory, "figuring out the population with a linear model." There are several reasons that we choose to situate the analysis at this level.

First, regardless of how many arguments the students had about the details of the model they were creating, they always seemed to come back to the "plan" of the model itself, that is, "multiply the number of seasons by the number of mice born per season." For example, the students began by figuring out how many seasons the mice reproduced. One might take this to be the trajectory the students are on. In fact, the group negotiated quite a bit about this issue. However, as soon as they had resolved that the mice reproduced eight times, they immediately turned to the next question of how many babies each mouse had (again, turns are compressed):

37	M	So there's eight. So there's eight times they reproduce (writing on the paper). And how many, (looking at next problem) there's five years here.
39	K	Do the first [one first
40	M	[Let's do the first one first. Yeah. So how many ...
41	K	How many times I mean how many babies do you think there ...
42	L	((looks up at K and says quickly)) Four. I think there are four.

The group spent time discussing this issue again, but as soon as they figured out how many babies were born each season (40), they immediately began to multiply 40 (number of mice per season) times eight (number of seasons).

The students then began to figure out how to graph their answer, season by season. As one group member was drawing the graph, another

realized that they had made a mistake. She suggested that they had forgotten a crucial aspect of the model, and the group agreed with her and
began to construct a new model. It was at this point, when the students
began to solve the problem using a different model (an exponential
model), that the trajectory changed (see transcript, lines 171 to 198).

Repairing the Birthrate as an Interactional Achievement

Examined closely as an achievement of talk-in-interaction, L's challenge
to and eventual repair of her group's birthrate for the population of
mice provides a nice example of how ongoing talk over different systems
of representation provides a setting for changes in understanding. As indicated in the previous analysis of this group's trajectory, her line of
questioning was already underway as M began to plot points in a
graphical frame they had jointly constructed (earlier turns, not shown).
L first asked (line 171) how M has arrived at 60 mice after the first breeding season, and when K (line 172) joined her in asking this question, attention shifted to the transition between seasons as a place where
arithmetic operations were difficult to understand (i.e., a particular interval of time within their shared situation model). Shifting briefly from
his focus on calculation, M explained that 40 were produced in the first
season, but that these then had to be added to the "twenty original"
adults (line 175) to get 60 animals. As M repeated the result (line 178), K
and L both appeared to understand why they got 60 animals at the end
of the first breeding season.

As M turned to plotting this value for the first season (line 180,
latched onset with L's line 181), however, L began narrated calculations
for the second season. It was while doing this that she apparently noticed something troubling (a 3-second pause, then "Wait a minute!" at
line 181). Unlike her earlier question, which recruited both K and M's attention, this utterance did not. Instead, M and K each continued what
appears to be an independent line of calculation, and they reached tell-
ingly different results. At line 182, K calculated 140 animals after (we
presume) the second season, whereas at line 183, M calculated a result
of 100 animals. One interpretation of these different values is that M
simply added another 40 newborns at the second season, resulting in
100 mice. On the other hand, K divided 60 animals into 30 breeding
pairs, then multiplied by a litter size of 4 newborns (their earlier agreement) to yield 120 newborns. She then may have added in the original
20 adults (as in M's prior explanation) to give 140 mice. Of course, we
have no way of knowing precisely why these numbers differ, but it appears that each student is doing something quite different. M moved
forward along a trajectory with a linear birthrate (i.e., adding 40 newborns each season). K correctly implemented a nonlinear birthrate, pair-
ing total mice for each next breeding season, but she may incorrectly
add the original mice to newborns at each season. L began a next season
of mice births, but she found something troubling and attempted again

to recruit the attention of her peers. Just what troubled L becomes clear in her next turn.

At line 184, L interrupted more forcefully, leaning into M's written workspace and beginning a series of iconic gestures that, together with her talk, created a simulation of one temporal slice out of the breeding cycle. Animated over the table surface and visually in front of M and K, L's simulation showed how adults would pair up (palms together) and then produce an even larger number of babies (hands flatten and spread over table surface, line 186). This enacted simulation of a transition to the next breeding cycle had a dramatic effect on K and M, who suspended their calculations and sat back, evidently realizing that they had underestimated (M more than K) the number of mice accumulating over seasons. In keeping with the earlier idea that their trajectory is changing, K announced they should "back up" (line 195), M ripped their in-progress graph off the pad of paper and (literally) out of collective vision (line 196), and L leaned back into shared interactional space to prepare for an alternative model (her repeated "no" at line 198).

Followed closely as an achievement in the structure of ongoing interaction, there are a variety of representational systems in play here, including forms of oral arithmetic (all three children are engaged with this), the graph frame being updated by M (eventually ripped out of the joint problem space), and L's complex gestural depiction of mice breeding over the table surface. One conjecture, in keeping with the semantic analysis offered earlier, is that plotting time-ordered points in the graph creates a material setting in which L's questions about how calculations work at the transitions between breeding seasons become newly relevant. In this sense, their earlier, single multiplication (what we have called a linear model of population growth) now needs to be unpacked into a series of time-ordered calculations that yield values for plotting. L's question about the first transition between breeding cycles (line 171) comes up again at the second season (line 181), where she apparently notices that the number of pairs breeding within each cycle is growing. As all the students suddenly realize, their mouse population is growing very quickly (i.e., L predicts "a lot of mice" at 194, then K expands this into "a lot of nasty mice" at 197). They go on (not shown) to calculate the number of mice at each season, ending with 87,480 mice at the end of 2 years.

L's talk and gesture opens up a single time slice in the world of breeding mice, and so expands a part of the represented world of mice that they had black-boxed in their earlier arithmetic calculations. Under this view, their earlier, linear model of growth was a consequence of getting stuck looking *at* a representational device (written arithmetic expressions, not shown). Building on L's insistent questions, eventually expressed in narrative and gestural depiction (a coordinated pair of representational devices), they were able to look through these calculations onto a finer-grained and more sensible model of the reproductive cycle. This model involved a new quantity—mice reaching reproductive maturity and ready to breed in the next cycle—and they were able to incorporate this into a scheme of calculations that implemented exponential population growth over eight seasons.

Predation Without Coordinated Representations (Episode 2, Pretest, Part 2)

The second episode that we discuss occurred when students were briefly interviewed just after the pretest. As evident in the following exchange, members of this group did understand the qualitative effect of predation, in the sense that cats eat mice and so reduce their population. But they had not yet developed a way to implement this understanding as a functional relation linking together their isolated, hand-calculated models (i.e., for mice and cat populations).

1	RH	So if the mice are eating grain …
2	M	Uh, huh.
3	RH	What are the cats eating?
4	L	[Mice.
5	M	[Mice.
6	RH	What does that do to the mouse population?
7	M	Reduce them.
8	RH	Ok, [so, as you were doing the mice calculations]
9	M	[Ah! Oh:::]
		((L and K look at M))
10	RH	Sounds like you were just kinda goin with, four per litter for the mice and letting them … go=
11	K	= Go, ok.
12	RH	So they're gonna be getting rubbed out by the cats, right?
13	M	[Uh huh.
14	K	[Right.

The absence of predation as a functionally explicit concept struck M first (line 9), then he and K agreed that their models allow cats to grow without bound. As they went on to acknowledge (not shown), this was something that violated the entire premise of the design challenge, and they were eager to get another chance at this kind of problem.

Learning Birth Rate: An Innovation That Goes Awry (Episode 3)

Again we choose an episode focused on an important concept in the domain of modeling biological populations, this time the composition of mathematical functions. When one function takes as its input the output of another function, the two functions can be composed into a single function with the input of the first and the output of the second.

Episode 3 took place near the middle of the unit (day 9 of 20). When the group brushed up against function composition, they were engaged in constructing one of their early models of a population. They had a worksheet entitled "Building the Birthrate" that gave them a scaffold consisting of questions and reference sources for calculating or making estimates for a number of important parameters for a situation in which fish breed in an enclosed tank (e.g., the size of different age cohorts within the population, birthrate, and survival rate). The pedagogical intent of this worksheet was twofold. First, questions in the worksheet were to help students complete a life table analysis that would explicitly consider reproductive maturity and fry survival as important influences on a composite birth rate for guppies. Second, students were to make different assumptions in this life table analysis and write about the consequences of these differences for the behavior of their population models. Parts of this worksheet and the computer interface are condensed into Fig. 1.2.

To complete the Building the Birthrate worksheet, the students were to follow four steps to calculate a guppy birthrate to use in their population model. The students then had to use that birthrate to calculate how many guppies they would have in their tank at the end of 2 years. One part of this process involved figuring out how many of the babies that are born in the first season actually survive (after birth approximately 95% of the baby guppies [fry] are eaten by their mother). In this episode M proposed that instead of calculating the birthrate, they should just make the birthrate 4%, because that's how many fry were actually going to survive. In other words, instead of going through all the calculations of having a large amount be born only to have most of them die, why not only have the number of fry who are actually going to survive be born? This idea—while a compelling innovation if one is hoping to teach the idea of function composition—is slightly flawed. Although the students are told that only a small percentage of the fry that are born survive, using this percentage as the birthrate (i.e., setting a birth rate of 4% for their initial model) ignores the fact that a very large number of fry are born each season. Relative to the size of the fertile adult cohort, even a small number of surviving fry give a much larger effective birthrate (i.e., a 51.6% birthrate for the assumptions shown in Fig. 1.2).

The worksheet specifies a sequence of activities, although this was not the sequence in which this group performed them. In the first step of the worksheet, students are expected to fill in the life table by combining their assumptions about fish with information from reference sources (e.g., the average fry per young or mature brood). This enables them to calculate the total number of fry born from all reproductive females during a cycle (bottom right of table in Fig. 1.2). At Step 2, the percentage survival rate is entered from a reference source and, at Step 3, applied to the total from the table to give a number surviving. The lines in Fig. 1.2 represent page breaks in the work booklet. Step 4 then converts the total surviving fry into a percent birthrate for the computer. The rel-

Building the Birthrate

	age	# males	# females	# fry	total
	young	2	1	4	4
Step 1	mature	4	2	50	100
	old	0	1	0	0
	total	6	4		104

Step 2 What percent of fry born survive? What happens to the ones who don't make it? *5% of fry survive. They are eaten*

Step 3 Use this survival percent and the total number born to calculate the number that survive. *5.16*

Step 4 So what's the birthrate? Now that you have calculated an assumed number of fry that survive past birth, you need to convert this into something that Habitech can use as a birth rate. As you know, Habitech works with percents or constant numbers. You will be using a percent birth rate.

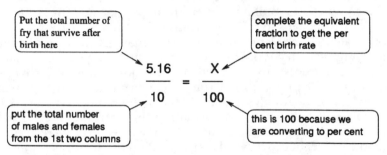

BASED ON YOUR ASSUMPTIONS YOUR BIRTHRATE IS | 4% |

Congratulations! Now take this birth rate and the death rate you will use and head to Habitech to make you model. Remember this birth rate is based on certain assumptions. If you change an assumption, it will affect your model.

Step 5 Entering numbers into the Habitech interface:

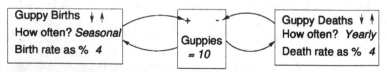

Recording of Models

Initial #	Birth rate %	Death rate %	Years	Descr.
10	4%	4%	2 year	< 13

FIG. 1.2. Parts of the worksheet and computer interface involved with Building the Birthrate. The numbers in the tables, equation, and italicized answers were entered by the students.

24

evant part of the interface—a population node connected to birth and death rates—appears next (this was not part of the worksheet, but it does reflect the need to enter rates into a network model of the sort shown in Fig. 1.1). The bottom table in Fig. 1.2 (a separate page in the worksheet) is to be used by students to keep track of alternative models. Fig. 1.2 shows the group's first model, although as the group continued working, this table held several alternatives (birthrates ranging from 4% to 51.6%).

The group's actual sequence of work was to start by fulfilling Steps 1, 2, and 3, followed by entering the result into the computer and recording the model. Step 4 was circumvented initially and was only filled in retrospectively the next day.

Heterogeneous Representations in Episode 3

Whereas the pretest episode (Episode 1) illustrated how heterogeneous representations may play a role in precipitating conceptual advance, this episode is chosen to illustrate heterogeneity of representation presenting problems for conceptual learning. The incident opened with M proposing to take a shortcut in the calculation. This was at first taken by L to be a mistake. She requested and received an explanation of the idea, although it is unclear whether she found this satisfying (see also the following analysis of the episodes' discourse for a discussion of this point). Although L appeared to appreciate that there was consequent bookkeeping that needed to be taken care of, she failed to deflect the group from continuing on to the entry of data into the computer model.

441	M	Hey wait, wait, wait …
443	M	No but listen. If 4% of the fry survive why don't we just forget about the fry survival and just put that amount for the, for how much are born …
445	L	Because the number born are not how much survived
446	M	Yes. Yes, the ones who survive are the ones we count, not the ones who are dead because we don't make room for the ones that are dead
453	M	Ok you know how 4% the who:::le fry who were born survive so why don't we just put 4% on the guppies birth because that's how many are going to survive
456	K	I get what you're saying because why put however many more guppies in when they're just going to die anyway?
459	K	So why not just put 4% because that's how many are surviving/ that's how many we're going to count
497	L	But what's that 4%?
498	K	The ones that survive

499	M	The ones that actually survive fryhood
501	L	Yeah, I know, but how many of the guppies are 4%?
502	M	We don't know, we'll let that mechanical thing work and tell us

At line 441, M opened with a proposal to collapse two stages of calculation into one. In fact, this proposal is perhaps something akin to what is embodied implicitly in the worksheet and is potentially a creative proposal involving a concept rather close to one of the core aims of this curriculum—the understanding of mathematical functions. M was proposing to compose two functions into a single function, taking the argument of the first and the value of the last. L objected to this proposal and justified her objection by pointing out that "the number born are not how much survived." In fact, we will see that in the terminology of the worksheet, the number of fry surviving expressed as a percentage of the whole population *is* the birthrate, which plays its part in this confusion. M appeared to understand the objection and explained his proposal's departure from the worksheet with some success. L accepted the sense of the innovation even though she expressed reservations about its coordination with the worksheet. The activity was turned over to the superior calculating powers of "that mechanical thing"—the computer program HabiTech.

Unfortunately, the "mechanical thing" did not understand the creative proposal; L's reservations were well motivated, but, lacking a clear understanding herself, her intervention did not deflect the group (read on for further analysis of the discourse dynamics). There are numerous problems of coordination between the representations in Fig. 1.2. The survival rate of 5% at Step 2 gets copied into the model table as 4% (possibly a memory error, or a correction later). But the serious error is in shortcutting the calculation at Step 4 and entering the 4% rate directly into the birthrate box at the end. The algebraic ratio part at Step 4 is returned to only later the next day when trying to comply with having the whole sheet filled in.

What went wrong as the group struggled with the welter of representations and numbers? It is hard to give a crisp interpretation of a murky confusion, but we can suggest some of the contributing factors. An important source may be a divergence of the ordering of biological events and the calculation events that refer to them; another is the terminology. In the fish world, fry are born, then the vast majority of these are eaten, and at the end of the season the survivors are counted. In the calculation world, first the number of births is calculated, then a survival rate is applied, and a census number of surviving fry results. So far so good. But turning the page after Step 3, and after recording model parameters in a labeled algebraic proportion (see Step 4), the students arrive at a further calculation of the "birthrate," where "birthrate" now means something like "birth-and-survival-to-year's-end rate."

What might students think the birthrate is at each step in this worksheet (i.e., conceptually, although "birthrate" is explicitly mentioned only in Steps 4 and 5)? At Step 1, the birthrate is a set of numbers representing the brood size of the average guppy at different ages (represented by the numerals 4, 50, 0); at Step 2, the birthrate is the number (represented by the numeral 104) of fry born to the whole population. In steps 3 and 4, the birthrate is the birth-and-survival-to-end-of-season rate expressed as a percentage of the whole population (represented by the numeral 4). The same idea, a very tangible idea, is represented each time by numerals, but each time the numeral counts different kinds of thing, and complex calculations constitute the inference rules that "move the idea from box to box."

Unfortunately, M's insight that two functions can be composed requires attendant housekeeping to keep the ontology—the things the numbers refer to—straight. Perhaps a contributing factor is that because the presurvival birthrate in Step 1 was never put into the form of a percentage (1040%), M did not appreciate that, after Step 3, it already had been implicitly composed with the survival rate, and the calculation at Step 4 was intended only to get back to a percentage form. The terminology unfortunately exacerbated this problem of "backward causality"—first calculating a survival rate (using births) and then calculating a birthrate from that figure. We return later to an episode that provides evidence that the confusions that arose here persist in their consequences at the posttest.

Discourse Dynamics in Episode 3

In this episode the same student who objected successfully in Episode 1 (L) again made an objection to the idea currently being discussed. In this third episode, however, although L's objections were taken up and discussed by the members of the group, she was not successful at changing the trajectory the group was on, and they instead continued along the same (mistaken) path. What was different in this episode? Why wasn't L successful at getting the group to understand the mistake they had made?

How Is an Objection Raised and a Discussion Opened?   In this episode, L's objection developed over several turns, rather than being fully formed and stated at once. As M's idea was initially introduced (lines 443–444), L objected to his proposal by pointing to an inequality in the formulation (line 445). In the face of strong disagreement, however, her objection took other, less specific forms, from confusion and digression to flat rejection. Toward the end of the episode, she returned to objections that were more closely grounded in the proposed idea itself, but these took the form of questions. Finally, her objections voiced confusion, and she was overridden.

This pattern is quite different from Episode 1, where L's objections grew stronger as the episode progressed. L was positioned quite differently in this interaction: the way she phrased her objections placed her in the role of questioner, rather than critical thinker.

There is another critical element to this interaction that differs from Episode 1. In this birthrate episode (Episode 3), the discussion the students were having rested primarily in terms of the problem model that they had constructed of the situation. They were talking mainly in mathematical terms, and although they made references to "guppies," none of the students successfully attempted to apply the mathematical model they were constructing to the real world: the mathematics was not applied to the situation. L's objections were also located primarily in the world of mathematics; they fell short of connecting the problem model and situation model to each other, as had been done in the pretest. Therefore, the group was not pushed to fit their problem model into the situation they were trying to represent, and they failed to see that they were not constructing their mathematical model accurately.

What Is the Trajectory and How Do We Know? At the beginning of the episode, the group had worked through the first three steps on the worksheet (how many guppies they would start with, how many of those were male and female, and whether the guppies were old, mature, or young). They had just agreed that 4% of guppy fry survive, with the rest eaten by the mother, when M proposed a new direction for them to take (see lines 441 and 443, presented earlier). From this point on, the group's trajectory became whether or not to accept M's idea and use 4% as the guppy birthrate. This trajectory ended, and a new one began, when M finally announced "Let's just try it out," and left the table to go to the computer.

During the course of negotiating whether to use M's idea of 4%, other lower level trajectories can be described, including trying to understand M's idea, teasing K, and getting clear about which number on the worksheet they were doing. Although these are identifiable paths of the group's interaction, the level that seems to best describe what is organizing their behavior is determining what the mathematical implications of M's suggestion are, and hence whether to act on it. We see evidence that this trajectory captures what the group considered itself to be engaged in. Following a digression of giggles in which L and M lightly tease K (not shown), K asserted, "I'd like to know what everyone thinks so that I can see where to base my decision." K accomplished (at least) two very important things with this act: She ratified the idea that they were in the process of making a decision; and she called them back to order. Furthermore, there is evidence that the group accepted this bid. L's response, marked by "ok," indicated both agreement with the trajectory and willingness to be called back into the work of deciding. M's subsequent response was an indication that he, too, was back to work. Thus, although the group could have dissolved into nonwork at this point, instead they were back on the track of determining whether to use M's proposal of 4% for the birthrate.

Interactional Achievement in Episode 3

As an alternative to asking how one of these students, L, fails to deflect M's proposed shortcut (i.e., to use the percentage of fry surviving as the birth rate), an analysis of interaction could also productively ask how M, and eventually K, manage to do a sufficient job of convincing L to drop her persistent questions about the meaning of the proposed shortcut. We take up this inverted question briefly, and the types of quantities put into juxtaposition across turns at talk in Episode 3 are critical for finding an answer.

M's initial proposal (line 443) was to "forget about" fry survival (a percentage) and to repurpose this quantity as "how much are born." L quickly countered (line 445), pointing out that "the number born" were not equivalent to "how much survived." M's next utterance (line 446) played a critical role by shifting the meaning of these quantities out from the represented world of fish alone (i.e., what happens to fish), to include a world of modelers who make decisions about "the ones we count" and fish "we don't [versus do] make room for." L's earlier nonidentity between types of fish (number born ≠ how much survived), reinterpreted by M to consider the purposes of modelers (i.e., these students, acting in their fictive capacity as biological consultants), added another layer of meaning that was accountable within the classroom. That is, not only is the world of fish being animated, but also a world of students, acting as biologists, who make decisions about which aspects of the world of fish need to be represented. From this perspective, the ongoing conversation was not so much about what happens among fish, but what should happen among students who make assumptions about, among other things, what is relevant to represent.

L's next turn (not shown) asked M to "repeat the question," acknowledging explicitly that "I'm kind of confused." As the conversation continued, M gave a more elaborate justification, checking in with both L and K on the distinction between fish born, fish dying (those "we don't make room for"), and fish surviving (those "we count"). Eventually, K took over the role of providing a justification to L (lines 456 and 459), as M prepared to implement their first model in the HabiTech™ environment.

As with the earlier analyses, students are struggling to coordinate a set of very different quantities. These include (directly from their talk): "number born," "ones who survive," "the ones we count," and "ones who are dead." These are put together into an argument for why it might make sense to leave out steps in the life table analysis, inasmuch as some of the quantities associated with these steps represent fish "we don't make room for." None of these quantities are "birthrates" as intended by "Building the Birthrate," but they are all quantities that have a sensible role in the life table at the center of this worksheet. In pursuing their own objectives in this episode, students are doing more than simply trying to be efficient. M, in particular, raises the possibility of acting as modelers—people who make decisions about what to bring in or leave out of a model.

Change in the Concept of Predation as the Reorganization of Representational Practice

In this section, we analyze several selections from this group's work near the end of the unit on population modeling, with a focus on how their understanding of predation (largely absent on the pretest, Episode 2) is reorganized as they work on more complex situation models and computer-based tools for implementing relations between quantities in these situations. Toward the end of the unit, student groups were asked to choose among a set of "extension scenarios" in which their fish population had been returned to a stream in Venezuela. In these extensions, students were to model the effects of a critical event of their choosing (e.g., upstream pollution and its consequences, the arrival of a predatory fish species, or rice farmers harvesting fish from the stream for mosquito control).

First we examine the MLKN group's elaborate response as fictional consultants to Venezuelan farmers, in the form of a "net wall" that served as a mechanical barrier to predatory fish. The group saw this as a solution to the problem of losing all the guppies, which Venezuelan farmers needed to control mosquito growth, to an exotic population of upstream predators (i.e., the wolf-fish). Then we examine their computational implementation of predation more closely, asking how their experiences during the unit may have contributed to a more sophisticated performance on the posttest design challenge.

Particularly important for our analysis of work at the interface between representing and represented worlds, these students appeared to be able to move fluidly between their roles as middle school collaborators (e.g., L asked for and her peers provided multiple explanations), technical designers (e.g., M and N implemented the network, but K followed and could explain their implementation), and observers/consultants for a Venezuelan stream environment (e.g., noticing the effects of predation on the posttest, L proposed that they add dogs to the barn environment to regulate the population of cats). How students moved between these figured worlds (Holland, Lachicotte, Skinner, & Cain, 1998) in ways that helped to develop and explore functionally explicit population models is a question for longitudinal analysis.

Coordinating Across Representations to Make Predictions About Predation and Population Growth

After successfully modeling the growth of a guppy population in captivity, the group chose an extension scenario in which predatory wolf-fish were released upstream from the guppies' pond, and farmers later noticed that these guppies were disappearing. The group predicted that the guppy population would flourish in the stream environment before the arrival of wolf-fish, then die out as guppies were eaten by newly arriving predators.

Engaging their fictional role as consultants to Venezuelan farmers, the group began working on solutions that would preserve the guppy population, eventually settling on K's proposal for a mechanical "net wall." In the following exchange, K reprised the idea of a net in which mesh openings captured wolf-fish but allowed guppies to swim through. By installing this net at the upstream boundary of the pond, she proposed they could catch and remove wolf-fish before they reached the farmers' guppies. Because aspects of these elaborated situation models are not presented on worksheets or at the computer interface, we need to augment our transcripts to convey some of the richness of student work. Transcripts for these segments mark the onset of relevant actions (gesture, gaze, work with inscriptions) using numbers in single parentheses. Action descriptions indexed by these numbers in parentheses then appear in italics below the transcribed turn at talk.

Segment 1: Blocking the Arrival of Wolf-Fish

1	K	[Ok, this is (1)the net, these are the guppies. (2) And they go sh:::, straight through the net. (3) And [the big fish go ... and they get caught

    (1) *R hand forms small opening*

    (2) *L hand, fingers wiggling, traces path through opening on "sh:::"*

    (3) R hand holds opening, L hand traces into opening and sticks

2	L	[(1)But the big fish are... caught, yeh. (2)And then, they, [they

    (1) *L hand holds opening; R hand traces into it*

    (2) *R hand flutters away, as if swimming*

3	K	[(1)Then we pull::: it up and then take it out.

    (1) *hands grab at center then rise on "pull::: it up"*

4	L	Why should we pull it out?
5	M	No::: [The stream is like fi::ve fee::t deep.
6	L	[Duh:::?
7	M	No not even five feet, three feet[... deep.]
8	L	[Ok, ok, ok, come on.]
9	M	You can just pick em out.
10	L	So, yeh yeh, so, so it should be like ... no no, we can't HIRE anyone to pick it out. It should like, flow::: naturally. Stuff like that, you know? You know, cause see the [guppies are
11	K	[(1)You gotta pull it out!

    (1) *hands grab at center and pull up*

12	L	No … (1)they won't be CAUGHT in there, (2)cause they're like, HUGE, ok? (3)The hole will be this big. They can't go in that. It will be like=
		(1) *L hand forms opening, R hand flows in and sticks*
		(2) *hands form object, larger than prior opening*
		(3) *L hand forms opening, R hand flows in and bounces back*
13	K	=They'll just be IN there.
14	L	They wouldn't be in there. (1)They would just hit it and go
		(1) *opening held with L hand; R hand flows in and bounces off to far right*
15	M	((to RH, at camera)) What is [the size::: of a wolf fish?

In this segment, during which a net wall was constructed, several phenomena are important for understanding how students shift between representing and represented worlds. First, a world of Venezuelan streams, farmers, and interacting fish populations was densely inhabited by members of the group. They literally constructed the stream, fish, and a mechanical barrier in the gestural stage between K and L, as M looked from "downstream." Fish, the stream, and human actors were all animated within this shared space (Goffman, 1979; Ochs, Jacoby, & Gonzales, 1994).

Second, while the technical details of the net wall barrier were still underway, the importance of isolating guppies from these predators was clearly their emergent goal. Animated from the perspective of a consultant to Venezuelan farmers (as in M's earlier animation of what students, as modelers, would need to "count" or "make room for"), this was a response to the consequences of predation, now articulated with the developing notion of a habitat that had semipermeable boundaries.

The importance of predation in MLKN's consulting proposal became clear later during this class meeting, when the group called the experimenter (Hall, or RH in transcript) over to discuss the boundaries of the stream environment. When asked about the effect of their net wall on a graph of the guppy population they had drawn earlier, K started a conditional response.

Segment 2: The Graphical Shape of Predation

1	RH	The graph of the guppy population. M thinks its gonna continue to … [(1)be wavy] and you all think its gonna, (2)its gonna go down and then [come back up.
		(1) *R pen traces path up and down*
		(2) *R pen dips down then rises*
2	M	[Be wavy.]
3	L	No we=
4	K	=It depends. (1)Are there still, like … wolf fish in here that are eating the guppies?

		(1) *R pencil points into drawing in field notebook*
5	R	HUm[::: you can
6	K	[If there is, (1)then its gonna go a little wavy. But if NOT, then the guppies are just ... gonna have their own ... (2)Like before, when ... like our other, um ... (3)thingie? It's gonna be like that. [Because the guppies are living all alone, and they'll be dying (on their own)
		(1) *R hand traces upward path on "go a little wavy"*
		(2) *R point to computer, behind the group on "before"*
		(3) *R point to hand drawn graph*
7	RH	[Ok ... I mean if you killed, if you get rid of ALL the wolf fish ... then the guppies should ... recover with no trouble.
8	K	=Yeh.
9	RH	=If there's still some wolf fish, [the wolf fish are gonna continue to grow and stuff.
10	K	[Then they're gonna ((hands trace oscillation))
11	RH	So you might think about how you're gonna get that, uh::: graph to come out of the software.
12	K	Ok.

According to K (turn 6; see Fig. 1.3), if any wolf-fish got through the net wall, the graph of the guppy population would "go a little wavy." This was because "there's still wolf fish in there eating them," as she mentioned several times. But if the net wall successfully closed the pond to wolf-fish, then guppies would grow in isolation "like before" (i.e., referring to their earlier model of guppies alone in the pond).

Another point is important for understanding how these students began to coordinate movement between representing and represented worlds. K's conditional explanation crossed worlds in the sense that shapes in the representing world (i.e., graph shapes coming out of their "thingie") depended on conditions in the represented world (i.e., the passage of fish through a net opening). As the beginning of an activity system that was intended by the curriculum (i.e., modeling population dynamics), types of outcomes, as graph shapes, were being associated with types of models, as determined by students' assumptions about habitat and relations between populations (i.e., was the pond open or closed to exotic predators). And critical to a broader understanding of modeling as such an activity system, these students saw that their results depend on starting assumptions.

Implementing Predation in a Computational Medium

The net wall consulting proposal was, in our view, an elegant solution to an emergent design problem, and it worked at several levels. Guppies would be preserved for rice farmers because the wolf-fish would be blocked from moving down-stream. And this could be done

K4: It depends. (1)Are there still, like…
wolf fish in here that are eating guppies?

K6: If there is, (1)then its
gonna go a little wavy.

(1) R pencil points into
drawing in field notebook

(1) R hand traces upward path
on "go a little wavy"

FIG. 1.3. When asked about the effect of their "net wall" on a graph of the guppy population, K begins a hypothetical contrast that links a drawing of the stream environment to alternative graphical shapes. Utterances are shown above, action descriptions below.

without killing any of these predators. As these students elaborated the fictional world of the task, this would also keep upstream Venezuelans happy (i.e., those who, according to L, must have owned wolf-fish). Up to this point, the group's work on this proposal was closely tied to a qualitative understanding of the effects of predation. Yet they were far from a functional implementation in computational media that could produce the graphs in question. As M announced at the beginning of their next class period, "Now how do we make it work?"

The next two conversational segments illustrate the kind of work these students undertook to construct a plausible (if not entirely correct) functional model of predation. In Segment 3, the group had already constructed a user-defined function that links caribou/wolf-fish[1] and guppies population nodes. With this stable network topology in view, they repeatedly adjusted node parameters and ran the model to produce what they saw as a reasonable number of guppies. Just before this segment started, L complained that they had a "river full of

---

[1]HabiTech™ provides named population nodes for Caribou, Wolves, Moose, and Guppies. Using Moose for Mice or Caribou for Wolf-fish appears to present students with no particular difficulty. Although there is possibly some hidden extra cognitive load, it is a very striking fact that adding a layer of indirectness does not cause more disruption.

not plants, not insects, but just fishes." In the following transcript, dynamic responses of the HabiTech™ computer interface are listed as turns at talk (HT).

Segment 3: Opening Boxes and Adjusting Parameters

1	L	Its not enough! (We're going to like) ten thousand, (1)so why don't (we do) like, thirty per cent.
		(1) *changes CaribouBirths to 30% every month, then runs*
2	HT	((shows huge guppy population in scientific notation again))
3	L	(1)It's still a lot. Um, there's something wrong … (2)guppies deaths. [(3)
		(1) *switches to Build mode*
		(2) *mouse over GuppiesDeaths*
		(3) *mouse over CaribouDeaths*
4	K	[Ok, that's the problem.
5	M	Yeh, you see, but the special two is gonna, doing ((yawning))
6	L	(1)Ok, uh … please explain this. What is that? hh
		(1) *mouse circles over then opens Special2*
7	M	Uh, explain what?
8	L	What's a … special two.
9	M	Special two is how many die because of the caribou.
10	L	OH! Really? [Wow, ok.]
11	M	[Yes.]
12	L	(1)I'll change this, right here (3 sec) Like this is … eighteen is um … how many guppies=
		(1) *selects expression 'Caribou * 18' and deletes '18'*
13	M	=No, let's do three … times thirty is … thirty, ninety. So do caribou times ninety.
14	L	((changes Special2 expression to 'Caribou * 90' and begins pulling on output arrow))
15	M	Because (inaudible) every month, now go … That's it, just … Go to build, go to the thing that says build. Then go:: to the end.
16	HT	((negative population value appears in Guppies node))
17	L	Negative?
18	M	Oh ok ((sighs))
19	L	That's a little too (much), (1)yeh hah.
		(1) *switches to Build mode and places mouse over Special2*
20	M	Now we need to reduce the births. Go to births. No, no don't touch that, do the births. [Reduce the births to ten percent every month.
21	L	[((resets Caribou births to 10% every month))
22	M	Now go:::

With the work of implementing predation in these particular computational media well underway, several phenomena are worth noticing. First, L had been adjusting model parameters without understanding how the predation function worked. When she asked "you guys" (M and N) for an explanation, M described what the node did as an explicit, computational relation to guppies: It is a type of death caused by caribou/wolf-fish (i.e., a functionally explicit version of predation).

Second, as L looked inside this function and questioned how many guppies were eaten by caribou/wolf-fish (turn 11), M proposed and L executed a change in how the predation node was defined. M's proposal unpacked the monthly value into a daily rate of consumption (i.e., 3 per day, times 30 days in a month, gives 90 guppies per caribou/wolf-fish per month).

This exchange was one of many in which students moved back and forth between changing model parameters and running their updated model (these are called "Build" and "Play" modes in the interface) to produce a new set of population values. Over the entire series, each adjustment was sensible within the network topology of their model, but none of these changes produced an outcome that the group found reasonable (e.g., negative assessments after turns 2 and 13). In the face of this stalled progress, M recalled from their earlier research that overcrowding would cause the guppy birth rate to fall. He reduced this parameter (evidently confusing discrete and continuous events) and ran the updated model.

Segment 4: Arriving at a Guppy Crisis

1	HT	((running Fast, values in nodes updating continuously))
2	L	Too much.
3	M	[No::: its not gone into the e's yet. And it hasn't.
4	HT	[(((Guppies value in population node rises for awhile, but becomes negative and ends with $-2.71826 * 10^6$ Guppies))
5	L	Negative?
6	M	((mouse pops open a graph))
7	HT	((graph shows Guppy crisis part way into third year))
8	M	Oh my [god:::
9	RH	[YES::::!
10	L	Oh, it's so funny! [What?
11	RH	[Yes:::
12	M	Yes what ?

L began to classify this as another unsuccessful run of their model (turn 2), but M, who had been monitoring the value displayed in the guppy population node, announced that the positive growth of guppies has not yet reached scientific notation (turn 3). Then as they watched the interface, the value displayed in the guppy population node went hugely negative (i.e., the software automatically shifted into scientific notation) and M opened a graph window (see Fig. 1.1, which shows the state of their HabiTech™ interface at this point in the interaction).

The graph shown in Fig. 1.1 was striking for members of the MLKN group, not only because it showed an extinction crisis for guppies, but also because it caught the researcher's eye (lines 8 and 10) as he was working with a group on the other side of the classroom. In a subsequent conversation about this network model and graph, M insisted on the influence of overcrowding in lowering guppies births, while both he and L recounted their decision to increase the level of caribou/wolf-fish predation. As a final part of their modeling effort, they implemented K's net wall as an emigration function (i.e., evacuating some percentage of the population on a yearly basis), something that was suggested by their teacher as a general strategy for modeling negative influences on population growth.

By the end of the curriculum unit from which the longitudinal selections in this chapter were drawn, the MLKN group had a sensible and fully implemented model of their consulting proposal, and its behavior was consistent with what they hoped to achieve in Segment 2 (i.e., K's conditional explanation, lines 4 and 6). As the net wall was implemented as a yearly reduction in the wolf-fish population (i.e., an emigration function, described earlier), these predators still made it into the pond environment. As a result, some level of predation was ongoing (i.e., this appeared as a scalloped or "wavy" graph of the guppies population over seasons). But the mechanical net wall, which they used to remove predators at a regular interval, reversed the outcome of their earlier crisis scenario (i.e., the guppies population grew steadily over the duration of their scenario).

Predation, as a concept that could be implemented within these particular computational media, was one among several influences in a more complex model of the Venezuelan pond habitat. These influences included (with varying levels of correctness): (a) the starting value established over an earlier period in which guppies lived alone in the pond, (b) the production of a guppy crisis after the unregulated arrival of predators, (c) the regulated influence of predation during smaller time cycles within the net wall model, and (d) the idea of birthrate suppression during conditions of overcrowding in the pond.

These explicit model components, worked out through repeated cycles of adjusting parameters and holding outcomes accountable to students' qualitative expectations, provided a rich set of resources for their activities on the post test design challenge.

Reusing an Algebraic Proportion for Birthrate Without Understanding Quantities (Episode 5, Posttest, Part 1)

We now present an incident from the posttest in which the group displays evidence that the confusion described in Episode 3 has not been fully resolved. Although in the intervening couple of weeks the group had made good progress in understanding population models, as illustrated in Episode 4, it was of some concern that the particular confusions surrounding the derivation of birthrate from raw data appeared to persist.

The group was working on the posttest problem of constructing a model for a mouse population preyed on by cats. This sample of utterances is from fairly early in the episode, when students were settling on a birthrate for mice and had not yet considered predation:

Segment 5:

76	M	Four, five or six? per adult?
77	K	If we're going to go four, five or six, let's go four.
78	L	Actually lets use five. Its four through six. Let's use five.
82	M	Ok, how do we find out the birthrate? ((grabs a piece of paper))We do the ... five is what we decided on. How many did we start out with (looks at the computer)
83	L	Twenty
86	M	I'm not sure that this is right ((as he writes $5/20 = X/10$))
87	M	What's 500 divided by twenty?
88	L	What are you doing?
89	M	Finding out the birth rate
90	L	Oh yeah.
91	M	What's 500 divided by 20? ((K hands him the calculator and M starts punching in numbers))
92	M	25% I could have figured that out myself ((K laughs; M goes back to the computer)) 25% right? ((enters this into the birthrate)) and how many die?

Heterogeneous Representations and the Persistence of a Confusion. Line 82 illustrates the pervasive struggle with the semantics of numbers. M accepts that they will use 5 (babies per litter per season), which one might think is a birthrate, but in this context, "birthrate" is a specific number that can be entered into certain boxes on worksheet and computer screen. The birthrate, in this sense, they correctly appreciate they do not have, and this is precisely where they had problems before. The number they seek is a percentage. At line 87, M has implicitly multiplied the 5 by 100 and is now explicitly going about dividing by 20 (the number in the initial population). L, not surprisingly, does not understand where the 500 came from and asks for clarification, but receives only the description at the completely unhelpful level "finding out the birthrate."

The problem is then accepted as a calculation problem, and the semantics is left unaccessed. Why should the number of babies in one litter divided by the total number of adults in the population multiplied by 100 yield a percentage birthrate? The answer would appear to be that the basis is some dim memory of a ratio formula (Step 4, Fig. 1.2).

The group is content to continue to the next stage of the problem and does not question the reasonableness of the figure of 25%. This is testimony to the insulation of the numbers from what they mean. If each couple has 5 babies, the actual number is 250%. But the group does not provide evidence of how they found this number, or acknowledge that adults have to be paired up. The group does not even apply the qualitative reasoning that inasmuch as the parents are outnumbered by their babies, the birthrate must be more than 100%. Such qualitative inferences are only available if what the numbers are treated as standing for is something other than themselves—numbers. Even when the model actually turns out to extinguish the mice in short order, the problem is not traced to the low birthrate. It is all too easy for the error to hide in a complex model. The whole point of models is that many parameters contribute to their outcome. This means that there are many possible culprits when the outcome is unacceptable.

In summary, this confusion about the calculation of birthrates arises at least partly because of an attempt to make a creative labor-saving innovation close to the heart of the understanding of mathematical functions. Learning founders because the calculative transformations that are necessary to keep the ontology straight are not modified in the way that the innovation would require, and because there appears to be failure to appreciate that the software cannot automatically adapt its ontological interpretation of its inputs. A notable teaching opportunity is missed here because no teacher is present who can understand the innovation the group attempts and help them do the extra work that is needed to make it work. It is noteworthy that the group does not penetrate beyond the calculative world of numbers—the operations of the formalism—to think in terms of what the numbers stand for. Without a teacher, resort to the semantics is the only available source of feedback.

This persistent failure raises the question of why there are not further ramifications in the groups' learning of the other concepts of population dynamics. In fact, as is seen from the other episodes cited here, the group makes considerable strides in mastering the modeling of populations. One reason why the misunderstanding does not do more damage may be that the current difficulty affects an isolated precalculation of inputs to the simulated models. The group makes strides understanding the relations between parameters of the models and their behavior, showing, for example, that they understand the qualitative relations between the signs of changes to inputs and the signs of changes to outputs. But all this learning can go on without a complete grasp of ontology of the numbers that are entered into the model. It does not really affect conceptual understanding whether percentage increases or absolute population increases are used. The important concept that is lost is the concept of a birthrate being relative to a survival time.

So we see the group in Segment 4 able to relate the plunge in the graph of population to the extinction of the population while simultaneously failing to clear up their misconception about birthrate calculations. Semantic grounding does take place at the more synoptic level of interpretation of the models while simultaneously failing to take place with regard to the calculation of inputs.

Coordinating Representations of Predation to Link Populations and Finding a Crisis (Episode 6, Posttest, Part 2)

As seen earlier, at the posttest design challenge, the MLKN group's understanding of population concepts was still unstable and dependent on particular means of implementation, but they *were* able to implement and explain a functional model of predation. For example, as M struggled to combine timelines for mice and cat populations into an integrated model, L recalled their earlier use of a "Special 2 thing" (i.e., a user-defined function) to model the predation of guppies by wolf-fish during the classroom design project. This recalled use of a special function provided a starting point for a fully explicit implementation of predation on the posttest.

In the following exchange, recorded near the end of the MLKN posttest, L asked K for an update on what they are doing, while M and N (silent) worked to repair an error with their combined timeline. As K explained, they started the combined model with too many mice, generated in an earlier model of mice living alone.

Segment 6:

1	**L**	((to K)) Could you run that by me?
2	**K**	Um, we ran the model for two years. But we forgot that one year, the cats were living with them. So then they were dying [(inaudible).
3	**M**	[Forty eight. ((resets Moose/Mice to 48))
4	**L**	((looking at interface)) Uh huh.
5	**K**	[(Not in this year.)
6	**M**	[Ok, so now … bring that … to negative. ((relinks Special 2 to Moose/Mice negative pole)) And we started with, how many? ((scrolls down to check Wolves/Cats)) Six, ok. Here we go. Now build … to two thousand and four. ((resets timeline)) Two thousand and four … Now, to the end. ((runs To End))
7	**HT**	((huge negative value for Moose/Mice population))
8	**M**	Oo:::
9	**L**	So how many … [That's only]
10	**M**	[After], after two thousand and four there's negative [mice.

11	L	[Can we bring in some dogs there! ((laughing))
12	M	Ok::: ((laughing, opens graph window)) Kaboom.
13	HT	((huge negative decline for Moose/Mice))
14	L	Oh gosh!

At the end of this design challenge, Hall (as a research interviewer) asked the group exactly when mice died off. The students' first idea was to narrow the timeline, a simplification that increased the resolution of their graph in both axes for time and population abundance. They eventually used this more fine-grained graph and a table of linked values to find that, in their implementation of predation, cats consumed all the mice after only one month.

Comparing pre- and posttest performances (Segments 1 and 6), it is clear that the concept of predation—along with technical means for implementing, using, and interrogating this concept—changed within the working capacity of the MLKN group. Although they neither mentioned nor implemented predation on the pretest, at the posttest they made several important advances: They (a) combined partial results from an investigation of mice to model the introduction of cats; (b) defined a predation function that explicitly linked cat and mouse populations; (c) displayed, investigated, and explained a resulting crisis in the mouse population; and (d) noticed that cats would, in turn, face a related crisis brought about by a lack of food.

DISCUSSION

The Birthrate Concept

How do Episodes 3 and 5, illustrating misconceptions, compare to the earlier successful conceptual breakthrough in Episode 1? In particular, how is the involvement of heterogeneous representations similar and different across these episodes? In the successful episode (Episode 1), there is evidence that the conceptual breakthrough is precipitated by the shift in representational modality from numerical calculation to graphical representation. In contrast, the confusions in the birthrate episodes (Episodes 3 and 5) center on details of the semantic interpretation of numbers representing birthrates in different ways. Initially, these levels of analysis seem to have little in common: How is a shift from equation to graph comparable to the changes of units and survival periods in the calculation of the birthrate?

We believe this presentation exaggerates the difference in analyses of success and failure episodes. In the successful pretest episode, the breakthrough does not come as a response to a constructed graph (a shift in external modality of representation) but as a consequence of a subtle ontological change in representation preparatory to drawing a graph. An ontology of "total annual population increase" (the cardinality of a set of animals) and a number of years is replaced by an ontology of processes in which sets of animals have offspring one year, there is a maturation process, and a new set of animals represents the breeding population in the next year. It is perfectly conceivable that this change might have been precipitated even if students had not chosen to construct a graph.

If the successful episode must be understood as resulting from a shift in ontology comparable to the shifts observed in the unsuccessful episodes, it is also true that the unsuccessful episodes might have had different outcomes if there had been an external directive to shift modalities of representation. One can imagine that the construction of some timeline representation of the births and numerous early deaths of several cohorts of fry could have served as a basis for teaching the concept of "birthrate, relative to census time" or "survival rate." Again, a shift in modality to graphing might not be essential, but it serves to clarify the ontological shift that has to be achieved by some means or other. At one level, the problem in the unsuccessful episodes may be seen as a problem of the details of the "units of measurement." At another level, the problem is the learning of the transformation rules that coordinate these units into a system. The learning in the successful episode is just the same in that it is the learning of a set of transformation rules, eventually reencapsulated in the behavior of exponential functions. The failure is a failure to incorporate required transformations.

What these analyses do make clear is just what a sea of semantic complexities the group swims in. They are awash with numbers, and those numbers have to travel from one representational system to another to achieve the problem-solving task at hand. As they travel, numbers change their meanings and their names and their values. Birthrate is rarely the same thing on two mentions. The whole system cannot be understood as anything other than heterogeneous, and the interpretations as anything other than highly local. If we were to go through the transcript spelling out after each occurrence of a numeral the type of the entities it enumerates, we should wind up with some splendid and totally incomprehensible sentences. Nor are numerals the only problem. Simply spelling everything out is *not* to be recommended, other than as a way of exposing complexity for the theorist. We cannot understand the students' problems until this complexity is exposed, but simply spelling out senses is not a pedagogical solution.

From a theoretical perspective, this may seem either banal or outrageous. Once we are fluent at the skills of transformation required for coordinating the subsystems of representation, the whole system appears to take on a transparency and homogeneity that is completely illusory. We cease to notice how the very same word (here *birthrate*) means something quite different from occurrence to occurrence, as do many of the other words. We therefore can either forget that the system is heterogeneous (and respond with outrage to the claim), or we can, as theoreticians, claim that there is nothing very deep in the coordinations that are required (and respond with a yawn).

The students do not have the luxury of mastery. For example, one of the banal consequences of the instability of the meanings of the numerals is that there is a huge memory load, as evidenced in the repeated misrecalls of numbers from sheet to sheet as students work. We do not believe that there is any way of avoiding heterogeneity. Learning mastery of the coordination of representation systems is a requirement of learning mathematics and science (and probably most other things). But what we can strive to do is to educate both teachers and students into the quirks of the representational furniture they find themselves surrounded by.

Our research experience in classrooms indicates that teachers are rather wary of taking an explicitly metalinguistic stance. They do not often point out the dangers of shifts in meaning of words during an argument. The critical thinking lecturer warns students about equivocation—the same term being used with different meanings in different occurrences in an argument—but only at college. Equivocation is treated as a fallacy, usually assumed to be eradicable, and therefore is perhaps thought to be eliminable from well-kept classrooms. Our analysis in terms of heterogeneity and localness of interpretation strongly suggests that equivocation is not eliminable. We cannot use a unique terms for every meaning, and should not if we could. The use of the same term is often essential to anchor the term to the shared concept as the details shift through its various guises. Perhaps signaling when this is likely to be a problem would help. And perhaps teaching teachers to detect the seams between systems that have become transparent for them is an important aim.

But these observations from the classroom are just as important for theories of the semantics of representations. The conventional response to the kind of observations of language we made here is that everyone knows that natural language is ambiguous. It is easy to acknowledge heterogeneity if a system contains language and diagrams, and here the heterogeneity is on the surface. But the idea that natural language consists of many heterogeneous subsystems is generally resisted and explained away as polysemy at the lexical level. There are at least two problems with this explanation. The number of polysemous readings required is essentially infinite, and the meaning of one word is systematically related to that of others. Words in these discourses do not function atomistically—they are part of subsystems. If *birthrate* is construed one way, then its contrasting terms such as *death rate* and *survival rate* will also be construed in related ways—at least until there is a shift to a different subsystem. Recently, (e.g., Moravcsik, 1998) theories of lexical meaning have paid more attention to the considerable distance between the generalities of the lexicon and the details of contextualized language use. These stratified theories are much more conducive to understanding real language use and the heterogeneous nature of most reasoning.

The Predation Concept

Despite the difficulties the group had coordinating the semantics and calculations connected with the term *birthrate*, the longitudinal record of group work reveals more complex forms of coordination appearing in the ways that students moved between representing and represented worlds. By the time they faced the posttest design challenge (Episode 6), and by comparison with their group capacity on the same question in the pretest (Episode 2), we argue that the MLKN group both constructed and learned how to participate in a new system of activity involving productive coordinations across diverse systems of representation. How this actually develops within the longitudinal record is, of course, a serious theoretical and empirical challenge for existing theories of conceptual change and mathematics learning and teaching. Our hope is to have produced at least some partial answers in our analysis of selected moments, both positive and negative instances of coordination, within the longitudinal record.

Although still far from a technical implementation of their model in computational media (Segment 1), students were able to develop an elegant solution to the problem of stopping or limiting predation. Their work included conversations carried out over a stream environment that was jointly constructed in a shared gestural stage. Also central in these conversations were processes of animation in which students spoke for (or as) fish in the constructed stream environment, Venezuelan farmers who had diverging interests in these fish, biological consultants concerned with finding a solution for the loss of guppies to predation, and middle school students working on a design project (i.e., as themselves).

As these elaborations of the represented world were carried into computational media, new forms of coordination were required (Segments 3 and 4). These included forms of explanation that linked computational media to aspects of worlds being modeled (e.g., K's conditional explanation associated graph shapes with physical events at the net wall in Segment 2, Fig. 1.3). As the structural components of their network model were settled, members of the MLKN group also managed to establish cycles of modeling activity in which they adjusted parameters and compared results with their qualitative expectations.

Through these kinds of activities, students encountered the need to simultaneously look at and through the interface between representing and represented worlds. As they worked through design problems, new conceptual understanding depended on putting existing concepts and a broader set of representational technologies into coordination. In this sense, concepts—as systems of activity—developed in ways that were inseparable from the representational technologies that implemented them.

What Do Different Analytic Perspectives Contribute to Understanding How Conceptual Change Occurs in the MLKN Group?

A foundational analysis of the semantics of representations provides a highly abstract characterization of what words (and diagrams, etc.) stand for and what inferences can be made from one representation to another. In analyzing conceptual learning, a foundational analysis can show how preexisting fragments of multiple representation systems get coordinated into a coherent system that allows new inferences to be drawn. This kind of analysis at least has the virtue of reminding us—as teachers and as analysts—how substantial this coordination problem is for the student. For all its abstraction, this kind of analysis is necessary for understanding the work students have to do, before we can set about studying how they actually achieve that work.

The modern guise of foundational semantic analysis as a mathematical discipline makes it easy to forget that in its origins, logic was an analysis of argument—a social phenomenon—that involved communication between parties misaligned as to concepts, meanings, knowledge, or belief. Logic can be seen as providing a highly abstract criterion for mutual understanding, but it certainly does not provide directions as to how to get there, nor even an operable test for being certain one has arrived. So the study of the dynamics of real argument is needed to supply some explanations as to why the group's discourse takes this or that trajectory. Participants may be unsatisfied by some move the group makes, but mere expression of dissatisfaction is unlikely to deflect the group. Even articulation of a contradiction does not provide a new direction. If an insight can be articulated that provides a new direction, then the group may be moved and new coordinations may be achieved. The dynamics are determined neither solely by personality nor solely by proposition.

An analysis of intergroup dynamics requires augmentation by analysis of regularities in different kinds of groups. Mathematical, biological, classroom, student group, and home discourses are different, and of course all themselves complex. School learning is importantly distinguished by the differentiation of disciplinary discourses. What would a mathematician do here? Something different from what a biologist would do, or a student in class or at home. Here one of the contributions of our analysis is to show how the discourse of actual learning is compound. Whereas a casual observer might expect the discourse of a project group to be homogeneous, involving students exclusively in their project-group roles, what we actually observe is talk that is compounded of the discourses of imagined experts, farmers, and even fish. This compounding plays a critical role in what is learned and how representational coordination is achieved.

By and large, academia is currently organized so that these three kinds of analyses are conducted as three separate discourses themselves.

Our purpose in bringing them together and exemplifying them in the same material is to challenge this separation. In our prime example of insight (Episode 1), a self-contained discourse of mathematical multiplication is intruded on by the facts of biological multiplication. The things that the numbers stand for reassert themselves, even to the extent that their affective properties come to the fore. The members of the group achieve this episode of conceptual change through discourse contributions that might easily have had a different conceptual outcome. It is not just that three separate analyses complement each other, but rather that coordination helps us, as a field, to make conceptual progress.

At many points in our work, this group of authors remarked on the analogies between our conceptual predicament and that of the MLKN group. Whether we have made as much progress is for the reader to judge. Our aim has been one of exemplification—to persuade the reader that, in the MLKN group's learning at least, all three perspectives are necessary, and that they are at least productively consistent each with the other.

REFERENCES

Barwise, J., & Etchemendy, J. (1994). *Hyperproof.* Stanford: CSLI Publications.

Brown, J. S., & Burton, R. B. (1980). Diagnostic models for procedural bugs in basic mathematical skills. *Cognitive Science, 4,* 379–426.

Brownell, W. A. (1935). Psychological considerations in the learning and teaching of arithmetic. In W. D. Reeve (Ed.), *The teaching of arithmetic: Tenth yearbook of the National Council of Teachers of Mathematics* (pp. 1–31). New York: Columbia University Press.

Clark, H. H., & Schaefer, E. F. (1989). Contributing to discourse. *Cognitive Science, 13*(2), 259–294.

Clement, J. (1989) Learning via model construction and criticism: Protocol evidence on sources of creativity in science. In G. Glover, R. Ronning, & C. Reynolds (Eds.), *Handbook of creativity: Assessment, theory, and research* (pp. 341–381). New York: Plenum.

Cobb, P., Yackel, E., & McClain, K. (1999). *Symbolizing and communicating: Perspectives on mathematical discourse, tools, and instructional design.* Mahwah, NJ: Lawrence Erlbaum Associates.

Dewey, J. (1985). How we think. In J. A. Boydston (Ed.), *The middle works of John Dewey 1899–1924* (Vol. 6, pp. 157–357). Carbondale IL: Southern Illinois University Press. (Original work published 1910.)

Engestrom, Y. (1993). Developmental studies of work as a testbench of activity theory: The case of primary care medical practice. In S. Chaklin & J. Lave (Eds.), *Understanding practice: Perspectives on activity and context* (pp. 64–103). Cambridge, UK: Cambridge University Press.

Engle, R. A., & Conant, F. R. (in preparation). *Design principles supporting productive disciplinary engagement: An emergent argument in a community of learners classroom.*

Engle, R. A., Conant, F. R., Wiebe, M., Erickson, F. D., & Greeno, J. G. (2000, April). *"We had this big old argument": The simultaneous construction of student identities and academic content in a population biology unit.* Paper presented at the annual meeting of the American Educational Research Association, New Orleans.

Goffman, E. (1979). Footing. *Semiotica, 25*, 1–29. (Reprinted in Goffman, E. [1981] *Forms of talk*. Philadelphia: University of Pennsylvania Press).

Goldman, S., Moschkovich, J., & The Middle-School Mathematics through Applications Project Team (1995). Environments for collaborating mathematically: The Middle-school Mathematics through Applications Project. In J. L. Schnase & E. L. Cunnius (Eds.), *Proceedings of CSCL '95: The First International Conference on Computer Support for Collaborative Learning*. Mahwah, NJ: Lawrence Erlbaum Associates.

Goodwin, C. (1994). Professional vision. *American Anthropologist, 96*(3), 606–633.

Gravemeijer, K. E. P. (1994). *Developing realist mathematics education*. Utrecht, The Netherlands: CD-Beta Press.

Greeno, J. G., & Hall, R. P. (1997, January). Practicing representation: learning with and about representational forms. *Phi Delta Kappa*, 361–367.

Greeno, J. G., Sommerfeld, M. S., & Wiebe, M. (2000). Practices of questioning and explaining in learning to model. In L. R. Gleitman & A. K. Joshi (Eds.), *Proceedings of the twenty-second annual conference of the cognitive science society* (pp. 669–674). Mahwah, NJ: Lawrence Erlbaum Associates.

Greeno, J. G., & The Middle-School Mathematics through Applications Project (MMAP). (1998). The situativity of knowing, learning, and research. *American Psychologist, 53*(1), 5–26.

Hall, R. (1996). Representation as shared activity: Situated cognition and Dewey's cartography of experience. *Journal of the Learning Sciences, 5*(3), 209–238.

Hall, R. (1999). *Case studies of math at work: exploring design-oriented mathematical practices in school and work settings*. Final Report to the National Science Foundation (RED–9553648).

Hall, R. (2000). Work at the interface between representing and represented worlds in middle school mathematics design projects. In L. R. Gleitman & A. K. Joshi (Eds.), *Proceedings of the twenty-second annual conference of the cognitive science society* (pp. 675–680). Mahwah, NJ: Lawrence Erlbaum Associates.

Hall, R., & Rubin, A. (1998). There's five little notches in here: Dilemmas in teaching and learning the conventional structure of rate. In J. G. Greeno & S. V. Goldman (Eds.), *Thinking practices in mathematics and science learning* (pp. 189–235). Mahwah, NJ: Lawrence Erlbaum Associates.

Hall, R., & Stevens, R. (1995). Making space: a comparison of mathematical work in school and professional design practices. In S. L. Star (Ed.), *The cultures of computing* (pp. 118–145). London: Basil Blackwell.

Hall, R., & Stevens, R. (1996). Teaching/learning events in the workplace: a comparative analysis of their organizational and interactional structure. In G. W. Cottrell (Ed.), *Proceedings of the eighteenth annual conference of the Cognitive Science Society* (pp. 160–165). Hillsdale, NJ: Lawrence Erlbaum Associates.

Hall, R., Stevens, R., & Torralba, A. (in press). Disrupting representational infrastructure in conversations across disciplines. *Mind, Culture, & Activity*.

Holland, D., Lachicotte, W., Skinner, D., & Cain, C. (1998). *Identity and agency in cultural worlds*. Cambridge, MA: Harvard University Press.

Latour, B. (1999). *Pandora's hope: Essays on the reality of science studies*. Cambridge, MA: Harvard University Press.

Leont'ev (1981). The problem of activity in psychology. In J. Wertsch (Ed.), *The concept of activity in Soviet psychology* (pp. 37–71). Armonk, NY: M. E. Sharpe.

Moravscik, J. M. (1998) *Meaning, creativity, and the partial inscrutability of the human mind*. Stanford: CSLI Publications.

Nathan, M. J., Kintsch, W., & Young, E. (1992). A theory of algebra-word-problem comprehension and its implications for the design of learning environments. *Cognition and Instruction, 9*, 329–389.

Nemirovsky, R. (in press). How one experience becomes part of another. In K. Beach (Ed.), Special issue of *The Journal of the Learning Sciences.*

Newell, A., & Simon, H. (1972). *Human problem solving.* Englewood Cliffs, NJ: Prentice-Hall.

Oberlander, J., Monaghan, P., Cox, R., Stenning, K., & Tobin, R. (1999). Unnatural language discourse: an empirical study of multimodal proof styles. *Journal of Logic, Language and Information, 8,* 363–384.

Ochs, E., Jacoby, S., & Gonzales, P. (1994). Interpretive journeys: How physicists talk and travel through graphic space. *Configurations, 1,* 151–171.

O'Conner, K., & Michaels, S. (1996). Aligning academic task and participation status through revoicing: Analysis of a classroom discourse strategy. *Anthropology & Education Quarterly, 24*(4), 318–335.

Resnick, L. B., & Omanson, S. F. (1987). Learning to understand arithmetic. In R. Glaser, (Ed.), *Advances in instructional psychology* (pp. 41–95). Hillsdale, NJ: Lawrence Erlbaum Associates.

Saxe, G. B. (1991). *Culture and cognitive development: Studies in mathematical understanding.* Hillsdale, NJ: Lawrence Erlbaum Associates.

Saxe, G. B., & Guberman, S. R. (1998). Emergent arithmetical environments in the context of distributed problem solving: Analyses of children playing an educational game. In J. G. Greeno & S. V. Goldman (Eds.), *Thinking practices in mathematics and science learning* (pp. 237–256). Mahwah NJ: Lawrence Erlbaum Associates.

Sayeki, Y., Ueno, N., & Nagasaka, T. (1991). Mediation as a generative model for obtaining an area. *Learning and Instruction, 1,* 229–242.

Schwartz, D. L., & Black, J. B. (1996). Shuttling between depictive models and abstract rules: Induction and fallback. *Cognitive Science, 20,* 457–497.

Schwartz, J. L., Yerushalmy, M., & Wilson, B. (Eds.). (1993). *The geometric supposer: What is it a case of?* Hillsdale, NJ: Lawrence Erlbaum Associates.

Sfard, A., & Kieran, C. (2001). Cognition as communication: Rethinking learning-by-talking through multi-faceted analysis of students' mathematical interactions. *Mind, Culture, and Activity, 8*(1), 42–77.

Stenning, K. (1999). The cognitive consequences of modality assignment for educational communication: The picture in logic teaching. *Learning and Instruction, 9*(4), 391–410.

Stenning, K., Cox, R., & Oberlander, J. (1995). Contrasting the cognitive effects of graphical and sentential logic teaching: Reasoning, representation and individual differences. *Language & Cognitive Processes, 10*(3–4), 333–354.

Stenning, K., & Sommerfeld, M. (2000) Heterogeneous reasoning and learning to model. In L. R. Gleitman & A. K. Joshi, (Eds.), *Proceedings of the twenty-second annual meeting of the Cognitive Science Society.* Mahwah, NJ: Lawrence Erlbaum Associates.

Stevens, R., & Hall, R. (1998). Disciplined perception: learning to see in technoscience. In M. Lampert & M. Blunk (Eds.), *Talking mathematics in school: Studies of teaching and learning* (pp. 107–149). Cambridge, UK: Cambridge University Press.

Tudge, J., & Rogoff, B. (1989). Peer influences on cognitive development: Piagetian and Vygotskian perspectives. In M. H. Bornstein & J. S. Bruner (Eds.), *Interaction in human development* (pp. 32–56). Hillsdale, NJ: Lawrence Erlbaum Associates.

Wertheimer, M. (1959). *Productive thinking.* New York: Harper.

Chapter 2

Modeling in Teaching and Learning Elementary Physics

Jacques Vince
Andrée Tiberghien
UMR GRIC, Université Lumière Lyon 2

This chapter deals with physics teaching and learning by students at the high school level. As is very well known, physics is considered to be a difficult discipline to learn, and nowadays at university level and even at high school level, the scientific disciplines are not among the favorite disciplines in terms of students' choice. This social context emphasizes the necessity of analyzing which physics aspects are so difficult to learn and how the teaching sequence and associated teaching materials can help to overcome such difficulties. The study presented here contributes to this analysis. We first present the two aspects of our approach related respectively to the knowledge to be taught and to students' learning. Then we present a simulation software program that is designed for modeling sound.

HOW TO ANALYZE THE KNOWLEDGE TO BE TAUGHT AND THE STUDENTS' KNOWLEDGE?

Our analysis is based on two choices: (a) A major process of physics knowledge is modeling the material world. Consequently, we consider this process as an essential aspect in physics teaching. (b) Another fundamental aspect deals with the students' difficulties in physics learning.

In this part we first present these two aspects, then we discuss our categorization of the knowledge involved in physics teaching and learning. All the examples of teaching and learning situations deal with sound.

The Modeling Activity in Physics

The nature of the modeling activity in physics is not developed here, as this kind of analysis has been made by several epistemologists (e.g., Bachelard, 1979; Bunge, 1975; Giere, 1988). Bunge (1975) stated that, in the case of physics:

[With a general theory framework or theories on specific physical systems] we cannot speak of a very particular type of objects (nucleus surrounded by protons or turbulence of liquids) without having constructed a model of these objects, that is a schematic idealization of the real thing in which such or such characteristic is emphasised. (p. 61)

In our case, we consider a very elementary view on the process of modeling—material objects and observable events are interpreted and/or predicted by a theoretical set including theories and model. This choice is justified to the extent that we are not dealing with research in physics but with physics teaching and learning at an elementary level (Tiberghien, 1994).

Students' Difficulties in Learning Physics

To illustrate characteristic difficulties, we use an example from the study of a teaching sequence on sound at an upper high school (Besson et al., 1998; Tiberghien, 2000; Vince, 2000a). The students are introduced to the concepts of amplitude and frequency, two physics concepts that have to be related respectively to loud/faint or high/low pitched sound. After the teaching sequence on sound, the students have to answer the following written question (see Table 2.1).

TABLE 2.1

A Written Question Asked After Teaching About Sound in Different Schools at the First Year Level of Upper Secondary School (15-Year-Olds)

Very often, it is stated that a sound has three characteristics: the acoustic level (loud/faint), the pitch (high/low) and the timbre (more or less rich). Give a physics concept (or a physics parameter), dealing with the sound vibration which corresponds to each of the following properties.

Sound characteristics	acoustic level	pitch	timbre
Physics parameter	...of the vibration	of the vibration	of the vibration

By making complete each sentence, tell how this parameter should evolve (increasing or decreasing for example) to obtain the indicated result;

	must ...... in order that the sound be louder	must ...... in order that the sound be high pitched	must ...... in order that the sound be richer

Correct answer

Sound characteristics	acoustic level	pitch	timbre
Physics parameter	*amplitude* of the vibration ...	*frequency* of the vibration ...	*spectrum* of the vibration ...

Note. The teaching content is not our teaching sequence for half of the sample.

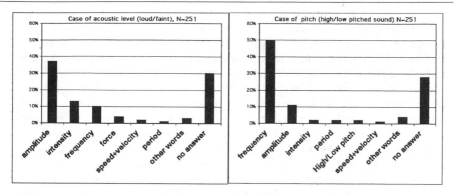

FIG. 2.1.   Types of students' answers to the question given Table 2.1 (in French there is a single word: "vitesse"; this is why the item is speed + velocity).

Figure 2.1 gives the percentage of words used by the students in the cases of acoustic level and pitch. Out of the 251 answers, less than 40% relate amplitude of vibration with the correct perceptual character of sound (loud/faint). In the case of the frequency, half of the population establishes the right relation between the concept and the perceptible character of sound (high/low pitch).

These fundamental relations between perceivable events and physics concepts, which are necessary to study sound from a physics point of view, are not acquired by half of the students (15 years old) at the end of 3 months teaching about sound. This result is not isolated; many other results in different domains (electricity, mechanics, etc.) confirm such difficulties in learning physics. Some people with a good physics education deny such results, thinking that in everyday life the correct distinction is made. In fact, in everyday life, very frequently sound is described in very general terms—loud can be associated with high or low pitched sound depending on the situations and/or the individual. This result can be interpreted in the following way: *establishing relevant relations between the physics model and the observable objects and events is a very difficult task*. However, such relations are the meaningful core of physics. Based on this interpretation, we propose to analyze the physics knowledge that needs to be taught and students' knowledge to better understand these difficulties and to be able to design relevant teaching situations to help students establish such relations.

Categorizations of Knowledge

We present two types of categorization.

Categorization Based on Modeling.   The previous example illustrates that a major difficulty in physics learning is to establish meaningful links between parts of the physics theory and models on one hand and the material objects and events on the other hand. At the same time, establishing these links is a fundamental process in physics. This leads us to introduce two main categories in knowledge analysis: the world of theory and model, and the world of objects and events (Fig. 2.2). We need to keep in mind that this categorization aims to analyze the knowledge to be taught, the knowledge that is *actually* taught, and students' understanding of the knowledge. Then this categorization deals with the oral, gestural, or written productions, that is, knowledge involved in communications. This choice leads us to specify what we mean by the world of objects and events. In this world the verbal and gesture productions are categorized in terms of what is directly perceived in the material world. This categorization is not absolute; it depends on the context of the production. Some productions like "the amplitude of the vibration can change without changing frequency" or "this sound is loud" are easily categorized as belonging to the world of theory and model and the world of object and events, respectively. Other verbal productions cannot be categorized so easily.

This example (Fig. 2.1) also illustrates the role of students' everyday knowledge in interpreting or predicting such material situations. More generally, the students' explanations or predictions can be based on diverse explanatory systems (Carey, 1985; Vosniadou & Brewer, 1994). Thus the explanatory systems, which are called a theoretical framework, are not unique—individuals draw on frameworks according to the objects and events in question, as well as the social situation. However, these frameworks are rather general to the extent that they can be applied to a variety of situations.

Consequently, in this categorization we have two main categories both for physics knowledge and everyday knowledge dealing with the material world: the theory/model world and the objects/event world. In each world, we differentiate the aspects of knowledge that are specific to physics and those that deal with everyday knowledge (Fig. 2.2).

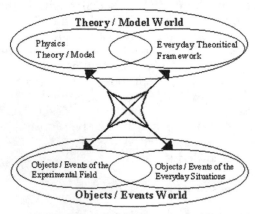

FIG. 2.2. The two worlds of categorization of knowledge based on modeling the material world.

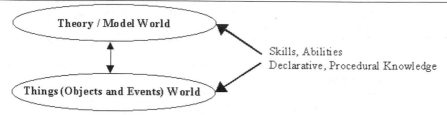

FIG. 2.3.   Categorization of knowledge based on a modeling activity.

Compared to other categorizations of knowledge, such as the classification into procedural and declarative knowledge that is very often used in problem-solving research, our categorization is transversal. That is, both worlds can include declarative and procedural knowledge. Consider, for example, the statement "the membrane of the loudspeaker is moving." This statement, in itself, involves declarative knowledge in the world of objects and events. By contrast, the statement "the wavelength increases because the frequency of the vibration decreases" is also declarative, but is categorized in the world of theory/model (Fig. 2.3).

Semiotic Registers.   Another way of decomposing knowledge is to take into account the semiotic aspects of the situation. Duval (1995) used the concept of semiotic registers. Graphs, algebra, geometrical mathematics, natural language, and drawings are all different registers. These registers constitute the degrees of freedom at the disposal of a person to transform an idea, as yet unclear, into an object of thinking for himself/herself (see p. 21). From this perspective, a hypothesis on learning is that an individual's understanding of a concept (or, more generally, an idea) develops when relations are established between different semiotic registers associated with the idea.

Analysis of the Types of Concepts Involved in Modeling

Constructing a meaning for the physics concepts introduced in the teaching sequences is the main aspect of learning that we want to study. If we suppose that the students construct a meaning of the new physics concepts from what they already know, then in the case of sound we consider that their previous knowledge is "everyday."

Following a French linguist, Gentilhomme (1994), we make a distinction between what he calls *notion* and *concepts* where "notion" corresponds to the everyday concept and "concept" to the scientific one. As Cornuéjols, Tiberghien, and Collet (2000) wrote:

> notions and concepts can be distinguished from a linguistic point of view,
> considering the properties of the linguistic items themselves, and their be-

haviour pattern within verbal productions. Though everyday language and scientific language cannot easily be separated from each other, some criteria are still fit for use. Here is a short list of characteristics for notions (everyday concepts):

- Their meaning is fixed by the requirements for social communication, and shared by all speakers.
- Their meaning is *flexible*. Figures of speech are possible and quite frequent, such as metaphor, metonymy, play on words, that can alter the meaning in various and gradual ways. Notions can also evolve by adjunction of modalities.
- Notion can be reformulated. The notional level allows the use of synonyms and various re-formulations .
- Notions can be altered when translated from one language to another.

The "flexible" characteristic of notion is very important when considering the relations between the two worlds. For example, the word *sound* can have a lot of attributes (loud, high pitched, but also pleasant, etc.).

In the teaching sequence mentioned earlier (Besson et al., 1998; Vince, 2000a), the aim of the first session is that students construct a first notion of vibration by inducing what is common to all the events creating sound. They can touch and get a sensory perception of back and forth movement and of sound in different situations (e.g., for low frequency, sound is not perceived but back and forth movement can be seen; this movement can be perceived by touch for higher audible frequencies). The concept of vibration becomes relevant to describe sounds that therefore are associated with two classes of events in a relationship: back and forth movement, and the emission of sound.

In this session, the students extend the meaning of sound and vibration through trying to understand the following situation: When the students are manipulating the Low Frequency Generator and observing and touching the membrane of the loudspeaker, a student says:

Ni (TP1, 198):[1] *You know […] if you put a sound with high or low pitch, the sound it does not move the same, it propagates the air differently, the sound it is a propagation of the air.*

Later, when starting to write the report on this experiment, Ch, who is working with him in the dyad, says:

Ch (TP1, 219): [the source of the sound] *emitted by the loudspeaker it is thanks to the membrane, to the movement*

…

Ch (TP1, 221): *is thanks to the movement vibration*

And **Ni** concludes (TP1, 231) [is thanks to] *vibrations of the membrane.*

---

[1]The first two letters (Ni or Ch) indicate the name of the students; TP means "Travaux Pratiques" (Laboratory activities); the number (1) indicates the order of the teaching session; the last number (605) indicates the dialogue turn in the dialogue in a given session.

In the first part of this extract, the sound is identified with the propagation itself. Such an interpretation tries to describe what cannot be directly perceived and yet takes place. In that case, the flexibility of the notion of sound associated with propagation without being clearly differentiated (sound propagates) is a help to the verbalization.

In the second part, the students associate the sound perception with the movement of the membrane and spontaneously introduce the notion of vibration. In this case, which is representative of most of the students' productions, this notion is compatible with the relevant physics concepts.

Still in the same first session of the teaching sequence, specific concepts like frequency and amplitude of the vibration are introduced and their definition should not allow the flexibility to invent a meaning that is not compatible with the very precise definition.

The students have to measure the frequency of the vibration of the loudspeaker's membrane (around 1 to 3 Hertz) by directly observing the membrane and using a chronometer. Then the frequency is increased.

Ni (TP1, 605): [the teacher asks them to count the number of back and forth movements of the membrane of the loudspeaker] *it makes the heart....*

Ni (732): *more the frequency of the vibration is rapid, is high*

Ch (733): *yeah high is better*

Ni (734): *yeah ... more the sound is high pitched*

....

Ni (738): *but it [the membrane] still vibrates ... it is like the heart you know it is like the vein of the sound*

This example illustrates the relation established by the students between the concept of frequency under construction and the object and events (high-pitched sound). Here the meaning of the frequency corresponds to relations with the observables (Fig. 2.4). However, most of the scientific concepts—as Cassirer (1977), a German epistemologist

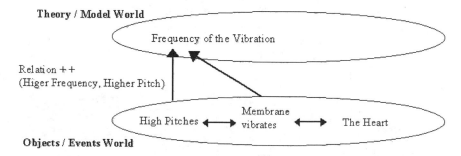

FIG. 2.4.   Relations established by the students during teaching. The frequency is mainly related to elements of the object/event world.

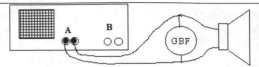

FIG. 2.5. Experimental setting during laboratory activity (GBF corresponds to the French name of Low Frequency Generator).

from the beginning of the 20th century stated—are relational, that is, they are defined by the relations established with other concepts. Cassirer distinguished this type of concept from the *categorical concepts* that are defined by a set of invariant properties. Here the frequency is more categorical than relational. This is associated with a close relationship between the two worlds. This is in line with the definition itself based on the invariant extracted from observations of the material world even if the invariant is the result of a choice.

Later in the teaching sequence, the same students are studying the shape of the curve on the oscilloscope according to the adjustment of the Low Frequency Generator (LFG) for frequency and amplitude (Fig. 2.5).

Ni (TP3, 93): *the amplitude ... the frequency of the voltage stays constant*

Ch (TP3, 94): *there ... there this is the frequency and this it is the amplitude* (touches the LFG)

Ni (TP3, 95): *then/ to increase then to decrease the amplitude of the electrical voltage / yeah but to increase then to decrease the amplitude therefore we have to stay at 500* [hertz (frequency)]

Ch (TP3, 96): *yeah*

Ni (TP3, 97): *yeah right ... / yeah louder and less loud / yeah go right*

In this example as it is shown in Fig. 2.6, the frequency is in relation with other concepts in the sense that it is distinguished from amplitude, is associated with vibration, and it has a value with a measurement unit. The teaching sequence aims at developing the following concept of vibration.

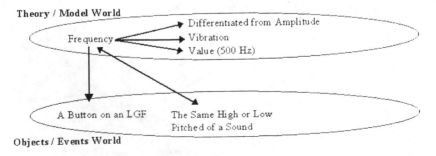

FIG. 2.6. Relations established by the students during teaching. The frequency is related to other elements of the theory/model world.

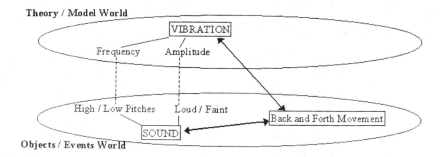

FIG. 2.7.   (cf. Vince, 2000, p. 320). Modeling activity based on the model of vibration.

In the whole teaching sequence, the concept of vibration is developed and related to the other concepts of frequency and amplitude, as shown in Fig 2.7. The different aspects of the concepts, relations with other concepts, and with objects and events are called, later in this chapter, *facets of concept.* In this teaching sequence as usual in physics, the students are introduced to other semiotic registers than that of natural language. In everyday life natural language is used most of the time to deal with sound. In the teaching sequence a variety of semiotic registers are introduced. In the examples given previously, numbers are introduced, the drawing of the back and forth movement, the graphs given by the oscilloscope. A microscopic representation of the propagation of sound is given, too. Then the students have to establish links between these representations, which for us is a way in which the students construct their understanding.

On What Knowledge Can Science Learning Be Constructed?

This previous analysis shows the essential differences between physics knowledge and everyday knowledge concerning:

- The type of concepts or notions and concepts according to Gentilhomme (1994). On the scientific side, the specificity of the concepts in both worlds, the different types of concept (relational/categorical) in each world, in the theory/model world their relational character, the associated formalisms, and the necessity of the associated knowledge to establish relations with elements of the objects/events world. On the everyday side, the notions are flexible with a few types of associated representation and in both worlds most of the concepts are of the same type, categorical.
- The type and the variety of semiotic registers. In everyday life, in the two worlds the semiotic registers are mainly natural language

and some analog representations. In physics, there are a variety of formal representations in the theory/model worlds, and even in the objects/events world the numerical register is involved with measurement via various readings.

- The relations between the two worlds. On the scientific side the relations are an object of knowledge, they are not direct, whereas in everyday life they are spontaneous and direct. This is not surprising inasmuch as a relational concept can be defined through relations with other concepts, and then its relation with the objects/events world has to be found. Most of the categorical concepts of everyday life are defined through invariant relations between the perceived objects and events, and then the relations with them are intrinsic to the concept itself.

These differences lead us to consider that learning physics has a high cognitive cost. Consequently, if scientific education for all is wanted, it is necessary to select the aspects of scientific knowledge that are learnable with a reasonable cost and that allow the learner to acquire a meaningful approach for a significant number of relevant material situations. In this case, it is necessary to know what aspects of everyday knowledge are useful to start learning physics according to the facets of the concepts that are to be acquired.

This approach also shows as others have shown (Buty, 2000; Leach & Scott, 1995; Minstrell, 1992) that it is necessary to analyze both the knowledge to be taught and the students' knowledge at a fine grain of analysis. In the following section we give an example of teaching materials for which the design is based on our knowledge categorizations and hypotheses about learning. This is a software program about sound that involves simulation.

DESIGN OF THE TEACHING RESOURCE: *SimulaSON*

SimulaSON is a simulation software program that aims at "staging" physics models in an interactive way (Vince, 2000a, 2000b). We follow Grémy (1985), who considers simulation as experimentation with a model. Simulation is a process of scientific research that consists of carrying out an artificial reproduction (model) of a phenomena to be studied, in observing the behavior of this reproduction when actions are exerted on the simulation, in inducing what would be going on in the reality under the influence of analog actions.

The *SimulaSON* software program is designed to help students to construct meaningful links between the theory/model of sound and the object and events relative to sound—in particular, the multisensory perception of sound (Vince & Tiberghien, 2000). Consequently, *SimulaSON* presents two main aspects of sound: vibration and propagation. It also should be used by the learners with a text and schemas giving the physics model (see Appendix). It is also designed on the hypothesis that the relations between different representations of the same concept favor the learner's construction of concepts.

Thus we propose the use of simulated objects and events in order to give representations of concepts dealing with vibration and propagation. Elaborating such representations implies a "manipulation" of those concepts. The objects of the simulated world are neither real objects, nor elements of theories or models. They are intermediaries that facilitate the links between the world of objects and events and the world of theory and models through the activity of problem solving: In the following description we call what is represented on the screen the simulated world. With Beaufils, Durey, and Journaux (1987), we think "the notion of modeling [...] should constitute one of the objectives of the use of simulation in teaching" (p. 327). The simulation not only aims to give a representation of a model but also to give a meaning to the model owing to the representation of the simulated phenomena. This representation introduces the mechanism of the behavior of the particles; it has a meaning in itself even if relations with other worlds are necessary.

A major objective of *SimulaSON* is to provide an animated representation that explicitly involves simulated objects. Next we discuss how *SimulaSON* "stages" the concepts of vibration and propagation.

Vibration

SimulaSON is supposed to be used by students when they have constructed a first notion of vibration, by inducing what is common to all the events that create sound. In our teaching sequence, this first acquisition is at least partly done after the first session (Vince, 2000b, Besson et al., 1998). However, *SimulaSON* aims to develop this basic teaching objective in linking a sound and a vibration, which also implies the establishment of links between an auditory event and a mechanical one.

The next step consists of establishing relations between the sound perception of high/low pitch and the frequency of vibration. It is extremely difficult to attain this objective with only material objects because their behavior cannot be directly related to the frequency and amplitude of the vibrations. The simulation introduces a dynamic representation of the concepts; it allows us to display (make visible) the effects of the respective variations of frequency and amplitude of the back and forth movement of a vibrating simulated surface (relation 1 in Fig. 2.8, see also the screen snapshot Fig. 2.9, on p. 63).

There is a moving line on the screen. The movement is slow enough to be observed and the indicated values are those of the simulation. In the case of amplitude, the value is in centimeters. Then it can be directly checked by observation of the screen (Fig. 2.9). To evaluate the frequency and check the value on the screen, a chronometer is included in the software.

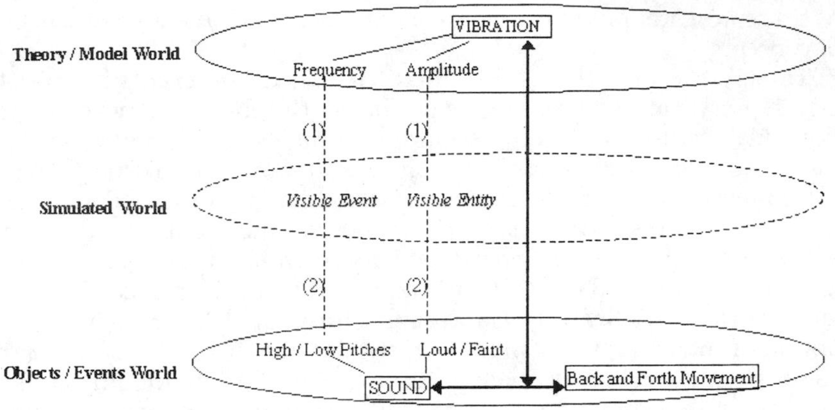

FIG. 2.8. Relations between the different worlds in the case of vibration.

Then *SimulaSON*, simultaneously but via different sense perceptions (hearing and eyesight), presents the simulated objects and the "observable" events (audible). On the interface, the user acts on the simulated objects, in particular on the amplitude and the frequency of the movement of the vibrating line, and simultaneously the user can hear a sound (relation 2 in Fig. 2.8). The links between the action on the screen and the sound emitted by the computer are the following:

- for the amplitude, the link is purely qualitative, the sound intensity rises or decreases when the amplitude of the vibrating line on the screen is increased or decreased via the user's action on the interface;
- for the frequency, the explicit link is semiquantitative because the frequency of the perceived sound is, at each instant, 1,000 times more than the frequency of the observed movement (the step of the sound frequency is 50 Hz).

Propagation

SimulaSON simulates the behavior of particles that obey a microscopic model. Such a model is considered as a help to better understand the phenomena of propagation, in particular the distinction between space and time. We make the hypothesis that a particulate model can help learners to interpret and predict macroscopic events related to sound. *SimulaSON* represents the compressions and expansions of the air when a sound is propagating and that corresponds to a sound wave model. This representation is based on a particular model, allowing the observer to distinguish what is going on in space and in time (see Vince, 2000b for a detailed presentation of the implementation of this model). Then the particles appear as simulated ones; the possible actions on these particles are impossible in the real world (e.g., coloring one of them). From the set of particles, it is possible to observe the zones of compression and expansion (space aspect) and the modification of the state of a given zone from a compressed state to an expanded one (time aspect). The physical quantities of the model—velocity and wavelength—are also available to the student at each instant. If the relevance of a physical quantity such as the wavelength to describe the propagation of sound and the state of the air in space is obvious for the physicist, this is not the case for beginners. The students can construct a meaning for the conceptual tool "wavelength" only when the mechanism of the propagation is at least partly understood in the sense of making a distinction between what is going on in time and space. Consequently, *SimulaSON* allows the student to get the values of the three physical quantities, period, velocity, and wavelength that are those corresponding to the representation on the screen and not those of the sound that can be heard. Measurements can be done by the students (a chronometer and a rule are integrated into the interface (Fig. 2.9) and the students can obtain these quantities by themselves.

Representation of Concepts and Display of the Information

The development of *SimulaSON* necessitates specifying the representations of the objects involved in the software. In order that students can establish relations between diverse semiotic registers of the same concept, it is necessary to clearly distinguish the representations. Our implementation takes these distinctions into account (display on the screen, color associated to each screen, etc.). When it is possible, the modification of a representation implies modifications of the others.

The user, via a button (Fig. 2.9), calls each window (except the graph). Table 2.2 describes the different windows and the representations used.

Table 2.3 gives an example of how the different "facets" of the concept frequency and amplitude (from the physics point of view) are involved in the representations and which specific information it gives.

Organization of the Different Windows and Representations

To organize the different windows we use the following learning hypothesis: the learner has to establish links between the different semiotic registers corresponding to concepts in order to construct the meaning of concepts. This is why each facet of a concept appears in a separate window, and each window has a color of reference. All the windows can be opened or closed, depending on the learner's choice, except the window representing the graph of the frequency on the X-axis and the amplitude on the Y-axis (a choice in agreement with the conventional representa-

TABLE 2.2
Description of the Different Representations

Windows	Semiotic register	Objects and represented concepts	Allowed actions	Associated Colour
Graphic	graph (non analog)	– frequency (X axis) – amplitude (Y axis)	modifiable	Red
Numerical values (parameters of the vibration)	expression algebraic + unit (non analog)	– frequency (Hz) + period (s) – amplitude (cm)	none	Yellow
Sound	sound	– auditory perception (high/low pitch; loud/faint)	none	Green
Vibration	diagram (analog)	– vertical line moving – amplitude (fine vertical line) + frequency of displacement	pause, animation	Blue
Microscopic	diagram (analog)	– simulated source (reprise including the "vibration") – "particles" + "specific particles"	pause, animation, step by step	Grey
Sensor/ Screen	graph (non analog)	2 curves (with shape, amplitude and frequency) linked to an object of the microscopic model	displace- ment of sensors	Black

tion of the spectrum). The parameters "frequency" and "amplitude" can only be changed from this window, which is the "control console" of the quantities. The other windows can be opened by a click of a button that has the same color as the window (Fig. 2.9).

Some links between these representations explicitly appear on the screen. This is the case for the microscopic simulation and the vibration because the movement of the vibrating line is exactly the same as the movement of the source line in the simulated cavity. Moreover, the window "sensor and screen" can be opened only when the microscopic representation is on the screen. The explicit links between the different windows are illustrated in Fig. 2.10.

TABLE 2.3

Facets of the Concepts "Frequency" and "Amplitude" and Associated Registers

Facets of <frequency>	Facets of <amplitude>	Associated register
physical quantity which can evolve qualitatively by an action on an axis	physical quantity which can evolve qualitatively by an action on an axis	graph
physical quantity with value and unit	physical quantity with value and unit	Numerical values (+ unit)
rapidity of vibrator (non materialised, to be observed)	Half of the distance covered by the vibrator during on back (or forth) movement	Animated register: – vibration – microscopic representation
concept which can be defined in natural language	concept which can be defined in natural language	Natural language

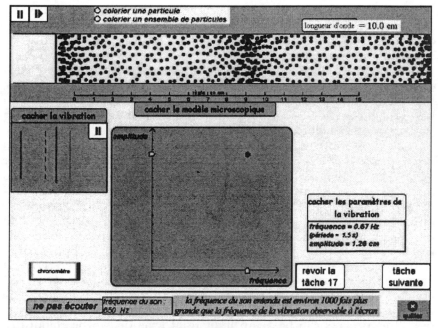

FIG 2.9.   Example of *SimulaSON* screen (experimental version).

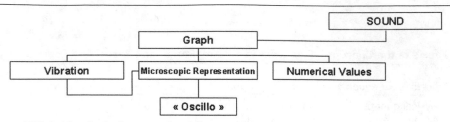

FIG 2.10. Links between the different windows.

CONCLUSION

This design of *SimulaSON* shows that theoretical hypotheses about learning associated with hypotheses about knowledge and its representation are operational. They allow making choices about the representations and the actions at the interface. The main underlying hypothesis is that understanding concepts implies establishing links between different elements, which implies a distinction between elements of knowledge. Modeling is a relevant process in physics for the categorization of knowledge dealing with the inanimate material world. Another complementary approach for categorizing knowledge is based on the semiotic registers used.

SimulaSON is operational and has been used for experimentation by students. The first results show that it can be used easily. It allows students to discuss and make predictions; in that sense, it is a tool for constructing understanding.

Our approach to analyze the knowledge involved in the use of educational software such as *SimulaSon* deals with two dimensions. The first dimension is *modeling, which here is taken as a process* with which knowledge functions. However, only the part of knowledge dealing with the material world is relevant for this dimension of our approach. This is a limitation, but at the same time, it gives us a new insight into any type of knowledge, scientific or everyday knowledge. As a matter of fact, any individual's production dealing with the material world from his or her point of view can be taken into account in our approach. For example, this approach allows us to take into account the different individuals' perceptions of the same material situation, in particular between the students and the teacher; the recognized events can be completely different. This approach does not presuppose "right knowledge," or even a specific content of knowledge as reference. It presupposes a process of constructing or dealing with a "model" in reference to a material situation (or a class of situations), this model being composed within an explanative framework or a specific theory. Moreover, this process can be at an individual level or can be elaborated within a group in a given situation.

The other dimension is in terms of the semiotic registers. It is more general in the sense that it is not limited to the knowledge dealing with the material world. However the semiotic registers are not sufficient to analyze the understanding involved in a situation.

These two dimensions are complementary, they give relevant constraints to designing software, as we showed in our analysis of students' productions in a situation; however, they are not sufficient as, in particular, they necessitate an introduction of the meaning of the knowledge involved.

REFERENCES

Bachelard, S. (1979). Quelques aspects historiques des notions de modèle et de justification des modèles [Some historical aspects of the notions of model and justification of models]. In P. Delattre & M. Thellier (Eds.), *Elaboration et justification des modèles* (Vol. 1, pp. 3–18). Paris: Maloine.

Beaufils, D., Durey, A., & Journaux, R. (1987). L'ordinateur en sciences physiques, quelles simulations? [Computer in physics sciences, which simulations?] *IXèmes journées sur l'Education scientifique*. Paris: Université Paris VII.

Besson, G., Chastan, J. M., Colonna, A. M., Guettier, C., Tiberghien, A., & Vince, J. (1998). *L'enseignement du son. Propositons du groupe SOC [Teaching sequence on sound: Proposals of the SOC group]*. Rapport interne No. 15. Lyon, France: UMR GRIC, équipe COAST, Université Lumière Lyon 2 (Available from: http://www2.ac-lyon.fr/enseigne/physique/docs/soc/index01.html).

Buty, C. (2000). *Etude d'un apprentissage dans une séquence d'enseignement en optique géométirque à l'aide d'une modélisation informatique* [Study of learning in a teaching sequence in geometrical optics with a computer model]. Thèse, France: Université Lumière Lyon 2.

Bunge, M. (1975). *Philosophie de la physique* [Philosophy of physics]. Paris: Le seuil. [traduction de *Philosophy of physics* (1973). Derdrecht-Holland: D. Deidel Publishing Co.].

Carey, S. (1985). *Conceptual change in childhood*. Cambridge, MA: MIT Press (Bradford Books).

Cassirer, E. (1977). Substance et fonction. Eléments pour une théorie du concept [Substance and function. Elements for a theory of concept]. Paris: Editions de Minuit (traduction française).

Cornuéjols, A., Tiberghien, A., & Collet, G. (2000). A new mechanism for transfer between conceptual domains in scientific discovery and education. *Foundation of Science, 5*, 129–155.

Duval, R. (1995). Sémiosis et pensée humaine, registres sémiotiques et apprentissage intellectuels [Semiosis and human thought, semiotic registers and intellectual leaning]. Berne: P. Lang.

Gentilhomme, Y. (1994). L'éclatement du signifié dans les discours techno-scientifiques. [Dividing up the signified in technoscientific discourse]. *Cahiers de lexicologie, 64*, 1994–1, Paris: Didier édition.

Giere, R. N. (1988). *Explaining science: A cognitive approach*. Chicago: The University of Chicago Press.

Grémy, J. P. (1985). Simulation. *Encyclopédie Universalis*, Corpus 16.

Leach, J., & Scott, P. (1995). The demands of learning science concepts: Issues of theory and practice. *School Science Review, 76*(277), 47–52.

Minstrell, J. (1992). Facets of students' knowledge and relevant instruction. In R. Duit, F. Goldberg, & H. Niedderer (Eds.), *Research in physics learning: Theoretical issues and empirical studies. Proceedings of an international workshop* (pp. 110–128). Kiel: IPN (Institut für die Pädagogik der Naturwissenschaften an der Universität Kiel [Institute for Science Education]).

Tiberghien, A. (1994). Modeling as a basis for analysing teaching–learning situations. *Learning and Instruction, 4*(1), 71–87.

Tiberghien, A. (2000). Designing teaching situations in the secondary school. In R. Millar, J. Leach, & J. Osborne (Eds.), *Improving science education: The contribution of research* (pp. 27–47). Buckingham, UK: Open University Press.

Vince, J. (2000a). Approches phénoménologique et linguistique des connaissances des élèves de seconde sur le son. Contribution à l'élaboration et l'analyse d'un enseignement et au développement d'un logiciel de simulation [Phenomenological and linguistic approaches of students' knowledge on sound at the 10th grades]. Thèse, France: Université Lumière Lyon 2.

Vince, J. (2000b). *SimulaSON.* (available from http://gric.univ-lyon2.fr/gric3/Home/jvince/index.html)

Vince, J., & Tiberghien, A. (2000). Simuler pour modéliser. Le cas du son [Simulating to model. Case of sound]. *Sciences et techniques éducatives, 7*(2), 333–366.

Vosniadou, S., & Brewer, W. F. (1994). Mental models of the day–night cycle. *Cognitive Science, 18*(1), 123–183.

APPENDIX

Model of Vibration for Sound

When a sound is perceptible, the object (or part of it) that creates the sound vibrates. This object is called the source of sound.

Each source of sound contains a vibrating part.

A vibration is a regular back and forth movement.

The source vibration is characterised by frequency and amplitude. These are two independent physical quantities.

Definitions:

The *frequency* f of the vibration is the number of back and forth movement during one second. The unit is *Hertz* (Hz).

The period T is the duration of one back and forth movement.

The relation between frequency and movement is $T = \dfrac{1}{f}$, where f is in *Hertz* and T in *second*.

A given number of back and forth movements per second can occur with a variable displacement: this is characterised by the quantity *amplitude of the vibration*. The amplitude of the vibration is the distance between the position of the source without vibration and its position when its direction changes (see schema).

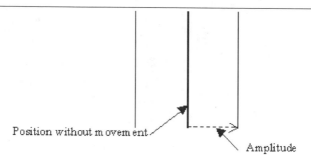

Position without movement

Amplitude

The sound wave: properties

The source of sound excites (compresses or dilates) the air around it and **this excitation is propagated** from one particle to the next **with the velocity V**, without any matter moving.

If the source vibrates with the period T, it is going to excite (compress and dilate) the air around it regularly, for each period.

Simultaneously, each compression and dilatation are going to be propagated after their creation. Then, for a sinusoidal wave, in the medium, <u>at a given time</u>, we have a **succession of compressed and dilated areas spaced out regularly**.

If we look at what happens <u>at a given place</u>, we will see compressions and dilatations arriving regularly. **At this place, the air alternately changes from the compressed state to the dilated state**, and the air is in its initial state at regular intervals T.

That is what we call vibration of the air.

This vibration is the cause of the sensation of a sound (hearing something).

The propagation of this vibration constitutes a sound wave.

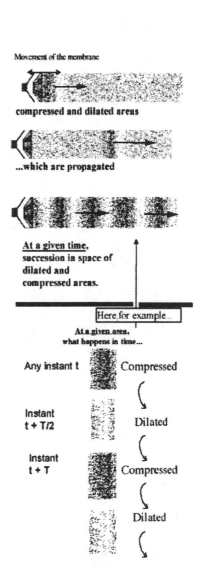

Movement of the membrane

compressed and dilated areas

...which are propagated

<u>At a given time,</u> **succession in space of dilated and compressed areas.**

Here for example...

<u>At a given area,</u> **what happens in time...**

Any instant t — Compressed

Instant t + T/2 — Dilated

Instant t + T — Compressed

Dilated

Conceptualizing and Constructing Linked Models: Creating Coherence in Complex Knowledge Systems

John R. Frederiksen
University of Washington

Barbara Y. White
University of California at Berkeley

Science domains are typically understood through the use of multiple models, where by model we mean a representational and reasoning system that allows one to describe, predict, or explain domain phenomena. Different forms of models serve different purposes and are designed to capture different aspects of a physical system. Nonetheless, these models can be coherently linked with one another. Science teaching typically incorporates multiple models, but it seldom addresses differences in their nature and purposes or develops the conceptual linkages among these alternative models. The result is a set of impediments to learning science due to the complexities associated with nonintegrated collections of models that have different forms, reasoning processes, and purposes.

We begin our discussion of this problem by identifying what, from our experience, are the primary conceptual difficulties that students face when they encounter the variety and complexity of models used by scientists in modeling physical systems These include: (a) the *abstractness* of the representations used to portray objects, events, and relationships in the model, (b) the *complexities* of the reasoning processes required for model-based reasoning, (c) the *linkages* and relationships among alternative models, (d) the *purposes* that are served by different models, (e) the *applicability* of models to multiple domains, and (f) the *epistemological status* of models in inquiry.

In the next section of this chapter, we propose an instructional approach that seeks to develop students' familiarity with a wide range of modeling techniques, their purposes, utility, and relations to one another. Understanding a wide variety of model forms and how they function in creating a scientific account of domain phenomena is a difficult challenge for science teaching and learning. We believe many of these difficulties stem from instructional practices that emphasize subject-matter knowledge, not how it is produced, and that fail to include an examination of the nature and purposes of scientific models and how these influence their form and function. By engaging students in a comparative analysis of the forms and functions of alternative models and how they can be coherently linked, we should be able to alleviate these impediments to learning. We also believe that a comparative study of model forms will promote students' learning of new models and help them in learning new domains of science. Our instructional approach is (a) to introduce to students scientific terminology, representations, and processes for reasoning using models, (b) to formulate cognitive goals for students' inquiry into the nature and purposes of models and relations among them, (c) to scaffold students as they collaboratively pursue these goals, and (d) to rely on the affordances of goal-directed, collaborative activity to focus students' conversations on creating the understandings we wish students to construct.

Following the theoretical development of our pedagogical approach, we present the results of an instructional experiment we carried out to test these ideas (Frederiksen, White, & Gutwill, 1999). This study is concerned with students' learning about electricity and electrical circuits, a domain that is particularly difficult for most students (Brna, 1988) and even science teachers (Cohen, Eylon, & Ganiel, 1983). We show how students develop knowledge of a series of linked models and learn to use them for reasoning about electrical systems. They also learn the reasons for using differing modeling techniques, how multiple models cohere with one another, and how one reasons with models to solve problems. We show how this effort paid off in their having substantially less difficulty in learning a new model—the standard quantitative circuit theory—at the end of the curriculum. Finally, drawing on discussions among students, we describe some conversational practices that appear to be necessary if students are to understand the linkages among the models they encounter.

In the final section of the chapter, we consider how our instructional approach addresses the six conceptual difficulties we have highlighted. We conclude by exploring the implications of our results for building cognitive theories of how students come to understand scientific models and modeling. Our results draw attention to a need for cognitive theories that explain how working with a variety of models and mapping their interrelationships enables students to develop a better understanding of and ability to use particular models, such as quantitative circuit theory. This requires theories of learning and of expertise that elucidate the abilities of students to cross the boundaries of multiple modeling forms and representational and reasoning systems.

SOURCES OF DIFFICULTY IN UNDERSTANDING AND USING MODELS OF ELECTRICITY

We begin by describing the characteristics of scientific models that we have identified as presenting particular sources of difficulty for students as they attempt to develop a conceptual understanding of physical systems. Our evidence and examples for these difficulties are based primarily on instructional studies we have carried out (Frederiksen, White, & Gutwill, 1999; White, Frederiksen, & Spoehr, 1993) and on studies of the models that are used by students or experts for reasoning about the behavior of electrical circuits (Frederiksen & White, 1992, 1998; White & Frederiksen, 1990). The models we observed and developed vary greatly in their purpose and form. In Fig. 3.1, we illustrate seven types of models used to represent electrical circuits, with each being applied to a simple circuit made up of a lamp, a switch, and a battery. For each model, we illustrate its methods for representing the circuit and also draw attention to the reasoning system employed in running the model. Each of these models (with the exception of the physical model) is generic, that is, it is capable of being generalized to new situations (e.g., more complex electrical circuits) or even new physical domains (e.g., thermodynamics). Thus, each model can serve as a general structure for representing and reasoning that can be used to guide inquiry into the nature of a new situation or even a new domain.

There are a number of sources of difficulty that arise from the multiplicity of model types used to understand a single physical system. Sources of difficulty we encountered in our instructional experiments with students are presented below.

Abstractness of Representations of Objects and Relations

Representations of objects and relations are abstractions chosen to depict particular aspects of a domain that are most relevant to the functions of that particular model. For instance, iconic descriptions abstract away nonessential pictorial elements in order to represent entities that are important within a particular theoretical framework. In the schematic diagram of Model 2 shown in Fig. 3.1, a lamp is represented by a thin, curly line (standing for the filament) enclosed within a boundary (standing for the evacuated glass enclosure), with each end offering a point of connection to the circuit. In depicting the circuit, lines are drawn showing conductors that connect each of the two sides of the lamp to a separate terminal of the battery, which provides a source of voltage within the circuit. This form of representation draws attention to particular properties of objects (such as the lamp having appreciable resistance and its being capable of heating up greatly with-

1. Physical Model

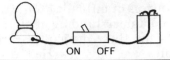

Physical enactment

Memory of resulting behavior

2. Schematic Diagram

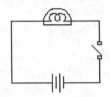

Recognizing spatial schemata (e.g., a complete circuit with no opens or shorts)

Spatial circuit tracing

3. Quantitative Model

R_L = Resistance of Lamp

R_S = Resistance of Switch
   = 0   if Switch is closed
   = huge value if Switch open

V = Voltage of Battery = 4.5 Volts

R_T= R_L + R_S (equivalent resistance)

$I = I_L = I_S$ (Kirchhoff's current law)

$I = V / R_T$ (Ohm's law)

Write attributes of objects as equations

Write equations for circuit

Manipulate equations

4. Particle Interactions

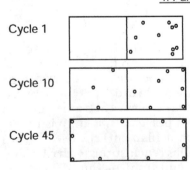

Cycle 1

Cycle 10

Cycle 45

Quantize time and space

Particles repel one another

Visualize movement of charged particles (spreading out)

Iterate until a steady state is reached

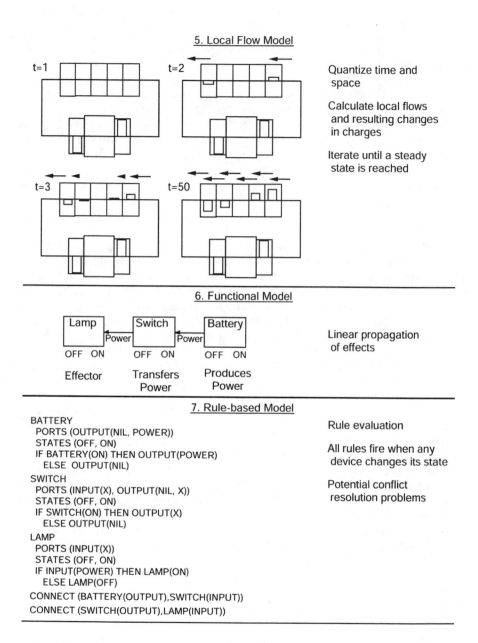

5. Local Flow Model

t=1

t=2

t=3

t=50

Quantize time and space

Calculate local flows and resulting changes in charges

Iterate until a steady state is reached

6. Functional Model

Lamp	Switch	Battery
Power	Power	
OFF ON	OFF ON	OFF ON
Effector	Transfers Power	Produces Power

Linear propagation of effects

7. Rule-based Model

```
BATTERY
  PORTS (OUTPUT(NIL, POWER))
  STATES (OFF, ON)
  IF BATTERY(ON) THEN OUTPUT(POWER)
    ELSE OUTPUT(NIL)
SWITCH
  PORTS (INPUT(X), OUTPUT(NIL, X))
  STATES (OFF, ON)
  IF SWITCH(ON) THEN OUTPUT(X)
    ELSE OUTPUT(NIL)
LAMP
  PORTS (INPUT(X))
  STATES (OFF, ON)
  IF INPUT(POWER) THEN LAMP(ON)
    ELSE LAMP(OFF)
CONNECT (BATTERY(OUTPUT),SWITCH(INPUT))
CONNECT (SWITCH(OUTPUT),LAMP(INPUT))
```

Rule evaluation

All rules fire when any device changes its state

Potential conflict resolution problems

FIG. 3.1. Multiple ways of modeling a simple electrical circuit. For each model, the representational forms it employs are shown on the left and the reasoning processes are illustrated on the right.

out burning up) and to functionally important patterns of interconnection (such as there needs to be a complete circuit loop containing the lamp and a voltage source for the lamp to light). Thus, understanding a representation such as this one requires an understanding of the underlying model that it accompanies. Such a representation must be appreciated as a kind of shorthand, invented to be useful for supporting certain kinds of reasoning. For instance, by tracing connections on the diagram, one can see whether conditions needed to complete the circuit between the lamp and the battery are met. In addition, when certain drawing conventions are adhered to (such as laying out connections on a grid), it becomes fairly easy to recognize subcircuits that have a known functionality (such as when two lamps in a branch are connected in parallel or in series).

At a much higher level of abstraction are quantitative circuit models, illustrated by Model 3 in Fig. 3.1. Rather than picturing the devices in a circuit, these models represent devices in the form of equations that describe their quantitative electrical properties. For example, a lamp has a fixed resistance (R) and its behavior is to allow a current (I) to flow through it that is directly proportional to the voltage (V) applied to it and inversely proportional to its resistance. This is stated by Ohm's Law: $I = V/R$. In addition to their use in characterizing devices, symbolic equations are used to specify the relations among the devices that are connected within a circuit. An example of a circuit equation is the description of the combined resistance of two lamps connected in series ($R_T = R_1 + R_2$). A particular circuit is therefore represented by a system of equations describing the objects and their interrelationships. Manipulating these equations allows one to derive new relations among circuit quantities and to solve for particular numerical values. These methods are used in solving circuit problems, such as finding the value of the current through a lamp when a switch is closed. Taken individually, the equations may be used to describe a wide range of circuit configurations. However, an appropriate symbolic description must be constructed for each circuit on the basis of recognizing circuit patterns or reasoning qualitatively about the circuit. A drawback is that looking at the resulting set of symbolic equations does not easily allow one to visualize the circuit that the equations are being used to describe. Systems of equations are, once they are set up correctly, useful in seeing the constraints on circuit quantities and in solving for the values of unknown quantities in terms of known quantities.

Still another way of representing circuits is in terms of functional models, such as Model 6 in Fig. 3.1. Functional models are often used in troubleshooting electrical systems (Frederiksen & White, 1998; Roberts, 1993). Rather than describing electrical systems in terms of electrical quantities, they describe the influences among interacting components by breaking them down into cause–effect relations among the states of circuit components. Thus, in the illustration, a source of power is connected to a switch that controls the transfer of power to a lamp, which takes on particular behaviors when power is applied or not applied. Reasoning about the circuit takes the form of tracing chains of causal influences. Treating circuits in this way reduces the complexity of the system description, which is particularly important when trying to troubleshoot a complex system, where one needs to keep track of which devices are operating correctly and which are malfunctioning.

These different choices of ways for representing a system vary in the aspects of the system they choose to emphasize, in their degree of abstraction in representing objects and relations, and in the particular ways of thinking about the system's behavior that they favor. These intentional design decisions for representing objects and relations are seldom made explicit for students as a fundamental aspect in building models of physical systems.

Complexities of the Reasoning Structures Embedded in Models

Models differ in the forms of reasoning they employ (Mellar, Bliss, Boohan, Ogborn, & Tompsett, 1994). Examples include reasoning about spatial configurations, evaluating behavior based on parallel processes (e.g., Resnick, 1996), causal reasoning about device interactions (e.g.,White & Frederiksen, 1990), and algebraic reasoning using equations (e.g., Halloun & Hestenes, 1987). For instance, in reasoning using a schematic diagram (Model 2 in Fig. 3.1), students learn how to recognize spatial schemata, such as a complete circuit loop containing a voltage source (battery) and an active device (e.g., a lamp). They also use spatial circuit tracing to verify that there are no opens or shorts within the circuit loop (White & Frederiksen, 1990).

In investigating the particle interaction model (Model 4 in Fig. 3.1; Frederiksen, White, & Gutwill, 1999), students reason about changes in the spatial distribution of charge over time that are due to electrical repulsion among mobile, like-charged particles. The objects in this model are small particles carrying an electric charge. They are free to move about on a surface but are confined to it and to the adjacent surfaces to which they are connected. The charged particles repel one another following Coulomb's Law, which states that the force between two like-charged particles is inversely proportionally to the square of the distance between them. Students observe a computer simulation showing the actions of such particles and develop rules to characterize the aggregate behavior of the particles, such as "they spread out to be as far as possible from each other." The range of behaviors of such models can be quite complex, as in Sherwood and Chabay's (1991) or Härtel's (1982) simulations of complex circuit configurations.

In another dynamic model, the Local Flow Model (Model 5 in Fig. 3.1; see also Fig. 3.2; White, Frederiksen, & Spoehr, 1993), students learn to reason about parallel events occurring throughout a circuit and their cumulative effects on the distribution of electric charge throughout a circuit. In the Local Flow Model, the local interaction rule is much simpler than in the Particle Model (where the acceleration of each particle

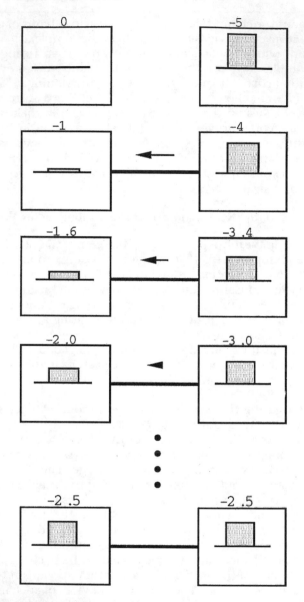

FIG. 3.2. An illustration of successive cycles of the Local Flow Model for two connected resistive slices.

must be calculated by combining forces exerted on it from all the surrounding particles), and this allows students to actually carry out simulations for simple circuits. The local-interaction rule states that the amount of charge that moves between adjacent sections of a resistor in a unit of time depends on the amount of charge in the two sections. The movement is from high levels of charge to lower levels of charge, and the amount of charge transferred is proportional to the difference in charge between the sections. Students observe a computer simulation that follows these rules and verify its behavior by running it step by step. For instance (see Fig. 3.2), they observe how the "static electric" charge on two conductors becomes equalized over time. In a circuit containing a battery (see Model 5 in Fig. 3.1) that moves charge between its positive and negative terminals to maintain a fixed charge differential between them, students discover that circuits containing such a voltage source also reach a steady state in which the charges on all sections of the circuit remain constant, but they see that in such circuits, charge continues to flow (a dynamic equilibrium has been reached).

In quantitative circuit analysis (Model 3 in Fig. 3.1), students reason using constraint satisfaction under the guise of algebraic manipulation of equations representing devices and relations within the circuit. Schematic diagrams are often the starting point in presenting quantitative circuit problems to students. Such problems have the property that they involve reasoning based on several models (i.e., spatial reasoning about the circuit structure and/or qualitative reasoning about voltages and currents within the circuit, combined with constructing systems of equations to represent the circuit devices and their relations).

Finally, in functional and rule-based models (Models 6 and 7 in Fig. 3.1), reasoning is about the propagation of effects occasioned by a change in the functional state of a device (e.g., White & Frederiksen, 1990; Roberts, 1993). For instance, when a switch is closed, this triggers a reevaluation of the states of the circuit's devices. In the example, the power producer sends power to the switch, which, if its state is on, then transfers the power to the lamp, which, since it receives power, enters the "on" state. In Model 6, the reasoning structure is simpler, involving a propagation of effects along a circuit path, although in more complex systems, these paths need to be located. In a more complex rule-based model, such as Model 7, when one device in the system changes its state, all other connected devices are reevaluated to see if there have been any resulting changes in their states. This process of propagating functional influences continues until no further changes in device states occur.

Linkages and Relationships Among Models

The multiple models of electricity students encounter can be related to one another by deriving linkages among them (Frederiksen, White,

& Gutwill, 1999; Gutwill, Frederiksen, & White, 1999; White, Frederiksen, & Spoehr, 1993). This involves mapping the objects, object interactions, and reasoning processes across pairs of models that represent the behavior of a system in different ways and/or at a different level of abstraction. To do this, students study a model, such as the Local Flow Model (Model 5 in Fig. 3.1), in a variety of circuit contexts and carefully observe the behavior of the model. While doing so, they formulate a set of "laws" or rules to describe the behavior of the model at a higher level of abstraction. They are then introduced to a new model (Model 3, the Quantitative Model) that is based on the same set of rules that they used to describe more abstractly the emergent properties of the prior model. By making these relations explicit, the objects and interactions within the higher level model are "mapped" to the objects and behaviors of the prior model. This is the process we call *model derivation*.

For example, consider the behavior of the Local Flow Model for the circuit shown in Fig. 3.1, Model 5, which contains a battery and a resistor connected in series. The students discover that the simulation reaches a steady state and that, in this final state, they can describe the relation between the current flowing through and the voltage across the resistor using Ohm's law. When they later begin working with Model 3, the Quantitative Model, Ohm's law is introduced as a basic rule governing the operation of the model. Thus, the students have already derived the fundamental circuit equations used in the Quantitative Model while they were studying the Local Flow Model.

In Table 3.1, we present a mapping of the full set of relations between these two models. The notions of a charge at a point in the circuit, of batteries having fixed voltages, and of connections among circuit components are directly mapped across the two models. Some circuit components in the Quantitative Model, such as the resistor, are defined in terms of sets of objects in the Local Flow Model (the resistor is made up of a set of connected areas in the Local Flow Model). The notion of a resistor having a fixed resistance in the Quantitative Model corresponds to the number of connected areas it contains within the Local Flow Model. Circuit equations within the Quantitative Model are based on rules used to describe the behavior of the Local Flow Model. For instance, Ohm's law in the Quantitative Model is derived from the finding that, when the steady state is reached in the Local Flow Model, the current through the resistor is directly proportional to the voltage across the resistor and inversely proportional to the total resistance. Finally, the control structure of the Quantitative Model (constraint satisfaction using algebraic reasoning) follows from the observation that the Local Flow Model reaches a steady state in which a set of consistent relations can be identified that are not time related. In these ways, the objects and emergent behaviors of a lower level model are mapped to the objects and processes of a higher level model.

TABLE 3.1
Relations Between the Local Flow Model and the Algebraic Model

Local Flow Model (Model 5)		System of Equations or Quantitative Model (Model 3)
Direct Mapping of Elementary Objects		
Aggregate charge within a unit area	$\rightarrow$	Electrical charge or potential (V)
Batteries with fixed voltage	$\rightarrow$	Batteries with fixed voltage
Connections as conductive paths	$\rightarrow$	Connections as conductive paths
Mapping of Emergent Objects/Properties		
Circuit components as sets of connected areas (resistors, switches)	$\rightarrow$	Circuit components (resistors/switches)
Total resistance depends on number of areas connected	$\rightarrow$	Resistors have a fixed resistance (R)
Mapping of Emergent Relations and Control Structure		
Currents and Voltages are constant when the circuit is in a steady state	$\rightarrow$	Algebra can be used to describe the steady state of a circuit
There are lawful relations among charges and currents (e.g., there is a constant current flow through a resistor that depends on its resistance and the voltage across it)		Equations can describe relations among circuit variables (e.g., Ohm's Law relates voltage, resistance, and current through a resistor)

Purposes of Different Models

Models having different forms address different purposes for modeling. Purposes for creating models of electrical systems include (a) representing and explaining electrical circuits at different levels of granularity (e.g., the particle, local flow, schematic, and functional models of electrical systems), (b) accounting for different characteristics and phenomena (e.g., circuit structure using schematic diagrams, circuit dynamics using local flow models, device interactions through functional models, and quantitative features of circuits using systems of equations), and (c) solving different kinds of problems (e.g., troubleshooting and circuit design). For instance, if one is trying to troubleshoot a complex system, functional and rule-based models are the most useful because they have the most appropriate level of granularity and the device-centered propagation of effects they make use of supports the application of general troubleshooting heuristics (Frederiksen & White, 1998). If one is trying to solve for the values of voltages and currents within a circuit, the circuit equations of the Quantitative Model make this possible. The scientific purpose of creating explanations and making predictions generally requires multiple models that describe circuits at multiple levels of granularity in order to account for both the dynamics and steady states of circuits. Likewise, the design of complex circuits makes use of models at different levels of abstraction.

Applicability of Models to Multiple Domains

In order to see how particular forms of models can be applied to new domains and situations, the models need to be developed using concepts and representations that are abstract enough to be mapped to objects and processes in other situations. Students also need to have practice in applying such generalizable models to new domains and situations. Learning how to apply models to new situations (e.g., understanding a new circuit) involves creating a mapping of objects and relations within that particular situation to objects and relations defined within the model, and applying the model to reason about the circuit for purposes of explaining its behavior, changing its design, or, perhaps, troubleshooting it. This means that the reasoning strategies used (e.g., troubleshooting) also need to be stated in terms of model-based entities, that is, they also need to be generalizable. Applying models to new domains (e.g., applying particle and flow models to heat conduction or gas diffusion) is closely linked to scientific inquiry. In inquiry, the scientist—or learner—makes use of existing models as schemas for creating provisional models in a new situation or domain and then refines those models if they lead to incorrect predictions of the new domain's behavior. In science instruction, and for purposes of inquiry, models from a familiar domain are introduced as analogies for understanding a new domain (Clement, 1993; Duit, 1991; Dupin & Joshua, 1989). This exercise can lead to clarifications as to what are appropriate mappings for objects and relations across domains (Gentner, 1989).

Epistemological Status of Models in Inquiry

Models need to be seen as epistemic forms for understanding physical systems (Collins & Ferguson, 1993). Students need to learn that models are a useful way to represent physical systems, within particular boundary conditions, but are not correct, ahistorical, and unassailable statements of truth (Nadeau & Desautels, 1984). Thus, in introducing models within a domain, students and teachers need to have conversations about what domain objects and processes the model is supposed to represent and what phenomena the model is constructed to characterize, predict, and explain. Students should learn how one tests the adequacy of a model's predictions against the observed behaviors of the phenomena that are being modeled. Further, they should learn that one can make use of models developed in one domain as a provisional basis for understanding another domain. All of these practices depend on students developing a mature epistemological stance on the nature of scientific knowledge and the role of modeling in scientific inquiry (Carey & Smith, 1993; Grosslight, Unger, Jay, & Smith, 1991; Schwarz, 1998; Smith, Maclin, Houghton, & Hennessey, 2000).

In our view, this set of six sources of difficulty that students face in learning complex science topics needs to be regarded as integrated, not as a set of discrete problems to be addressed separately. This is because the six factors are closely intertwined. Representations have little meaning apart from the phenomena they are trying to account for and the methods of reasoning that are used to give that account. Models are intentionally constructed to be useful for certain situations and are validated through their success in predicting system behaviors within those situations. Models may be linked when one is looking for mechanisms at a lower level that may explain behaviors at a higher level of analysis. All of these practices of the model builder need to be seen as aspects of scientific modeling and inquiry, and as practices that are equally appropriate for learners of science as well. Developing an understanding of these related aspects of scientific models, their construction, and their use should be important goals of science education. Our research suggests how this might be achieved by focusing learning on the forms, functions, and relationships among multiple models for a domain.

LEARNING BASIC ELECTRICITY BY CONSTRUCTING MULTIPLE LINKED MODELS

We chose to investigate how students can learn elementary DC circuit theory, because understanding the behavior of electrical circuits is known to be notoriously difficult for students (Cohen, Eylon, & Ganiel, 1983; Fredette & Clement, 1981). It requires students to reason about electrical potentials at different locations within a circuit and the flow of electrical charge caused by differences in these electrical potentials. Students also need to be able to envision how changes in the conductivity of any circuit component will have nonlocal effects, causing changes in electric potentials (voltages) throughout the circuit that, in turn, produce changes in current flows in different circuit branches. This "voltage centered" model is the expert or target form of reasoning that students need to develop (White & Frederiksen, 1990).

Unfortunately, most electricity curricula seldom provide any physical mechanism for explaining circuit principles such as Ohm's Law or how current is propagated within a circuit. In addition, introductory instruction in electrical circuits is typically centered around the solution of quantitative circuit problems. The type of reasoning that is involved in solving such problems is constraint-based reasoning and takes the form of manipulating algebraic equations. The difficulty is that students are not shown how the quantitative circuit theory is related conceptually to a causal model of what is happening within the circuit. Instead, abstract concepts such as voltage are often simply treated as variables in an equation. The student is left with the notion that physical systems can be understood only through mathematical equations, and that these equations cannot be understood in terms of any underlying physical mechanism.

Rather than considering what is happening within a circuit, students learn to use the circuit diagram and problem statement as cues to access equations that they think "fit" the problem, to manipulate these equations algebraically to solve for the required result, and then to substitute given quantities into the equations to calculate an answer (Larkin & Chabay, 1989). There is thus a disjunction between an understanding of what is happening within a circuit and the quantitative circuit theory (Eylon & Ganiel, 1990; Frederiksen & White, 1992; White, Frederiksen, & Spoehr, 1993).

We investigated how one might remedy these problems by introducing students to basic electricity and circuit theory through presenting them with a chain of linked models (White Frederiksen, & Spoehr, 1993). The models in the sequence were increasingly abstract and designed to connect microscopic circuit behavior (e.g., electrons repelling one another) to macroscopic circuit behavior (e.g., voltage distribution within a circuit). The model sequence therefore included the Particle Model, the Local Flow Model, and the Quantitative Model (quantitative circuit theory). The Particle Model was designed to serve as an anchor, or starting point, for the other models. In this instructional study, we compared students who were given the full sequence of models with a second group who were not given the initial, mechanistic model as an anchor. The results provide evidence that anchoring students' learning of the Local Flow and Quantitative Models to an initial mechanistic model of how particles move had a significant effect on their later learning, with the major impact being on their ability to reason about voltage and charge distributions within an electrical circuit.

This finding led to some new research questions: Was this beneficial effect due to our providing a mechanistic, anchoring model that is understandable to students (as in Clement, Brown, Zietsman, 1989), and/or to our providing students with a diverse set of models (as in Gutwill, Frederiksen, & White, 1999), and/or to our enabling students to create a meaningful derivational pathway through the models in the progression? To further investigate the latter possibility, we carried out a second instructional study (Frederiksen, White, & Gutwill, 1999), summarized here.

The second study provides evidence of how creating a coherent derivational chain among a set of scientific models can benefit students' learning, understanding, and problem solving. The instructional sequence in this study again introduces students to three linked models: the Particle Model, the Local Flow Model, and the Quantitative Model. The first two models in the sequence were presented to students using a dynamic, computer simulation that shows the changes that occur within the circuit over time. In studying each model, the computer simulation is applied to a series of particular situations (circuit configurations) for students to study. Students make predictions about the behavior of the model in each situation and then run the simulation to observe and reflect on its behavior. They are guided in this inquiry by workbooks that present "laws" or rules they can use to describe the behavior of the model in that situation. These rules are designed to describe the behavior of the circuit at a higher level of abstraction. The students then determine the accuracy of the rules by comparing their predictions with the actual behavior of the simulation. Over the course of working with a model, the complexity of the rules derived from the model is increased by increasing the complexity of the situations (types of circuits) that are being studied. The rules that are developed after studying the model's behavior over the range of situations then become the building blocks for the next model in the sequence.

We were particularly interested in how this form of instruction supports the learning of DC circuit theory, which was the third model in the sequence. For this reason, instruction for the third model, the Quantitative Model, followed the customary, problem-centered approach that is common in science curricula. The problems were presented using printed workbooks. The workbooks introduced the standard circuit laws and also described procedures for applying them in solving quantitative problems. The difficulty of the problems increased as the complexity of the circuits increased. The sequence of circuits exactly paralleled the sequence of situations that students encountered in their study of the Local Flow Model. The instructional idea was that applying the Quantitative Model to the same circuit forms that the students had studied using the Local Flow Model should help them make the connections from the rules they developed using the Local Flow Model to understand the quantitative circuit laws. In addition, seeing how alternative models can be used to describe similar situations should help students develop an appreciation of the purposes and advantages of each model and how each supports solving particular kinds of problems using methods provided by that model.

Understanding the linkages among the three models is crucial to our instructional and theoretical approach. The instructional goal is for students to characterize the emergent behaviors of a model in the form of a set of laws or principles that can then be used as the basis for constructing a more abstract, higher level model. To facilitate this learning process, several conditions must be met: (a) the lower level or "source" model must be understandable in its own right, which means that it must employ representations and forms of reasoning that are accessible to students, such as reasoning about discrete objects and events based on local mechanisms involving causal interactions (Frederiksen & White, 1992; White, 1993); (b) students must be able to run the source model in situations where the model's behavior illustrates the rules needed for the derived model; (c) students must explicitly formulate "laws" or rules to describe the behaviors of the source model that correspond to the basic operating principles of the derived model, and (d) students must construct the higher level, derived model by specifying its objects, relations, and control processes in terms of rules they have derived from studying the source model. One can regard these model-based derivations as analogous to mathematical proofs, with the steps in running the source model and characterizing its behaviors corresponding to steps of a mathematical investigation.

Design of the Instructional Study

The purpose of the instructional study was to establish experimentally the importance of having students develop a coherent chain of linkages among models that increase in their level of abstraction in representing the behavior of electrical circuits. In this study, all students were presented with the entire set of models, anchored to an initial, mechanistic model (the Particle Model). Our instructional manipulation was chosen to interrupt the derivational chain that linked the models in the sequence. We therefore compared two groups of students who differed in their opportunity to construct the linkage between the Local Flow Model and the Quantitative Model. We varied this aspect of their learning by controlling students' exposure to the dynamic, computer simulation of circuit behavior while they were studying the Local Flow Model. Students in one group (the Transient Group) studied the behavior of the Local Flow Model by seeing it actually run through various transient states until it reached the steady state, whereas students in the second group (the Steady-State Group) were shown only the starting and ending states of the simulation. In every other way, we made sure that the instruction presented the models in the same way and that the same instructional materials were used to developing the set of rules for describing the models' behavior.

In choosing this instructional manipulation, our hypothesis was that it is necessary for students to see and reflect on the dynamic simulation in order to understand how, in the Local Flow Model, local differences in electrical potential cause local current flows and how these lead, over time, to a final, steady state of the circuit. Seeing the dynamic simulation of the local flow process should also help students make the connection between the representation of voltages and currents within the Local Flow Model (using bar graphs and arrows) and the dynamic flow of particles seen within the Particle Model. Our prediction was, therefore, that students in the Transient Group would perform better on assessments of their ability to reason qualitatively about the relative magnitudes of voltages and currents within circuits and, as a result, they would also develop a better knowledge and use of the quantitative circuit theory. We expected the students' use of circuit equations would be less prone to error and that they would also be less rigid in following the particular solution procedures presented in the instructional workbook.

The participants in this study were 32 high school students who had not taken a physics course. The students attended a 2-hour, after-school session each day for 2 weeks. They worked in pairs throughout the study except when they completed the assessments.

Effects of the Instructional Treatments

We provide an overview here of our analyses of differences between the Transient and Steady-State Groups. We report results for posttests that addressed students' understanding of the models developed in the curriculum and thus were designed to reveal differences in knowledge gained by the two groups. The results are summarized in Table 3.2. A fuller presentation of our results can be found in Frederiksen, White, and Gutwill (1999).

Assessments of the Particle and Local Flow Models. The first two assessments were included to see if the two groups of subjects differ in their understanding of the Particle Model and the Local Flow Model. To assess their understanding of the Particle Model, the students were given a paper-and-pencil test containing problems in which they identified or described what would happen when charged particles were free to move on conductive surfaces. The results are presented in the first row of Table 3.2. As expected, there were no significant differences between the two groups.

To assess their understanding of the Local Flow Model, the students were shown configurations of two or three connected areas with various charges on them and were asked to predict the final amounts of charge on each section after they are connected. In these test items, charges were depicted using the bar graph representation. The items also asked students to explain their responses. Our hypothesis was that students in the Transient Group would be better able to understand and predict the steady-state distributions of charges and current flow, because they saw how the final distributions of charges were derived from the Local Flow Model as it was used to simulate the transient processes that occur as circuits go from one steady state to another. Results bearing on this hypothesis are presented in the second row of Table 3.2. Students in the Transient Group significantly outperformed those in the Steady-State Group. Using the Local Flow Model simulation to dynamically illustrate the behavior of the model clearly helps students see how differences in the charge distributions lead to current flows that, in turn, alter the charge distributions. Moreover, the students could see how, over time, this cyclical, local-flow process leads to a steady state.

Qualitative Reasoning Assessment. The next issue is to test whether understanding this local flow process and linking it to the properties of a circuit when it reaches a steady state help students to develop a better ability to reason about the relations among voltages and currents within a circuit. To test this ability, we had both groups of students complete an assessment of qualitative reasoning in which they

TABLE 3.2

Results of Linking Models of Electricity on Postinstructional Performance

Assessment	Sample Question	Transient Group M (SE)	Steady State Group M (SE)	t_{26} (p)	Effect Size
Particle Model	What happens and why?	65.7 (4.3)	61.5 (4.3)	.69 (n.s.)	.2
Local Flow Model	What happens and why?	56.7 (3.5)	43.7 (3.5)	2.56 (.01)	.9
Qualitative Reasoning	Which resistor has a greater voltage difference?	71.3 (4.8)	54.8 (4.8)	2.40 (.01)	.9
Quantitative Reasoning	Find the voltage difference across each resistor.	42.9 (4.9)	24.1 (4.9)	2.69 (.006)	1.1

were asked questions about the relative magnitudes of voltages and currents in circuits that have reached a steady state. During instruction, both groups of students were given the same set of instructional materials for drawing out a set of qualitative rules for predicting voltage differences and currents when a circuit has reached the steady state. The only difference was that students in the Transient Group were shown how the iterative application of the flow equation leads to a final state of the circuit in which voltages and currents follow those laws. Our hypothesis was that this model derivation exercise should enable students to apply rules they had developed in that context to reasoning about the relationship between voltage differences and current flows within circuits. It should also enable them to develop a better conception of the distinction between the transient and steady states of a circuit, and of the abstract notion of constraints (circuit laws) as a means of describing the unchanging features of the steady-state world. The results are shown in the third row of Table 3.2. Students in the Transient Group significantly outperformed those in the Steady-State Group. This result supports our hypothesis that the learning of circuit theory is enhanced when students' complete the hierarchical linking of particle behaviors to the local flow of charge within a circuit, and of the local flows to more global descriptions of circuits based on relations among circuit quantities when a circuit has reached a steady state.

Quantitative Reasoning Assessment.   Finally, we predicted that students in the Transient Group would outperform those in the Steady-State Group when they were asked to solve quantitative circuit problems, due to their greater understanding of the relationship of voltage difference and current flow. Results bearing on this hypothesis are given in the last row of Table 3.2. There is a significant difference between the groups on quantitative problems in which students had to calculate voltages and currents for various circuits, even though the Quantitative Model instruction was the same for both groups of students. These results clearly indicate that completing the full sequence of model derivations has helped students make sense of the formulas.

We also examined how students in the two groups made use of the circuit equations in solving problems. We looked at how pairs of students working together went about solving a particularly difficult, voltage divider problem that was presented to them in their instructional workbook. We found that all of the eight pairs of students in the Transient Group solved the problem correctly and three of the pairs solved the problem in a novel way—they used a method that differed from the method that had been shown to them in the workbook. One pair actually solved the problem two ways. In contrast, only six of the eight pairs of students in the Steady-State Group solved the problem correctly, and all eight of them used the same procedure that had just been shown to them. The two pairs of students who were unsuccessful both lost track of the meaning of one of the equations they were using, and this led to their calculating a meaningless result. It appears that they had either lost sight of the most important variable, voltage difference, or they did not understand what the formulas actually meant. A full presentation of these problem-solving protocols can be found in Frederiksen, White, and Gutwill (1999).

Students' Conversational Practices

We share the now generally held view that students' conversational practices are instrumental in their learning (Baker, Hansen, Joiner, & Traum, 1999; Lemke, 1990; Vygosky, 1978). Our instructional approach is to shape these conversations by introducing explicit cognitive goals for students' collaborative inquiry, such as using a model to predict the behavior of a physical system and explaining discrepancies between these predictions and the observed behaviors of the actual system itself. Students engage in collaborative activities and conversations as they pursue such goals. Our view is that by providing explicit cognitive goals along with scaffolding to support their attainment, and by introducing terminology and representations for talking about models, students' conversations will be directed toward our general learning goals, which include creating a shared language for talking about models and reasoning about their behavior. Such a discourse community also provides opportunities for participants to test their reasoning and ideas with one another and to coconstruct arguments and explanations. These are widely useful abilities that can perhaps be developed most naturally within a discourse community.

In our observations of students interactions during learning (which were video taped), we found that the students' discussions served a number of critical functions in their developing models of electricity and understanding how the models are linked to one another. (See Frederiksen, White, and Gutwill (1999) for an extended protocol that illustrates most of these functions.)

Establishing Reference. Conversations helped students establish the referents for scientific terms—what entities and phenomena are being referred to in the scientific terminology. An example is the notion of a "steady state" of a circuit (which is distinct from situations where features of the circuit's behavior are constantly changing). Students' initial notion of the concept was overly restrictive in that they thought of it as a situation in which all aspects of a circuit were unchanging (charges in all of the circuit stayed the same and no current was flowing). When the simulation software reported that a "steady state has been reached" for a complete circuit containing a resistor and battery (see the fourth panel for Model 5 in Fig. 3.1), they were mystified until, over an extended sequence of utterances, they figured out that it is the quantities of charges in each section of the circuit that are invariant.

Expressive Use of Terminology. Students make use of scientific terminology to express their ideas; the terms are not just used receptively in reading a problem or an explanation composed by another person. This is seen in the students' willingness to dive in and use the terminology before they have fully appreciated its technical meaning. Through their ongoing use of scientific terminology in describing situations and reasoning about the circuit, they cooperatively build an increasingly adequate use of the terminology, as in most communities of practice (Schön, 1982).

Testing Their Reasoning. In their communication, students implicitly use each other to test the plausibility and adequacy of their predictions, observations, and descriptions. They are continuously testing the soundness of their reasoning whenever they explain their reasons for a particular interpretation or conclusion to their partner. The partners are continuously giving verbal ("Huh?" "Oh, why?" "I think I get it.") and nonverbal signs that indicate their degree of comprehension of their partner's contributions.

Co-constructing Arguments. There are many examples of pairs of students coconstructing arguments through coordinated reasoning. We see this when students are attempting to construct model-based explanations for a circuit's behavior they have encountered. An example can be seen in the following short excerpt from the protocol. The students are looking at the computer simulation of a complete circuit containing a resistor and a battery (similar to that in panel 4 of Model 5 shown in Fig. 3.1) and they are puzzled as to why a complete circuit still has current flowing in it when the computer says it has reached a steady state. They have used the Local Flow Model to calculate the result that currents between sections of the resistor are everywhere the same, but they see another problem: Why are the charges in a particular section of the resistor no longer changing when charge is still flowing?

Jerry: That tells us that charge is still flowing at uh. This is what I thought it would be, all moving the same in relation to one another.

David: Right.

Jerry: So.

David: So the flow—

Jerry: So flow is coming [points to the section of the resistor that is connected to the battery's negative terminal]. This is the only one I don't understand.

David: But the flow is coming [in from the battery terminal] at the same time that it's balancing out. I see. Cause the charge is just shifting.

Jerry: Yeah. And this is coming, this [he now points to the negative terminal] is staying the same because this [points to the electrolyte of the battery] is giving it electrons but this—

David: This tells us right here. [He reads the computer message:] "A steady state has been reached because there's no *change* in the charge of any section." That doesn't mean the charge isn't flowing, it just means there's no change in the charge.

Jerry: That's why you've been hearing that so much and we don't get it. Oh!

David: Thank you Mr. Computer.

Evaluating Evidence.   Students often help each other in evaluating their rule-based predictions and calculations against evidence to see if they are consistent with one another. This also includes choosing relevant evidence and checking its accuracy. This occurs in working with the computer simulation, where rounding errors can sometimes make the results somewhat imprecise. It is even more prevalent when we observe students working on real-world experiments (White & Frederiksen, 1998).

DISCUSSION

We have identified a number of what, on theoretical grounds, appear to be critical conceptual impediments to learning complex, interrelated models for understanding a scientific domain, and have shown how instruction that addresses many of these bottlenecks can greatly improve students' learning. Here we consider how the instructional approach we adopted addressed each of these conceptual needs in learning science.

1. *Abstractness*. We addressed the problem posed by the abstractness of the representations used to portray objects, events, and relationships in models by choosing what White (1993) termed *intermediate abstractions*. The Particle Model portrays the behavior of mobile, charged particles within a conductive medium and their changes in position over time. It is a causal model that unpacks a physical mechanism. The basic interaction among particles within this model is the Coulomb interaction (like charges repel). Students can investigate the properties of a system that incorporates such a mechanism by moving to a higher level of abstraction. To facilitate this, we introduced students to the Local Flow Model, which incorporates more abstract representations of the charge of a slice (i.e., the vertical bars shown in Fig. 3.2) and the transfer of charge from one slice to another (i.e., the horizontal arrows shown in Fig 3.2) based on the flow equation. The Local Flow Model is a generic model of a transport mechanism that represents the aggregate behavior of particles. It is more abstract than a model of the movement of individual particles, and less abstract than models based on steady-state principles such as $V = IR$. By the use of this intermediate abstraction, and stepping through time, students infer simple relationships, such as "the larger the difference in charge density between two adjacent slices, the greater the current flow between those two slices." The explanation for why charge flows is reductionistic, based on the motion of particles and their interactions as shown in the Particle Model. If one puts together a complete circuit, like the one shown for Model 5 in Fig. 3.1, and lets the Local Flow Model run until it reaches a steady state, students see how the steady-state, noncausal laws (such as Kirchhoff's laws) are emergent properties of a system whose basic flow process was derived from interactions among particles following Coulomb's law (see Model 5 in Fig. 3.1). The Local Flow Model

thus links the behavior of individual particles (the Particle Model) with the steady-state system equations (the Quantitative Model) by providing a causal model at an intermediate level of abstraction.

2. *Complexities.* We addressed the complexities of model-based reasoning by making the reasoning processes explicit. This was accomplished by implementing them within a computer simulation that students could run. The computer simulation, particularly that for the Local Flow Model, was designed to be as transparent as possible. Students could run the simulation in step-by-step mode (in addition to continuous mode) and verify "by hand" the calculations that it was performing on each step. In fact, we found that students devoted a great deal of effort in using their calculators to verify—and understand—the operation of the simulation. This effort seemed to be very important to them. Although the computer software included a speech synthesis device that could explain each local calculation when asked to, many students were not satisfied until they had verified the calculations for themselves. Because students worked in pairs, they talked through points that were not clear to them. The workbooks had students make predictions, evaluate them in terms of the behavior of the simulation, and work with rules for describing the emergent behaviors they observed. In each of these tasks, the students would share their predictions, observations, and ideas, and try to reach a consensus. Students also devoted a great deal of effort in verifying that the behavior of the simulation was reasonable under the rules of the model. The stimulus for these conversations was often a situation where the students encountered an unexpected result, such as when they first encountered a circuit in which there was still current flowing when it reached a steady state (it reached a dynamic equilibrium). As we have seen, this set off a protracted discussion in which the reason for this result was derived by the students using the basic principles of the model and by verifying its calculations. This act of deriving the result had a purpose and authenticity to the students because, at first, they did not believe it.

3. *Linkages.* The instructional strategy was to rely on students' ability to create linkages among models at increasing levels of abstraction. This ability was not assumed in our curriculum but carefully nurtured through workbook exercises in which students were presented with rules to describe the behavior of the simulated systems they were studying. These rules became the fundamental principles for the next model in the sequence, which described and modeled the electrical circuit at a higher level of abstraction. Students were able to make use of abstract concepts and rules (e.g., Ohm's law) because they had seen how it was a result of the operation of an earlier model that they felt they understood. Our view is that this process of creating and linking models needs to become a visible and important aspect of inquiry in science instruction. Further, it cannot be assumed that an explanation by a teacher or textbook will ensure

that students successfully accomplish this linking of models. Explicit attention needs to be given to teaching students how to carry out these derivational activities for themselves.

4. *Purposes*. Students' understanding of the multiple purposes that are served by different models (e.g., reasoning about dynamic processes, showing steady-state relationships) was addressed as the fundamental motivation for creating models at higher levels of granularity and abstraction. The students knew that, as one student said, "real electricity" was about circuits with continuous current flowing. Characterizing the behavior of the steady state relationships among voltage, current, and resistance using equations was viewed as the final objective. The students clearly recognized that this model would also allow them to solve some problems they might encounter in the "real world" and that they would certainly encounter in a physics course. Furthermore, the workbooks illustrated what sorts of reasoning each model would support and its likely utility.

5. *Transfer*. Although the curriculum did not address the applicability of models to multiple domains (e.g., applying dynamic models, like the Local Flow Model, to electrostatics, gas diffusion, and thermodynamics), it was our intention in our choice of representations and rules that the forms of models students develop would be at a level of abstraction that could support their application to new domains. In developing a full science curriculum around the principles of modeling we are espousing, curricular activities could be developed to explicitly address this issue.

6. *Epistemological status of models*. Our curriculum introduced students to a mature epistemological view of models and of their status in the process of scientific inquiry. Models were introduced as conceptual constructions that embody theories that can be useful for solving problems. Students worked with alternate forms of models for a single physical system, each focusing on different objects and interactions as elementary units of analysis, and each employing a different type of reasoning process. They also saw how models representing alternative perspectives on a physical system can nonetheless be coherently linked. They learned about the nature of the mappings among models through the characterization of emergent properties of lower level models in models at a higher level in an abstraction hierarchy. Whether students in our study developed metacognitive awareness that incorporates such sophisticated expertise about the epistemological status of models is unknown, inasmuch as this was not assessed. It may be that, for students to become aware of the processes of scientific inquiry and modeling and of the epistemological status of models, additional instructional activities and materials are required. These activities could, for example, engage students in reflecting on the modeling process itself and thereby explicitly foster such metalevel knowledge (as in Schwarz, 1998; White & Frederiksen, 1998; White & Schwarz, 1999; White, Shimoda, & Frederiksen, 1999).

Schwarz (1998) has shown that such expertise plays a central role in enabling students to learn about scientific modeling and inquiry, as well as in their development of subject-matter expertise.

CONCLUSIONS

Our results raise problems for cognitive theorists seeking to understand how complex models in science are learned. Models can employ widely varying forms of representation and reasoning, and they can be built to portray and explain different phenomena. Accordingly, the theoretical descriptions of the expertise they embody vary from model to model. Yet, our results show that success in learning is strongly related to students ability to link models having diverse representations and reasoning systems. This means that our cognitive theories need to capture these linkages among models and explain how they influence learning.

In their pioneering work, Gentner and her colleagues (Gentner, 1989; Gentner & Markman, 1997; Tenney & Gentner, 1984) have shown that, to understand students' use of analogy, one needs to address the mapping of relational structures, not just object mappings. Our results suggest that this attention to mapping applies more generally, and needs to be expanded to address mappings across models at widely different levels of abstraction. This mapping work needs to consider how students can create descriptions of emergent behaviors of models, and how these description can be used to build new, theoretically linked models that may differ in the objects they contain, the processes or interactions among objects they depict, and the reasoning techniques they utilize. Yet, despite (or because of) their differences, these linked models become an important means for making sense of models at higher levels of abstraction in terms of causal mechanisms. In addition, we have seen that they alter the way in which abstract models, such as quantitative circuit theory, are understood and used. Adding further to the complexity of building a cognitive theory is the fact that models are intentionally built to make certain phenomena easier to understand and certain forms of problems easier to solve. In addition, understanding this intentional purpose of constructing models requires a clear epistemological stance that recognizes the constructed nature of scientific knowledge and how it is verified.

There is a great deal of work needed, in the spirit of Gentner's work on analogy (Gentner, 1989), to provide a rich theoretical characterization of these processes for model-based explanation, learning, and problem solving. This will require extensive collaborative analysis on the part of cognitive scientists, discipline specialists, and science educators to characterize the space of possible models and determine the relations among them, as well as to develop pedagogical activities that can foster an understanding of models and the process of modeling (as in Schwarz, 1998; White & Schwarz, 1999; Wilensky, 1999). Finally, we need to understand more fully how shaping the cognitive goals, language, and representations used within collaborative learning groups can lead to profitable discourse practices.

REFERENCES

Baker, M., Hansen, T., Joiner, R., & Traum, D. (1999). The role of grounding in collaborative learning tasks. In P. Dillenbourg (Ed.), *Collaborative Learning: Cognitive and computational approaches* (pp. 31–63). Amsterdam: Pergamon.

Brna, P., (1988). Confronting misconceptions in the domain of simple electrical circuits. *Instructional Science, 17*, 29–55.

Carey, S., & Smith, C. (1993). On understanding the nature of scientific knowledge. *Educational Psychologist, 28*(3), 235–251.

Clement, J. (1993). Using bridging analogies and anchoring intuitions to deal with students' preconceptions in physics. *Journal of Research in Science Teaching, 30*, 1241–1257.

Clement, J., Brown, D., & Zietsman, A. (1989). Not all preconceptions are misconceptions: Finding "anchoring conceptions" for grounding instruction on students' intuitions. *International Journal of Science Education, 11*(5), 554–565.

Cohen, R., Eylon, B. S., & Ganiel, U. (1983). Potential difference and current in simple electric circuits: A study of students' concepts. *American Journal of Physics, 51*(5), 407–412.

Collins, A., & Ferguson, W. (1993). Epistemic forms and epistemic games: Structures and strategies to guide inquiry. *Educational Psychologist, 28*, 25–42.

Duit, R. (1991). On the role of analogies and metaphors in learning science. *Science Education, 75*(6), 649–672.

Dupin, J., & Joshua, S. (1989). Analogies and "modeling analogies" in teaching: Some examples in basic electricity. *Science Education, 73*, 207–224.

Eylon, B. S., & Ganiel, U. (1990). Macro–micro relationships: The missing link between electrostatics and electrodynamics in students' reasoning. *International Journal of Science Education, 12*(1), 79–94.

Frederiksen, J., & White, B. (1992). Mental models and understanding: A problem for science education. In E. Scanlon & T. O'Shea (Eds.), *New directions in educational technology* (pp. 211–226). New York: Springer-Verlag.

Frederiksen, J. R., & White, B. Y. (1998). Teaching and learning generic modeling and reasoning skills. *Interactive Learning Environments, 5*, 33–51.

Frederiksen, J. R., White, B. Y., & Gutwill, J. (1999). Dynamic mental models in learning science: The importance of constructing derivational linkages among models. *Journal of Research in Science Teaching, 36*(7), 806–836.

Fredette, N., & Clement, J. (1981). Student misconceptions of an electric circuit: What do they mean? *Journal of College Science Teaching, 10*(5), 280–285.

Gentner, D. (1989). The mechanisms of analogical learning. In S. Vosniadou & A. Ortony (Eds.), *Similarity and analogical reasoning* (pp. 199–241). London: Cambridge University Press.

Gentner, D., & Markman, A. B. (1997). Structure mapping in analogy and similarity. *American Psychologist, 52*, 45–56.

Grosslight, L., Unger, C., Jay, E., & Smith, C. L. (1991). Understanding models and their use in science: Conceptions of middle and high school students and experts. *Journal of Research in Science Teaching, 28*(9), 799–822.

Gutwill, J., Frederiksen, J., & White, B. (1999). Making their own connections: Students' understanding of multiple models in basic electricity. *Cognition and Instruction, 17*(3), 249–282.

Halloun, I., & Hestenes, D. (1987). Modeling instruction in mechanics. *American Journal of Physics, 55*(5), 455–462.

Härtel, H. (1982). The electric circuit as a system: A new approach. *European Journal of Science Education, 4*, 45–55.

Larkin, J., & Chabay, R. (1989). Research on teaching scientific thinking: Implications for computer-based instruction. In L. Resnick & L. Klopfer (Eds.), *Toward the thinking curriculum*. Association for Supervision and Curriculum Development.

Lemke, J. (1990). *Talking science: Language, learning, and values*. Norwood, NJ: Ablex.

Mellar, H., Bliss, J., Boohan, R., Ogborn, J., & Tompsett, C. (Eds.). (1994). *Learning with artificial worlds: Computer based modeling in the curriculum*. Washington, DC: The Falmer Press.

Nadeau, R., & Desautels, J. (1984). *Epistemology and the teaching of science*. Toronto, Canada: University of Toronto.

Resnick, M. (1996). Beyond the centralized mindset. *Journal of the Learning Sciences, 5*(1), 1–22.

Roberts, B. (1993). Constrained learning environments for intelligent tutoring. In P. Brna, S. Ohlsson, & H. Pain (Eds.), *Artificial intelligence in education 1993: The world conference in AI and education*. Charlottesville, VA: Association for the Advancement of Computing in Education.

Schön, D. (1982). *The reflective practitioner*. New York: Basic Books.

Schwarz, C. (1998). *Developing students' understanding of scientific modeling*. Ph.D. thesis, University of California, Berkeley.

Sherwood, B., & Chabay, R. (1991). Electrical interactions and the atomic structure of matter: Adding qualitative reasoning to a calculus-based electricity and magnetism course. In M. Caillot (Ed.), *Learning electricity and electronics with advanced educational technology* (pp. 23–35). New York: Springer-Verlag.

Smith, C., Maclin, D., Houghton, C., & Hennessey, M. (2000). Sixth grade students' epistemologies of science: The impact of school science experiences on epistemological development. *Cognition and Instruction, 18*(3), 349–422.

Tenney, Y., & Gentner, D. (1984). What makes analogies accessible: Experiments on the water-flow analogy for electricity. In *Proceedings of the International Workshop on Research Concerning Students' Knowledge of Electricity*. Ludwigsburg, Germany.

Vygotsky, L. S. (1978). *Mind in society*. Cambridge, MA: Harvard University Press.

White, B. (1993). Causal models and intermediate abstractions: A missing link for successful science education? In R. Glaser (Ed.), *Advances in instructional psychology* (pp. 177–252). Hillsdale, NJ: Lawrence Erlbaum Associates.

White, B., & Frederiksen, J. (1990). Causal model progressions as a foundation for intelligent learning environments. *Artificial Intelligence, 42*, 99–157.

White, B., & Frederiksen, J. (1998). Inquiry, modeling, and metacognition: Making science accessible to all students. *Cognition and Instruction, 16*(1), 3–118.

White, B., Frederiksen, J., & Spoehr, K. (1993). Conceptual models for understanding the behavior of electrical circuits. In M. Caillot (Ed.), *Learning electricity and electronics with advanced educational technology* (pp. 77–95). New York: Springer-Verlag.

White, B., & Schwarz, C. (1999). Alternative approaches to using modeling and simulation tools for teaching science. In W. Feurzeig & N. Roberts (Eds.), *Computer modeling and simulation in science education* (pp. 226–256). New York: Springer-Verlag.

White, B., Shimoda, T., & Frederiksen, J. (1999). Enabling students to construct theories of collaborative inquiry and reflective learning: Computer support for metacognitive development. *International Journal of Artificial Intelligence in Education, 10*(2), 151–182.

Wilensky, U. (1999). GasLab—an extensible modeling toolkit for connecting micro- and macro-properties of gasses. In W. Feurzeig & N. Roberts (Eds.), *Modeling and simulation in science and mathematics education* (pp. 151–178). New York: Springer-Verlag.

II

Provoking More
Effective Modeling

Construction and Abstraction: Contrasting Methods of Supporting Model Building in Learning Science

Rosemary Luckin
Benedict du Boulay
University of Sussex

Interactive Learning Systems can offer students a range of representations, tools, environments, and assistance to construct a model that reflects their understanding of a situation that exists in the real world. They can also offer a range of possibilities for learners to improve their communicative competence and articulate their understandings to themselves, to others, or to the system itself. However, the relationship between interactivity, learning, and communication is complex and can involve humans, artifacts, or a combination of both. Theories based on the promotion of productive interactivity between humans in order to engender individual learning development, such as that of Vygotsky (1978; 1986) can be found at the heart of much work on the design of Interactive Learning Environments (ILEs; Guzdial et al., 1996; Jackson, Stratford, Krajcik, & Soloway, 1996; Luckin & du Boulay, 1999; Rosson & Carroll, 1996; Wood & Wood, 1996, for example). But what do we mean by *interactive* and what is the relationship between *interactivity* and *communication?* Clarifying these concepts should help us build systems better able to support learners in their search for understanding. A definition of *interactivity* that we have found useful is as follows:

> Interactivity is the cycle of operational or conceptual exchange between two or more parties, one of which may be a digital system. *Operational exchange* refers to functional activity: the entering of information through a keyboard and the resultant response from the system, entering a number on the screen for example. Essentially operational interchange is at the level of individual key presses or mouse movements together with their

corresponding character level or cursor movements on the screen, in the case of a computer, and individual words, spoken and heard, in the case of people. *Conceptual exchange* refers to activity involving the concepts of the particular topic being studied. This might involve the solution of a screen based problem activity by a user, or discussion about where chemical elements belong in the periodic table involving a teacher and learners completing a computer based task.

Interactivity can be considered in terms of *range*: It may involve interactivity with and between individuals, small or large groups, groups that are local or distributed. It can also be considered in terms of its *locus*: Interactivity can occur both at and through the interface between interlocutors. The system's interface in the systems we describe in this chapter is a computer screen. Interactivity *at* the interface is deemed operational and as such, it should be straightforward and intuitive. Interactivity *through* the interface requires interactions between users and the subject matter concepts that make up the discipline of study. This distinction is similar to that made by Laurillard (1993).

In this chapter we discuss two very different approaches to the design of ILEs for science education in the classroom. The first system, Ecolab, is designed for use by an individual learner aged 10–11 years. It allows him or her to construct different mini-ecosystems through the availability of modeling tools and to examine different views of the model being built. The system itself also attempts to help the learner construct viable and *runnable* models that accurately reflect the relationships between organisms in the real world. The second example, Galapagos, is drawn from a system designed for use by groups of older learners, aged 15–21, who need to collaboratively write a description of the process that has led to the evolution of different variations of the same species of organism. Although the material that learners can draw on to write an answer is varied, rich, and multimedia, the representation that they can use to formulate their model of the process is *static*: a textual notepad.

The two systems supported contrasting kinds of modeling and communicative activity. In the first the models were runnable and could be constructed from a predefined kit of objects and actions. These could be assembled into mini-ecosystems and observed running. The modeling activity was essentially a "bottom-up" process of building an understanding of a complex system by first understanding its parts and then understanding how those parts interact in models of increasing complexity. Learning support for this endeavor was provided by the tools for guiding the development of the sequence of runnable models and for observing them from different viewpoints. In this instance, communication was between computer and a single learner, although the system could have been used by groups (but was not). In the second system the theory of evolution was presented through text, diagrams, pictures, and video clips. The modeling activity of the students was to build a nonrunnable descriptive model. This meant that they had to abstract away from the rich detail of the learning materials to "reveal" the bare bones of the underlying evolutionary processes. Learning support for this activity was provided by the interactions with the other students as they struggled to articulate to each other and themselves the nature of the theory. Here the partial and imperfect descriptions of the other students functioned in a similar way to the tools for observing models from different perspectives provided in the first system. Interaction and communication was between individual members of the group and each other, individuals and the system, and the group and the system. We use case studies of both systems to tease out some of the factors that have proved successful in linking support for learning as communicative competence and for the process of modeling.

Our view of learning science is that both kinds of modeling are important. The young scientist needs to work with "formal" tools such as mathematics or simulations, as in Ecolab, that focus attention on central concepts, crucial variables, and important relationships. In other words, the detail and "messiness" of the real world needs to be stripped away to reveal essential structures and an underlying simplicity. But to really understand this simplicity, learners *also* need to take part in the activity of "stripping away complexity," typically through discussion. It is through discussion that they can come to understand how the simplified model stands in relation to the more complex reality, and embed the understanding of these phenomena in the wider context of their other knowledge.

This chapter has three parts. The next section describes the Ecolab adaptive system, able to adjust itself to an individual learner and designed to support one-to-one interaction. This interaction was largely concerned with modeling within a simulation. This section describes how three different variants of the system produced different kinds of modeling behavior in their users. The following section describes the adaptable system Galapagos, again implemented as three variants, and again producing rather different modeling behaviors. This system was designed to support groups of learners and to provoke focused discussion. The final section compares the two methodologies.

CASE STUDY 1: THE Ecolab: MODELING AN ECOSYSTEM

The Ecolab Software

The first case study involves the Ecolab software that provides 10–11-year-old children with the facilities to model feeding relationships in a simulated ecology laboratory environment. Ecology is a subject that involves the study of relationships between organisms within an environment. These relationships can be extremely complex, but they can also be introduced in a simplified manner through concepts such as food chains and food webs. These form the foundations of more complex ecosystems and are part of the curriculum for primary school children in the United Kingdom. In the Ecolab children can select animals and plants and then build, activate, and observe the relationships that exist between members of a simple food web in a woodland ecosystem. This environment can be viewed from several different perspectives, including:

- World—a picture of a woodland environment and the organisms the child has chosen to place within it.
- Web—a traditional textbook style diagram of the organisms in a food chain and food web.
- Energy—a graphical representation of the energy levels of the organisms currently "alive" in the Ecolab (see Fig. 4.1).
- History—a linear narrative of what has happened in the Ecolab world to date, which animal has eaten which other animal, for example.

As already stated, the nature of the relationships that can exist between organisms in the real world can be very complex. The software was designed to allow each of the children using it to learn about relationships at a level of complexity that was appropriate to them. It was built in a manner that allows children to learn about relationships ranging from the simplest, between just two single organisms, up to the more complex network of relationships that could exist even in a very

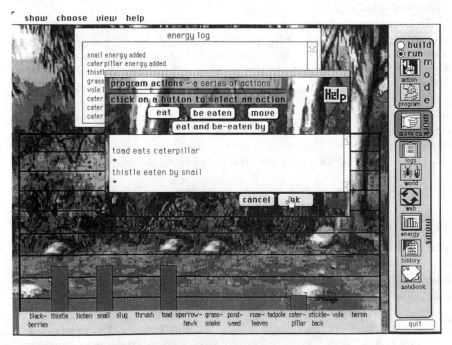

FIG. 4.1.   Ecolab Energy view.

simple ecosystem with populations of organisms. The complexity of the relationships represented within the Ecolab can be varied at any stage during the child's interaction with it. It is also possible to alter the abstractness of the terminology used to describe the organisms in the Ecolab so that a snail, for example, can be described by the words *herbivore, primary consumer,* or *consumer* as well as by the word *snail.*

In addition to this simulated laboratory environment, the system offers each learner a collaborative learning partner that can provide assistance of the following sorts:

1. *Extension* of the learner's knowledge through increasing the complexity of the relationships that she or he is asked to study and/or the abstractness of the terminology used to describe what is happening in the Ecolab.
2. *Collaborative Support* that can take the shape of *activity differentiation;* in the form of alterations to the difficulty of the activities the learner is asked to complete, or *context sensitive help* of variable levels of quality and quantity.

The theoretical foundations underpinning the design of the Ecolab can be found in the Zone of Proximal Development (Vygotsky, 1978; 1986). Great emphasis is placed on the importance of collaboration between more able and less able members of an interactive learning partnership. The partnership in the Ecolab is between the system and an individual learner; the system acting as the more able partner with a responsibility for giving the learner opportunities to tackle challenging activities as well as support to ensure their successful completion. The Ecolab, therefore, provided its child users with modeling tools and opportunities to enter into a collaborative partnership. Communication between partners (i.e., the system and the child) is through the interface in the shape of the commands invoked by the child and the visual feedback provided by the system. The following scenario illustrates the type of interactions that could occur:

> Helen is a novice, both in terms of her use of this system and in terms of her knowledge of food webs. The initial task that faces Helen is the selection of some plants and animals for her community. She is offered a selection of organisms and as each one is chosen it is added to the screen representation of the world. The availability of a choice of organisms is designed to promote the possibility that those chosen will be familiar to Helen and a part of her informal knowledge of ecosystems. For example, Helen's first choice is a sparrow hawk, which now appears in each of the different Ecolab views: as a picture, an energy meter, and an element of the food web puzzle. Further selections are made, the system offering feedback about what each organisms eats and is eaten by.
>
> The first activity that Helen undertakes is an investigation for which the underlying rule is: Energy is transferred from food to feeder when the food is

eaten. Helen is asked to use the world to answer questions of increasing difficulty, for example:
- What happens to the energy level of the sparrow hawk when it eats the thrush?
- Why does the thrush eat the snail?
- How does the snail get enough energy to live?

Helen can change the mode of the system to "run" in order to investigate the answers to these questions. She can select from a range of action commands to run elements of the model such as the sparrow hawk eating the thrush. If the action is legitimate, it is simulated and the state of the Ecolab world changes to reflect the effects. In this example the thrush would be eaten in world view, the energy level of the sparrowhawk would increase in energy view, the arrow between thrush and sparrow hawk would be instantiated in web view, and the statement "the thrush has been eaten by the sparrowhawk" would be added to the narrative in history view. As an alternative to instigating single action commands, Helen could use the program option and link action commands together.

That brief description illustrates how Helen can interact with the Ecolab, and it explains the types of activities that she encounters. However, what is not clear from this text is how the system acts as a more able collaborative learning partner. This will now be clarified. As has already been identified, there are two basic types of assistance available. First, there are help statements that can be of five different levels of specificity. For example, if Helen has difficulty in answering the investigation questions, the system can prompt generally with "try setting the world to 'run' and see what happens" or, more specifically, with "try using the action commands to make the sparrow hawk eat the thrush and look in the energy view to see the changes." The most specific help, in which the system takes the greatest control, would be a demonstration of selecting the action command to make the sparrow hawk eat the thrush and then switching to energy view to see the outcome.

The second category of assistance consists of the manner in which the activity presented to Helen can be adjusted. The adjustments possible in the current implementation are organized into two levels. The first level incorporates two types of adjustment. First, the number of organisms used in the activity is restricted to those that exhibit the relationship or features that are currently the subject of instruction. Second, when the child is required to select an answer or construct an answer from its constituents, the number of possible wrong answers or constituents is reduced. The second level of adjustment also encompasses two kinds of alteration in addition to those utilized for level one. First, some of the elements of the activity are already completed and, second, any rule refinements are ignored. In the current example this would mean that Helen would be introduced to the rule that energy is transferred from food to feeder, but not that some of the energy is dispersed.

Once Helen has completed this activity, a new activity of appropriate complexity will be needed. If she has found the current task straightforward, then a more challenging activity will be needed; alternatively if this one has proved tough, then an easier option is needed. It might also be appropriate to alter the nature of the terminology used to describe the plants and animals Helen has selected. A move to more abstract terminology will mean that in the next and future activities Helen will be required to manipulate concepts such as carnivore rather than sparrowhawk. She will need to understand the relationships that exist between the organisms in terms of their roles rather than in terms of their category instances. Such roles are likely to be less familiar to Helen and therefore more difficult. If, however, such a move presents Helen with an unreasonable degree of difficulty, then the level of abstraction can be lowered again.

Although we have stipulated that the interactions that occur in the Ecolab are between a system and a single learner, we have not specified which of these partners is responsible for making decisions about what the learner should do next, how difficult it should be, and how much help the system should give. In fact, the Ecolab is not a single system: There are three system versions in which this responsibility and the manner in which collaboration from the system was offered to the learner is varied. The three system variations are: VIS (Vygotskian Inspired System), WIS (Woodsian Inspired System) and NIS (Nontheoretically Inspired System). The way in which each of the system variations adopts a different approach is described in more detail in Luckin (1998) and is summarized in Table 4.1.

Empirical Evaluation: Modeling and Collaborating With the Ecolab

An exploratory evaluation study of the Ecolab software was conducted with a class of children aged 10 and 11 years. More detail about the methodology and results can be found in Luckin (1998). Here we focus on the types of interactions children had with the system, the nature of the models they constructed, and the collaborative communication that occurred between system and child. Twenty-six children completed all parts of the study that involved two sessions using the Ecolab, a written and verbal pre- and post-system-use-test, and a delayed posttest 10 weeks later. The children's school assessments were used to allocate each child to one of three ability groupings: high, average, and low. One aspect of the evaluation looked at whether the different variations of the Ecolab had been more or less effective in increasing the child's learning gain in terms of his or her understanding of the feeding relationships that exist in a food web reflected in the pre- and posttest data. This indicated that ability and the system variant that the child used was relevant to his or her subsequent learning gain. The VIS system produced the best overall learning gains, the WIS system produced the highest learning gains for the most able students, and the NIS system produced the highest learning gains for the least able group (see Luckin & du Boulay, 1999 for a detailed discussion of these results).

TABLE 4.1

Collaborative Support Within **Ecolab**

	VIS	WIS	NIS
Levels of Help Available (different levels provide differing qualities of help—5 represents the greatest and 1 the least)	5	5	2
Decision about Level of Help made by	system	system and child	child
Levels of Activity Differentiation Available	3	3	3
Decision about type of Activity and Differentiation level made by	system	child—system makes suggestions	child
Extent of Learner Model maintained by the system and used to make decisions about the support to be offered to the learner.	Bayesian Belief Network (BBN) of values representing the system's beliefs about child's ZPD formed from its knowledge about the amount of collaborative support used to date.	Record of help used to enable contingent calculation of next help level. Record of curriculum nodes visited maintained to permit suggestions.	Record of Curriculum nodes visited maintained to help child keep track.
Abstractness of Terminology selected by	system	child	child
Area of the Curriculum and complexity of the next activity selected by	system	child—system makes suggestions	child
Ecolab View selected by	mostly child	child	child

Each time a child used the **Ecolab**, his or her activity was logged. It is the analysis of these logs that we concentrate our attention on, and within those logs, it is the character of the interactions between each child and the system that we focus on here. For each child, an annotated summary record of his or her interactions was produced from the detailed logs maintained during the two sessions of system use and this was used to build up a picture of the types of interactions each child experienced with the system (for full information, see Luckin, 1998). The analysis of these annotated interaction summaries of children's experiences with the Ecolab software enabled us to classify children according to the nature of their experiences with the system. Two aspects of this classification appropriate to the current discussion are *Interaction* and *Collaboration*, with the children who took part in this study being categorized into *Interaction Profiles* according to the character of their interactions with the Ecolab, or *Collaboration Profiles* according to the nature of the collaborative support provided by the system for the child.

Interaction Profiles

Interaction profiles were organized along three dimensions: *busyness–quietness*, *exploration–consolidation* and *hopping–persister*. Each child was allocated a position along each of these three dimensions. The terminology for the dimensions was chosen for its evocativeness: the terminology is not intended to be judgmental.

The three dimensions of categorization—Busy/Quiet, Exploration/Consolidation, and Hopper/Persister—bear some similarity to features found in other categorization systems. Pask's (1976) differentiation of "top- down" holists from "bottom-up" serialists shares some common ground with the Hopper/Persister characteristic, for example. The differentiation of exploration from continuing activity at a level of consolidation is likewise similar to the challenge–safety division of Groat and Musson (1995). However, the motivation for the analysis reported in this chapter was not the presentation of a generally applicable categorization system. The aim was twofold: to investigate the relationship between interaction style and learning gain, and to examine how each of the system variations of the Ecolab supported and encouraged particular learning styles.

Busyness was considered to be a characteristic of interactions in which the child completed an average or above average number of actions of any type, such as adding an organism to their Ecolab world or making one organism eat another. The interaction summaries of these children contained an above-average number of events. The opposite of Busyness is referred to as *quietness*.

Exploration was considered to be a characteristic of an interaction if the child had been involved in some sort of action that allowed him or her to experience more than one level of complexity or more than one level of terminology abstraction, beyond her initial starting levels. The opposite of exploration is referred to as *consolidation*.

Some children also switched frequently from one type of interaction to another. For example, they might switch from attempting to make one animal eat another, to looking at their organisms in a different view, to accessing a new activity entirely. Their interactions contained no, or few, series of repeated actions of the same type. They were particularly prone to frequent changes of view. These users have been characterized as *hoppers*. Other learners exhibited a more persistent approach, with sets of actions of a similar type grouped together. These users have been referred to as *persisters*.

These three binary characteristics allow each child to be categorized into one of eight possible Interaction Profiles. Children fell into six of the eight possible Interaction Profile groups. The distribution within these groups is illustrated in Table 4.2. The following subsection illustrates the largest of these interaction profile categories, namely that of *Busy— Exploring—Persisters*. Details of the other of the members of the other profiles can be found in Luckin (1998).

Interaction Profile Example.   S10 (Gene) was a typical example of the *Busy–Exploring–Persister* style of interaction. Her first action was to switch from world view to energy view and then back to world view. She then added 15 organisms to the Ecolab and visited the energy view again. On switching back to world view, she made one of her organisms eat another, switching to energy view to see the effect. This pattern of making organisms act, either eating or moving, and looking at the effect in an increasing number of different views continued. Introductory, investigative, and rule-definition activity types were completed for the first two nodes in the curriculum before her first session drew to a close. She chose not to save her current Ecolab world, which meant that at the start of her next session her first actions were the addition of organisms. Once again she added all 15 and then moved into the next phase of food web complexity and used more abstract terminology to view her organisms. Although the nature of the actions she completed was now more advanced and several instances of help were used, her pattern of activity remained one of initiating an action or actions appropriate to the evident goal. Actions were often completed in pairs and were followed by viewing the result from different perspectives (most commonly, energy, web, and world). She did not experiment with writing a program or attempt to "escape" from completing the activities offered to her.

TABLE 4.2

Interaction Profile Membership (*N* = 26)

Profile Description	% of children in Profile group
Busy–Exploring–Persister (BEP)	28%
Busy–Exploring–Hopper (BEH)	12%
Busy–Consolidating–Persister (BCP)	8%
Busy–Consolidating–Hopper (BCH)	12%
Quiet–Consolidating–Persister (QCP)	20%
Quiet–Exploring–Persister (QEP)	20%

This profile group contains only high and average ability children from the VIS and WIS system user groups. In terms of performance at posttest, there was a tremendous spread: A *Busy–Exploring–Persister* learner attained the lowest learning gain (–4.1%), another, the second highest learning gain (32.5%). To put these figures in context, the mean learning gain across all users was 11.8%, although the interaction profile cell sizes were too small to compute significant differences. The high ability children within the group all achieved an above-average learning gain (12.6%, 17%, and 32.5%), but within the average ability children there was a wider spread of learning gain scores (24.8%, 12.3%, 4.2%, and –4.1%). Membership of this group was limited to VIS and WIS users, of whom the VIS users both achieved above-average posttest learning gains (24.8% and 12.6%), including the highest learning gain within this user group.

Collaboration Profiles

Two characteristics were found to be the most useful for categorizing collaborative style within the interactions: amount of support and depth of support used. These collaboration characteristics were used to group the children into one of four Collaboration Profile groups.

1. *Amount* of support: the average amount of activity differentiation and the average number of help instances for the experimental group was calculated. An above-average amount of either activity differentiation or instances of help was the criteria necessary for a child to be considered as using "lots" of collaborative support.

2. *Depth* of support: this characteristic was based on the level of help and level of differentiation used. Once again the average levels used within the experimental group were calculated. Help or differentiation above the average level resulted in a child being considered as using "deep" or higher level support.

Interactions could be grouped into all four of the possible Collaboration Profiles. The first group was the largest and was further divided in accordance with the type of support that was most prevalent. The distribution of children into these groups is illustrated in Table 4.3.

Collaboration Profile Examples.   S1 (Jason's) use of the available support was typical of the *Lots and Deep* profile group and of a user of above-average amounts of both help and activity differentiation. He used level 4 help early in his first session of system use to achieve success in making organisms eat each other. His initial activities were completed with maximum differentiation of level 3. This was gradually reduced and then increased again. During his first session of system use, he completed a range of activities for three nodes in the first phase of the curriculum. All instances of successful help were at level 4 or level 5. Fewer

TABLE 4.3

Distribution of Children Within Collaboration Profile Groups (N = 26)

Profile Description	% of children in Profile	Profile subgroup Description	% of children in Profile subgroup
Lots and Deep (LD)	53%	Differentiation and Help	19%
		Differentiation	19%
		Help	15%
Lots and Shallow (LND)	12%		
Little and Deep (NLD)	16%		
Little and Shallow (NLND)	19%		

activities were completed during his second session. However, these activities were at a lower level of differentiation and there were fewer instances of help.

The *Lots and Deep* Collaboration Profile group was the largest and was subdivided to account for the type of support used. Only VIS and WIS system users shared the profile. Jason was a member of the subgroup that used above-average amounts and levels of both activity differentiation and help. This subgroup again consisted only of high and average ability children whose mean learning gain was above the average for the whole class (16% as compared to the class average of 11.8%). The subgroup of children who used greater levels of differentiation than help contained children from all ability groups. This second subgroup also produced above-average learning gains at posttest (18% as compared to the class average of 11.8%). The last subgroup of children, who used greater amounts of help than differentiation, were all average ability children. Their average learning gain was well below the class average (3.9% as compared to the class average of 11.8%).

So far little has been said about the NIS user group; they have not belonged to either of the Profiles used in the examples. Recall that NIS was the system variant where the child had the *most* autonomy about selecting what to do next and about choosing the degree of assistance (see Table 4.1). In fact, all the NIS users belonged to a Consolidating Interaction profile; there were no explorers in this system user group. In addition, and as was previously mentioned, no NIS users were in the *Lots and Deep* Collaboration profile group.

S9's (Tim's) Interaction profile, which was that of a Quiet, Consolidating Persister, was typical of a NIS system user. His initial session consisted of adding a single snail and then making 11 view changes to look at this organism from all perspectives. This initial stage was followed by a series of organism adding (commonly in blocks of four); single actions, such as "move" or "eat" commands, in blocks of one to five; and view changes that were almost always in pairs. In session 2 he adopted the commonly seen approach of adding a considerable number of organisms to start (in this case 12) and then, once again, completing single actions and view changes.

Likewise S26 (Karlie's) Collaboration profile, reflecting low use of all types of help (Little and Shallow: NLND), was typical. She placed herself at the far extreme of food web complexity and started dealing with populations of organisms straight away. She only completed one type of action during both sessions of computer use: she built food webs using the *build web* command. Initially she made errors and used only occasional low-level feedback, persisting until successful. The children in this profile group were all of high or average ability, but their average learning gains were well below average (5.2% as compared to the class average of 11.8%)

A further difference found within the NIS user group relates to the relationship between ability and learning gain. In the VIS and WIS user groups, it was the higher ability children who achieved the greatest learning gains. By contrast, among the NIS users, none of the high ability children made an above-average learning gain; in fact, the only learners who made above-average learning gains were the low ability children. Although the numbers are small and the study exploratory, this result is interesting and is certainly informing our current research. We had expected that of all three systems, the one that left most control within the hands of the learner would be most effective with the more able learners. Our results indicate that the opposite was, in fact, the case in our study.

WHAT DOES THIS CASE STUDY TELL US ABOUT MODELING AND COMMUNICATION?

The children in this study were not always effective at selecting activities that were appropriately challenging or at seeking the appropriate amount of assistance from the system. It was possible to influence the nature of their modeling activities: the complexity of the models they ran, for example, and the nature of the collaboration that occurred between system and child through manipulating the role played by the computer. Indeed, a Pearson Chi-squared statistical test revealed that the system variation a learner used had a greater impact on their membership of an Interaction or a Collaboration profile than their ability. There was a significant association between System variant membership and Collaboration Profile membership (Chi-square = 28.52, df = 6, $p < .0001$), and between System variant membership and Interaction Profile membership (Chi-square = 25.79, df = 10, $p < .01$). Table 4.4 sets out the number of children in each of the Interaction and Collaboration profiles by System variant.

These results suggest that the nature of the modeling was very sensitive to the variant of the system and to the ability of the particular child. VIS and WIS were able to adjust the degree of abstractness of the termi-

TABLE 4.4
Membership of Profile Categories ($n= 26$)

Profile	VIS	WIS	NIS
Busy exploring persister	2	5	0
Busy exploring hopper	1	3	0
Busy consolidating persister	0	0	2
Busy consolidating hopper	1	0	2
Quiet consolidating persister	0	1	4
Quiet exploring persister	4	1	0
Lots and Deep	9	5	0
Lots and Shallow	0	0	2
Little and Deep	0	4	1
Little and Shallow	0	0	5

nology used, but none of the systems were in a position to react mean-ingfully to children's explanations in their own words about what they were modeling. In fact, the children were asked to explain various con-cepts as part of the posttest and a delayed posttest, and in general they were able to make better explanations after their experience with the system (of whichever variant). So although some features of the com-munication between child and computer were under the control of ei-ther the child or the system, there were, in the end, strong limitations in the extent to which the children could explicitly contextualize with and through the system what they were learning against the background of what they already knew about ecology.

Our second case study begins to address this issue. Here the students worked in groups, discussing with each other, and writing a freeform tex-tual answer to a given question. These students could engage in unre-stricted communication with each other, and an aspect of interest in the second case study is how system features affect that communication. Of course, the second system has its weak points; too, notably that students cannot test their understanding by running and debugging a simulation.

CASE STUDY 2: GALAPAGOS: DISCUSSING MODELING

The Galapagos CD-ROM

The second case study we discuss involves a CD-ROM called Galapagos. This was developed as a research tool to aid our investigations into the impact of narrative on children's learning with Multimedia Interactive Learning Environments (MILEs). It provides learners with a multimedia account of Darwin's visit to the Galapagos Islands and the theory of evolution he developed as a result. Learners are set the task of using the resources provided on the CD-ROM to construct an explanation of the variations in the wildlife on the islands in an on-line notepad. The notepad is the location of the modeling activity in this case study, and the form of the model is a textual narrative rather than a runnable simulation as in Ecolab. The elements that learners can use to construct this text are the resources on the CD-ROM and the resources each of them brings to the situation and shares. In this example, as in Case Study 1, learning is collaboration, but the parties involved are different. They are the learners working as a group around the computer with the CD-ROM. The system does still provide some scaffolding to assist the learner's progress, but in this instance the support is adaptable *by* the learners rather than adaptive *to* the learners.

The resources on the CD-ROM are also of a different nature from the action commands and runnable model elements of the Ecolab. There are eight sections of content material on the CD-ROM, each of which deals with a particular aspect of Darwin's visit. For example, there is a section that describes his arrival and first impressions of the Galapagos Islands, and sections about the identity of the different islands and the different varieties of finch that lived in these different locations. The full set of sections is as follows; the section numbers are used to refer to sections throughout this chapter, but were not part of the structure presented to our users.

> Introduction
> Section 1: About Darwin's visit
> Section 2: About Islands
> Section 3: Island Formation
> Section 4: Island Location
> Section 5: Trade Winds
> Section 6: Currents
> Section 7: About the Birds
> Section 8: Explore the Islands

As well as having a role within the overall story about Darwin's work on evolution, each of these sections also offers its own possibilities for interaction, in the form of movies to play or images to click on for feedback. In addition to these sections of content material, users can access the following five features to assist them via a tool bar at the bottom of the screen as illustrated in Fig. 4.2. (For more detail about all the Galapagos features, see Luckin et al., 1998):

1. A reminder about the task they have been asked to complete at the outset of their interactions with Galapagos.
2. An editable notepad in which they can take notes and write their answer: the focus of their modeling activity in this case study.

3. A model answer, which is a sample of an acceptable answer to the task they have been set and which can only be accessed when they have written 50 words in the notepad.
4. A script window that contains the transcript for all audio material in the CD–ROM.
5. Some navigation options that allow navigation to be varied in accordance with the actions selected by the learners as appropriate to the subgoal with which the group is currently operating.

We used **Galapagos** with groups of students, aged between 15 and 21 years, all of whom were studying for a national examination in biology. A session using **Galapagos** and completing the task (to explain the variation in the wildlife on the Galapagos Islands and write the answer in the notepad) to their own satisfaction typically took about 45 minutes. The following scenario describes the sort of experiences learners had with **Galapagos**:

> The first thing that Mark, Claire, and Louise do after the initial introduction (which includes the specification of the task) is to access the task again and discuss what it is they have got to do. They then return to the introduction, which involves hearing the task again. Between 2.19 minutes and 14.37 minutes (34% of the total session time), the group starts to construct a notepad answer. They access the guide and through this facility they move on to content section 8 of the CD-ROM. They open the notepad and then section 2 of the CD. Initially (2.19–5.29 minutes), talk is about what completing the task involves. This is followed by a move back to the introduction and therefore another experience of the task. At 4 minutes the search engine is used and section 2 of the CD-ROM is accessed. Activity between 4.09 and 14.37 minutes (29% of total session time) consists of alternating between section 1 of the CD-ROM and the notepad, with one look at the task as well. As they watch section 1 of the CD-ROM, they start to type into the notepad and the discussion is about what they should write, picking up points from the audio track. At 14.54 minutes they go back to the introduction again and then to the task, and in this way they hear the task twice. At 14.54 minutes the search engine is used to reach section 7 of the CD-ROM. Discussion is about how the section on the different birds relates to the task. The notepad is not used after this, but is opened again at 19.09 minutes after the guide has been used and section 2 of the CD viewed. They talk about the importance of the Galapagos being an island and how this relates to the task. Until the model answer is opened at 28.04 minutes, activity consists of using the guide to access sections 3, 5, and 6 of the CD-ROM, and further completion of an answer in the notepad. About 50% of the talk is about the completion of the task. The features of the CD-ROM section and their relationship to the model answer are discussed. Once the model answer is accessed, section 2 of the CD-ROM is opened and some revisions made to the notepad.

As in the **Ecolab** system in Case Study 1, **Galapagos** was implemented as three different system versions. However, in this case the manipulation is with respect to the presentation of the same content material. Spe-

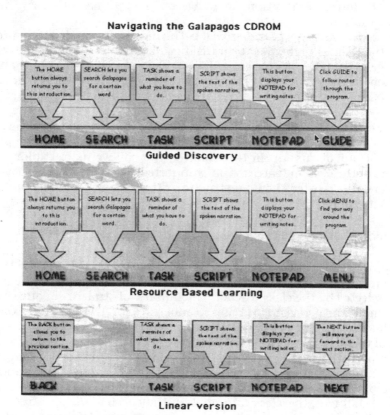

FIG. 4.2. Galapagos tool bars.

cifically, it relates to number 5 in the list, *navigation options*: the amount of guidance the system provides to users to help them navigate through the available material is varied. The three Galapagos versions are called *Linear, Resource-Based Learning*, and *Guided Discovery Learning.*

1. *Linear*: When the material on this version is first viewed, the system moves automatically between the content sections. After this, learners can elect to go back to certain selected points within this presentation and from there, they can move either backward or forward between the different sections of content. It provides no full menu or search facility and no overview of the structure of the CD-ROM. The navigation options available on the tool bar of this system variation are *back* and *forward*.

2. *Resource-Based Learning* (RBL): Learners have free access to all sections of the CD–ROM through a menu and free text search facility.

The navigation options available on the tool bar of this system variation are *menu* and *search*.

3. *Guided Discovery Learning* (GDL): The menu is expanded into a textual guide that breaks the initial task down into subtasks and suggests the relevant sections of the CD-ROM to access for information about these subtasks. The navigation options available on the tool bar of this system variation are *guide* and *search*.

These three versions were developed to enable us to observe the impact of presentational variation on learner interaction. For the purposes of our discussion in this chapter, they allow us to explore the nature of the system features that supported communication between learners and assisted their construction of an answer: a model of their understanding.

Empirical Evaluation: Interactions Around **Galapagos**

The groups of learners using **Galapagos** each used only one of the three system versions. Each group consisted of three learners of differing abilities, selected by the class teacher. The number of students in our study was small, and it was not our aim to adhere to a pretest/posttest experimental methodology but rather to concentrate on process issues. As part of their course of study, 36 learners used **Galapagos** at a time when it was pertinent to their curriculum objectives. The interactions around the computer were complex, and we wanted to increase our understanding of the process learners went through when they used the CD-ROM. It was, therefore, our goal to study each of our groups in detail and we used video as one of our sources of data. We recorded every group session from two videosources: one recorded the group of learners at the computer to capture talk, movement, gesture, and machine interaction; the other was the screen image, taken from the computer via a scan converter.

Video provides a flexible source of data for analysis. However, the richness of the data, although enormously valuable, can be overwhelming. In order to cope with the overwhelming density of information and to try to ensure that (a) particularly interesting moments in the interactions can be located quickly at a later date, and (b) sufficient contextual information about these moments can be found quickly, we developed a number of charts and graphs as tools for representing different aspects of the interactions (see Luckin et al., 1998, for more detail about the methodology and analytical tools used). In this chapter, we concentrate our discussion on dialogue analysis in combination with one of these representations: Answer Construction Records (ACR). ACRs record the time and content of each text entry made by the group into the notepad and the system features used around this text entry.

The Dialogue Between Learners as They Use Galapagos

The dialogue was transcribed and categorized. The categories used were informed by our early observations of commercial CD-ROMs and the questions we wanted to explore. With respect to educational focus, these categories enabled us to:

- differentiate the times when learners are focusing on the medium of communication: on procedural or operational issues, from the times when they are involved in the pragmatics of answer construction, and to determine the times when they are trying to construct an understanding of the underlying concepts about evolution.

There is a wide variety of work that considers the structure of the exchanges within dialogue, the nature and quality of the argumentation, or the negotiation that occurs between participants (Chi, 1997; Pilkington, Treasure-Jones, & Kneser, 1999; Quignard & Baker, 1999; Ravenscroft & Hartley, 1999, for example). It would certainly be interesting to explore the structure of the dialogues surrounding the use of Galapagos, but such work has been beyond the scope of our analysis to date.

Two researchers acting independently but using the same system of categorization completed all coding of dialogue. Discrepancies were few and were discussed in order to reach a consensus about the final coding category to be used. The dialogue was categorized initially into *Nontask*, *Task*, and *Content*.

1. The Nontask category encompasses navigational and operational talk other than that which relates specifically to using the notepad or model answer (e.g., "click on one" "play" for video or audio clips). This category focuses on the use of system features and learners' interactions with the operational aspects of the system rather than the content.
2. The Task category includes dialogue about the pragmatics of answer construction, about getting the task done rather than what to put in the answer. For example, discussions about how and when to use the notepad (e.g., "Shall I type?"). The focus here is on specific software features such as the notepad and model answer. Here learners are negotiating the use of tools, which should enable them to interact with the content and construct an understanding of these concepts.
3. The Content category of talk includes all discussions about Darwin, the Galapagos Islands, and evolution, both specifically related to constructing a group's answer and in general.

There were very few examples of instances where dialogue fell into more than one category. These were entirely restricted to humorous comments that might, for example, be flippant and yet relate to content.

Each of these categories was then subdivided for a more detailed analysis. Discussion of this is beyond the scope of this chapter, but can be found in Plowman, Luckin, Laurillard, Stratfold, and Taylor (1999).

WHAT SUPPORT DID GALAPAGOS PROVIDE FOR MODELING AND COMMUNICATION?

The goal of our analysis was to construct an understanding of what was happening at the system interface, what was happening between individual learners in the group, and what sort of an understanding individual learners were constructing as a result of these collaborative interactions. Here we concentrate on how the system supported communication and model building in the notepad.

Did Learners Focus on Domain Concepts or Interface Operation?

In order for learners to construct a model of their understanding, they need to interact with the concepts of the domain rather than the operations of the medium. The discussions conducted by all groups of learners contained twice as much Content type talk as talk categorized as Nontask or Task. Likewise, with respect to notepad use, over 25% of the total discussions between learners took place when the notepad editor was open on the screen and more than 10% when the model answer had been accessed and was open on the screen. Talk about navigational and operational issues (i.e., categorized as Nontask dialogue) for all groups occurred throughout all but one content section of the CD-ROM as learners discussed when and how to play a particular video clip, for example. Discussion about how to complete the task (i.e., categorized as Task dialogue) was, however, less evenly distributed among these same content sections.

The following transcript excerpt is taken from a group of learners using Galapagos and illustrates conversation clearly focused on the current task.

A: Do you want to make notes on this—did you hear what they said?

B: The islands are tips of volcanoes.

A: Is it Notepad ...

C: Yeah

B: Under the sea ...

C: Under the sea—but that's got nothing to do with variation.

B: But that's nothing to do with the variation of the wildlife—is it? Well ...
   Video of the islands forming from volcanoes

B: When they first came they were—or do we not really need that?

C: I don't know.

A: No—oh, you can say that it got there from ocean currents and trade winds and, these are the factors in how.... OK—The islands, the wildlife got there....

The learners had been asked to explain the variation in the finches on the Galapagos Islands. The group searched for information relevant to their task and when they found it, they recognized its relevance and continued to construct a narrative of their understanding of how the variations in the Galapagos wildlife occurred.

How Did Learners Use Their Own Articulations to Coconstruct Their Descriptive Model?

All the groups of learners using Galapagos were required to construct their answers as a collaborative effort. There were many clear instances of productive collaborations. The following transcript is taken from a group who had just viewed a video clip about ocean currents and were starting to construct their text in the notepad. During the latter part of this conversation, the following text was entered: "*the wildlife's population increased because of ocean currents, trade winds. the islands were formed from volcanic action underneath the sea so they were just rocks.*"

B: Ocean currents, trade winds—right, you remember one of them, I'll remember ocean currents

A: I'll remember trade winds

B: and you remember island formation
Notepad opened on screen and text entered

A: because of—

B: ocean currents

A: trade winds

C: and island formation

The teacher later assessed the unattributed written response and commented of this group, "I like this answer a lot. This is obviously written in their own way, rather than taking chunks from the video, and they go through it in a very ordered manner." The clear statement of the goal allowed the learners to keep it in mind while constructing their response, helping them to avoid getting side-tracked. The notepad allowed them to record each of their contributions within the answer, and the constant availability of the task provided a reminder.

How Did Learners Use the System's Model of an Answer to Revise Their Own Articulation?

The model answer was designed to offer feedback on learners' conceptions, motivate reflections on their response, encourage collaboration, and allow revisions to the learners' own answer. Attempting to open the model answer before sufficient text was entered into the notepad resulted in learners being advised that they could only access the model answer when they had typed 50 words into the notepad editor. Only one of the groups who accessed the refusal message had started to enter text prior to this point, and in all cases the notepad was opened and text entered within a very short period of time (under 3 minutes). The extract in Table 4.5 is an ACR extended to include dialogue. It illustrates the activity of one group of users following the model answer refusal message that was seen after 9 minutes of CD-ROM use. The students open the task window, read the task aloud, then open the notepad and start to enter their answer.

The existence of a model answer motivated learners to start constructing an answer of their own but, once opened, it also prompted revisions. The following dialogue extract illustrates how one group discussed these revisions. The model answer is accessed after 33 minutes of system use. The notepad and the model answer are open on the screen and this dialogue occurs in the next couple of minutes. The group adds the following sentences to the start of their own answer: "*The island was created by Volcanic activity. This means no wildlife was there to start off with. The islands are on the Equator so there are strong winds and water systems. The wildlife now found on the islands probably drifted over on rafts from America.*"

> **B:** (*speaks aloud while writing*) OK, activity, er what else is it? …… That water, isn't it, water?
>
> **A:** The birds came across by reeds or something
>
> **C:** (*Pointing at model answer on screen, reads something aloud*).
>
> **B:** (*Reading*) The islands are in the equator with strong winds and water systems - OK. (*Turns to look at C who apologizes that her tummy is rumbling and says she is really hungry.*)
>
> **C:** There was the strong winds as well
>
> **B:** Yeah …… And was it water currents? Water systems

In these brief examples we have paid attention to the communicative processes revealed within the dialogue among the groups of students as they collaborate to produce a coconstructed textual narrative. Different groups of learners adopted different approaches and varied in the way they used the available resources, both those provided by the CD-ROM and those provided by each other.

TABLE 4.5

Learner's Activity After Accessing Model Answer Refusal

Time	Notepad text entered	Dialogue	Screen
(mins)	The animals on the island varie	A: The animals on the islands all vary, C: the animals on the islands vary, um	Notepad open
11.29		— (B types and is told to use two hands by C)— A: The animals on the island all vary. C: Yeah that will do (laughter) .... What did you do that for	
11.56		B? B: Where did it go? A: what are you trying to do, delete something?	
12.15	due to	B: There you are .... – due to? A: I dunno, something like evolution or something to sound good B: Due to the change in habitat	
	change in habitat	B: - due to habitat - A: Oh brits is getting along there	
12.32		A: Due to the habitat and, and what I don't know	
	climate	C: Habitat, weather A: Climate, climate and C: Habitat climate and what's the other one - ?	
12.49	and prediters	A: Predators C: Yeah predators	

What Differences Did the Three Versions of **Galapagos** Have on Learner Interaction?

So far we have considered learners' interactions with Galapagos without taking into account the existence of the three different versions. Next we consider the impact of these variations and summarize their effects on learner interaction and communication.

The Menu in the *resource-based* version provided free access to all sections of the material, but, unlike the Guide (in the *guided discovery* version), it gave no guidance on how sections related to each other.

This left less confident learners without support for linking the parts together to construct their own textual representation and did not motivate sufficient discussion of these relationships between learners to compensate. These *resource-based* learners were further disadvantaged as they were more likely to miss key sections of the material, being entirely self-directed via the Menu. This meant that the groups of learners neither interacted with the information in these sections, nor discussed the concepts presented. In contrast, both *linear* and *guided discovery* learners were exposed to all of the material. The *resource-based* version was highly interactive, requiring students to be very pro-active in what they spent time on. They *felt* they had learned a lot, although in fact learners with low prior knowledge could not complete the full analysis required for construction of the answer. This was further compounded by the fact that in several cases they had not covered all the material. The tools provided in this version were insufficient to support these learners in their model building activity and left them vulnerable to misconception.

The predefined Guide in the *guided discovery* version tended to focus learners' notes on the essential activities and thus aided abstraction. The more open-ended choices of the *resource-based* version elicited notes on incidental facts that were more difficult for less able learners to integrate into their own understanding. As with the *resource-based* version, we found that not all the students who had little prior knowledge were able to build the top-level answer with the *guided discovery* version. They were, however, able to use the Guide to construct the building blocks beyond the simple facts, namely, to the level of the component relations identified in the subgoals offered (such as the differences observed between birds on the islands and those on the mainland, and the different weather conditions on the islands relating to variations in species).

The continual requirement to decide on the next action, in both *resource-based* and *guided discovery* versions, encouraged learners to open the Notepad early and take notes as they progressed, and begin to build their own articulated account. This was totally absent for the *linear* groups. Learners were much more likely to refer back to other sections as they constructed their answers within the learner-controlled *resource-based* and *guided discovery* versions, and therefore tended to use quotes from the material in their notes, which *linear* users did not do.

The *linear* version certainly did engage learners in the preconstructed narrative. In fact, they never disturbed the sequence and did not use the Notepad until they had seen all sections. This did, however, leave some learners unable to articulate their own understanding except as recall. There was very little communication between learners about either operations or concepts until the sections had been viewed once and the answer construction process began. In the individual audio-recorded follow-up sessions, we found that only those students with good prior knowledge of evolution were able to maintain the link between this high-level narrative line and the specific information provided in the multimedia material. For the others, the full control by the program for the sequence, and hence the lack of requirement for them to plan their own investigation or articulate their understanding, reduced their clarity about the relationship between the immediate information and their overall goal.

Clearly the nature of the direction provided by the system has an impact on the usefulness of particular system features as tools in the answer construction process. Variations in this direction can also motivate different quantities and qualities of communication between learners about the concepts at the root of that answer.

DISCUSSION

At the start of this chapter we defined *Interactivity* as the cycle of operational or conceptual exchange between two or more parties, one of which may be a digital system. We stressed the importance of Interactivity *through* the interface between users and the subject matter concepts that make up the discipline of study. We used case studies of both systems to tease out some of the factors that have proved successful in linking support for learning, as communicative competence, and the process of modeling. Both systems have been evaluated using methodologies that yield a rich source of data about the way in which students used the systems as well as the models they constructed. This allows us to explore similarities and differences, and to focus in particular on the nature and role of the communicative interactions engendered by these systems. In the first, communication is between learner and system; in the second, the system's role is different and is to motivate communication between users around the system. In both cases there is an explicit attempt to engender conceptual interactivity with the scientific concepts of the domain through the features of the system. A striking factor of both case studies is that the majority of the learners were both engaged and hard working. Another striking factor was that differences between system variants produced differences in the manner of working. In Ecolab, NIS users were consolidators rather than explorers, and a similar phenomenon was found with Galapagos where the linear version produced the most constrained traverse of the material.

Neither system was designed to support fully all aspects of modeling in science. Ecolab provided the tools for pupils to manipulate a simplified world. It acted as the more able partner in an interactive interchange where it could make adjustments of various kinds so as to maintain the learners in "vigorous mental activity." It is not unreasonable to regard the interchange between pupil and the system as communication, where each partner in this communication was responding to and adjusting to their perceptions of the other partner. The nature of these adjustments on the system side had strong effects on the collaborative element of that communication as well as indirect effects on the kind of interaction that ensued.

In the case of Galapagos, the communication between system and student was not subject to dynamic changes on the system side. None of the three variants maintained any kind of internal model that would have allowed adjustments in the Ecolab sense. The variants offered differences in interactivity that were essentially fixed for the duration of the session. Nevertheless, different variants produced different kinds of interactive behavior. In any case, the primary focus in this study was not on the communication between the students and the system but on how that communication interacted with the communication between the students, a factor missing in the Ecolab study.

The differences in interactivity between the Ecolab variants was largely conceptual and occurred *through* the interface. Thus some variants of the system varied the level of specificity of the help that they offered, adjusted the level of complexity of the tasks they set, chose what task to do next, and adjusted the degree of abstractness of the terminology used by the system. By contrast, the designed-in differences between the variants of Galapagos were largely operational, *at* the interface. These consisted of differences in the way that the material on the CD-ROM could be accessed. There is some overlap between conceptual and operational interactivity, but these two case studies indicate that both types of interactivity can have effects on the nature of the communication through the interface and as provoked between participants around the interface.

We return to a point we made earlier. Learning science effectively is a complex process, and system design to support this is tricky. Small changes in the interactivity implicit in the design can have large changes on the kind of modeling that takes place. By offering case studies that describe both an adaptive and an adaptable system, we indicate that both kinds of system have a useful role to play and that in both cases, attention to the interactivity made possible through the design can crucially affect outcomes.

ACKNOWLEDGMENTS

The Ecolab system was developed with the aid of a grant from the Economic and Social Research Council. The research described in the second case study was conducted as part of MENO (Multimedia, Education, and Narrative Organisation), funded by the Economic and Social Research Council's Cognitive Engineering Programme, grant no. L127251018. The project was conducted in collaboration with Diana Laurillard, Lydia Plowman, Josie Taylor, and Matthew Stratfold. The Galapagos CD-ROM was developed by Matthew Stratfold. We are indebted to the schools, teachers, and students who made this research possible and to the reviewers, for detailed and valuable comments.

REFERENCES

Chi, M. T. H. (1997). Quantifying qualitative analyses of verbal data: A practical guide. *Journal of the Learning Sciences, 6*(3), 271–315.

Groat, A., & Musson, T. (1995). Learning styles: Individualizing computer-based learning environments. *Association for Learning Technology, 3*(2), 53–62.

Guzdial, M., Colander, J., Homely, C., Narayanan, H., Carlson, D., Rapine, N., Hubscher, R., Turns, J., & Newstetter, W. (1996). Computer support for learning through complex problem solving. *Communications of the ACM, 39*(4), 43–45.

Jackson, S. L., Stratford, S. J., Krajcik, J., & Soloway, E. (1996). A learner-centered tool for students building models. *Communications of the ACM, 39*(4), 48–50.

Laurillard, D. (1993). *Rethinking university teaching: A framework for the use of educational technology.* London: Routledge.

Luckin, R. (1998). *'ECOLAB': Explorations in the Zone of Proximal Development.* (Thesis: CSRP Technical Report 486): School of Cognitive and Computing Sciences, University of Sussex.

Luckin, R., & du Boulay, B. (1999). Ecolab: The development and evaluation of a Vygotskian design framework. *International Journal of Artificial Intelligence and Education, 10*(2), 198–220.

Luckin, R., Plowman, L., Gjedde, L., Laurillard, D., Stratfold, M., & Taylor, J. (1998). An evaluator's toolkit for tracking interactivity and learning. In M. Oliver (Ed.), *Innovation in the evaluation of learning technology* (pp. 42–64). London: University of North London.

Pask, G. (1976). Styles and strategies of learning. *British Journal of Educational Psychology, 46,* 128–148.

Pilkington, R. M., Treasure-Jones, T., & Knesser, C. (1999). *Educational chat: Using exchange structure analysis to investigate communicative roles in CMC seminars* (Tech. Rep. No. 99/6). Leeds, UK: Computer-Based Learning Unit, University of Leeds.

Plowman, L., Luckin, R., Laurillard, D., Stratfold, M., & Taylor, J. (1999, May). Designing multimedia for learning: Narrative guidance and narrative construction. *In the proceedings of CHI 99* (pp. 310–317). Pittsburgh, PA: Association for Computing Machinery.

Quignard, M., & Bakes, M. (1999). Favoring modelable computer-mediated argumentative dialogue in collaborative problem-solving situations. In S. Lajoie & M. Vivet (Eds.), *Artificial intelligence in education* (pp. 129–136). Amsterdam: IOS Press.

Ravenscroft, A., & Hartley, R. (1999). Learning as knowledge refinement. In S. Lajoie & M. Vivet (Eds.), *Artificial intelligence in education* (pp. 155–162). Amsterdam: IOS Press.

Rosson, M. B., & Carroll, J. M. (1996). Scaffolded examples for learning object-oriented design. *Communications of the ACM, 39*(4), 46–47.

Vygotsky, L. S. (1978). *Mind in society. The development of higher psychological processes.* Cambridge, MA: Harvard University Press.

Vygotsky, L. S. (1986). *Thought and language.* Cambridge, MA: MIT Press.

Wood, D., & Wood, H. (1996). Vygotsky, tutoring and learning. *Oxford Review of Education, 22*(1), 5–16.

Chapter 5

Cognitive Support in Computerized Science Problem Solving: Eliciting External Representation and Improving Search Strategies

Zvia Fund
Bar-Ilan University

This study examines cognitive support for science learning while problem solving in a computerized environment. Science problem solving in a computerized learning environment requires the learner to be engaged in complicated and complex modeling tasks. Concurrently with the problem solving, while in the computerized learning environment, the student should be learning scientific material as well as acquiring appropriate problem-solving strategies. Both might be achieved by re-modeling the computerized environment itself (Brna, 1999), by relating the computerized phenomena to previously acquired concepts and knowledge, or by establishing meaningful relationships between such phenomena and the student's concomitantly emerging explanatory system (Tiberghien, 1999).

Studies on education in the domains of artificial intelligence and computers in education suggest that such learning is difficult for learners, most of whom require guidance and support (Davis & Linn, 2000; Njoo & de Jong, 1993; Swaak, van Joolingen, & de Jong, 1998). Such assistance is assumed to facilitate the problem solving in several ways, which include eliciting an external representation (ER) of the problem-solving process and the problem itself and reducing the cognitive load on the learner. Inasmuch as ERs are the means by which students develop their conceptual understanding of physical phenomena, we might expect that such support would increase understanding of the scientific material as well (Brna, 1999). Guidance leading to these results (i.e., freeing up cognitive resources, enabling better concentration on the problem, improving understanding, and fostering the acquisition of general cognitive and metacognitive skills) may be subsumed under the term *cognitive support*. This may simultaneously offer the learner a continuing challenge of discovery and enable the concurrent construction of solutions and appropriate problem-solving strategies (Andriessen, 1999). Hence, our current enterprise with a computerized learning environment is twofold: to examine appropriate facilitating mediators for the complex modeling tasks, and to construct a research tool to describe and analyze such modeling activities during science problem solving. The latter is described elsewhere (Fund, 1996, 1999, 2001, 2002a), and the former is discussed in this chapter.

A series of guiding principles for the design of an effective learning environment has emerged from the available literature. The learning environment should induce and support constructive, cumulative, and goal-oriented acquisition processes in all learners by providing a good balance between learning by discovery and learning through systematic instruction and guidance. The learning environment should foster students' self-regulation of learning processes and should, as much as possible, embed acquisition processes in authentic contexts possessing personal meaning for students. In addition, in view of the complementary role that domain-specific and domain-general knowledge are assumed to play in learning and thinking, science problem solving in a computerized learning environment should integrate the acquisition of general cognitive and metacognitive skills within the specific domain(s) of the subject matter (De Corte, 2000).

Application of these ideas to science problem solving in a computerized learning environment raises the need for identification of the most appropriate means of cognitive support. Based on our search of the scientific literature, we describe four support components found to be effective in a computerized learning environment for science problem solving.

THE COMPONENTS

Recent research addresses some of the factors that affect science problem solving. In order to design a more effective approach to instruction, Reif (1995) examined the underlying thought processes required to deal with science. He proposed that thought processes, such as monitoring and self-assessment, as well as providing explanations during science problem solving, should be taught more explicitly and consequently be implemented more frequently by students. Bielaczyc, Pirolli, and Brown (1995) found that students, when learning LISP programming, could be successfully trained to give more and better self-explanations. Chi, De Leeuw, Chiu, and LaVancher (1994) stressed the importance of self-explanation during the problem-solving process as a metacognitive process that promotes understanding. Chi, Glaser, and Farr (1988), in comparing the problem solving of experts and novices, found that the main difference was in the well-organized procedural knowledge and domain-specific knowledge of the experts. This enabled the experts to use their knowledge, as well as their cognitive and metacognitive skills of self-monitoring and self-assessment, in a much more effective way.

A study of guidance for the acquisition of inquiry skills, as well as for self-assessment and reflection, under conditions of the computerized simulation of an "intelligent discovery world" proved that the guidance was helpful with specific content as well as with the development of general strategies for inquiry (Glaser, Schauble, Raghavan, & Zeitz, 1992).

The Computer as Learning Partner project used sentence-starter prompts to foster reflection and encouraged students to make predictions and reconcile their data with those predictions (Linn & Songer, 1991). This was found to promote improved understanding. The Knowledge Integration Environment software and curricula, which were developed as a result of the Computer as Learning Partner research (Bell, Davis, & Linn, 1995), used reflection prompts of two kinds: (a) self-monitoring prompts, which encourage planning and reflection upon activities, and (b) activity prompts, which guide the inquiry process. The former were found to be more successful than the latter in helping students demonstrate integrated understanding of relevant scientific knowledge (Davis & Linn, 2000).

From these and other studies, we categorized the various forms of prompts and guidance as having three main components:

1. A *structural* component provides a general framework for problem solving or a suggested sequence of steps to solve the problem (e.g., De Corte, 2000; Glaser et al., 1992; Guzdial, 1994). Guzdial (1994), for example, described students programming scientific contexts in a computerized learning environment under two conditions of scaffolding (instructional supports): (a) macro scaffolding, which suggests a general structure for performing the programming, and (b) micro scaffolding, which guides specific steps in the programming. In a scientific domain the structural component might include identifying goal(s), identifying given and missing information, collecting data, writing down the answer, and explaining the solution. Supplying such a structured framework, this component supposedly fosters cognitive skills and strategies that are important for the performance of any learning task.
2. A *reflection* component provides a framework for metacognitive skills such as monitoring and control, self-assessment, and self-regulation to be applied during the problem-solving process or at its end (e.g., Bielaczyc et al., 1995; Davis & Linn, 2000; Reif, 1995; Scardamalia & Bereiter, 1991; Zellermayer, Salomon, Globerson, & Givon, 1991).
3. A *subject-matter* component addresses domain-specific general guidance or specific instructions and provides prompts for solving problems (see for example, De Corte, 2000; Glaser et al., 1992; Goodyear, 1992; Leutner, 1993; Pirolli & Recker, 1994).

In this study, an additional component that we called *enrichment* was introduced in accordance with the "infusion approach" of Swartz and Parks (1992). This component guides the student to think about the solved problems and to sense possible applications.

These components, adjusted to problem solving in computerized environments, served as the building blocks of the instructional programs offered in this study and are further discussed in this chapter.

Much work has been done on the prompts and guidance needed for problem solving in general and within computerized learning environments in particular. We felt, however, that systematic work of two kinds was still lacking. There is a need for (a) the design and implementation of programs of cognitive support, which suggest different reasonable combinations of the support components and compare their effectiveness; and (b) research that examines learning outcomes of the support at four relevant levels: knowledge and understanding, cognitive skills, metacognitive skills, and motivational aspects.

Therefore, instructional support programs were constructed for the present research by creating different combinations of these four components, in accordance with three models of human teaching (Scardamalia & Bereiter, 1991), as described later. This study examines the four outcome levels of these support programs. We confine ourselves here to measures of only one facet of the cognitive and metacognitive skills matrix—that which stems from individual interviews and observation of problem-solving activities within a computer environment.

Thus, the main purpose of this chapter is to present the cognitive support programs and some resulting modeling activities involved in science problem solving in a computerized learning environment, namely the production and utility of external representation (ER), and search strategies used in problem solving in the computerized learning environment. The findings are discussed theoretically at the conclusion of this chapter, with particular reference to the structural and reflection components, which were found to be of the greatest importance. (For details concerning the learning effects at the achievement level see Fund, 1996, 2002c. The learning effect of some facets of the cognitive and metacognitive levels are described in Fund, 1996, 1999, 2002b).

THE STUDY

The research was carried out using a problem-solving computerized environment in science called Inquire and Solve (Educational Technology Center, Israel), implying that an inquiry process is required in order to solve the problem.

Inquire and Solve is a microworld that combines a problem-solving environment with a simulation of laboratory experiments. It consists of 60 qualitative science problems, 42 of which were found to be adequate for the present research population (seventh grade). Each problem presents a question represented by textual and graphical components. Four such sample questions are:

- Which vessel contains the greatest amount of air—1, 2, or 3?
- One of the coils in this system is made of copper, another of iron, and a third of aluminum. What is coil no. 2 made of?
- In which gas compound—1 or 2—do the particles move more quickly?
- What is the spoon made of?

Using the computerized learning environment tools, the learner is able to determine the answer by "performing" the experiment, observing its results, collecting missing data from available sources, and deciding which data are relevant to the problem.

Various tools, represented by icons, were provided. The most important are:

- Camera: enabled movement from one episode of the simulation to another. All the episodes together reflected the entire experiment (2–5 episodes per problem).
- Magnifying glass: provided information about specific graphical parts of the experimental system (e.g., "the liquid is water," "the electric current in the circuit is 0.5 Ampere," "the height of the water entering the column is $\frac{2}{3}$ of the column's height"). In each episode the user could get more information or more refined information by using the magnifying glass.
- Data pages: a simulation of a data book gave as many as six kinds of information for each problem as needed. Examples included boiling point, density, tendency to be notched, and scales of proportional values for physical properties as electrical or thermal conductivity. The user was required to choose the relevant data and then observe tabular information concerning those data. On this basis, the user usually had to compare the values of the relevant compounds or elements and reach a conclusion. Thus, for example, the compound with the lower boiling point boils first; the compound with greater thermal conductivity gets hotter first; the compound with greater electrical conductivity enables a higher electric current, and so on.
- Watch: a series of measuring tools (e.g., thermometer, voltmeter, current meter, manometer, etc.) from which the student could choose to measure relevant values.
- Answer flag: upon presenting the suggested solution, the user received the appropriate feedback (correct/not correct).

The Support Components

To enable the researcher to control the support components for each learner, the four support programs were implemented by appropriate worksheets. Hence, each support program included 42 specific worksheets, one for each problem of the Inquire and Solve computerized environment. The four identified support components served as building blocks for these specific worksheets, which were constructed as follows:

1. The *structural* component was implemented by the prompts in Fig. 5.1.

a. The problem to be solved:_____

b. The important data: _____

c. The correct answer: _____

d. Explain your answer and how you obtained it: _____

FIG. 5.1.   Structural prompts.

By completing the worksheet on this component, learners are encouraged to provide their own ER at every stage of the solving process. The structural component imposes no constraints on the form of ER. Hence, any "free" ER might be constructed at any point: while identifying the goals (prompt a), while searching the simulated experiment for given or missing data (prompt b), when concluding the answer (prompt c), and when explaining the solution (prompt d). The constructed ERs might assist the user to remember the fine details collected while answering prompt a and b and hence reduce the cognitive load. Alternatively, ERs might serve as scaffoldings to facilitate the reasoning cognitive process of concluding the answer (prompt c) or explaining it (prompt d).

2. The *reflection* component encourages metacognitive processes, implemented in the worksheets as shown in Fig. 5.2.

e. Proposed answer: _____

f. Did you give a correct answer? (Use the flag) yes/no

g. If you proposed a wrong answer, how does it differ from the correct answer? Explain why you were wrong _____

FIG. 5.2.   Reflection prompts.

This component provides a general framework for predicting an answer (prompt e), assessing solutions (prompt f), and explaining difficulties and mistakes (prompt g). Any previously constructed ER is useful in the cognitive process of identifying the error by supplying some sort of an overview of the problem and the data. Documentation of the assessing process is also recommended.

(These first two components are content-free and therefore are identical for all problems.)

3. The *subject-matter* component clarifies ideas and concepts relevant to each problem. This component was provided in two modes: a hierarchical subject matter mode, directing attention to both general guidance and specific instructions (Fig. 5.3, h + i), and a linear subject-matter mode (only i) that directs attention only to specific instructions. The two modes reflect the importance of knowledge organization, and the superiority of hierarchical over linear knowledge organization (see Eylon & Reif, 1984; Reif, 1995). These modes are illustrated in Fig. 5.3, for the following question: One of the coils in this system is made of copper, another of iron, and a third of aluminum. What is coil no. 2 made of?

---

h. General guidance: each of the three coils is connected to the contacts of an electrical circuit. You should find out what each coil is made of, by measuring the current. The higher the current the better the coil conducts electricity. Then you can relate the metals to the coils, using the "data pages" tool.

i. The important data:
  • What are the components of the electric circuit? _____
    _____
  • What is the current intensity with coil no. 1? _____ With coil no. 2? ___ With coil no. 3? _____
  • Which coil is the best conductor? _____ Which is the worst? _____
  • Use the "data pages" to complete the conductivity scale of: copper _____; iron _____; aluminum _____
  • Which given metal is the best conductor? _____
  • Which is the worst? _____

FIG. 5.3.   Subject-matter components.

Specific instructions in both modes include "short guiding questions" (i.e., the guiding questions in prompt i, to which the student replies while collecting data and solving the problem), eventually producing a "structured" ER. The general guidance (prompt h), which is included only in the hierarchical subject-matter mode, consists of a textual explanation to be read before beginning the solution, and is therefore assumed to have almost no influence on the ER.

4. The *enrichment* component includes questions that relate the specific problem to other relevant subjects. Specific enrichment questions were presented for each problem, to be answered after the original problem had been solved. The use of ERs is not addressed in this component.

Whereas the structural and the subject-matter components activate different aspects of ER, the reflective component favors existing ER and documentation.

The Support Programs

The four components already described—structure (1), reflection (2), subject-matter (3) and enrichment (4)—were combined to construct four treatment programs, presented in Table 5.1. These support programs were implemented by appropriate worksheets for every problem in the Inquire and Solve computerized learning environment, to be completed by the students while solving the problems.

The "integrated support" program was constructed on the basis of the first "knowledge-based" teacher model, the human (i.e., noncomputer), teaching models of Scardamalia and Bereiter (1991), and includes all the components (1, 2, 3, and 4). The "strategic support" program includes 1, 2, and 4 of the components and was constructed according to the second teacher model of Scardamalia and Bereiter (1991), which avoids giving domain-specific support. The "operative support" program was constructed in accordance with the "task model" teacher (Scardamalia & Bereiter, 1991), who puts emphasis on solving tasks; hence, this support program includes components 1, 3 i, and 4. The fourth program is the "enrichment nonstructural" one, which includes only enrichment questions.

As shown in Table 5.1, three of the treatment programs contain the structural component and are thus structural programs, whereas the

TABLE 5.1
The Four Support Programs

Integrated support program	Strategic support program	Operative support program	Enrichment nonstructural program
Structure	Structure	Structure	
Reflection	Reflection		
Subject-matter (hierarchical)		Subject-matter (linear)	
Enrichment questions	Enrichment questions	Enrichment questions	Enrichment questions

enrichment program is non-structural. In addition to the four treatments described here, a basic treatment was used that gave no cognitive support at all. Instead, the students were directed to keep notes in their notebooks at their own discretion.

We examined the effect of each treatment on content knowledge (subject-matter achievement), cognitive and metacognitive skills (problem-solving strategies and other measures), and motivational aspects (evaluated through interviews and attitudinal scales). The treatment effects were compared with one another and with the basic condition. In this chapter we describe only those parts of the resulting cognitive skills manifested by external representation (ER) and by search strategies of given and missing data.

The Sample

The subjects of the analysis were 187 students from among 473 seventh-grade students in three Israeli junior high schools. The larger sample, comprising all of the students in 16 classes, was randomly divided into five groups (four experimental "support program" groups and one "basic" group). All groups were represented in each school. All groups used the same textbook and worked within the Inquire and Solve computerized environment. Each experimental group was assigned a different support program by completing the appropriate worksheets. The treatments were conducted for a period of approximately 6 months, as part of the regular class program. The subjects of this analysis, comprising almost half of the students in each experimental group and the basic group, were the subsample who were interviewed at the end of the study and whose problem-solving activities in the computerized learning environment were observed.

Instruments

For the large-scale research ($n = 473$), three open-ended subject-matter questionnaires, tapping knowledge and understanding of the studied material, were distributed at different times during the research period. In addition, an attitudinal scale and a questionnaire testing scientific thinking were administered on two occasions. This chapter is based on data obtained from 187 participants in the course of observations and interviews conducted at the end of the research.

Each student was interviewed individually, after being observed while solving about three problems with the computer. Such a session lasted for about 25 minutes. Before beginning to solve problems during the observation, students were given a blank sheet of paper and asked to use it during the solving process whenever needed. In the subsequent interview they were asked to describe how they had usually worked in the computerized learning environment. At the end of the interview, three structural worksheets of a certain problem were presented to them and they were asked to state their opinion about every prompt in each worksheet. The observed problem-solving activities in the computerized learning environment, including spontaneous remarks, questions, and explanations of the student, were carefully transcribed. The transcribed activities of each student were then analyzed using the scheme for analysis of science problem solving in a computerized environment (Fund, 1996, 1999, 2002a), as described next.

QUANTITATIVE MEASURES

A scheme for analysis of science problem solving in a computerized environment (Fund, 1996, 1999, 2002a) was derived from Reif's (1995) three general stages model. This scheme includes 11 main skills (categories) subdivided into specific subskills, a total of 11 skill categories (see appendix), of which eight are cognitive and three are metacognitive. The detailed subskills enable us to detect even the smallest activities in the course of the solving process. In the solving stage, for example, our specification allows us to see the personal ER produced by the student, as well as the number of such ERs generated. We also noted whether or not the student paid attention to the evolving ER while proceeding toward a solution. All of these activities reflect the modeling processes experienced by students while solving problems in a computerized learning environment and are analyzed and presented in this chapter. Some of the analyses of the qualitative data are conducted by straightforward counting (number of occurrences of certain codes), whereas others are based on measures derived from the codes describing problem-solving protocols. The effects of the cognitive support programs on search strategies (random, linear, or hierarchical search) and on the external representation (ER) of the problems are also presented.[1]

The derived measures discussed in this chapter are mainly the search mode and the external representation (ER). The former analyzes the way the student addresses the problem with regard to the sequence of steps followed (discovering the goals of the problem, scanning it, and looking for missing data). The latter, which includes written self-explanations, remarks, or data recorded by the learner while solving the problem, is an explicit measure allowing the observer to detect the student's implicit thinking processes and understanding of the problem and its solution,

---

[1]Our research integrates qualitative and quantitative methods. Qualitative methods generally refer to research conducted in natural settings such as classrooms, and rely on the researcher as the main observer in both the data gathering and the analysis (Chi, 1997, p. 279). Quantitative methods refer to experimental design, and the data gathered are usually of a quantitative nature that can be subjected to precise statistical tests (Chi, 1997, p. 280). In this chapter, the student activities are both observed and coded, and the derived measures are statistically analyzed. Thus, the two methods are blended, and the subjectivity of the qualitative method is removed while at the same time the qualitative nature of the data is maintained. The result is a richer and deeper understanding of the situation, as suggested by Chi (1997).

yielding some sort of transparency of the solving process. During the interview and observation, the student had a blank paper for note taking, but had no working sheet (thus no cognitive support). The notes that each student made on the blank paper while solving the problems were analyzed. The simplest ER measure that we used is quantitative—the number of ERs (henceforth NER), that is, the number of times the student made use of the opportunity to record notes while approaching a solution. A more qualitative analysis of the ER reflected the typical form of a student's ER (henceforth FER), defined as random or systematic. These measures (search, NER, and FER) and their results are presented in the next section, and the main conclusions follow.

SEARCH AND EXTERNAL REPRESENTATION

The measures referred to as Search and ER are interrelated, inasmuch as writing is a natural accompaniment to approaching the problem, and both are therefore presented in this section. Nevertheless, we assume that the amount and quality of ER depend on the given cognitive support, where each component elicits a different aspect of ER. Hence, the manner in which the students produced ER using the note-taking blank paper, while being observed solving problems at the conclusion of the research, reflects their internalization of a need to use ER, when guided by the specific styles of cognitive support used in this study. The basic treatment might serve as a baseline reference (reflecting the natural tendency to use ER while working in a computerized learning environment) for comparison with other treatments.

In the following comparison of the results of treatment, the predominant finding is that students in the integrated and strategic support groups did better than those in the operative support group, and the latter in turn did better than or equaled the achievements of those in the enrichment and basic support groups. For simplification, the common components of these groups are presented in Fig. 5.4.

The terms used in Fig. 5.4 are used in the following presentation and discussion of the research findings.

Analysis of Problem Search

An overview of all the observations reveals that searching the problem may be categorized in three different ways:

1. Random search, a nonsystematic scanning of the problem with or without the computerized tools. In this search the observer cannot anticipate the student's next step, as the student has no clear idea of exactly what to look for in the problem.
2. Linear search, in which the student goes systematically from one "episode" of the problem to the next, usually examining each epi-

Integrated support (1)	Strategic support (2)	Operative support (3)	Enrichment support (4)	Basic treatment (5)

Reflection groups		Non-reflection groups		

Structural groups		Non-structural groups		

FIG. 5.4. The common support components of the groups.

sode with the available computerized tools. The following description (from an interview) gives an example of such a search: "First I copy the question. Then I take 'magnifying glass' [a tool allowing the episode to be seen in detail] to see episode 1. Then on to episode 2, and so on. I then take data from 'data pages' [a tool supplying needed external information] and match it to the data I already have. Now I get the answer."

3. Hierarchical search, in which the student scans the problem in two phases. The first phase is a short overview of the problem's episodes, to gain an idea of what the problem is about. The second phase is a linear search, aided by revisiting a known situation. This hierarchical mode is often accurately described by the students themselves. The following description serves as an example: "Usually I read the question first, then go to the pictures [episodes]. I read the question again to know what exactly they want from me [global first phase, Z.F.]. Then I take 'magnifying glass' to understand everything that happens in the experiment. Then with 'data pages' I get information about the materials [detailed second phase, Z.F.]. Then I think about the answer, and check myself with the 'flag' [a tool showing the correct answer]."

The frequency of search modes by experimental group is presented in Fig. 5.5. Significant differences between the groups are revealed by χ^2 tests ($\chi^2 = 53.16$; $df = 8$; $p < .001$).

As shown in Fig. 5.5, frequencies of the search mode differ between the five treatment groups. The linear search mode is predominant in

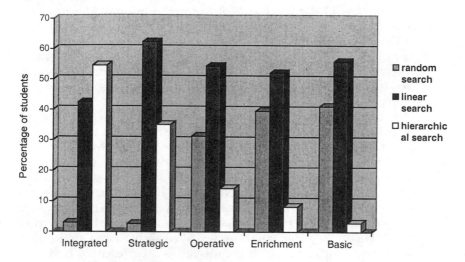

FIG. 5.5. Frequency of search modes by experimental group.

most of the groups, except in the integrated group, where most of the students used a hierarchical search. In addition, the figure shows that among the groups that do not include a reflection component, about 40% of the students search randomly, whereas in the two groups that include reflection there is almost no random searching. Additional χ^2 tests show that the two reflection groups differ from the other three groups. If the basic group serves as a reference for the spontaneous natural search while solving problems in a computerized learning environment, we can conclude that the two reflection groups have experienced two crucial changes: the random search has all but vanished, and the hierarchical search has become important, with around 55% of the students of the integrated group and 35% of the strategic group implementing it. The linear search remains almost the same. Special attention to this finding is given in our concluding discussion.

Analysis of External Representation

The ER produced by the student is described by four measures:

1. The number of times the student wrote on a note-taking blank paper while solving a problem (NER). In this study, over all the observations, this ranged from 0 to 9 times. For each student, NER is assigned a value corresponding to the maximum number of written entries recorded on the blank paper for any one problem.

2. The purpose of the produced ER—representation of the problem, or of the collected data, or of the missing data, or transplantation of the collected data in the problem.
3. The quality of the written ER, described either as random (with a few words or numbers here and there) or as systematically formalized (with the important data organized in full sentences or as a "story").
4. The complementary measure—a 1/0 flag, which denotes the answer to the question: Did you use the written data while solving the problem? 1 stands for "yes," 0 for "no." The recorded notes are considered to have been used if, at least once while solving the problems, the student has read the question or the data from the page, or self-assessed the collected data while looking at the handwritten notes. This measure was detected using the corresponding codes in the Science Problem Solving in a Computerized Environment scheme (see appendix), as described earlier (see Quantitative Measures). The results of these measures are presented next.

Quantity of ER. Differences in NER (number of times an ER was produced) between the groups, examined by one-way ANOVA, were significant: $F(4,182) = 24.95$; $p < .001$, with high means for the two reflection groups (Integrated: $M = 3.79$, $SD = 2.62$, $n = 33$; Strategic: $M = 4.19$, $SD = 3.45$, $n = 37$), and much lower means for the other groups (Operative: $M = 1.40$, $SD = 2.05$, $n = 35$; Enrichment: $M = 0.17$, $SD = 0.56$, $n = 48$; Basic: $M = 0.88$, $SD = 1.79$, $n = 34$). A Kruskal-Wallis test, carried out because the standard deviations were quite high, also showed a significant difference between the groups ($\chi^2 = 72.92$; $df = 4$; $p < .001$).

These results show that the students in the two reflection groups write much more than the students in the other groups, whereas the two nonstructural groups produced almost no ER. A Scheffe paired comparison test confirmed that the reflection groups differed in this respect from the three other groups.

Purpose(s) of ER Production. The complementary information on the NER measure asks in which categories (see appendix) an ER is produced. It is natural that the ER should be produced mainly in certain categories that reflect the purpose of the ER. These include reading the question, collecting data for problem description (both belong to the first stage of initial problem analysis); collecting missing data, using the collected data in the problem ("transplanting" the data), and concluding the answer (both belong to the second stage of solution construction).

A χ^2 analysis was carried out for the students producing any ER in each of these categories, over the five treatment groups. The results are shown in Table 5.2.

As shown in Table 5.2, there are significant differences between the three structural and the two nonstructural groups on the one hand, and between the two reflection groups and the operative group on the other

TABLE 5.2

**Frequency of ER Production for Five Categories, by Treatment Groups,
for Some Problem-Solving Activities, and χ^2 Analysis**

Categories[a]	Integrated program $n = 33$	Strategic program $n = 37$	Operative program $n = 35$	Enrichment program $n = 48$	Basic group program $n = 34$	χ^2 $df = 4$
Reading the question	72.7	59.5	37.1	8.3	23.5	45.10*
Collecting data	72.7	67.6	37.1	10.4	20.6	49.57*
Collecting missing data	60.6	43.2	37.1	4.2	20.6	34.60*
Using the data	54.5	27.0	2.9	0	0	61.45*
Concluding the answer	63.6	48.6	8.6	0	0	74.33*

See Appendix
* $p < .001$.

hand. Students in the reflection groups produced much more ERs than those in the other groups in all five categories; the operative group produced more ERs than the non-structural groups in only three categories, with almost no ER in the other categories. Examination of these categories shows that students in the nonreflection groups produced ERs mainly when using the computerized tools (reading the question, collecting data for problem description, or missing data); thus, this ER is mostly "technical," for memorization purposes to reduce the cognitive load. Students in the two reflection groups, apart from producing much more technical ERs, also produced ERs when performing thinking processes, like using the collected missing data in the problem or concluding an answer. Usually such processes involve implicit reasoning, and the accompanying "thinking ER" turns them into explicit and transparent reasoning processes. These results confirm the contribution of the structural component, and especially of the reflection component, to ER production.

Quality of ER.   Differences in the quality of the overall ER produced were examined by defining three groups: No ER, random ER (only a few words or numbers), and ER characterized by systematic and organized formalism, with full sentences, including most of the important data.

A χ^2 analysis carried out over the five treatment groups shows a significant difference in the quality of ER between the groups ($\chi^2 = 78.30$; $df = 8$; $p < .001$). The results are presented in Fig. 5.6.

As shown in Fig. 5.6, most of the ERs produced by the students in the reflection groups are of the systematic type (high quality ER), whereas those in the other groups mostly produced "no ER" or "random ER." Approximately 50% of the students in the operative group produced no ER and equal amounts of low and high quality ER. The basic group exhibits a similar profile to that of the operative group, and both were better than that of the enrichment group.

Extent to Which the Produced ER Is Used During Problem Solving.
The activity of writing is only the first stage of ER. In the next stage, this ER is used while solving the problem. This involves reading the ER, adding the names of materials to data or vice versa, or self-assessing the answer (hence "using produced ER"). A χ^2 test shows a significant difference between the groups in using produced ER ($\chi^2 = 60.50$; $df = 4$; $p < .001$). Approximately 70% of the students in the reflection groups used the produced ER at least once, whereas in the other groups more than 70% did not. The same trend was found in the quality of ER, that is, the majority of students in the reflection groups, and a minority in the other groups, showed high quality (systematic type) ER.

A χ^2 test demonstrated a significant link between the search mode and the use of produced ER ($\chi^2 = 24.50$; $df = 2$; $p < .001$). Among the students exhibiting a random search, only 8.7% used their written notes at least once. While solving the problems, written notes were used at least

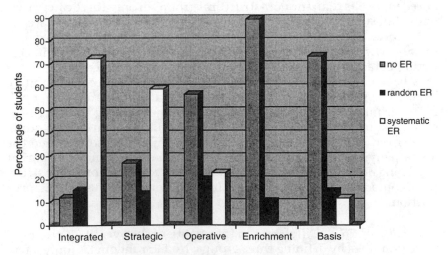

FIG. 5.6. Percentages of students showing no ER, random ER, and systematic ER in each experimental group.

once by 40% of students whose search mode was linear, and by 58.8% of those showing hierarchical search.

As shown here, students in the reflection groups carried out a more efficient search and produced a higher quality of ER (which was later used to support the problem-solving process) than students in the other groups. ERs of high quality might be an effective external support, bolstering the thinking process, whereas low-quality ERs do not adequately support the problem-solving process and are therefore unused. In a previous study, participants often had difficulties with representation construction as well as with reading off results from their representations (Cox & Brna, 1995). A possible conclusion is that those who search hierarchically produce higher quality ER, which in turn serves to support the problem-solving process, hence they become "good solvers." These good solvers belong mostly to the two reflection groups, not to the nonstructural groups. The students in the operative group are mostly mediocre solvers. This implies that cognitive support affects strategies of problem solving, including search strategies and the production and use of effective ER, with support of the structural-reflection type yielding the best results.

In the enterprise of modeling the modeler, we should consider the contributions of the reflective and structural components in the cognitive support in order to assess their function as supporting mechanisms in problem solving in a computerized learning environment. These issues are addressed next.

DISCUSSION

A summary of the main results of this study is presented in this section:

1. The search modes of students in the reflection groups were mostly linear and hierarchical, whereas those of students in the nonreflection groups were mostly linear and random.
2. The amount of ER produced, as measured by the numbers of written entries, in decreasing order by treatment program was: Strategic ≈ Integrated >> Operative > Basic > Enrichment.
3. To support the problem-solving process, the produced ER was used at least once by most of the students from the two reflection groups (around 70%), whereas it was not used at all by most of the students from the other groups (more than 70%).
4. All or most of the ER of students from the nonstructural groups was technical, produced while using computerized tools. Students from the reflection groups, in addition to producing technical ER, also produced "thinking ER," accompanying implicit thinking processes.
5. High quality ER was produced by most of the students from the two reflection groups (more than 70% from the integrated and 60% from the strategic groups), but by only 20% of students from

the operative group and a low percentage from the nonstructural groups.

6. The trend in these results was mainly reflection groups > operative group > nonstructural groups.

Because the two reflection groups exhibited almost the same results in terms of ER production, which was higher than that of the nonreflection groups, we can conclude (a) the contribution of the subject-matter component (included in only one of them and in the operative group) is limited, as indicated by the lack of difference between the integrated and the strategic groups; (b) the structural component has an important influence, hence the ER production by students in all three structural groups is higher (and some other measures are better) than in the two nonstructural groups; nevertheless, the structural component on its own cannot account for this difference, as the operative group was much lower, in most measures, than that of the other two structural groups; and (c) the combination of reflection and structural components, common to reflection groups, might explain the superiority of the latter groups in most measures.

Why do the reflection and structural components elicit better search strategies and induce much higher quality ERs? To answer this question we examine their implementation in the working sheets, along with theoretical discussion regarding their subcomponents.

The Structural Component

The structural component consists of the following subcomponents: (a) writing down the question to be answered (termed "the question"); (b) "important data," prompting the production of "free ER", that is, the student can produce any ER he wants in order to represent given or collected data; (c) writing down the answer ("the correct answer"); (d) explaining the answer ("justify the answer and explain its principles"). These subcomponents are discussed next.

"The Question."   Many students have difficulty in reading a problem so as to extract the relevant information and visualize the situation (Reif, 1995). Because correct initial analysis of a problem can make it much easier to solve, whereas the effect of erroneous analysis is usually disastrous, activities such as writing down or copying the question might aid comprehension and initiate its data processing. Cox and Brna (1995) recommended encouraging the student to spend more time on problem comprehension. One way to achieve this is to provide a "problem summary" window into which the student has to post information concerning the problem itself. Abstracting elements of the problem into the summary window might have the function of increasing the extent to which the student reflects on the problem, resulting in improved compre-

hension (Cox & Brna, 1995). The same functions might be served by writing down the question or its main keywords in the structural component. This subcomponent was favored by most of the students (80%) from the three structural groups, but by only 2% of students from the enrichment group, who were not presented with the "the question" subcomponent ($\chi^2 = 117.88$; $df = 6$; $p < .001$). Some of the reasons given for including this subcomponent were: "Sometimes, when I copy the question, I begin to think about the question, that it might be this or that" (M. from the operative group). "Copying the question helps me to understand what the goals are and what should be found in the question" (L. from the strategic group). These comments are in line with previous research and confirm the assumption that even the simple activity of writing down the question can promote initial processing of the question. Those who did not write down the question (mostly students from the nonstructural groups) could not appreciate the importance of doing so.

"Important Data." This structural subcomponent enables the students to produce ER in their own way, while collecting the given and missing data, and consequently to appreciate the importance of ER in easing the cognitive burden and thus facilitating problem solving. As one student remarked, "The 'important data' helps me a lot since it makes me write things down. When I take another look at what I wrote, I understand the question better and it's easier to get to the answer." Comments such as these suggest that this subcomponent endows the students with efficient learning strategies, causing them to produce ERs that otherwise would not have occurred to them, and this in turn helps them to comprehend all the data and thus solve the problem. Therefore, although any ER can be expected to improve problem-solving efficiency, "free" ER has a particular advantage in this respect. Self-constructed representations have been shown to be more effective than prefabricated ones (Grossen & Carnine, 1990).

It is interesting to note that a few students from the strategic group claimed that they had no need of ERs in solving the problems, as they were able to remember the data. Some examples follow: "I think this subcomponent is unnecessary because I keep the data in my head, and when I write them down on the page it interrupts my line of thought." "It helps to find out the data, but I don't think I have to write them down because I keep them in my head." Such remarks came mostly from students with a high academic level, whose need to lighten the cognitive load is less critical than in others because of their talent for processing information.

The structural "important data" subcomponent (i.e., without operative specific guiding questions) induces the learners to devote more effort in solving the problems and enables them to experience inquiry and discovery. Students from the strategic group generally favor this approach, as shown by their comments: "Writing down the data by myself, in my own way, is the best way for me to understand the problem."

"I prefer to find the data by myself; it takes more time but it's much better." "I want to find out by myself." "When I do it by myself, without the small questions, it sharpens my mind." "On a blank paper [in the interview, Z.F.] it's much easier to answer the question. I write down just the data I want to, what I think is important to write" (this from a student from the integrated group, used to working with operative-specific instructions). Yet, most students from the other support programs prefer to use operative-specific instruction as an easy way to solve the problem, although it prevents them from experiencing self-discovery. These students belong either to the integrated and operative groups, whose support programs included operative-specific instructions, or to the nonstructural groups, where no such support was provided. Their comments include the following: "It's the easiest way to solve the problem." "It's the best way [the integrated program] to solve the problem, because you hardly have to work." "The small questions [the specific-operative instruction] are actually what help me." "The small questions are the most important part of the work sheet; they organize everything." These remarks suggest that the specific guiding questions develop some dependency on the support to do the work, whereas the use of "free" ER increases the challenge and motivation by making the problem-solving process more demanding.

"Free" ER poses certain difficulties, however, such as the need to decide what data should be written down, or to distinguish between important and irrelevant data. One student (from the operative group) commented, for example: "In this version [the strategic program] you have to write things down by yourself, and you might omit some data. I wouldn't know what's important, and I'd be delayed." Some of these difficulties disappeared once the students became familiar with the computerized learning environment: "At the beginning I didn't write anything down, because I didn't think I needed it. As time went on I realized that it's important and I began to write down all the data." Or (a student from the strategic group): "Sometimes I didn't know exactly what to write down, whether I should write everything. Sometimes I could not distinguish between what is important and what is not, so I wrote either half or everything." In answer to the interviewer's question, this last student claimed that after some time she was able to decide quite easily what to write.

The students from the strategic group developed personal strategies that helped them to decide what needed to be written down. For example: "According to the magnifying glass [a computerized tool, Z.F.] I see the changes in the experiment, let's say in the current-meter, then I write them down. When a few materials are involved, I write down what happens to them." Or: "I write down things I really have to remember, like the scales of coils, not according to whether the data are important or not." Or: "I decide what's important to write down according to what they ask me in the question." Such statements suggest that producing an appropriate ER requires general strategies, which the students develop with time. They further imply that the integrated support might facilitate the work during the first few weeks, until the students become accustomed to the computerized learning environment, after which time they might derive more benefit from the strategic support. A similar idea was suggested by one student: "This version [integrated program] is preferable at least during the first 2 months, as it makes it easier to get used to the courseware."

In contrast, the small specific-operative questions (in the subject-matter component) that lead to more structured ER were found to be of limited help (see Fund, 1996, 1999 for details). Moreover, these specific-operative instructions had some severe disadvantages. In some cases they caused students to focus on details of the problem while neglecting the global aspect, leading to "narrow-minded" solving strategies. The ability to form connections between relevant concepts or subjects was consequently inhibited. In describing how they solved the problems, students from the operative group said that they read each specific-operative question and answered it in the worksheet, and that this led them to the solution. One student said: "I write down each 'small question' they ask, without first organizing the information in my head." When shown the strategic model, he claimed that with such support he would have formulated for himself "similar questions, but first I would have organized the data in my head, and only afterwards written them down on the page" (for details see Fund, 2002a). This "organization in my head," which was missing in the operative support, refers to the organization of knowledge for the purposes of processing it and anchoring it in previous knowledge, an important stage for improving understanding and for constructing robust knowledge.

Relying on the small specific-operative questions reduces the student's ability to conduct an independent inquiry, as mentioned earlier, or to reach conclusions without such guidance, inasmuch as "it prevents you from thinking, it tells you what to do." These students became less confident while solving the problems, for example in identifying the subject of a problem when no support was supplied. Approximately 35% of the students in the subject-matter groups (integrated and operative) asked the interviewer some "helping" questions to be sure that their identification was correct, whereas only a few students from the other groups asked such questions (even when they could not identify the subject). Consequently, solving the problems with the operative-specific instructions, which "makes life easier," was favored mostly by the integrated, operative, and enrichment groups, and much less by those from the strategic group, who were used to working "hard" and preferred the challenge.

Motivation, not discussed in this chapter, is negatively affected by the specific-operative instructions (see Fund, 1996).

"The Correct Answer."   This encourages students to assess their answers, while acquiring habits of writing full answers.

"Justify the Answer and Explain Its Principles."   Requiring students to give a written explanation of the answer is thought to play an important role in improving understanding and cognitive skills. This is because it assists them to gain a deeper understanding of the problem. Students expressed it thus: "When you write down the explanation it makes every thing clear to you." "If I can explain, it means I understand it." According to explanation-based learning theory and studies on self-explanations' effects, explaining the solution creates links between previous and newly acquired knowledge (Bielaczyc et al., 1995; Chi et al., 1994). Writing down the explanation supports construction of a coherent model of the domain, which in turn facilitates the acquisition of cognitive skills. At the information-processing level, writing a text implies complex cognitive abilities and activities (Andriessen, 1999). During the writing process, an internal dialogue takes place, improving knowledge construction and understanding (Scardamalia & Bereiter, 1991). Such a process occurs when students write down an explanation of their solutions.

Thus, the explanation subcomponent is an essential part of the structural component, where its role is to promote connections between previous and new knowledge, thereby improving understanding, knowledge construction, and acquisition of cognitive skills. The "important data" subcomponent, which promotes "free" ER during the problem-solving process, facilitates the cognitive burden on the one hand, and reflects the student's understanding of the problem on the other. Both of these subcomponents serve to organize the information flow between two resources: knowledge and thinking resources of the learner (the "learner's resources"), and the resources and tools of the computerized environment (the "environment's resources"). This is achieved through the creation of work patterns, such as producing effective ER, using it effectively, and performing elaborated search strategies (hierarchical vs. linear or random search), found to be much more frequent in the reflection groups than in the other groups (see Figs. 5.5 and 5.6).

Yet, in comparing the three structural groups to the two nonstructural groups with respect to the quality and quantity of ER production and the search mode, the structural component was found to be necessary for most measures, but was insufficient, as the reflection component was needed as well. Next we will attempt to explain these findings.

The Reflection Component

Addition of the reflection component to the structural support (as in the two reflection groups) resulted in a dramatic improvement in most measures, including the quality and quantity of ER and the search mode. In trying to determine what makes the reflection component, and in particular the winning combination of structural and reflection components, so effective, we turn to Sternberg's (1990) human intelligence model. According to this model, acquisition of new declarative and procedural knowledge in all domains occurs in three main stages:

1. Selective encoding, which involves sifting relevant from irrelevant information and recognizing only the pieces of information relevant for the learner's purposes.
2. Selective combination, in which the selectively encoded pieces of information are combined into integrated knowledge.
3. Selective comparison, where newly acquired knowledge is related to knowledge acquired in the past. Without this activity, the new knowledge is useless. The encoding and combination of new knowledge are guided by the retrieval of old information, thus enabling integration of the new knowledge into the cognitive schema.

We now proceed to determine which stages in our learning situation (i.e., problem solving in a computerized learning environment with cognitive support) serve as engines to drive Sternberg's stages. Writing down an explanation of the answer (in the structural component), by articulating the main aspects of the problem, serves as the "selective encoding" of the new knowledge to be gained from solving the problem, in choosing the essential part to be learned—the first of Sternberg's stages. This stage, although necessary, is insufficient, according to Sternberg as well as the research findings. To enable all three of Sternberg's stages to be performed, the whole cycle of scientific inquiry "predict–observe–compare–explain" is required. In a computerized learning environment, this cycle should be changed into "observe (and examine the problem and its computerized simulated experiment), predict (the answer), compare (the predicted with the correct answer of the courseware), and explain (the correct or wrong answer)." It implies a need for the three main subcomponents of reflection, namely predicting the answer, assessing it, and giving reasons for errors when the answer is wrong. Predicting an answer makes it possible to selectively combine the new pieces of information while comparing the prediction with the correct answer and trying to explain the causes of error correspond to Sternberg's "selective comparison."

This theoretical discussion offers an explanation for the construction of (declarative) knowledge as a result of science problem solving, or in other words, from the procedural knowledge. The reflection component encourages metacognitive processes during problem solving. These processes play a crucial part in knowledge construction, and in turn affect understanding as well as other cognitive and even affective measures. A further consideration of the reflection subcomponents is presented next.

"Proposed Answer."   The need to predict an answer, as part of the cycle "observe–predict–compare–explain" (OPCE), requires a global scanning of the solved problem, thus selectively combining the new pieces of information (Sternberg's second stage). It also activates rele-

vant concepts as well as adjacent linked concepts. Activated concepts are processed better (according to "spreading activation" of Anderson, 1984), and predicting an answer begins a chain of concept activation, which in turn improves understanding and enhances construction of robust knowledge.

Predicting an answer has affective outcomes as well. It acts as a challenge, stimulating learners' interest in each solved problem, and thus makes the students more eager to solve the problems. This was corroborated in this study by our observations and from the attitudinal scales, as well as from the comments of the students themselves. Every correct prediction increases the intrinsic motivation and enjoyment from the work.

"Did You Give a Correct Answer? (Use the Flag)."   Comparing the predicted answer with the correct one, as part of the OPCE cycle, serves as the third stage in Sternberg's theory (the selective comparison), thus completing the construction of (declarative) knowledge from the solved problem. At the same time, every successful prediction increases motivation and enjoyment by supplying intrinsic reinforcements. When the predicted answer is incorrect, it causes the student to think of possible reasons for the error, an activity that is further articulated in the next subcomponent (error explanation). When students from the reflection groups were asked if they felt angry or frustrated when their answers were wrong, their replies showed that they did not even think about such feelings, but only about "why I was wrong." Internalization of self-assessment (i.e., the need to assess any answer or predicted answer during the solving process) was also found to be an outcome of this subcomponent, but is not described in this chapter.

"If You Gave a Wrong Answer, How Does It Differ From the Right Answer? Explain Why You Were Wrong."   As already mentioned, trying to explain the errors completes the selective comparison of Sternberg's third stage. The student has to explain not only what he has done (as he does when explaining a correct answer, in the structural component), but why he has done it, a metacognitive process that elicits self-assessment, which in turn encourages the production of effective ER and the performance of elaborated search strategies.

The need to find reasons for incorrect predicted answers also develops tolerance toward making mistakes, giving the feeling that it is legitimate, because you can learn from your mistakes and thus benefit from them. Students verbalized this, saying: "It helps me understand what is wrong, so I learn from my error." "It helps me to understand why I was wrong, so I can learn from it and won't make the same mistake again." When students are not required to explain their mistakes, they feel as if they have failed to solve the problem each time they do not know the answer, and this has a negative effect on their confidence in themselves as problem solvers and on their attitudes toward computerized problem solving. These negative feelings might explain the decline in attitudes among the operative group (discussed in Fund, 1996).

Although most of the students in the reflection groups did not actually write down the reason for their mistakes on the worksheet, they claimed that this subcomponent (trying to explain errors) made them think of possible reasons. They said, for example: "Because of this [subcomponent] it occurred to me why students might go wrong here, even when I made no mistake." Thinking of the mistake itself, not the verbalized self-explanations, presumably contributes to the impressive differences found between the reflection groups and all the others. Berardi-Coletta, Buyer, Dominowski, and Rellinger (1995) confirmed the truth of this claim by demonstrating that the positive effects of verbalization (on solution transfer) were not due to verbalization per se but to the metacognitive processes involved in the effort required to produce explanations for solution behaviors. The requirement to give an explanation shifts the focus of the students to an examination of their actions, thoughts, and reasoning.

CONCLUSIONS

The research findings show significantly richer ER (measured both quantitatively and qualitatively) and a significantly more hierarchical search mode in students from the reflection groups than in students from the other support programs. The three main conclusions are:

1. The combination of structural and reflection components (e.g., the strategic program in the present study) has a powerful influence on problem-solving strategies, including ER construction.
2. In the two groups that include a reflection component, it is this component that is mainly responsible for these results. Analysis of the reflection subcomponents showed that their contribution to all measures is due to the metacognitive processes they impose on the learner, which might involve merely thinking metacognitively about the solving process.
3. The limited contribution of the subject-matter component might be typical of environments whose subject-matter is built into the system and operates according to certain rules, as in the present computerized learning environment or other computerized simulations. It is possible that in other types of computerized environments, the subject-matter support component would become more important.

The main practical claim of this study is that science problem solving with a computerized learning environment should include strategic support. Such support is remarkably easy to prepare and to integrate in any computerized learning environment. It should supply the learner with a structural working pattern and with a "notebook" tool for writing or drawing data and ERs of the problems as well as for explaining the solution. The support should also provide reflective guidance; the learner should be encouraged to predict an answer after collecting all the needed information, and to give reasons for wrong answers.

Whether or not this form of support should be expanded by the additional inclusion of a subject-matter component depends on the nature of the computerized environment (with or without built-in subject-matter), and on the learner's experience in working with the computerized learning environment. In the first stage of working in the computerized learning environment, additional subject-matter support (e.g., an integrated program) might be helpful until the learner becomes accustomed to the computerized learning environment, after which it could be gradually withdrawn.

ACKNOWLEDGMENTS

This chapter is partly based on the author's Ph.D. dissertation, carried out at the School of Education, Bar-Ilan University, Israel. I would like to express my thanks to Prof. Jossef Menis, School of Education, Bar-Ilan University, and to Prof. Bat-Sheva Eylon, Science Teaching Department, The Weizmann Institute of Science, Israel, for their helpful contributions to this study. This chapter was supported by the Schnitzer Foundation for Research on the Israeli Economy and Society.

REFERENCES

Anderson, J. R. (1984). Spreading activation. In J. R. Anderson & S. M. Kosslyn (Eds.), *Tutorials in learning and memory: Essays in honor of Gordon Bower* (pp. 61–90). San Francisco, CA: W. H. Freeman.

Andriessen, J. (1999). *Collaborative learning with computers.* Paper presented at the "Roles of Communicative Interaction in Learning to Model in Mathematics and Science" conference of the Leeds University Computer Based Learning Unit, Corsica, France.

Bell, P., Davis, E. A., & Linn, M. C. (1995). The knowledge integration environment: Theory and design. In *Proceedings of the Computer Supported Collaborative Learning Conference* (CSCL '95: Bloomington, IN) (pp.14–21). Mahwah, NJ: Lawrence Erlbaum Associates.

Berardi-Coletta, B., Buyer, L. S., Dominowski, R. L., & Rellinger, E. R. (1995). Metacognition and problem solving: A process-oriented approach. *Journal of Experimental Psychology: Learning, Memory, and Cognition, 21*(1), 205–223.

Bielaczyc, K., Pirolli, P. L., & Brown, A. L. (1995). Training in self-explanation and self-regulation strategies: Investigating the effects of knowledge acquisition activities on problem solving. *Cognition and Instruction, 13*(2), 221–252.

Brna, P. (1999). *Modeling the modeler: Communicating about content through shared external representation.* Paper presented at the "Roles of Communicative Interaction in Learning to Model in Mathematics and Science" conference of the Leeds University Computer Based Learning Unit, Corsica, France.

Chi, M. T. H. (1997). Quantifying qualitative analyses of verbal data: A practical guide. *The Journal of The Learning Sciences, 6*(3), 271–315.

Chi, M. T. H., De Leeuw, N., Chiu, M. H., & LaVancher, C. (1994). Eliciting self-explanations improves understanding. *Cognitive Science, 18*, 439–477.

Chi, M. T. H., Glaser, R., & Farr, M. J. (Eds.). (1988). *The nature of expertise.* Hillsdale, NJ: Lawrence Erlbaum Associates.

Cox, R., & Brna, P. (1995). Supporting the use of external representations in problem solving: The need for flexible learning environments. *Journal of Artificial Intelligence in Education, 6*(2/3), 239–302.

Davis, E. A., & Linn, M. C. (2000). Scaffolding students' knowledge integration: Prompts for reflection in KIE. *International Journal of Science Education, 22*(8), 819–837.

De Corte, E. (2000). Marrying theory building and the improvement of school practice: A permanent challenge for instructional psychology. *Learning and Instruction, 10*, 249–266.

Eylon, B. S., & Reif, F. (1984). Effects of knowledge organization on task performance. *Cognition and Instruction, 1*(1), 5–44.

Fund, Z. (1996). *Models of written cognitive support for science problem solving in computerized environment: The effects on learning of "structure," "reflection" and "subject-matter" components.* Unpublished doctoral dissertation, Bar-Ilan University, Ramat-Gan, Israel.

Fund, Z. (1999). *Models of written communication as a cognitive support for computerized science problem solving.* Paper presented at the "Roles of Communicative Interaction in Learning to Model in Mathematics and Science" conference of the Leeds University Computer Based Learning Unit, Corsica, France.

Fund, Z. (2002a). *Construction of a computerized science problem solving scheme for the analysis of science problem solving in a computerized learning environment.* Manuscript submitted for publication.

Fund, Z. (2002b). *Science problem-solving with cognitive support in computer-based learning environments: Effects on cognitive and meta-cognitive skills.* Manuscript in preparation.

Fund, Z. (2002c). *Cognitive support models in science problem solving and achievement outcomes.* Manuscript in preparation.

Glaser, R., Schauble, L., Raghavan, K., & Zeitz, C. (1992). Scientific reasoning across different domains. In E. De Corte, M. C. Linn, H. Mandl, & L. Verschaffel (Eds.), *Computer-based learning environments and problem solving* (pp. 345–371). Berlin, Heidelberg: Springer-Verlag.

Goodyear, P. (1992). The provision of tutorial support for learning with computer-based simulations. In E. De Corte, M. C. Linn, H. Mandl, & L. Verschaffel (Eds.), *Computer-based learning environments and problem solving* (pp. 391–409). Berlin, Heidelberg: Springer-Verlag.

Grossen, G., & Carnine, D. (1990). Diagramming a logic strategy: Effects on difficult problem types and transfer. *Learning Disability Quarterly, 13*, 168–182.

Guzdial, M. (1994). Software-realized scaffolding to facilitate programming for science learning. *Interactive Learning Environments, 4*(1), 1–44.

Leutner, D. (1993). Guided discovery learning with computer-based simulation games: Effects of adaptive and non-adaptive instructional support. *Learning and Instruction, 3*, 113–132.

Linn, M. C., & Songer, N. B. (1991). Teaching thermodynamics to middle school students: What are appropriate cognitive demands? *Journal of Research in Science Teaching, 28*(10), 885–918.

Njoo, M., & de Jong, T. (1993). Exploratory learning with a computer simulation for control theory: Learning processes and instructional support. *Journal of Research in Science Teaching, 30*, 821–844.

Pirolli, P., & Recker, M. (1994). Learning strategies and transfer in the domain of programming. *Cognition and Instruction, 12*(3), 235–275.

Reif, F. (1995). Millikan lecture 1994: Understanding and teaching important scientific thought processes. *American Journal of Physics, 63*(1), 17–32.

Scardamalia, M., & Bereiter, C. (1991). Higher levels of agency for children in knowledge building: A challenge for the design of new knowledge media. *The Journal of the Learning Sciences, 1*(1), 37–68.

Sternberg, R. J. (1990). *Metaphors of mind: Conceptions of the nature of intelligence.* New York: Cambridge University Press.

Swaak, J., van Joolingen, W. R., & de Jong, T. (1998). Supporting simulation-based learning: The effects of model regression and assignments on definitional and intuitive knowledge. *Learning and Instruction, 8*(3), 235–252.

Swartz, R., & Parks, S. (1992). *Infusing critical and creative thinking into secondary instructions: A lesson design handbook.* Pacific Grove, CA: Midwest Publications.

Tiberghien, A. (1999). *Learning modeling activities in elementary physics learning* Paper presented at the "Roles of Communicative Interaction in Learning to Model in Mathematics and Science" conference of the Leeds University Computer Based Learning Unit, Corsica, France.

Zellermayer, M., Salomon, G., Globerson, T., & Givon, H. (1991). Enhancing writing-related metacognitions through a computerized writing partner. *American Educational Research Journal, 28*(2), 373–391.

APPENDIX

The Main Skills in the Computerized Science Problem Solving Scheme, (Fund, 1996, 1999, 2002a).

Stages	Main Categories
I. Initial problem analysis	*Initial analysis:*
	1. Finding the goals of the problem
	2. Collecting data for problem description
	Translation into scientific language:
	3. Global: identifying the subject
	4. Specific: mapping the subject to natural language
II. Construction of a solution	5. Collecting missing data
	6. Using the collected data in the problem (reasoning is needed)
	7. Concluding the solution
III. Checking the solution	8. Self-assessing of problem solving process
	9. Assessing final answer
	10. Explaining the method of solution
	11. For incorrect solution: finding the error and its causes

Chapter 6

Interactive Model-Building Environments

Anders Bouwer

Vania Bessa Machado

Bert Bredeweg

University of Amsterdam

Computers are becoming increasingly important as tools for articulating and communicating information and knowledge. At the same time, theories on human learning strengthen the hypothesis that learning is an active process during which knowledge is constructed[1] as opposed to just received via some communication channel (Fiske, 1990). This article combines both these themes as it discusses the notion of interactive model-building environments. Two aspects are of prime interest to this work: first, the development of model building tools that support learners in articulating their understanding of the (physical) reality in a machine readable form; second, for the computer, how to use this knowledge, what inferences to make, and how to communicate the results back to its users.

Usage of computers in modern educational settings is often limited to data storage, retrieval, and presentation means. Take, for instance, an average science project. Typically, learners search the Internet, communicate and collaborate with each other (using e-mail and chat rooms), and write, possibly as a group, a document that describes the phenomenon they have been studying. Although by itself this is an interesting development, it does by no means exploit the full potential of modern computers. The problem is that computers can only process the information units, manipulated by the learners, from a technical point of view. That is, the computer can transport a collection of bits over the Internet, use it to drive a visualization on the screen, provide

---

[1]This type of work is inspired by theories on constructivism (Bruner, 1966) and situated learning (Brown, Collins, & Duguid, 1989).

tools for the user to modify it, and so forth. But the computer cannot access the content (or knowledge) captured by these units, because the computer does not have a formal, knowledge level (Newell, 1982) representation of this content. As a result, computers cannot be used as *knowledgeable agents* to support the learner with the knowledge construction process. This is undesirable, because guidance is one of the most important requirements for effective learning (e.g., Elsom-Cook, 1990; Hulst, 1996).

In our research we use artificial intelligence technology to develop an interactive model-building environment by means of which students can learn by constructing simulation models. We use the computer as an intelligent agent (e.g., Bradshaw, 1997), knowledgeable about the domain and the model building process, and therefore capable of providing support. Our work combines three strands of research: simulation-based learning, qualitative reasoning, and learning by building models. Simulation is a powerful tool for learning, because it allows us to mimic (model) reality in a way that is optimized for specific tutoring goals (e.g., Jong, 1991). For instance, some scientific phenomena are difficult to witness in reality and hard to replicate in a physical experiment, but can be simulated by a computer model. This is particularly true for processes that have a large time scale (e.g., ecology) or a very short time scale (e.g., chemistry). Second, the simulation models we use are qualitative (e.g., Weld & Kleer, 1990). The ontology underlying such models provides a rich vocabulary for reasoning about system structure and behavior. This allows not only inspecting simulation results, but also searching for causal explanations. Third, learning by modeling is based on the idea that scientific phenomena are better understood when one tries to make explicit one's understanding into a format that can be communicated to others. Choosing the right abstractions, making the right assumptions, and capturing those aspects of structure and behavior that matter are the skills necessary to build a good model (e.g., Bental & Brna, 1995). This model construction can be done using a computer as an articulation device that, among other things, allows running simulations for inspecting the status of the model. The model and its simulation results can also be communicated to other learners, for example, by using the Internet.

LEARNING AND SIMULATION MODELS

This section elaborates on the idea of using interactive simulations as tools for humans to learn about systems and their behavior. First, the basic idea behind this approach is presented. Second, requirements are formulated with respect to the kind of insights learners should acquire. Third, the need for knowledge-based simulation models to address these requirements is emphasized. Fourth, qualitative models are briefly discussed. Finally, different ways of interacting with simulations are pointed out.

The Basic Idea

When interacting with the physical world, people often perform tasks to manipulate systems and their behavior. Typically, this involves three classes of tasks: controlling the behavior of existing systems, constructing new systems with new behavior, and repairing broken or malfunctioning systems. The specific nature of these tasks can be further detailed by taking into account the kind of domain a system belongs to (e.g., physics, ecology, or medicine) and whether a system is an artifact or a natural system. For humans, who in general have to perform at least some of these tasks, it is necessary to learn what kind of systems exist and how they behave. Computers provide interesting opportunities to act as intelligent agents capable of teaching humans important parts of that knowledge (Fig. 6.1).

In order to construct such computer-based knowledgeable agents, two aspects are crucial. First, the computer should be equipped with models (possibly simulations) that capture the behavioral aspects relevant to the system that is the subject of teaching. These models should be detailed and explicit with respect to the phenomena that must be learned by the learner. To stress the notion of being explicit and sufficiently detailed, these models are often referred to as *articulate simulation models* (Bredeweg & Winkels, 1998; Falkenhainer & Forbus, 1991;

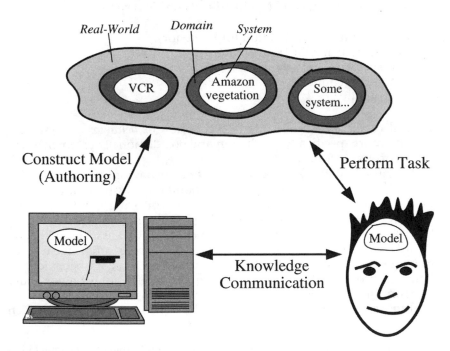

FIG. 6.1.   Learning about systems and their behavior.

Koning, Bredeweg, Breuker, & Wielinga, 2000). Second, the computer should have means to communicate the details captured by these models to learners. However, it is usually not sufficient to just show the results generated by running a simulation. It is well known that without sufficient guidance, learners may spend lots of time without learning much. Some coaching, such as helping to focus an exploration, providing accurate summaries, giving assignments, or providing explanations is therefore essential (e.g. Elsom-Cook, 1990; Hulst, 1996).

What Do Students Have to Learn?

Following projects such as STEAMER (Hollan, Hutchins, & Weitzman, 1987), QUEST (White & Frederiksen, 1990), and ITSIE (e.g., Sime, 1994), we take the approach that learning proceeds in steps. When learning, humans first acquire insights in the functioning of partial systems. Further learning elaborates these insights or focuses on other partial systems. Learning also modifies and integrates insights in order to accommodate for different perspectives and levels of abstraction. However, understanding exactly how humans learn is still a subject of current research.[2] What we do know is "what learners have to learn," that is, the requirements that should be fulfilled in order to have the insights that are needed to effectively interact with systems and their behavior. The following issues can be pointed out in this respect:

- Prediction and postdiction (of behavior).
- Deriving behavior from structure.
- Perspectives and assumptions.
- Causal accounts.
- Reusability.

Central to these requirements is the notion of *behavior analysis* (Fig. 6.2), or, more specifically, prediction and postdiction of system behavior (e.g., Forbus, 1984).

As argued by Breuker and Velde (1994), behavior analysis is an important subtask within many tasks dealing with systems and their behavior, such as designing, planning, monitoring, and diagnosis. Behavior analysis starts with "deriving behavior from structure" (e.g., Kleer & Brown, 1984), which refers to the ability of associating behavioral features to structural constellations. There is often not a single mapping between a particular structural unit and its behavior. Repairing a broken traffic light system requires a different behavior analysis from deciding on whether, and how, to cross the street with that broken traffic light system. Moreover, the structural units that are iden-

---

[2]An interesting enumeration of competing theories on learning can be found in TIP (Kearsley, 1994–2000).

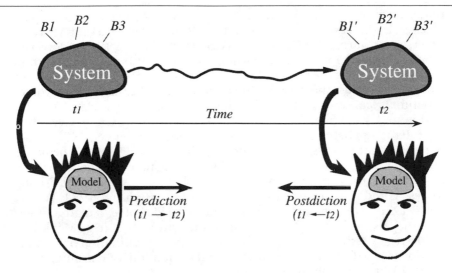

FIG. 6.2. Behavior Analysis: Prediction and Postdiction.

tified and taken into account may be different. In general, an appropriate behavior analysis depends on the tasks and the goals of the humans involved. In computer programs this flexibility in reasoning about system behavior is often implemented by using the idea of assumptions (e.g., Falkenhainer & Forbus, 1991; Rickel & Porter, 1997; Sime & Leitch, 1992). Another important aspect of behavior analysis concerns causal accounts. The insights that humans learn should identify the quantities that are most crucial for the typical behavior of the system and specify how they are related, that is, understand how these quantities affect each other and thus explain the overall behavior of the system. Finally, there is the issue of reusability. The insights that humans learn should be applicable to a wide range of situations and not only to some specific structural constellation. The insights should be domain independent, at least to a certain extent. The concept of friction, for instance, applies to all kinds of systems that move from one place to another.

Simulations as Knowledge Models

Mathematical models are important building blocks for modern science. In educational settings, teachers often use such models to explain the behavior of systems, particularly at the university level. Given the increasing computational power of computers, a logical next step was to use mathematical models as interactive models that allow learners to learn about real-world phenomena simulated by these models. The usefulness of this approach in educational settings has been pointed out by many authors, and powerful software tools are available to support teachers in this respect, such as MATLAB (Pratap, 1999), STELLA (Grant, Pedersen, & Marin, 1997) and SIMQUEST (e.g., Kuyper, 1998). However, when it comes to interactive learning environments, in which certain tutoring activities are automated, mathematical models are not always sufficient. For instance, precise information may be missing and therefore numerical simulation not possible. Other problems relate to explanation and subsequent knowledge communication issues relevant to the interaction between learner and environment (Wenger, 1987). Also, mathematical models require considerable knowledge of mathematics and as a result are usually not suitable for secondary school curricula. Coping with the previously mentioned problems was one of the driving forces behind research on qualitative reasoning (Bobrow, 1984; Weld & Kleer, 1990). For generating explanations, the idea of articulate simulation models (or knowledge models) became important (e.g., Winkels & Bredeweg, 1998),[3] but the problem of simulating without precise information is also seen as an important goal of qualitative reasoning (e.g., Kleer & Williams, 1991).

Maybe even more interesting than using qualitative knowledge to overcome the limitations of mathematical simulations is the use of qualitative models for their own sake. That is, qualitative models have characteristics that make them particularly suited to address specific learning activities. For instance, when teaching to solve physics problems, teachers emphasize the need for learners to first understand the (problem) situation. Before trying to apply equations, learners should build a conceptual model (e.g., Mettes & Roossink, 1981) of the initial-state, the end-state, and the possible transition trajectories between the two. In fact, it is considered naïve (beginners' behavior) if learners jump to applying formulae without making a proper analysis of the problem situation (e.g., Elio & Sharf, 1990). Expert problem solvers excel because they spend a significant amount of time on making a conceptual model before using equations. Analyzing (problem) situations is close to the idea of making an *envisionment*, that is, a mental simulation of what happens, or may happen (Kleer & Brown, 1984).

Qualitative models are also relevant in specific domains (often less formalized) where domain experts try to uncover the causal dependencies that govern a system's behavior. After understanding the causal dependencies, the experts may try to apply the formulae that are appropriate for the system. In fact, the causal model helps them to find the appropriate equations. Experts often do not even bother about the equations. Instead, developing a conceptual model is a goal in itself; that is, discovering the physical constituents of the system, identifying the relevant quantities, and understanding how these interact in determin-

---

[3]The work on self-explanatory simulations (Forbus & Falkenhainer, 1992) is an interesting example of combining quantitative simulations with qualitative knowledge to automatically generate explanations.

ing the system's behavior. Qualitative models are well suited to help domain experts in articulating and formalizing their insights (e.g., Salles, 1997). If we think of how this kind of knowledge can be communicated to (new) trainees in the field, qualitative models are again crucial.

Qualitative Models

As already argued, qualitative models should be seen as knowledge models of systems and their behavior. For technical details of such models, see Bobrow (1984) and Weld and Kleer (1990). In our research we use GARP (Bredeweg, 1992), a simulator written in SWI-Prolog. GARP takes as input a scenario and generates a graph of qualitative distinct behaviors for the situation described in that scenario. GARP uses model fragments and transition rules to construct this graph. Model fragments have conditions and consequences. If the conditions match the scenario and are consistent with other model fragments that match the scenario, they are added to the state of behavior. States of behavior transform into successor states when inequalities between quantities change or when quantities reach a different value in their quantity space. Such changes are the result of influences introduced by model fragments (of types *process* and *agent*). These influences propagate via proportionalities and affect the derivatives of quantities. In other words, they change the quantities, and this is modeled as derivatives being positive or negative. Quantity spaces represent the values that quantities can have. Each quantity has a unique quantity space. A quantity space captures the relevant distinctions for a quantity, such as the temperature of a substance being below, at, or above the boiling point. When developing a simulation model in GARP, a model fragment is often used to represent a particular concept relevant to the domain that is modeled; for instance, a population (ecology), a heat-flow (thermodynamics), or a pressure-area (meteorology).

How to Interact With Simulation Models?

If students learn by using simulation models, what kind of interaction styles between learners and such models should be established? We distinguish three major categories and refer to them as *assignment-based*, *assembling-from-library*, and *self-building*. The difference between these categories relates to the status of the simulation model the learner interacts with. Assignment-based is probably the default approach when thinking about simulation-based learning (e.g., ITSIE, Sime, 1994; SIMQUEST, Kuyper, 1998). There are many forms of the assignment-based approach, but they all have in common that the simulation is not made by the learner. Instead, the model is built by the developers of the interactive simulation and the learner can only interact with the simulation. This interaction can then take many specific forms (see e.g., Jong, 1991), such as answering prediction questions, controlling the simulation (as in a flight simulator), setting up experiments and discovering what happens, finding explanations for observed behaviors, and many more. The idea is that by interacting with the simulation, possibly taking into account a set of assignments, a learner will eventually understand the behavioral insights captured by the simulation and thus understand the real system's behavior (or at least partly).

A somewhat different approach could be called assembling-from-library. In this case, the simulation is not fully available, but has to be assembled by the learner. Typically, the learner is given a library of partial models or components (e.g., as a set of icons on the screen) from which he or she has to select the ones relevant to the situation (scenario) for which a model has to be constructed (e.g., CYCLEPAD, Forbus et al., 1999). Selecting and connecting the parts is not always enough to get a simulation running adequately. Often learners have to provide additional detail, such as initial values, value-range limits, and possibly modes of operation in the case of components. Also, remodeling the initially selected set of partial models may be necessary when the model does not produce the desired behavior results. Notice that the assembling-from-library approach is a kind of design task, one where all the building blocks, from which designs can be made, are predefined. Also notice that this approach can easily be augmented with ideas from the assignment-based approach, for instance, providing a "hypothesis scratch-pad" to help the learner with organizing his or her ideas concerning behavioral features captured by the partial models and their interactions (e.g., Joolingen & Jong, 1991).

The third approach is probably the most difficult one from a learning perspective. In the case of self-building, the learner has to build the simulation by himself or herself and by doing so acquire the insights relevant to the system's behavior. Obviously, a learner needs to master a considerable amount of detail of the real system's behavior in order to build an adequate simulation model. Typically, the self-building approach starts with a model building tool (e.g., STELLA) that can be used to construct a model. These building blocks differ from the ones in the assembling-from-library approach in that they are much finer grained and usually domain-independent. They refer to concepts used in science and science teaching (in fact, theoretical constructs) to model a wide range of systems (e.g., System Dynamics). Often the language underlying these concepts has a close relation to mathematics, particularly with differential equations. The self-building approach is mostly used in higher education, such as universities. When building a model, learners have to perform important but difficult abstraction steps in order to map the real system's behavior onto the building blocks provided by the model building tool that is used. Building a model also includes filling out many technical details in terms of the underlying mathematical equations. Depending on the tool, parts of this process may be automated.

In our approach we use both the assignment-based and the self-building approach. In contrast to most of the simulation programs previously referred to, we use qualitative models of systems and their behavior. This will become clear in the remainder of this chapter, which includes the following. The VISIGARP tool, described in the next section, is primarily meant as a tool for inspecting model contents and simulations results (e.g., in the context of solving assignments). MOBUM, on the other hand, embodies the self-building approach, by supporting learning by building simulation models. It is our plan to integrate tools like VISIGARP and MOBUM in order to create interactive model-building environments which actively support (communities of) learners in building and experimenting with simulation models.

COMMUNICATING MODEL CONTENTS AND SIMULATION RESULTS

How to communicate the contents of qualitative simulation models to a user? The output generated by the GARP simulation engine consists of a large amount of complex propositional statements in Prolog code format, which is hard to read, search, and oversee, except for experienced knowledge engineers. Therefore, we designed a tool, VISIGARP, that supports investigation of the simulation model and results. VISIGARP offers a number of views, each of which focuses on certain kinds of information while using others to form the context or to provide links to more detailed information. Because the knowledge is highly structured and cannot be captured easily in linear text, we mainly use graphical representations, such as block diagrams, trees, and graphs. These visualizations make structural aspects of knowledge explicit, which can facilitate internalization of complex concepts. Our visualization ontology consists of circular, rectangular, and oval shapes of variable sizes for different kinds of entities, and lines, arrows, inclusion, ordering, and indentation for different kinds of relations. Because our approach is generic and does not use domain-specific pictures or symbols, text labels are used to denote specific entities and relation types. For each view, we designed a mapping from the ontology of qualitative simulation to the ontology of visualization primitives, to facilitate specific reasoning tasks (identifying, searching, counting, associating, and sequencing) and interaction types (reading, selecting, dragging, resizing, etc). Multiple views can be opened simultaneously, allowing users to navigate between global overviews and more detailed descriptions and to switch between different types of reasoning.

Components of the Model

VISIGARP offers views for all types of components of the simulation model: the entity-relationship graph, the causal model (or dependency graph), the is–a hierarchy of entities, and three different views on model fragments. The entity-relationship graph (see Fig. 6.3) shows the instances of system elements as labeled rectangles; relationships between entities are shown as labeled arcs. This view is deliberately kept simple, which makes it useful as a graphical introduction to the system model. The is-a hierarchy (also shown in Fig. 6.3) is a separate view, showing subtype relationships in a left-to-right tree format. Because the hierarchies are usually wider than they are deep (in terms of nesting), and there are often multiple branches with long strings as labels, a top-to-bottom format would very soon take too much space along the horizontal dimension. The levels below a certain entity node can be collapsed and opened up again by clicking on it, to allow viewing at different levels of generality.

A more detailed view, including also aspects of system behavior, is offered in the causal model, or dependency graph. Figure 6.4 shows a screenshot of the causal model for state 1 in a simulation of the Brazilian Cerrado vegetation with three populations (grass, shrubs, and trees), and fires. In the diagram, all quantities are shown, together with the dependencies between quantities, between quantity values, and quantity derivatives. As shown, all quantities belonging to the same entity are grouped together within the block representing that entity. This facilitates recognition of dependencies within subsystems, and dependencies crossing subsystem borders. Alongside the diagram, radio buttons are supplied that can be turned on or off to show or hide specific types of information. This way, the value, the quantity space, and the derivative of quantities can also be shown. If turned on, the quantity space is dis-

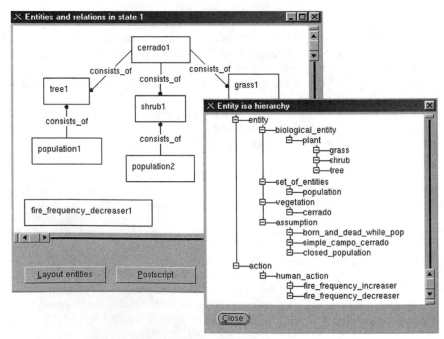

FIG. 6.3. Entity-relationship graph and Entity is-a hierarchy for an ecological model of the Brazilian Cerrado vegetation.

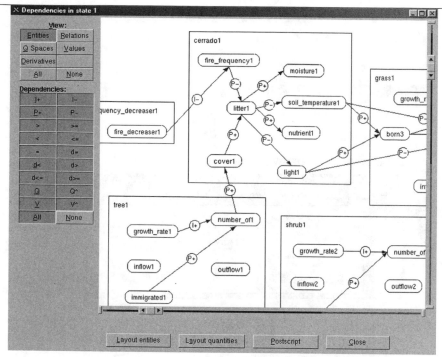

FIG. 6.4. The causal model view for state 1 of the Cerrado simulation, showing quantities within the entity they belong to, and relationships as labeled arrows. The I-relations denote influences; P-relations denote proportional relationships.

played within the quantity node in vertical orientation, with the current value highlighted and an arrow beside it, indicating increase or decrease. In addition, it is possible to show or hide the entities and relationship to clarify the system structure.

To investigate the role of the different model fragments during a simulation, a view is supplied that lists all model fragments that apply in a particular state (see Fig. 6.5). Such a list gives a high level overview of what is true and what is happening in that state. A model fragment can be selected, and more details can be requested in a structured text format, or a graphic format based on the causal model view, with color used to highlight the contents of the specific model fragment. This gives an overview of the context while drawing special attention to the specific knowledge introduced by that model fragment.

It is also possible to view how the different model fragments are structurally related to each other in the model library. Two views (not shown in this chapter) are supplied for this purpose: the is-a hierarchy of model fragments, which shows the hierarchical subtype-relationships between model fragments, and the applies-to hierarchy, that

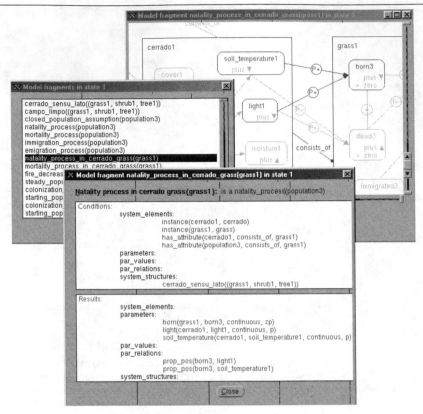

FIG. 6.5. The list of model fragments that are active in state 1. The contents of the selected model fragment *natality process* for the *grass population* are shown in detail, both in text and graphics format.

shows which model fragments are conditional for which other model fragments. In both views, a model fragment can be selected for further inspection.

Because this kind of knowledge is a bit more abstract than the kinds described previously, it should not be used before students have had some experience with the more concrete aspects of the simulation model. It is especially useful, however, for the system modeler or students learning to model.

Running the Simulation

Running a simulation leads to processes becoming active or inactive, quantity values changing, and qualitative states terminating and transforming. The behavior graph, or state-transition graph, shows an overview of the progress of the simulation in terms of states and state transitions (see Fig. 6.6). Alongside the diagram, buttons are provided to control the simulation: a state can be selected to pursue the simulation in one direction only, or, alternatively, all branches can be pursued until no further progress is possible (the Full Simulation button). Terminations, which have not (yet) resulted in a state transition, are shown as tiny circles, connected to their originating state. States, terminations, and transitions can be investigated in more detail by selecting them and clicking one of the other view buttons. When two or more states are selected in Path-mode, a path through these states (if one exists) is automatically selected. This is especially useful for the transition history and the quantity value history views because they show behavioral aspects of multiple transitions/states in a single screen.

The transition history button pops up a small screen with a short textual description of all terminations/transitions in the selected path or connected to the selected states (partly visible in Fig. 6.6). This gives a brief overview of all events that triggered a state transition. A more detailed description of individual terminations is also available by selecting one in the popup window. In the quantity value history view (the fore-

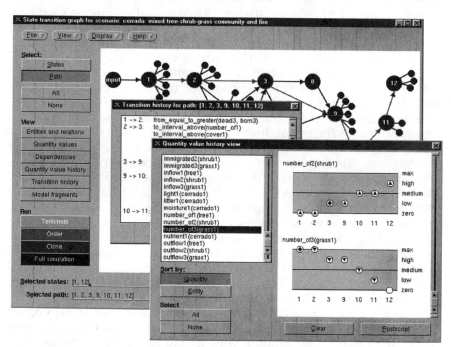

FIG. 6.6. State-transition graph for the Cerrado simulation. For the selected path between state 1 and 12, the transition history is opened, as well as the value histories for the quantities denoting the amount of shrubs and grass: *number_of2(shrub1)* shows an increase from zero to high, while *number_of3(grass1)* shows an decrease from max to zero.

most window in Fig. 6.6), quantities can be selected from a list—when selected, the values of this quantity will be plotted over time (the sequence of states selected in the behavior graph).

Like a traditional x–y graph that plots a dependent variable against time, a graph format is used with the quantity space on the y-axis and the state sequence on the x-axis. Point values are plotted on horizontal lines indicating specific value points, whereas interval values are plotted between two lines, corresponding to the values bordering the interval. Note that connecting these points to form a line graph would suggest too much, because the exact slope of ascent/descent within intervals is unknown in our qualitative simulation framework.

Working With Visualizations of Qualitative Simulations

One of the educational goals that can be supported by VISIGARP is learning to make predictions and to test their accuracy. Given a certain simulation scenario starting state (including a structural description of the system and the causal dependencies between its quantities), a possible exercise is to predict the possible changes of one or more quantities, and in what order they might occur. In order to test the hypothesis, the student can run a complete simulation. The simulation engine then produces all possible successor states, including alternative branches when the situation is underdetermined. By looking at the state transitions and the order in which they occur in the behavior graph, the student can test the accuracy of his or her predictions. A common mistake is to consider only one or a few possibilities, when in fact underdetermination leads to multiple branches, hence unforeseen results.

In addition to making and testing predictions, the system also supports the search for explanations for particular results of the simulation. For example, if state 12 (which may be an end state, or intermediate state) of the simulation shows that a certain population dies out (*number_ of* = zero), the student may be asked to find out how this happened. This forces the student to trace back from state 12 (there may be multiple paths leading there) to earlier states to check for state transitions and other differences that may have occurred. To find out why a certain state transition occurred, the student will have to look into the causal model for the originating state to find out how all quantities involved are related to each other. Contrary to events in the real world, events happening in the simulation can always be traced back to a starting state, providing at least a kernel for explanation.

It is important to note that the figures generated by our system do not contain domain-specific symbols or pictorial representations. One may argue that this is a weak point because it may be hard for students, especially novices, to relate the model to reality. Other work in simulation-based learning has incorporated domain-specific symbols, icons, or pictures to help students understand the correspondence between the model and the system modeled (e.g., Forbus et al., 1999; Kuyper, 1998).

Nevertheless, due to their flexibility, more abstract representations can actually provide advantages, as research in diagrammatic reasoning indicates (e.g., Kulpa, 1994). After a learning phase, students can directly read off characteristics of the simulation by looking at the diagrams. This way, they can find out whether there is ambiguity in the simulation or a feedback loop in the causal model, for example. Also, an overall estimation of complexity and relative importance can be given by just glancing at the diagram layout: a diagram with lots of lines going back and forth suggests a complex system; clutter around a certain quantity may suggest that it serves an important role in the system. These kinds of reasoning with diagrams can prove very useful because they go beyond the possibilities of text as a medium for knowledge communication.

It is also important to note that the diagrams in our system are created at the moment a student wants to see them, in the context he or she has chosen interactively. They can be extended and modified at the student's will, within the scope of the current interface options: adding extra details, extending behavior paths, highlighting fragments, modifying the layout. This may well lead the students to see that diagrams are not necessarily static figures (as is the case in books), but external representations with which you can interact to facilitate reasoning. Furthermore, once students learn to use abstract representations in one domain, knowledge of how to use them can be transferred to other domains. When the goal is not only to learn about a specific domain, but also to learn more general skills, like learning to model scientific phenomena, abstract representations are even necessary.

Current Status and Future Work

VISIGARP is implemented in SWI-Prolog/XPCE (Wielemaker & Anjewierden, 1992). Other members of our group have implemented some of these ideas on visualization in JAVA.[4] All figures in the screenshots in this section were automatically generated by VISIGARP, using a large simulation model developed for GARP by Salles and Bredeweg (1997). This mechanism works for any GARP model in any domain, for example, a piston system with a heat-flow, a balance system with a liquid flow (Koning, 1997), and the ecology of Brazilian Cerrado populations with different growth and migration processes (Salles, 1997). Preliminary evaluation with 25 undergraduate students has shown that these subjects can use VISIGARP to help them complete exercises asking for simple qualitative knowledge in a domain unfamiliar to them (for details, see Bouwer & Bredeweg, 2001). However, reasonably large models (such as the Brazilian Cerrado ecology model employed in this study) can still lead to complex diagrams, with

---

[4]For example, http://www.swi.psy.uva.nl/projects/GARP/index.html. GarpApplet is an online visualization prototype, implemented in JAVA 1.2. It runs in both Explorer and Netscape.

suboptimal layout. Possible improvements to the system are smarter layout algorithms, or alternative browsing techniques (e.g., automatic zooming or hyperbolic browsing). However, a more promising direction we are investigating is to automatically select and abstract the most interesting aspects of the simulation model, before visualization. For example, it can be helpful to show the most important values in every state in a state-transition graph, or to show the important differences between two states in terms of model fragments. For the automatic realization of such support, we can build on research dealing with aggregation and abstraction mechanisms (e.g., Koning et al., 2000; Mallory, Porter, & Kuipers, 1996). A third avenue for further work addresses the question of how to enhance the graphics with textual explanations, and how the visualizations can be used in a dialogue between system and student. Automating these processes may benefit from work in multimedia generation such as that by Mittal, Moore, Carenini, and Roth, (1998), who generated figures and their captions automatically, and Wahlster, Andre, Profitlich, and Rist (1993), who focused on planning a complete interactive presentation. Also, research on automated explanatory dialogue may prove useful in this respect (see Moore, 1995; Pilkington & Grierson, 1996).

LEARNING BY BUILDING MODELS

As argued earlier, building a model can also be a learning experience. Enabling this type of learning requires adequate model building environments. One of the main bottlenecks in the construction of knowledge models is the absence of easy-to-use, domain-independent tools to support the average learner in the realization of complete and manageable models. To address this problem we have implemented a prototype, MOBUM, that allows users to interactively build qualitative simulation models. This section discusses the details relevant to the construction of this tool.

Constraints for the Design of Workspaces

Building a simulation model is a complex activity that involves many tasks, subtasks, and interdependencies between tasks (e.g., Schut & Bredeweg, 1996). An important issue, therefore, concerns the decomposition of this overall activity into smaller parts that can be performed more or less independently from each other. These parts can thus be supported by separate, and possibly dedicated, interface constructs (referred to as *workspaces*). As a starting point, we used the simulation model ontology on which GARP is based (Bredeweg, 1992) and remodeled it using an object-oriented approach. A summary of this model is shown in Fig. 6.7.

Without going into all the details, notice that the system model (that is, the simulation model as a whole) consists of a hierarchy of model

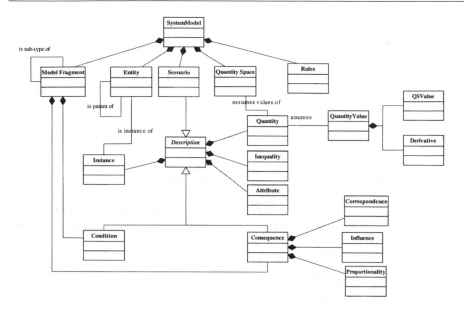

FIG. 6.7.   Simulation model ontology of the GARP qualitative reasoning engine.

fragments, a hierarchy of entities, a scenario, quantity spaces, and rules.[5] Both model fragments and scenario use *descriptions*, which implies that the latter have to exist (or have to be created) when creating a model fragment or a scenario. Entities and quantity spaces, on the other hand, do not use other model parts (but they are used as inputs when creating other model parts).

Description is a model construct used to group sets of model parts that are reused in other model parts. Although not shown in Fig. 6.7, it turns out that these description parts are highly interrelated. For instance, a quantity always belongs to an entity, an attribute always exists between two instances, a proportionality always exists between two quantities, etc. Moreover, the specific descriptions that a learner may want to formulate always depend on the specific model fragment he or she is constructing. For instance, a liquid-flow process between two containers should only become active when those two containers exist, are filled with an amount of liquid, have unequal pressures, and are connected by a pipe that facilitates the flow (see also Fig. 6.10). Putting these insights together and making them available under the correct conditions is precisely what constructing a model fragment is all about. It is therefore necessary (i.e.,

---

[5]In the current implementation of MOBUM, a set of default rules (domain independent) is provided. Rules are therefore not further discussed in this chapter.

logical) to have the interface facilities, for creating the descriptions, available in the context of creating a model fragment.

Constraints such as these have resulted in defining four builders (main workspaces) and sets of tools that are available within each workspace. Table 6.1 enumerates the builders that exist in MOBUM.

Tools exist for creating, modifying and organizing the model parts (mainly the descriptions in Fig. 6.7) within each builder.[6] For instance, within the model-fragment builder the following tools exist (see also Fig. 6.10, column on the right, read from top to bottom):

1. Pointer tool (move icons on the screen with the workspace)
2. Instance tool (add entities to the workspace)
3. Modify tool (e.g., change a name)
4. Delete tool (permanently remove something from the workspace)
5. Attribute tool (make structural relations between entities, e.g. container *contains* a liquid)
6. Quantity tool (add a quantity to an entity)
7. Influence tool (define an influence constraint between two quantities)
8. Proportionality tool (define a proportionality constraint between two quantities)
9. Correspondence tool (define a correspondence constraint between two quantities)
10. Inequality tool (define an [in]equality constraint between two quantities)

TABLE 6.1
Learner Workspaces in MOBUM

Entity Builder	In this workspace the learner models the (physical) objects that represent the domain. The hierarchical relationships between these objects are modeled here as well.
Scenario Builder	In this workspace the learner defines the situations that can be simulated. Notice that by definition this can only be a "selection" of the model parts defined elsewhere in the model. For instance, there is no point in specifying an entity in a scenario that is not used in any model fragment.
Model Fragment Builder	In this workspace the learner constructs the knowledge about the behavior of entities. This includes the specification of features of instances, such as quantities, the values these have, and the dependencies that exist between the quantities.
Quantity Space Builder	In this workspace the learner creates an ordered set of quantity values that quantities may have. These values are a sequence of alternating points and intervals.

---

[6]Most tools are called *makers* in the user interface of MOBUM (e.g., the quantity tool is referred to as the *quantity maker* (see also Fig. 6.10).

11. Reuse model fragment tool (add an already defined model fragment as a condition)
12. Reuse instances tool (reuse parts of a conditional model fragment in order to further refine)

Notice that most of these tools are also available in the other builders, such as the quantity tool in the scenario builder (in fact, the tools 1, 2, 3, 4, 5, and 6 from this list are available within the scenario builder).

To further constrain the design of MOBUM, we used the notion of task analysis (e.g., Preece et al., 1994; see also Fig. 6.8). Mainly by detailing each of the subtasks within a workspace in terms of inputs–outputs, and thus their relative order, an additional set of requirements and constraints emerged.

Case: Create Quantity, apply a Quantity Space and assign a value to the quantity

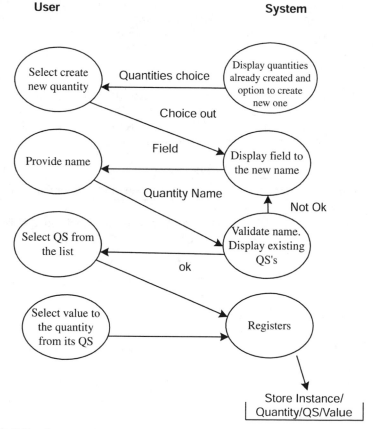

FIG. 6.8. An example task analysis for making a new quantity.

Input–output dependencies determine whether a subtask can be performed and thus can be used to govern the availability of tools within a workspace. For instance, the quantity tool cannot be used unless at least one instance has been added to the workspace of the model fragment being built (and before that, the learner must have created the entity as an element in the entity builder). Table 6.2 enumerates the minimum requirements for using a tool within the model fragment builder.

When these basic requirements are fulfilled (and at least one tool can be used), the input–output dependencies within the subtask, supported by that tool, can be used to determine whether the learner has performed the task correctly or at least sufficiently (that is, syntactically speaking). For instance, within the quantity tool the learner always has to select the instance to which the new quantity must be applied. The task is not sufficiently completed without that information and thus closing the task should be made impossible (of course, it can be cancelled). On the other hand, some information may not be crucial yet. For instance, the quantity space of a quantity may be added later. For each tool, the minimum required steps have been identified. They have been used in the design of the tools within MOBUM to support the learner in always performing the task to a sufficiently complete level.

User Interface Design

The overall user interface design for the MOBUM environment starts with the notion of builders and tools. Tools are displayed on the right side of the screen and automatically change when the learner chooses to work with a different builder (i.e., workspace). Opening a builder can be

TABLE 6.2

Minimum Requirements for Using a Tool in the Model Fragment Builder.

Instance tool	One entity must have been created (in entity builder)
Attribute tool	Two instances must exist (in workspace)
Quantity tool	One instance must exist (in workspace)
Influence tool	Two quantities must exist (as consequence in the workspace)
Proportionality tool	Two quantities must exist (as consequence in the workspace)
Correspondence tool	Two quantities must exist (as consequence in the workspace)
Inequality tool	Two quantities must exist (in workspace)
Reuse model fragment tool	Other model fragment must have been created (with MF builder)
Reuse instances	A reused model fragment must exist (in workspace)

done by clicking on the icons in the main toolbar, at the top of the overall interface. Builders can also be opened using the menu options. Multiple builders can be opened, but only one tool can be active. Although from a technical point of view multiple tools can be provided, the idea is that it is better to support learners in performing focused model building steps. Allowing only one tool to be active forces learners to first finish this task, or cancel it, before moving on to the next. Having multiple builders open is essential, because next to supporting a model building step, these builders also provide the learners with overviews of what has been built so far (see Fig. 6.9).

Figure 6.9 shows a screenshot of a model building session in MOBUM. Two builders are open, the entity builder and the quantity space builder. The learner is working within the latter and uses the point/interval maker. This is a tool that allows the user to add values to a quantity space. On the left side in Fig. 6.9, the model browser is shown (system model view). This browser provides an overview of the model building activities by showing the model parts that have been created so far. The browser can also be used for navigation and to open specific model parts and the corresponding builders (by double clicking on the name label).

Next to the overall design, the internal design of the different workspaces has to be determined. Some choices are rather straightforward, such as using combo-boxes to present the user with a list to select from (e.g., instance selection in the quantity tool in Fig. 6.10). This is easier and prohibits typing errors. When the learner has to provide a new name, the words entered by the user are always checked against the already existing labels in order to prevent errors or undesired overlap. Less obvious design choices concern the icons and the spatial layout of some knowledge items on the screen. To start with the former, we tried to find insightful icons to refer to knowledge items in a builder. For instance, an entity is visualized as a cube, a quantity as a gauge, etc. These

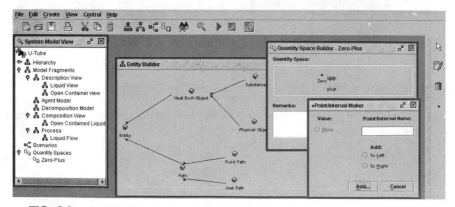

FIG. 6.9. A MOBUM session, showing: browser, entity builder and quantity-space builder.

choices are somewhat arbitrary. We do not yet know to what extent the MOBUM icon language will be interpreted correctly by the target users. However, most icons also have labels identifying them.

With respect to the spatial layout, most knowledge items (e.g., entities, instances, quantities, reused model fragments, points and intervals) are represented as nodes of a connected graph. They may be moved around freely by the learner allowing him or her to organize the model to his or her taste (using the pointer tool). An exception to this rule is formed by the quantities, which are organized in a tabular form, grouped together with the instance they have been assigned to. Included in this table are the quantity space, current value, and derivative for each of the quantities (see also Fig. 6.10).

Binary relationships between knowledge items are represented as lines connecting the two icons that visualize the knowledge items. The type of relationship is shown by an icon placed at the midpoint of the line (e.g., the > sign for an inequality, or an I+ sign for an influence, both shown in Fig. 6.10). A problem with this approach is that dependencies between quantities belonging to the same instance are somewhat difficult to represent, because they are lines from and to the same icon. Particularly in the case of many lines, this will become messy. Another approach would be to represent each of the quantities by a unique icon and then connect it, using lines, to the instance it belongs to. The problem with this approach is that it becomes more difficult to see what icons belong together. Also, in the case of many quantities, all the lines connecting all the icons make the overall picture pretty messy. More research is needed to find a good solution for this problem.

Another discussion concerns the *conditions* and *consequences* part of a model fragment. How to visualize this? In MOBUM we decided to have

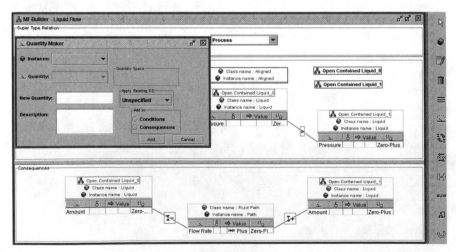

FIG. 6.10. Model fragment builder: User starts adding a new quantity to the liquid-flow process.

separate fields within the builder for this (see Fig. 6.10). Obviously, it is immediately clear whether an icon is in the condition or in the consequence part. But there is also a problem, and that is using the same knowledge item both as condition and as a consequence. In the MOBUM approach this leads to a full copy of the instance (knowledge icon) into both the conditions and the consequences, and then add quantities relevant to each part (in Fig. 6.10 pressure is added in the conditions and amount plays a role in the consequences). From the resulting visualization in the model fragment builder, it is not obvious that both icons refer to the same instance; the user really has to understand the underlying details. Another approach would be not to have separate fields, but to visualize the condition versus consequence role by means of a color. Again, more research is needed to resolve the issue.

Notice that the previous section, about VISIGARP, already hinted at possible solutions for the problems mentioned above. However, it should be pointed out that the visualizations for VISIGARP and MOBUM are designed to support different tasks, and may therefore need to look different.

Current Status and Future Work

MOBUM is a fully operational prototype that has been implemented in JAVA. In the current implementation there is no direct communication with the simulator. Instead, the learner has to save the model into files and then run the simulator (GARP) as a separate program. To be used in practice with real learners, this will not be sufficient. For that purpose, MOBUM and the simulator must be fully integrated, at least from a user's perspective.

Despite the fact that MOBUM has not yet been evaluated with the target users, three points for improvements can be pointed out.

1. Intermediate modeling support: Often when building a model, the persons building the model define intermediate models before they write down the final model. MOBUM does not support this process, it only supports the latter step. Improvements for MOBUM could focus on supporting and maintaining intermediate models for the user.
2. Horizontal views: When building a model in MOBUM, it is difficult to see how all the model fragments that have been created will interact. There are no tools/builders/views that provide the user with a global overview of certain model parts (except for the model browser). For instance, it may turn out to be helpful to provide the user with a "causal model viewer," similar to the causal model view in VISIGARP (shown in Fig. 6.4). This would allow the user to investigate if and how the causal dependencies, that have been defined in the different model fragments, are related (thus, without running the simulator first).

3. Model building support from a"content" point of view: MOBUM allows for building syntactically correct models, but the current prototype has no knowledge of the model construction process and the status of the model. In order to coach learners in building models beyond the syntactic level, MOBUM should be extended in this respect.

TOWARD A NETWORKED MODEL-BUILDING COMMUNITY

Integration of the prototypes discussed in the previous sections takes us close to the goal of interactive model-building environments, which incorporate intelligent support for both model building and inspection of simulation models. But we believe that the combination of these two will prove to be even more powerful for educational purposes than just the sum of their individual functionalities. If models of scientific phenomena become easier to produce and inspect, they can also be shared more easily. And it is exactly the sharing of understanding, made explicit in the form of (qualitative) simulation models, that creates a huge potential for learning. Imagine, for example, that two students get the same assignment of modeling a particular system, but solve it differently. Would there be a better way to exchange their different views than to let them exchange models and experiment with them? Or imagine a whole classroom working together on a model of a large complex system, dividing tasks among subgroups to model different parts or different aspects of the system. Or, on an even larger scale, imagine several classrooms separated by many kilometers in space, yet connected via the Internet. They could build models of systems that are important, maybe omnipresent, in their part of the world, but largely unknown to others (like the Cerrado vegetation in Brazil, or electricity generators based on water-wave energy in northern Europe). By exchanging models, people could learn about systems they do not have access to in their own part of the world. Learning about distant places will become more interesting, we believe, when students will not only be able to read and hear about them, but also be offered ways of interacting with simulations of them. In this sense, our notion of a model building community resonates strongly with the work of Reichherzer, Cañas, Ford, & Hayes, (1998) on the Quorum project, although the form of knowledge representation they use is far simpler (i.e., concept maps) than in our case.

Of course, just exchanging models would not be enough to establish understanding, especially when cultural or language barriers are being crossed. Learning does not only entail model building and inspection, but also requires coaching, involving dialogue, exercises, and feedback. Additional communication channels, like personal contacts between teachers, project WWW pages, e-mail, and chat facilities between students, etc., will be necessary to establish real model building communities. When more people become involved in building a single model, specific tools for collaborative work will be required as well, to support both synchronous and asynchronous work, version management, search for differences and similarities, feedback on potential integration problems, etc. An example of this kind of work is C-CHENE, a structured computer mediated communication interface that supports reflective discussion between pairs of students building models in energy physics (Baker & Lund, 1997). Indeed, the idea of model-building communities introduces several interesting problems on our research agenda. While working on this agenda, more and more elements are being put in place, alleviating part of the shortcomings of today. Therefore, we believe that interactive model building environments based on a domain-independent modeling ontology will prove very useful for the communication of knowledge in the future.

CONCLUSIONS

This chapter has introduced the notion of interactive model-building environments for educational purposes. This notion is essentially based on two ideas. First, students can learn by interacting with an articulate simulation model, investigating the structure and behavior of a particular system in the real world by looking at a qualitative representation of that system and its behavior. A prototype, VISIGARP, has been implemented for this purpose. Using VISIGARP, students can experiment with simulations of systems, or situations that are difficult to replicate in reality. They can check predictions of what might happen and search for causal accounts of particular events in the simulation. Second, students can learn by building such models themselves, using tools that contain the necessary modeling primitives as building blocks and that support the model-building process. This is addressed by a second implemented prototype, called MOBUM. Using the right modeling abstractions and assumptions, students can articulate in MOBUM their intuitive ideas about some interesting phenomenon in the form of a qualitative model, which can be used to run simulations. Because the prototypes are domain-independent, support is available for modeling and model communication in various domains. Both prototypes are currently undergoing evaluation, and further work is necessary on several aspects. For the communication of model contents and simulation results, it is clear that the diagrammatic representations cannot be treated as explanations on their own—embedding them in an educational dialogue, and grounding them to educationally meaningful tasks is necessary. Concerning the support for the model-building process, the currently implemented tools and constraints are not sufficient; additional guidance is needed to ensure that the model-building effort turns into a useful learning experience.

When the functionality of the two current prototypes is combined, this will lead to interactive model-building environments, which empower students to articulate their thoughts, experiment with the results generated by their own model, and reflect on the outcomes. By making explicit their ideas, students may not only deepen their own conceptual understanding of a domain, but also share this with others because having a runnable simulation model means that it can be communicated to other users, too. This aspect of interactive model-building environments based on a principled modeling framework makes it possible to think about multiple users, building models together, or exchanging models between them. By realizing that knowledge can be articulated, and that the resulting model can be used to reason and communicate about system behavior, students may learn to view their knowledge of the world not as something static, but as dynamic and interactive, like the world itself.

ACKNOWLEDGMENTS

We would like to thank Joost Breuker and Bob Wielinga for their support and comments on the research presented in this chapter.

REFERENCES

Baker, M. J., & Lund, K. (1997). Promoting reflective interactions in a computer-supported collaborative learning environment. *Journal of Computer Assisted Learning, 13*, 175–193.

Bental, D., & Brna, P. (1995). Enabling abstractions: Key steps in building physics models. In J. Greer (Ed.), *Artificial intelligence in education: Proceedings of the AIED95 conference*, (pp. 162–169). Charlottesville, VA: Association for the Advancement of Computing in Education (AACE).

Bobrow, D. G. (Ed.). (1984). *Qualitative reasoning about physical systems*. Amsterdam, The Netherlands: Elsevier.

Bouwer, A., & Bredeweg, B. (2001). VisiGarp: Graphical representation of qualitative simulation models. In J. D. Moore, G. Luckhardt Redfield, & J. L. Johnson (Eds.), *Artificial intelligence in education: AI-ED in the wired and wireless future* (pp. 294–305). Osaka, Japan: IOS-Press/Ohmsha.

Bradshaw, J. M. (1997). *Software agents*. Cambridge, MA: MIT Press.

Bredeweg, B. (1992). *Expertise in qualitative prediction of behavior*. Doctoral dissertation, University of Amsterdam.

Bredeweg, B., & Winkels, R. (1998). Qualitative models in interactive learning environments: An introduction. *Interactive Learning Environments, 5*, 1–18.

Breuker, J. A., & van de Velde, W. (Eds.). (1994). *The CommonKADS library for expertise modeling*. Amsterdam: IOS Press.

Brown J. S., Collins, J., & Duguid, S. (1989). Situated cognition and the culture of learning. *Educational Researcher, 18*(1), 32–42

Bruner, J. (1966). *Toward a theory of instruction*. Cambridge, MA: University Press.

Elio, R., & Sharf, P. B. (1990). Modeling novice-to-expert shifts in problem-solving and knowledge organization. *Cognitive Science, 14*, 579–639.

Elsom-Cook, M. (1990). Analysis of a tutoring dialogue. In M. Elsom-Cook (Ed.), *Guided discovery learning: A framework for ICAI research* (pp.113–131). London: Chapman.

Falkenhainer, B. C., & Forbus, K. D. (1991). Compositional modeling: Finding the right model for the job. *Artificial Intelligence, 51*, 95–143.

Fiske, J. (1990). *Introduction to communication studies* (2nd ed.). New York: Routledge.

Forbus, K. D. (1984). Qualitative process theory. *Artificial Intelligence, 24,* 85–168.
Forbus, K. D., & Falkenhainer, B. (1992). Self-explanatory simulations: Scaling up to large models. In R. Leitch (Ed.), *Proceedings of the 6th International Workshop of Qualitative Reasoning* (pp. 22–35). Edinburgh, Scotland: Heriot-Watt University.
Forbus, K. D., Whalley, P. B., Everett, J. O., Ureel, L., Brokowski, M., Baher, J., & Kuehne, S. E. (1999). CyclePad: An articulate virtual laboratory for engineering thermodynamics. *Artificial Intelligence, 114,* 297–347.
Grant, W. E., Pedersen, E. K., & Marin, S. L. (1997). *Ecology and natural resource management: Systems analysis and simulation.* New York: Wiley.
Hollan, J. D., Hutchins, E. L., & Weitzman, L. (1987). STEAMER: An interactive inspectable, simulation-based training systems. In G. Kearsley (Ed.), *Artificial intelligence and instruction: Applications and methods* (pp. 113–134). Reading, MA: Addison-Wesley.
Hulst, A. van der. (1996). *Cognitive tools. Two exercises in non-directive support for exploratory learning.* Doctoral dissertation, University of Amsterdam.
Joolingen, W. R., & de Jong, T. (1991). Supporting hypothesis formation by learners exploring an interactive computer simulation. *Instructional Science, 20,* 389–404.
Jong, T. de. (Ed.). (1991). Computer simulations in an instructional context [Special issue]. *Education and Computing, 6*(3/4).
Kleer, J. de, & Brown, J. S. (1984). A qualitative physics based on confluences. *Artificial Intelligence, 24,* 7–83.
Kleer, J. de, & Williams, B. C. (1991). Qualitative reasoning about physical systems 2. [Special issue]. *Artificial Intelligence, 51.*
Koning, K. de. (1997). *Model-based reasoning about learner behavior.* Amsterdam: IOS Press.
Koning, K. de, Bredeweg, B., Breuker, J., & Wielinga, B. (2000). Model-based reasoning about learner behavior. *Artificial Intelligence, 117,* 173–229.
Kearsley, G. (1994–2000). *Explorations in learning & instruction: The theory into practice database.* [On-line]. TIP: http://www.gwu.edu/~tip/
Kulpa, Z. (1994). Diagrammatic representation and reasoning. *Machine GRAPHICS & VISION, 3*(1/2), 77–103.
Kuyper, M. (1998). *Knowledge engineering of usability: Model-mediated interaction design of authoring instructional simulations.* Doctoral dissertation, University of Amsterdam.
Mallory, R. S., Porter, B. W., & Kuipers, B. J. (1996). Comprehending complex behavior graphs through abstraction. In Y. Iwasaki & A. Farquhar (Eds.), *Proceedings of the tenth international workshop on qualitative reasoning* (pp. 137–146). Menlo Park, CA: AAAI Press.
Mettes, C. T. C. W., & Roossink, H. J. (1981). Linking factual and procedural knowledge in solving science problems: A case study in a thermodynamics course. *Instructional Science, 10,* 333–361.
Mittal, V., Moore, J., Carenini, G., & Roth, S. (1998). Describing complex charts in natural language: A caption generation system. *Computational Linguistic, 24*(3), 431–467.
Moore, J. D. (1995). *Participating in explanatory dialogues: Interpreting and responding to questions in context.* Cambridge, MA: MIT Press.
Newell, A. (1982). The knowledge level. *Artificial Intelligence, 18,* 87–127.
Pilkington, R. M., & Grierson, A. (1996). Generating explanations in a simulation-based learning environment. *International Journal of Human–Computer Studies, 45,* 527–551.

Pratap, P. (1999). *Getting Started with MATLAB 5: A quick introduction for scientists and engineers*. Oxford, UK: Oxford University Press.

Preece, J., Rogers, Y., Sharp, H., Benyon, D., Holland, S., & Carey, T. (1994). *Human–computer interaction*. Reading MA: Addison-Wesley.

Reichherzer, T. R., Cañas, A. J., Ford, K. M., & Hayes, P. J. (1998). The giant: A classroom collaborator. In *Proceedings of the ITS '98 Workshop on Pedagogical Agents* (pp. 83–86). San Antonio, TX: St. Mary's University.

Rickel, J., & Porter, B. W. (1997). Automated modeling of complex systems to answer prediction questions. *Artificial Intelligence, 93*, 201–260.

Salles, P. S. B. A. (1997). *Qualitative models in ecology and their use in learning environments*. Doctoral dissertation, University of Edinburgh, Edinburgh, Scotland.

Salles, P., & Bredeweg, B. (1997). *Building qualitative models in ecology*. In L. Ironi (Ed.), Proceedings of the International Workshop on Qualitative Reasoning, QR'97 (pp. 155–164). Pavia, Italy: Istituto di Analisi Numerica C.N.R.

Schut, C., & Bredeweg, B. (1996). An overview of approaches to qualitative model construction. *The Knowledge Engineering Review, 11*(1), 1–25.

Sime, J., (1994). *Model switching in intelligent training systems*. Doctoral dissertation. Heriot-Watt University, Edinburgh, Scotland.

Sime, J., & Leitch, R. R. (1992). *Multiple models in intelligent training*. Proceedings of the 1st International Intelligent Systems Engineering Conference (ISE'92) (pp. 263–268). Edinburgh, Scotland: Heriot-Watt University.

Wahlster, W., Andre, E., Profitlich, H.-J., & Rist, T. (1993). Plan-based integration of natural language and graphics generation. *Artificial Intelligence, 63*, 387–327.

Weld, D., & de Kleer, J. (Eds.). (1990). *Readings in qualitative reasoning about physical systems*. Palo Alto, CA: Morgan Kaufmann.

Wenger, E. (1987). *Artificial intelligence and tutoring systems. Computational and cognitive approaches to the communication of knowledge*. Los Altos, CA: Morgan Kaufmann.

White, B. Y., & Frederiksen, J. R. (1990). Causal model progressions as a foundation for intelligent learning environments. *Artificial Intelligence, 42*, 99–157.

Wielemaker, J., & Anjewierden, A. (1992). *Programming in PCE/Prolog*. University of Amsterdam.

Winkels, R., & Bredeweg, B. (Eds.). (1998). Qualitative models in interactive learning environments. *Interactive Learning Environment, 5*, 1–134 (Special issue).

Chapter 7

Enhancing Reflective Modeling Through Communicative Interaction in Learning Environments

Susan Bull
University of Birmingham

Vania Dimitrova
University of Leeds

Paul Brna
University of Northumbria at Newcastle

It would be hard to develop a model of some aspect of the world without an element of reflection. In terms of modeling, we ask about what is being reflected on, when reflection happens and, from a pedagogical perspective, how to guide relatively novice modelers into more productive reflection. In this chapter we examine two different kinds of modeling: In one sense, it is about building a model of some physical situation (how electricity works or how the solar system is formed) or some state of affairs (e.g., the world of finance markets), and the other sense of modeling is about building a model of one's own understanding through reflective thought as well as through discussion.

Reflection has an important role in theories of learning (e.g., Dewey, 1933; King & Kitchener, 1994; Kolb, 1984). It is more accurate to state that it has many important roles. For example, Kolb (1984) emphasized the role of experience in learning. He provided a model of experiential learning expressed as a cycle between the four processes of active experimentation, concrete experience, reflective observation, and abstract conceptualization. This stressed the reflective examination of experience, but there are many kinds of experience that might be the focus of such an inspection.

In a more developmental vein, King and Kitchener (1994) provided a stage-based account of the growth of reflective thinking in more epistemic terms. Their Reflective Judgement Model features a growth in reflective thinking as people move through seven stages of development with quasireflective thinking occurring in stages four and five, and more well developed reflective thinking at levels six and seven. Their work drew on that of Perry (1970), but especially appeals to Dewey's (1933) conception of reflective thinking and his notion that reflective thinking only arises once there is some recognition of an impasse or dilemma.

Focusing more specifically on modeling, if we regard the modeler as a *reflective practitioner*, then we can see (at least) three kinds of reflection: reflection-on-action, reflection-in-action, and reflection-for-action (Schön, 1987). If we follow Dewey here, all these forms of reflection may entail the recognition of some kind of dilemma. Thus the debate about reflection can be broadened to consider how to engineer such dilemmas. Winograd and Flores (1986), following Heidegger, went further and argued:

> We prefer to talk about "breakdowns." By this we mean the interrupted moment of our habitual, standard, comfortable "being-in-the-world." Breakdowns serve an extremely important cognitive function, revealing to us the nature of our practices and equipment, making them "present-to-hand" to us, perhaps for the first time. In this sense they function in a positive rather than a negative way. (pp. 77–78)

This suggests that unplanned breakdowns, as well as engineered ones, may well serve a pivotal function in realizing something important about the development of some model of (part of) the world.

In this chapter, we demonstrate that there is a class of learning environments designed to support reflection through a special kind of dialogic process. This process is promoted through the learner externalizing some part of his or her model of the world, which is then used to generate a model of the learner (student model).[1] Then this student model becomes the means by which reflection is stimulated.

The externalization process goes hand in hand with transformation because the expression that describes the elements of the model has to be constructed. Further, there are two important kinds of reflection that result from this process—reflection on one's own externalization, and reflection on some reflection on one's own externalization from some other person or some software agent. This kind of *reflection on reflection* has been commented on by Schön (1987) as a clearly symbolic process. In our framework, the system itself may propose a representation that

---

[1]Student models—data structures that represent characteristics of the student, their domain knowledge, and metacognitive skills—are crucial for building adaptive educational systems that "care" about their learners (Self, 1999). These systems are able to follow the needs of individual learners, providing appropriate feedback or adjusting the educational material to address specific pedagogical issues.

is intended to be close to that of the student's own representation if it were to be expressed. In this sense, the system has a provocative role.

This chapter primarily addresses this last kind of reflection, *reflection on reflection*, where students may examine their own reflections on actions and thinking processes as a method of understanding their own learning process. This is not the same as self-explanation (Chi, Bassok, Lewis, Reimann, & Glaser, 1989) but must be related in some way because the student reflects on an externalized fragment. However, in our framework, either the student or the system may propose a contribution to the student model.

The promotion of reflection is important. For example, Jackson, Krajcik, and Soloway (1998) argued for reflective scaffolding that provides support for thinking about the task (e.g., planning, making predictions, evaluating). Various researchers in artificial intelligence in education stress the importance of reflection and suggest methods for fostering reflective learning (e.g., Dillenbourg & Self, 1995; Goodman, Soller, Linton, & Gaimari, 1998; Self, Karakirik, Kor, Tedesco, & Dimitrova, 2000; White, Shimoda, & Frederiksen, 1999).

In our framework, the process of reflecting on reflection arises as a consequence of the interactions that take place between the learner, the externalized model, and another agent (human or software). Thus reflective modeling seems to be part of what Clancey (1992) argued—namely, that reflection is not something that occurs internally, in a hidden way, separate from some activity. It is always part of an ongoing activity, of a set of concerns, attitudes, and orientation toward what is important, what we are trying to do, what we are paying attention to.

The issue of externalization gets close to the important issue here, which is whether the systems we design can involve the student in a constructive dialogic process with themselves thinking about their models of the world with the active help of the system/other person. In this chapter, the term reflective modeling is to be understood in this way.

Reflective modeling is part of the process of learning to model. Following Vince and Tiberghien (chap. 2, this volume), modeling takes place when "a person or a group of persons makes an explanation of or an interpretation of or a prediction about the material world." In this case, two worlds are involved: a theory/model world and an objects/events world. The former is the core for a student's explanatory system, whereas the latter is generally concerned with the experimental field (the objects and events being investigated). Vince and Tiberghien argue that classroom situations that encourage learners to establish meaningful links between entities in the two worlds are critical in learning to model.

In this light, explanatory tasks (Vince & Tiberghien, chap. 2, this volume) and collaborative dialogues (Baker, chap. 11, this volume) have been successfully exploited. The reflective modeling approach we propose engages the student in an interaction that promotes articulating the model, validating the model, and challenging the robustness of the model. Hence, the students may be encouraged to think about their knowledge of the world, reconsider relationships in the model, recall entities and events in the world, and bring to mind links between elements of the real world and pieces of the model.

In the remaining part of this chapter we demonstrate how computer-based learning environments may provide the means for enhancing *reflective modeling* through communicative interaction. We present examples from four domain independent approaches illustrated by specific learning environments. In the first two—Mr Collins and STyLE-OLM—the computer system discuses the model with a learner, exemplified respectively in second language acquisition and terminology learning areas. The other two are PeerISM and I-Help. PeerISM is used in peer modeling situations where two learners discuss their models, with the interaction involving or being mediated by the computer system. In I-Help learners contribute to the user models of their peers, these then being used to match suitable partners for computer-mediated interaction. Finally, we consider the extent to which the different kinds of interaction provided by these systems fit learners' cognitive styles, and argue that an amalgamation of the approaches into a single system would allow for wider applicability to different kinds of learner.

MR COLLINS—COLLABORATIVE STUDENT MODELING

The aim of the Mr Collins student model (COLLaboratively maintained, INSpectable student model) is to aid in diagnosis and to support learning through reflective modeling. This is achieved by involving the student in the student modeling process and by using the student model as a learning resource for the student.

Although this is a general perspective,[2] it is here illustrated in a concrete implementation in the domain of second language acquisition, specifically weak object pronoun placement in European Portuguese, an area in which many students have difficulties. The approach described is *collaborative student modeling* (Bull & Pain, 1995).

It has been argued that an increased explicit awareness or consciousness of language form can facilitate second language acquisition (Ellis, 1992; Schmidt, 1990). Enabling learners to view information in their student model, together with expert information held in the system, helps learners to create a model of the target language that may later result in implicit knowledge. The approach of collaborative student modeling suits the kind of learner who wishes to "learn about the language" (Wenden, 1987), and it is reminiscent of the notion of the "learner as researcher" recommended by Wolff (1994).

As already stated, the aim of collaborative student modeling is to encourage greater learner involvement in the modeling process in order to

---

[2]The generality of Mr Collins is discussed in Bull, Brna, and Pain (1995).

obtain a more accurate student model, while at the same time promoting learner reflection. Reflection occurs as the learner is encouraged to view the student model and to collaborate with the system in its construction and repair. Students are required to explain and justify their views, providing a vehicle through which they may practice *self-explanation*. This differs somewhat from Chi et al.'s (1989) well-known experiment on self-explanation, for although our students may be trying to explain correct domain examples as in Chi et al's study, they may also be defending their own (mistaken) beliefs. Therefore, in addition to reflection on domain content, through interaction about the student model, learners also reflect on and become more aware of their learning and possible difficulties they have in the domain.

There are two kinds of task—both concerned with pronoun placement. In the first type the student is presented with a Portuguese sentence with the pronoun missing. The pronoun is given separately, and it must be placed correctly into the sentence. In the other kind of exercise, students are provided with an English sentence and must translate this into Portuguese (vocabulary is provided). The domain comprises rules of pronoun placement for 12 sentence types. To submit a sentence, the student must click on one of four "confidence" buttons: "very sure," "almost sure," "unsure," or "very unsure." This prompts self-evaluation and also provides information for the learner model, to be used in the negotiation of model contents.

Learner reflection is promoted by encouraging the student to view and negotiate the contents of their student model. This is designed to encourage reflection on the domain content, leading to a more accurate model of the domain, while also considering their knowledge and progress. Viewing the student model occurs as in Fig. 7.1.

There are two views on the learner's knowledge: the system's student model and the student's student model. If learners choose to inspect the student model (either after prompting if there is a conflict between student and system beliefs, or on their own initiative), statistical information is provided about their overall performance for each rule attempted. The learners are also given a summary of recent performance that is based on their last five attempts to use a rule. This is in order that assessment does not depend only on the very last attempt, nor may it be influenced by earlier attempts that may no longer be valid. This information is retrieved from the system's student model and presented via text templates in order to make it accessible to the student. Learner and system confidence measures for each rule are also displayed. This makes any incompatibilities salient to the learners, in order to prompt consideration of their model of the language. In the illustration in Fig. 7.1 of a learner who has attempted pronoun placement in negative sentences and in affirmative main clause statements, it is indicated that the system is very sure that the student knows the rule for pronoun placement in negative clauses, but the student himself is unsure. The system is unsure that the student knows the rule for

So far this session you have attempted 13 NEGATIVE sentences.
Your total number of correct sentences with this structure is: 9.
From your most recent performance the system believes you to have a perfect command of the rule used in NEGATIVE CLAUSES.

So far this session you have attempted 7 sentences with a DECLARATIVE VERB-PRONOUN structure.

Your total number of correct sentences with this structure is: 2.
From your most recent performance the system believes you to have a rather shaky knowledge of the rule for AFFIRMATIVE MAIN CLAUSE STATEMENTS.

The pronoun is:	YOUR CONFIDENCE (a - d)	SYSTEM CONFIDENCE (1 - 4)
Pre-verbal in negatives　e.g. Não os compra	unsure (c)	very sure (1)
Post-verbal in positive main clauses　e.g. Compra-os	almost sure (b)	unsure (3)

FIG. 7.1.　Inspecting the current student model.

the positioning of pronouns in affirmative main clauses, but the student is more confident (almost sure). As with the summary of the learner's performance, the confidence levels are also based on a learner's last five attempts to use a rule; that is, the learner's most recent five statements of confidence associated with sentences using a particular rule will be "averaged" to determine the learner's confidence in using this rule, and the actual performance over the last five attempts at the same rule will determine the system's confidence in the learner's use of the rule. This is not detailed further here, as the actual mechanisms of the student modeling process are not relevant: the approach of Mr Collins can be used in combination with any (successful) student modeling technique. The learner's confidence is indicated by the values a through d ("a" being the highest level), and the system's confidence in the student by 1 through 4 ("1" portraying the highest level of confidence).

The student and system belief measures could be viewed as similar to the outside boundaries in bounded student modeling (Elsom-Cook, 1986, 1988); that is, the "true" representation of the student is likely to be anywhere within the area defined by the two measures. The difference is that in collaborative student modeling, the aim is to reduce the area through negotiation.

In this example, the two confidence measures for negative sentences are incompatible—the learner has low confidence (c) in their knowledge of the rule, but their performance leads the system to be very confident (1) in their use of this rule. For positive main clause statements, although the belief values differ (3 and b), they are still close enough to be compatible (a step down for the system, or a step up for the students—that is, 4b or 3a would be necessary before the values became incompatible). The aim is that through discussion, the values should become identical (1a, 2b, 3c, or 4d), or at least within one value on the scale. This will not only result in a student model that is more faithful to the true situation (as the student may have information that the system alone cannot take account of), but will also encourage the students to reflect on their learning, thereby also contributing to their learning (ultimately resulting in increased student and system confidence measures).

If, after viewing information in the student model, the students disagree with either their own confidence level or that of the system, they may select the option allowing the possibility of changing the model. This occurs through menu-based discussion. If the learners choose to alter their own confidence measures, they are asked what level they wish to change this to. If the new value exactly matches that of the system, the system acknowledges that it agrees with the choice. If it almost matches (as in the example for main clause statements), the system will indicate that there is a difference between their two confidence measures (here, that the system is a little less confident), but it will acknowledge that this difference is not great enough to be incompatible. If the students were to change their confidence measure to a value that is very different from that of the system—in this example, where the system is "unsure (3)," if the student were to select "very sure (a)"—the system would state that the two belief measures were not compatible, and ask the students if they wish to ignore this incompatibility and maintain the new selection. The students may insist on their own choice (inasmuch as it represents their own belief) or may ask the system to justify itself, and then may or may not be convinced by the system's reasons. System justification involves presentation of the students' sentences, together with an assessment of their performance. Figure 7.2 shows part of a session with the system to illustrate students changing their own confidence measure to one that is incompatible with that of the system.

Up to this stage in the discussion of the student model, although the system has indicated which sentences contain an error through use of an asterisk, it has not indicated which type of error is involved. The system will explain errors at this point if the students request a justification of its assessment of their performance. Alternatively, the students may select to once again inspect the contents of the model in order to reconsider before making a final decision.

If the students disagree with the system's level of confidence in their performance, they may challenge the system in an attempt to make it alter its own representation in the student model. However, if then requested, the students must be willing to defend their beliefs explicitly. If they are unable to convince the system, it will maintain its own original confidence measure. The purpose here is to prompt the learners to re-

system:
Currently your own confidence in your use of the rule applicable in positive main clause statements is:
almost sure / b.   (system's confidence = unsure / 3)

What is your new confidence level?:
- very sure (a)   • unsure (c)   • very unsure (d)   • (cancel)

student: (selects)
very sure (a).

system:
You have changed your confidence measure from 'b' to 'a'. This new confidence value is a lot higher than that of the system. The two confidence measures are incompatible. Your last five attempts to place the pronoun in positive main clause statements were the following:

    *O Manuel a mostrou no mapa.
    *O Manuel mostrou a no mapa.
    O Manuel mostrou-a no mapa.
    *O homem o comeu rapidamente.
    O homem comeu-o rapidamente.

These recent attempts demonstrate that you are having difficulties.
Confidence measure 'a' is too high for your actual proficiency. What do you wish to do?
- system justify itself   • change my belief   • view student model   • keep new belief

FIG. 7.2.   Changing one's own confidence measure.

consider their model of this part of the language, alongside the knowledge that their model may be incorrect.

On challenging the system, students are first asked whether they are happy with the representation of *their own* confidence measure (as the system must be sure of the students' current views in order to know what it is defending itself against). Students are then asked what they feel the system's confidence in their ability should be changed to. An example attempt at changing the system's beliefs (again for affirmative main clause statements) is given in Fig. 7.3.

Because the student has selected a value for the system that is distant from the system's own view, the system will not automatically allow itself to be persuaded. The student is offered the option of simply accepting the system's decision without argument, of viewing the student model once more before making a decision, of accepting a compromise (here 2 is the midpoint between 1 and 3—had the system's confidence in the student been at level 4, no such compromise would have been offered as the distance between 1 and 4 is too great), or of system or student justification of their standpoint. If the student requires the system to explain its position, the system will present the student's most recent five attempts, together with its reasons for its assessment, as in this example. The student may or may not be convinced, and is again offered the aforementioned choices for how to proceed.

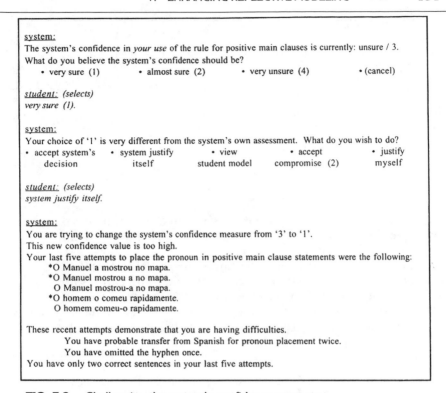

FIG. 7.3. Challenging the system's confidence measure.

If the students choose to justify themselves to the system, they will be offered a test sentence. If they are able to demonstrate to the system that their own claims about their proficiency are right (in this case that they can use the rule correctly), the system will be convinced by the argument. In the example in Fig. 7.4, the student is offered a test, and proves his or her argument by producing a correct sentence.

However, if the students are not able to demonstrate the validity of their claims (in this example, if they had been unable to produce a correct sentence), the system will try to confirm the correctness of its own representation by generating an identical sentence to that produced by the student, but based on the representations it has constructed in the student model. For example, in this case the system could predict that the student may use Spanish word order (e.g., *O João a confirmou*). Similarly, using the student model, the system could also predict that the learner may omit the hyphen with a correctly placed pronoun (e.g., *O João confirmou a*). If the student had offered either of these sentences as their response to the system's test, the system would have been satisfied that its own representation was correct, and therefore would not have

FIG. 7.4. Student justification.

allowed the student to override it. It was found that students will challenge the system in this way if they disagree with its representations in the student model (Bull & Pain, 1995).

An inspectable student model allows the model to be offered to the learner as a learning resource. Opening the model to learners for negotiation of their domain-focused beliefs supports their modeling of the target domain. In the following section we describe a system that extends the approach of collaborative student modeling demonstrated in Mr Collins, to a graphical environment.

STyLE-OLM—COLLABORATIVE STUDENT MODELING IN A GRAPHICAL ENVIRONMENT

STyLE-OLM addresses a conceptual understanding task, which is explored in learning technical terminology (STyLE-OLM is an Open Learner Modeling component in STyLE—a Scientific TerminologY Learning Environment). Understanding term meanings is important for comprehension and production of terminological texts, which follows a more general argument about the importance of word meanings in language learning (Singer, 1990). Generally, *concept learning research* refers to acquiring a domain conceptualization by applying correctly corresponding theories and methods; for example, generalization (inferring from examples), explanation (justifying certain properties), deduction (inferring specific knowledge about category exemplars), and analogy (reasoning using similarities) have been explored (Thagard, 1992). This is often not the case with learners who may misapply or fail to apply the correct classification rule. In educational contexts, both finding possible explanations for learners' conceptual errors and scaffolding learners' conceptual understanding play an essential role. STyLE-OLM addresses these tasks as demonstrated in a finance domain shortly.

STyLE-OLM (Dimitrova, Self, & Brna, 1999a) illustrates an interactive diagnostic approach where a learner and a computer system are involved in an ongoing dialogue about the conceptual model of the former.

It follows the collaborative student modeling demonstrated in Mr Collins and expands the interaction to allow both the learner and the system to use the same communicative means and to have reasonably symmetrical powers in maintaining the dialogue. STyLE-OLM adopts dialogue games for managing an interactive diagnostic dialogue in a graphical communication medium (Dimitrova, Self, & Brna, 1999b) and modal logic techniques for formally maintaining a jointly constructed learner model (Dimitrova, Self, & Brna, 2000a). Domain expertise encoded with conceptual graphs (Angelova, Nenkova, Boytcheva, & Nikolov, 2000) is imported.

The communication medium in STyLE-OLM is based on a graphical representation of conceptual graphs (Sowa, 1984). This medium takes advantage of the properties of diagrams to reduce the working memory load (Larkin & Simon, 1987), and facilitates both comprehending the model and performing the necessary inference (Stenning & Oberlander, 1995). Used as a language for system-learner communication, diagrams may bring forth additional cognitive processes activated by the learners' involvement in constructing external representations of their thoughts. The semantic properties of diagrams may affect the self-explanation provoking the learners to confront their problem comprehension (Cox, 1999). Furthermore, Cox argued that diagram construction "helps to turn one's initial internal representation into an external stimulus" (p. 353). Being a kind of semantic network, conceptual graphs are characterized by a high logical expressiveness (Stenning & Inder, 1995) and may be assumed to facilitate a potentially good mapping between the external representation and the learner's own (internal) mental model (Collins & Quillian, 1969).

STyLE-OLM provides two modes: DISCUSS, where learners can discuss aspects of their domain knowledge and influence the content of the learner model (Fig. 7.5), and BROWSE, where learners can inspect the current state of their learner model (Fig. 7.6).

The graphical tools on the top allow the students to manipulate the graph that will present the proposition of their communicative act. The learners add illocutionary force by selecting a dialogue move from the right area of the screen. STyLE-OLM adopts a flexibly structured communication in designing the interface, which has been found beneficial for promoting task-focused reflective interactions (Baker & Lund, 1997). Both the student and the system contribute to the discussion in the same way—by selecting a graph component and a dialogue move. The bottom text window shows a generated transcript of the dialogue. The learner can browse this textual form of the dialogue history or a graphical one. As the dialogue proceeds, the system makes plausible inferences about what else the learner believes on the basis of what is explicitly asserted, and from this, a dialogue strategy is determined. The dialogue is guided by general explanations of misconceptions, for example, that an entity may be believed to be a member of a class if it has some features of that class.

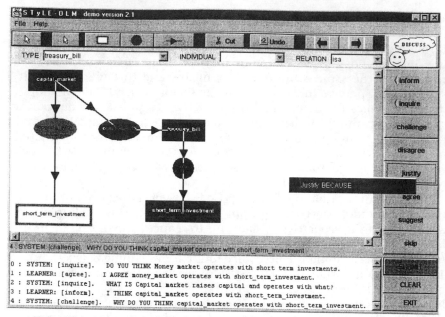

FIG. 7.5. STyLE-OLM in a DISCUSS mode—the learner is constructing a justification of their statement, after being challenged by the system.

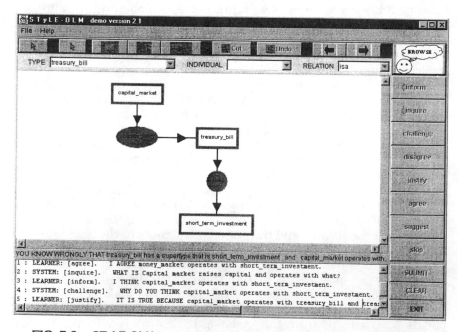

FIG. 7.6. STyLE-OLM in a BROWSE mode—the learner browses through their conceptual model.

The following example presents an example session with STyLE-OLM in a finance domain. STyLE-OLM is called in a situation where a learner is believed to know some aspects of the terms MONEY_MARKET and CAPITAL_MARKET but to often mix up these terms. The system initiates a dialogue to explore the learner's knowledge about these terms. The following is an extract from this interaction (note that this is a generated transcript—all communication actually occurs graphically, using the graph and menus):

STyLE-OLM[inquire] DO YOU THINK MONEY_MARKET operates with SHORT_TERM_INVESTMENTS.

Learner[agree] I AGREE MONEY_MARKET operates with SHORT_TERM_INVESTMENTS.

STyLE-OLM[inquire] WHAT IS CAPITAL_MARKET raises CAPITAL and operates with WHAT?

Learner[inform] I THINK CAPITAL_MARKET operates with SHORT_TERM_INVESTMENTS.

STyLE-OLM[challenge] WHY DO YOU THINK CAPITAL_MARKET operates with SHORT_TERM_INVESTMENTS?

Learner[justify] IT IS TRUE BECAUSE CAPITAL_MARKET operates with TREASURY_BILLS and TREASURY_BILL is a SHORT_TERM_INVESTMENT.

The screen shot in Fig. 7.5 depicts the environment at the moment when the learner constructs and submits his or her justification. STyLE-OLM challenges as the learner's statement is not completely correct:

STyLE-OLM[challenge] WHY DO YOU THINK CAPITAL_MARKET operates with TREASURY_BILLS and TREASURY_BILL is a SHORT_TERM_INVESTMENT?

At this time the student questions the robustness of his or her domain model. The learner switches to a browse mode to look through the current state of the learner model. Figure 7.6 presents this stage. The learner realizes that his or her belief that CAPITAL_MARKET operates with TREASURY_BILL and TREASURY_BILL is a SHORT_TERM_INVESTMENT is wrong. The system can now be requested to help in exploring the domain knowledge about these terms. The learner switches back to a discuss mode and asks:

Learner[inquire] IS IT TRUE TREASURY_BILL is a SHORT_TERM_INVESTMENT?

STyLE-OLM[inform] I KNOW TREASURY_BILL is a SHORT_TERM_INVESTMENT.

The learner now realizes that this belief is correct and challenges the other part of the wrong belief.

Learner[inquire] IS IT TRUE CAPITAL_MARKET operates with TREASURY_BILLS?

STyLE-OLM$_{[inform]}$ I DO NOT KNOW CAPITAL_MARKET operates with TREA-SURY_BILLS.

The learner has clarified the incorrect aspect of his or her beliefs. In following interactions the learner can possibly withdraw the claim that CAPITAL_MARKET operates with SHORT_TERM_INVESTMENTS ask what CAPITAL_MARKET does operate with, or explore his or her knowledge about SHORT_TERM_INVESTMENTS by making claims about other examples of SHORT-TERM INVESTMENTS.

STyLE-OLM has been used as an artifact to monitor reflective activities in interactive open learner modeling. An experimental study with seven postgraduate students at Leeds University was conducted; details of the study are given in Dimitrova, Self, and Brna (2000b). In sessions with STyLE-OLM, which lasted about 30 minutes, learners were asked to inspect their conceptual models (obtained from their presession drill performance), discuss, and possibly influence the content of these models.

Three kinds of situations promoting reflective modeling were identified: (a) the students render statements about their domain beliefs, thus they externalize their conceptual models; (b) the students go back to claims about their beliefs and (possibly) change these claims, thus they challenge the robustness of their models; and (c) the students investigate arguments to support their beliefs, thus they search for grounds and relationships in their models. The subjects were classified into two groups according to their initial models—*more knowledgeable* students (four subjects) whose conceptual models presented mostly known facts, and *less knowledgeable* students (three subjects) whose models incorporated mainly incomplete and erroneous knowledge.

The more knowledgeable subjects were relatively well-engaged in discussions about their models. They experienced on average a total of 12.5 ($SD = 4$) reflective activities in a session. Although the interactions with the less knowledgeable students were shorter and had frequent focus changes, these students browsed their models more often when provoked by the system's inquiries or challenges. As a result, the average total number of reflective activities that the less knowledgeable students were involved in is only slightly lower: 11.3 ($SD = 1$). Figure 7.7 presents the distribution of the reflective activities among the two learner groups.

Predominantly, learners rendered statements about their domain beliefs. The more knowledgeable learners were involved in more diverse types of dialogue exchanges. By contrast, typical situations where less knowledgeable subjects were provoked to externalize their models were sequences of a system's inquiry followed by the learners browsing through their model, ending with the learners' statement to change the information in the model (the last move could well change the discussion topic). Reflective activities of the second type were usually observed in situations where learners looked back at their claims both in the dialogue history and the obtained learner model, after they were challenged

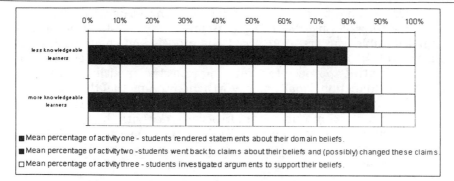

FIG. 7.7. Distribution of the three reflective activities monitored in the sessions with STyLE-OLM. For every learner the percentage of each type of reflective activity, in respect to all reflective activities that this learner has experienced, is calculated. Then, the mean percentage for the three reflective activities for both groups—less knowledgeable and more knowledgeable learners—are obtained.

by STyLE-OLM. The less knowledgeable learners experienced such situations more often because their claims were more frequently challenged by the system. These subjects tended to browse their models in order to check the correctness of the claims they had made. Some more knowledgeable learners did not go back to claims they had made. There was not significant difference in the number of justifications, included in the third group of reflective activities, made by each type of learner. However, regarding active inquiries where students grounded their domain beliefs by asking questions to clarify aspects of the domain relying on the system's domain expertise, our interaction analysis shows that more knowledgeable learners constructed questions exploring aspects not discussed yet, but following the preceding discourse (as in the earlier extract). In contrast, a common pattern with the less knowledgeable students was to "answer" a system's question by posing it back to the system (the reflectiveness of such inquiries is dubious).

The occurrence of the preceding situations in interactions with STyLE-OLM allowed us to make claims about the *presence of reflection.* Regarding its effectiveness, some factors have been monitored. We found that the scope of articulated beliefs has been extending in a coherent manner, hence, not only have the learners recalled aspects of their models, they have also been able to build a consistent picture connecting related domain facts. Various alternatives have been provided for the students to explore the domain (definitions, situations, exemplars of a more generic term, etc.), so that they could study the domain in depth, finding different aspects to expand their models. These factors are by no means comprehensive. The effectiveness of reflection in STyLE-OLM needs further investigation.

STyLE-OLM has been able to engage more knowledgeable learners in reflective interactions about the domain as well as to provoke less knowledgeable learners to inspect their models and challenge the robustness of these models. We may then argue that STyLE-OLM demonstrates a fruitful approach for fostering reflective modeling through a graphical interaction. Finally, it is worth mentioning that the subjects in our study did not agree regarding their preference for graphics or text as a basic method of communication. In accordance with this observation, a later section elaborates on the requirements suggested by different learner cognitive styles, and on the design of learning environments that promote reflective modeling.

PeerISM: HUMAN–HUMAN COLLABORATIVE STUDENT MODELING

Unlike Mr Collins and Style-OLM, peerISM (peer Inspectable Student Model) is completely domain independent (i.e., it is not a general approach implemented in a specific domain, but the implementation itself is domain independent). Examples have been described for linguistics (Bull & Brna, 1997) and French as a foreign language (Bull, Brna, Critchley, Davie, & Holzherr, 1999). As a contrast to the previous language domains, we here take the example of the formation of the Solar System as the target domain.

PeerISM is used by pairs of learners. Some students gain much from interaction through peerISM, whereas other pairs simply do not work together at all. To overcome the problem of the latter, an Artificial Peer was designed to work with individuals whose partner was missing (Bull et al., 1999). This is in some ways similar to the collaborative modeling described previously in this chapter. Therefore we here concentrate on human–human collaborative student modeling, the primary purpose of peerISM.

In order for students to use peerISM, tutors must supply questions to the system, which should be answered by the learners. No further tutor involvement is then required. The following describes an interaction with peerISM:

1. Students independently answer the tutor's questions in peerISM.
2. Students evaluate their answers on a four-point quantitative scale (very good, good, variable, problematic), and also makes notes for themselves if they wish.
3. Students view the work of their partners.
4. Students evaluate the answers of their partners, providing qualitative feedback and quantitative feedback (on the same four-point scale).
5. Student assess their confidence in the feedback they have given.
6. Each student views the peer evaluation received, together with his or her self-evaluation and answers, and comments from the system

based on both the self-assessment and the peer evaluation. These three components form the inspectable student model (Fig. 7.8).

7. Students may make comments to their partners, about the feedback presented in the student model; and they may comment to peerISM about the system's contribution to their student model, thus updating the model.

8. The two students come together to discuss their respective student models, preferably face-to-face.

9. Students may again update their learner model.

Reflection and domain modeling occur at all stages of the peerISM interaction. First, students are involved in formulating their responses to a set of tutor questions. Their work has a real audience—a peer who is working on the same topic and who will read their contribution thoroughly. In addition to writing their answers, students must evaluate these answers at least quantitatively. This is designed to ensure that students have fully considered their arguments before viewing those of a peer and have an explicit awareness of their own views, including areas where they lack knowledge or understanding.

In our example, the first question set for students is: What evidence is there that the sun, the planets and most of the moons in the solar system all formed at the same time? Student 1 (S1) offers *like rotation* and *radioactive dating* as arguments for the singular formation of the solar system. Student 2 (S2) also suggests *radioactive dating* as evidence when responding to the question. S2 also raises the point that *the moon contains materials found on Earth*, suggesting that it arose as a result of impact with the earth, whereby it was ejected and then trapped by the earth's gravitational field. However, S2 is not sure how important this fact is for the argument about the formation of the solar system. At this stage, learners each have their own separate model of the Solar System's formation, and the system has a simple representation for each student of his or her believed proficiency, based on his or her quantitative self-evaluations.

In the second stage, students view the work of a peer, possibly becoming aware of new arguments they had not previously considered. Learners evaluate their partner's answers quantitatively and qualitatively. Their partner's work may confirm their view of the domain, or they may find that to provide their evaluation they must try to reconcile conflicts between their own beliefs and those of their partner. The learners' awareness is raised of potential strengths and weaknesses in their models. Evaluating the feedback they give reinforces this reflection.

On receiving S1's answer, S2 sees that S1 considers *like rotation* to be important, and agrees with this argument. Thus S2's mental model is changed to some extent—at the least, to realize an area that requires further investigation. Similarly, S1 is prompted to consider the *composition of the moon*. The peer evaluations are a form of asynchronous communication designed to lay the foundation for later synchronous, face-to-face communication. Writing the peer assessment helps render the learners' mental models more explicit. Each learner now has a modified model of his or her own knowledge and a partial model of his or her partner's beliefs.

Self and peer assessment have been suggested to positively affect learning with useful formative applications (Mowl & Pain, 1995; Somervell, 1993; Stefani, 1994). As stated earlier, we use self-assessment in peerISM to ensure that individuals have thought through their own arguments fully, before viewing the work of a partner. Peer assessment is then employed to open up new possibilities to the recipient and giver of feedback and to reinforce previous learning. Thus, by the time students later view their respective learner models, which are created in part from this self and peer assessment, and progress to face-to-face domain-focused discussion, they have a strong foundation on which to base their interaction.

In the next stage, students receive feedback on their own work. Again there may be new insights or conflicts. Students view this feedback in the student model, alongside their own answers and self-evaluation, and system commentary derived from the two sets of evaluations (Fig. 7.8).

On viewing the student model, S1 and S2 are confronted with more information about each other's beliefs about the domain than they had from viewing and commenting on their partner's work. For example, S1 finds that although the argument about like rotation is relevant, it is more complicated than previously assumed (with Venus and Uranus, and some moons, apparently contradicting the argument). This may lead to renewed updating of mental models. PeerISM has now gained a further proficiency indicator for each student (which may or may not conflict with the first), provided by the quantitative peer evaluations.

Self and peer evaluations are definite—learners must choose between the values *very good*, *good*, *variable*, and *problematic* for the quantitative evaluations for each question. Elaboration is then provided through qualitative commentary. However, the system's evaluation is less precise. It is designed to provoke reflection, but as it is basing its assessment on potentially inaccurate evaluations, the language used is sometimes vague. In the example of the inspectable student model given here, the system knows there is a problem, because the self and peer assessments are different. However, it knows only that one of the learners is having trouble, but not which one. In cases where the evaluations are similar, it is more cautious, suggesting that there is "probably" a problem, or that the student "probably" understands the topic quite well. The role of the system's contribution to the student model is, then, to direct students' attention to areas of agreement and disagreement. Resolution through communicative interaction is the task of the students.

The facility is also available for students to provide additional information to update their learner model, which may be useful, for example,

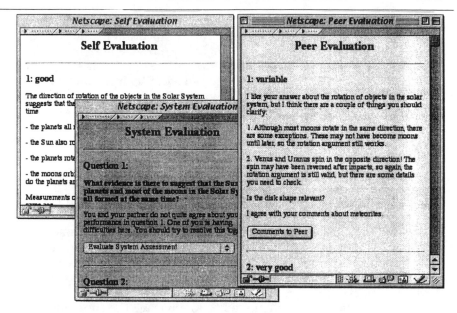

FIG. 7.8.   The peerISM human–human collaborative student model.

when students come to work on an area for which this is a prerequisite, or for future matching of partners in the course (see next section). Options include "My partner is right: I do not understand as well as I thought I did"; "Now I have discussed this with my partner, I understand it much better."

As has been seen, before viewing their respective student models, students are already aware of any differences between their self-evaluations and their models of their partner's knowledge. On viewing their student model, differences between their self-assessments and feedback received from their partners become salient. This is further supported by remarks from the system based on the underlying models formed from the quantitative self and peer evaluations. On viewing the student model, learners may also send comments to their partners, about the feedback they received. This is a further source of reflection for both partners.

Because, at this stage, all target material has been fully considered by all partners, with reference to their own knowledge and in comparison with their partners' beliefs, there is a strong foundation for face-to-face domain modeling to take place. Thus, after viewing their learner models separately, students come together to resolve any remaining problems. A good way to effect this is for the tutor to require a joint submission of the answers to the peerISM questions, taking the two student models as a starting point. Sharing student models in this way has been suggested to foster spontaneous peer tutoring (Bull & Broady, 1997).

It can be seen that during many stages of the interaction, learners are explicitly formulating their views for communication to and with their partners. This occurs in writing when they provide peer feedback for their partners' student models, and when they comment on information in their own student models, received from their partners. Writing comments allows time for reflection on the domain during the formulation of the comments. When learners come together face-to-face, the communicative interaction becomes more intensive as they discuss their learner models, and collaborate or tutor each other when a discrepancy is found.

In summary: peerISM engages pairs of learners in intensive content-based discussion and in content-based reflection. This is achieved in part through an approach that encourages students to help themselves through seeking to help one another.

In working with peerISM, students reflect on their own understanding—in the setting described in this chapter—of the formation of the solar system. They are able to propose a theory-based argument for the proposition that the solar system was formed at the same "moment" in time. To achieve this they must construct an internalized model of the formation of the solar system, and then envisage the consequences of this model. They have to externalize these models in the form of a list of arguments. Each argument has an associated student confidence that reflects the students' own understanding of their own model of the solar system. PeerISM provides support for this process.

PeerISM also provides support for students to improve their model of the solar system (in this example of its use) through peer discussion. By supporting a student giving feedback to another student, peerISM helps the learner to understand the process of learning through gaining insight into the doubts of another student as well as the advances made by the other learner. This experience has the effect of improving the participants' domain models, and aiding students in building their own models and comprehending the models that others have.

In the next section we introduce another system that uses human–human collaborative student modeling, but that focuses on the use of the resulting models to match suitable partners, rather than using the models as a source for promoting reflection.

I-HELP—MATCHING PARTNERS
BASED ON DISTRIBUTED USER MODELS

I-Help matches students having difficulty with some aspect of their course, with capable peer helpers, according to a variety of characteristics: knowledge level, helpfulness, eagerness to participate, availability, cognitive style, and preferred characteristics in a learning partner. I-Help differs from the previous systems in that the collaborative student modeling is not the focus of the interaction. Users do contribute to their own user model, and peers also contribute to the user models of other students. The major difference from the previously discussed systems is that these user models are used to facilitate peer matching, rather than themselves being an object of discussion. (Nevertheless, both helper and "helpee" are still expected to benefit through the reflection that takes place during a help session.)

I–Help is domain-independent. Examples have been described for computer science (Greer, McCalla, Vassileva, Deters, Bull, & Kettel, 2001), and medical education (Greer & Bull, 2000). Before usage of I–Help commences, tutors provide the topic areas of their courses. Learners then select the appropriate topic each time they submit a help request.

I–Help is intended for use by large numbers of students. I–Help users have their own personal agents to take care of their needs (Vassileva et al., 1999). I–Help user models are fragmented across the I–Help system and are computed only at the time the information is required, which is necessary because the models are continually being updated from a range of information sources (McCalla, Vassileva, Greer, & Bull, 2000). For each user model, these sources include: logs of activity in I–Help (for the eagerness measure); self-evaluation and preferences (for knowledge level, availability, cognitive style, and preferred characteristics in a learning partner); and peer evaluations (for knowledge level and helpfulness). Thus representations in an individual's user model may change even when he or she is not personally using I–Help because new peer evaluations may come in at any moment.

Figure 7.9 shows some of the methods of contributing information about oneself to the user model, and Fig. 7.10 illustrates peer evaluations, which are given after completion of a help session.

I–Help, therefore, differs from the previous systems. Its purpose is to use the distributed user models to locate appropriate peer helpers for students with a problem. This is further elaborated in the following section.

COLLABORATIVE STUDENT MODELING AND COGNITIVE STYLE— INTEGRATING THE APPROACHES

This section is more speculative. Here we consider how the four systems already introduced may be integrated to provide appropriate kinds of interaction for learners with different cognitive styles.

There has been a great deal of research into cognitive style, but this has focused mostly on the wholist–analytic aspect of cognitive style (Riding & Cheema, 1991), which is similar to field dependent–independent (Witkin, Moore, Goodenough, & Cox, 1977) and holist–serialist (Pask, 1976). In addition to the wholist–analytic dimension of their cognitive style classification, Riding and Cheema also defined an independent verbal–imagery dimension, measuring the extent to which individuals represent information verbally or in image form (as opposed to the processing of information, which relates to the wholist–analytic aspect). It is the verbal–imagery dimension that is most important to our argument in this chapter.

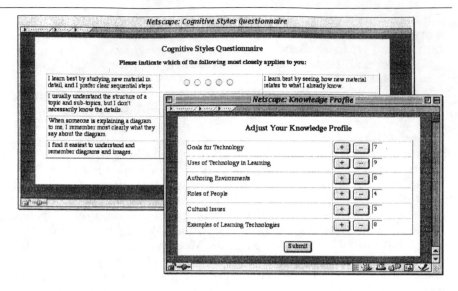

FIG. 7.9.   Self-assessment and cognitive style.

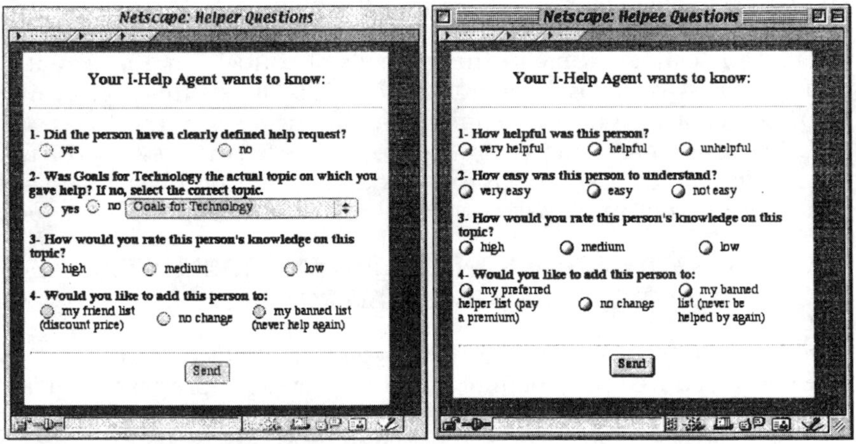

FIG. 7.10.   Helper and helpee evaluation questionnaires.

The interface for collaborative student modeling in Mr Collins is textual, as in the implemented example it is grammar rules that are being modeled. It is feasible that more visual components could be introduced, for example, using boxes and arrows to indicate the position of pronouns in different kinds of sentence. However, because the pronouns also undergo phonetic contractions, there must necessarily be some prominent textual components. Indeed, because we are dealing with the written language, it is impossible to reduce the textual component significantly.

In contrast, the interface of STyLE-OLM is more graphical, using conceptual graphs. Conceptual graphs provide an easy interpretation of information, although the concepts could also be rendered more textually for those learners who are located on the more extreme verbal pole of Riding and Cheema's (1991) verbal–imagery dimension. Similarly, some of the textual labels might be presented graphically, for more visual learners.

For domains that can be represented in textual or image form, some combination of the approaches of Mr Collins and STyLE-OLM would be useful, to allow better adaptation to the individual cognitive style of learners. However, further investigation would be required here; some studies have found that links between performance, cognitive style and presentation format are not straightforward. Indeed, in some cases these associations are even the reverse of what might be expected (McKay 1999a, 1999b). Thus, although it would be nice to allow the system to infer the interface to use in each case, students might instead be given the choice of a textual or graphical environment, in domains for which either may be appropriate.

The major difference between the aforementioned systems and peerISM is that the collaborative modeling of the former is between student and system, whereas collaborative modeling in peerISM occurs mainly between the students themselves, with some additional system input. The current implementation of peerISM uses only textual input. However, it could easily be developed to enable graphical interaction if learners so wish. This would require a consideration of matching learners on the verbal–imagery dimension to facilitate communication, inasmuch as individuals tend to answer questions using a graphical or written style compatible with their cognitive style—that is, verbalizers use fewer diagrams in their responses (Riding & Douglas, 1993). Furthermore, there is some evidence that students are at least implicitly aware of the kind of presentation they believe suits them best (Riding & Watts, 1997), and they may therefore become dissatisfied with their partners' interactions if their cognitive styles differ.

I-Help also includes peer modeling as one of its sources of user model data. In contrast to peerISM, I-Help does not assume that individuals are already paired. Indeed, as described in the previous section, one of the main aims of I-Help is to locate an appropriate peer helper to respond to a particular help request of a student. In addition to comprising self-assessment, peer evaluations, and system modeling, user modeling in I-Help is also concerned with different kinds of information about the student. These include knowledge levels, helpfulness, eagerness to participate, and cognitive style. I-Help uses both the verbal–imagery and holist–analytic dimensions of Riding and Cheema's (1991) cognitive style classification, each of these being more or less important for different kinds of help request and for different learners. Six question types were identified as relevant in the peer help scenario (Bull & Greer, 2000), one of which makes full use of the verbal–imagery dimension: "Can you suggest any good resources for … ?" Whereas I-Help allows only textual input, recommendations of materials from a helper may be for any kind of presentation. These recommendations may be URLs that the helpee can access directly, or textbooks and articles. It is assumed that a verbalizer will suggest resources suitable for another verbalizer, and an imager will suggest resources appropriate for another imager. A bi-modal on the verbal–imagery dimension should be able to adapt to the presentation of the materials recommended. (However, a bimodal can only recommend resources to another bimodal because they may suggest materials that are stronger on either text or graphics.) The argument for like-matching should hold true regardless of whether, at least in certain contexts, imagers learn best from graphical materials and verbalizers from text (Riding & Ashmore, 1980), or interactions of presentation format and cognitive style are more complex and unexpected (McKay 1999a, 1999b). Future work will examine the interaction between the matching of recommendations to cognitive style, to help clarify the inconsistencies in research to date. This will occur through comparing the cognitive style of individuals and the peer evaluations for this kind of question, which occur subsequent to a help session. In addition, the next version of I-Help will include a more graphical, a textual, and a mixed interface.

This flexibility in presentation is also recommended for a system combining the features of Mr Collins, STyLE-OLM, peerISM, and I-Help in a collaborative learner modeling context. The textual input style of Mr Collins might well suit certain learners (e.g., verbalizers—although more research is needed), whereas the graphical approach of STyLE-OLM would suit others (e.g., imagers). This is because, despite the uncertainty of the effects of presentation mode on performance for different cognitive styles, some individuals tend to produce graphics in their own responses, whereas others use purely textual representations (Cox, 1999; Riding & Douglas, 1993). PeerISM provides the context for human–human collaborative student modeling for pairs of students who prefer interaction with another person. I-Help provides the match-making service to ensure that peerISM partners are suited according to cognitive style and task requirements. I-Help can also run alongside this new integrated system to provide peer help for those who wish to make a help request.

Another important factor to consider is the kind of interaction preferred by individuals. For example, Riechmann and Grasha (1974) distinguished between collaborative and competitive learners—the former believe that they learn best by interaction and sharing, and would perhaps gain much from the peerISM or I-Help approach; the latter learn in order to outperform peers. Such students are less likely to share their knowledge in peerISM; they may seek help in I-Help, but may not accept many help requests from others. For them, the approaches of Mr Collins and STyLE-OLM may be more suitable. Other distinctions made by Riechmann and Grasha included independent learners who like to think for themselves, preferring to work alone, but willing to listen to the ideas of others. Independent learners might prefer Mr Collins and STyLE-OLM. Participant learners do not undertake much work outside of the course requirements, but do take part in class activities. They participate with others if this is one of the requirements. Such learners may or may not choose the approach of any of the systems discussed here, and any choice made will not necessarily be the most effective for them. Dependent learners also learn only what is required, and similar usage patterns might be found as for participant learners. Avoidant learners are either disinterested or overwhelmed by the classroom. Disinterested individuals are unlikely to use any of the computational approaches; however, those who are overwhelmed might indeed use the systems described here, in particular, Mr Collins and STyLE-OLM.

Given the individual differences in cognitive style (Riding & Cheema, 1991) and learning style (Riechmann & Grasha, 1974) presented here, we propose an integrated system combining the approaches of Mr Collins, STyLE-OLM, peerISM, and I-Help. As described previously, Mr Collins and STyLE-OLM will provide textual and graphical interfaces respectively, whereas peerISM will offer a more social alternative. I-Help will manage the matching of individuals in the peerISM component, and help others decide between the Mr Collins and STyLE-OLM approaches. Standard I-Help help sessions will also be available alongside the other approaches. In some domains, one or two of these may be appropriate; in others, perhaps all will be relevant. Assuming the modeling and the domain allow each of the approaches, different instantiations of the system might still be used in the same way by some individuals, as it appears that cognitive styles are stable (Riding, Glass, Butler, & Pleydell-Pearce, 1997). However, others, such as participant or dependent learners (Riechmann & Grasha, 1974), might still use only those approaches that have been explicitly prescribed.

SUMMARY

This chapter demonstrated how intelligent learning environments may be used to promote reflective modeling in learners. The approaches described focused on different aspects of collaborative student modeling, each of which encourages learners to become more explicitly aware of their beliefs about a domain, and helps guide the student toward a more accurate domain model.

Approaches were described that use a textual interaction in the collaborative modeling process (Mr Collins, peerISM, and I-Help), and a graphical collaborative modeling environment was also presented (STyLE-OLM). Some of the interactions occur between the student and the system (Mr Collins and STyLE-OLM), whereas others involve student–student distributed interaction (peerISM and I-Help), or face-to-face interaction (peerISM).

These systems are each useful for certain kinds of learner, but no single one is likely to be the best approach for all learners. We therefore concluded that using the cognitive style identification in I-Help, learners could be matched not only with other learners as occurs currently in I-Help, but could also be guided toward one of the other systems as would be most suitable according to their cognitive style.

ACKNOWLEDGMENTS

Mr Collins formed part of the first author's PhD research, funded by the Economic and Social Research Council. The supervision of Helen Pain is gratefully acknowledged. The research on STyLE-OLM is being carried out as part of the second author's PhD studies supported by the British ORS program. John Self's supervision on this work is greatly appreciated. STyLE-OLM is part of the Leeds team's work on the EU-funded LARFLAST project aimed at developing intelligent tools for learning scientific terminology. I-Help is an ongoing project of the ARIES Laboratory at the University of Saskatchewan. Many people have been involved in the work, in particular Ralph Deters, Jim Greer, Lori Kettel, Gordon McCalla, and Julita Vassileva. I-Help is funded by the Canadian Telelearning Network of Centers of Excellence.

REFERENCES

Angelova, G., Nenkova, A., Boytcheva, Sv., & Nikolov, T. (2000). CGs as a knowledge representation core in a complex language learning environment. In B. Ganter & G. W. Mineau (Eds.), *International conference on conceptual structures* (pp. 45–58). Berlin: Springer.

Baker, M. J., & Lund, K. (1997). Promoting reflective interactions in a computer-supported collaborative learning environment. *Journal of Computer Assisted Learning, 13*, 175–193.

Bull, S., & Brna, P. (1997). What does Susan know that Paul doesn't? (and vice versa): Contributing to each other's student model. In B. du Boulay & R. Mizoguchi (Eds.), *Artificial intelligence in education: Knowledge and media in learning systems* (pp. 568–570). Amsterdam: IOS Press.

Bull, S., Brna, P., Critchley, S., Davie, K., & Holzherr, C. (1999). The missing peer, artificial peers and the enhancement of human–human collaborative student modeling. In S. P. Lajoie & M. Vivet (Eds.), *Artificial intelligence in education— Open learning environments: New computational technologies to support learning, exploration and collaboration* (pp. 269–276). Amsterdam: IOS Press.

Bull, S., Brna, P., & Pain, H. (1995). Extending the scope of the student model. *User Modeling and User Adapted Interaction, 5*(1), 45–65.

Bull, S., & Broady, E. (1997). Spontaneous peer tutoring from sharing student models. In B. du Boulay & R. Mizoguchi (Eds.), *Artificial intelligence in education: Knowledge and media in learning systems* (pp. 143–150). Amsterdam: IOS Press.

Bull, S., & Greer, J. (2000). Peer help for problem-based learning. In S. S. Young, J. Greer, H. Maurer, & Y. S. Chee (Eds.), *Proceedings of the international confer-

ence on computers in education/international conference on computer-assisted instruction (pp. 1007–1015). Taiwan: National Tsing Hua University.

Bull, S., & Pain, H. (1995). "Did I say what I think I said, and do you agree with me?": Inspecting and questioning the student model. In J. Greer (Ed.), *Artificial intelligence in education, 1995: Proceedings of AI-ED'95—7th world conference on artificial intelligence in education* (pp. 501–508). Charlottesville, VA: Association for the Advancement of Computing in Education.

Chi, M. T. H., Bassok, M., Lewis, M. W., Reimann, P., & Glaser, R. (1989). Self-explanations: How students study and use examples in learning to solve problems. *Cognitive Science, 13,* 145–182.

Clancey, W. J. (1992). Representations of knowing: In defense of cognitive apprenticeship. *Journal of Artificial Intelligence in Education, 3*(2), 139–168.

Collins, A., & Quillian, M. (1969). Semantic hierarchies and cognitive economy. *Journal of Verbal Learning and Verbal Behavior, 8*(2), 7–240.

Cox, R. (1999). Representation construction, externalised cognition and individual differences. *Learning and Instruction, 9,* 343–363.

Dewey, J. (1933). *How we think: A restatement of the relation of reflective thinking to the educative process.* Lexington, MA: Heath.

Dillenbourg, P., & Self, J. A. (1995). Designing human–computer collaborative learning. In C. O'Malley (Ed.), *Computer supported collaborative learning* (pp. 254–264). Berlin: Springer.

Dimitrova, V., Self, J. A., & Brna, P. (1999a). STyLE-OLM—an interactive diagnosis tool in a terminology learning environment. In R. Morales, H. Pain, S. Bull, & J. Kay (Eds.), *Proceedings of workshop on open, interactive, and other overt approaches to learner modeling* (pp. 25–34). Available as Technical Report 99/9. Computer-Based Learning Unit, University of Leeds.

Dimitrova, V., Self, J. A., & Brna, P. (1999b). The interactive maintenance of open learner models. In S. P. Lajoie & M. Vivet (Eds.), *Artificial intelligence in education—Open learning environments: New computational technologies to support learning, exploration and collaboration* (pp. 405–412). Amsterdam: IOS Press.

Dimitrova, V., Self, J. A., & Brna, P. (2000a). Maintaining a jointly constructed student model. In S. A. Cerri & D. Dochev (Eds.), *Artificial intelligence: Methodology, systems, and applications* (pp. 221–231). Berlin: Springer.

Dimitrova, V., Self, J. A., & Brna, P. (2000b). *Applying interactive open learner models to learning technical terminology.* Technical report 00/15. Computer Based Learning Unit, University of Leeds, England.

Ellis, R. (1992). *Second language acquisition and language pedagogy.* Clevedon: Multilingual Matters.

Elsom-Cook, M. (1986). *Artificial intelligence and computer assisted instruction.* CITE Report No. 4, Institute of Educational Technology. Milton Keynes, UK: The Open University.

Elsom-Cook, M. (1988). Guided discovery tutoring and bounded user modeling. In J. A. Self (Ed.), *Artificial intelligence and human learning* (pp. 65–178). London: Chapman and Hall.

Goodman, B., Soller, A., Linton, F., & Gaimari, R. (1998). Encouraging student reflection and articulation using a learning companion. *International Journal of Artificial Intelligence in Education, 9*(3–4), 237–255.

Greer, J., & Bull, S. (2000). Computer support for collaboration in medical education. *Clinical and Investigative Medicine, 23*(4), 270–274.

Greer, J., McCalla, G., Vassileva, J., Deters, R., Bull, S., & Kettel, L. (2001). Lessons learned in deploying a multi-agent learning support system: The I-Help experience. In J. D. Moore, C. L. Redfield, & W. L. Johnson (Eds.), *Artificial intelligence in education* (pp. 410–421). Amsterdam: IOS Press.

Jackson, J. L., Krajcik, J., & Soloway, E. (1998). The design of guided learner-adaptable scaffolding in interactive learning environments. *ACM'98 Proceedings of human factors in computing systems* (pp. 187–194). New York: ACM Press/Addison-Wesley.

King, P. M., & Kitchener, K. S. (1994). *Developing reflective judgement.* San Francisco: Jossey-Bass.

Kolb, D. A. (1984). *Experiential learning: experience as the source of learning and development.* Englewood Cliffs, NJ: Prentice-Hall.

Larkin, J. H., & Simon, H. A. (1987). Why a diagram is (sometimes) worth ten thousand words. *Cognitive Science, 11,* 65–99.

McCalla, G., Vassileva, J., Greer, J., & Bull, S. (2000). Active learner modeling. In G. Gauthier, C. Frasson, & K. VanLehn (Eds.), *Intelligent tutoring systems* (pp. 53–62). Berlin, Heidelberg: Springer-Verlag.

McKay, E. (1999a). An investigation of text-based instructional materials enhanced with graphics. *Educational Psychology, 19*(3), 323–335.

McKay, E. (1999b). Exploring the effect of graphical metaphors on the performance of learning computer programming concepts in adult learners: A pilot study. *Educational Psychology, 19*(4), 471–487.

Mowl, G., & Pain, R. (1995). Using self and peer assessment to improve students' essay writing: A case study from geography. *Innovations in Education and Training International, 32*(4), 324–335.

Pask, G. (1976). Styles and strategies of learning. *British Journal of Educational Psychology, 46,* 128–148.

Perry, W. G. (1970). *Forms of intellectual and ethical development in the college years: A scheme.* New York: Holt, Rinehart & Winston.

Riding, R. J., & Ashmore, J. (1980). Verbaliser–imager learning style and children's recall of information presented in pictorial versus written form. *Educational Studies, 6*(2), 141–145.

Riding, R., & Cheema, I. (1991). Cognitive styles—an overview and integration. *Educational Psychology, 11*(3–4), 193–215.

Riding, R., & Douglas, G. (1993). The effect of cognitive style and mode of presentation on learning performance. *British Journal of Educational Psychology, 63,* 297–307.

Riding, R. J., Glass, A., Butler, S. R., & Pleydell-Pearce, C. W. (1997). Cognitive style and individual differences in EEG alpha during information processing. *Educational Psychology, 17*(1–2), 219–234.

Riding, R. J., & Watts, M. (1997). The effect of cognitive style on the preferred format of instructional material. *Educational Psychology, 17*(1–2), 179–183.

Riechmann, S. W., & Grasha, A. F. (1974). A rational approach to developing and assessing the construct validity of a student learning style scales instrument. *The Journal of Psychology, 87,* 213–223.

Schmidt, R. W. (1990). The role of consciousness in second language learning. *Applied Linguistics, 11,* 129–158.

Schön, D. A. (1987). *Educating the reflective practitioner.* San Francisco: Jossey-Bass.

Self, J. A. (1999). The defining characteristics of intelligent tutoring systems research: ITSs care, precisely. *International Journal of Artificial Intelligence in Education, 10,* 350–364.

Self, J. A., Karakirik, E., Kor, A. L., Tedesco, P., & Dimitrova, V. (2000). Computer-based strategies for articulate reflection (and reflective articulation). In S. S. Young, J. Greer, H. Maurer, & Y. S. Chee (Eds.), *Proceedings of the international conference on computers in education/international conference on computer-assisted instruction* (pp. 3–12). Taiwan: National Tsing Hua University.

Singer, M. (1990). *Psychology of language: An introduction of sentence and discourse processes*. Mahwah, NJ: Lawrence Erlbaum Associates.

Somervell, H. (1993). Issues in assessment, enterprise and higher education: The case for self-, peer and collaborative assessment. *Assessment and Evaluation in Higher Education, 18*(3), 221–233.

Sowa, J. (1984). *Conceptual structures: Information processing in mind and machine*. New York: Addison-Wesley.

Stefani, L. A. J. (1994). Peer, self and tutor assessment: Relative reliabilities. *Studies in Higher Education, 19*(1), 69–75.

Stenning, K., & Inder, R. (1995). Applying semantic concepts to analyzing media and modalities. In J. Glasgow, N. H. Narayanan, & B. Chandrasekaran (Eds.), *Diagrammatic reasoning: Cognitive and computational perspectives* (pp. 303–338). Menlo Park, CA: AAAI Press.

Stenning, K., & Oberlander, J. (1995). A cognitive theory of graphical and linguistic reasoning: logic and implementation. *Cognitive Science, 19*, 97–140.

Thagard, P. (1992). *Conceptual revolutions*. Princeton, NJ: Princeton University Press.

Vassileva, J., Greer, J., McCalla, G., Deters, R., Zapata, D., Mudgal, C., & Grant, S. (1999). A multi-agent design of a peer help environment. In S. P. Lajoie & M. Vivet (Eds.), *Artificial intelligence in education—Open learning environments: New computational technologies to support learning, exploration and collaboration* (pp. 38–45). Amsterdam: IOS Press.

Wenden, A. (1987). How to be a successful language learner: Insights and prescriptions from L2 learners. In A. Wenden & J. Rubin (Eds.), *Learner strategies in language learning* (pp. 103–117). London: Prentice Hall.

White, B., Shimoda, T., & Frederiksen, J. (1999). Enabling students to construct theories of collaborative inquiry and reflective learning: Computer support for metacognitive development. *International Journal of Artificial Intelligence in Education, 10*, 151–182.

Winograd, T., & Flores, F. (1986). *Understanding computers and cognition: A new foundation for design*. Cambridge, MA: Addison Wesley.

Witkin, H. A., Moore, C. A., Goodenough, D. R., & Cox, P. W. (1977). Field-dependent and field-independent cognitive styles and their implications. *Review of Educational Research, 47*, 1–64.

Wolff, D. (1994). Computers in classroom research. *Computers and Education, 23*(1–2), 133–142.

III

Collaboration
and Language

Modeling the Modelers: Communicating About Content Through Shared External Representations

Paul Brna
University of Northumbria at Newcastle

Mark Burton
ARM, Cambridge

WHY MODEL THE MODELERS?

We model when we learn about the world around us, and learning to model includes describing the world in a variety of ways, being able to predict the consequences of changes in conditions, and knowing how to make links between theoretical constructs and the world. Modeling the modeler is about understanding how people learn together and how they interact with the world. In this chapter we examine some aspects of the ways in which modelers work together as they coconstruct a model of a fragment of the world. We do this by describing a computational model that we built of a group of learners interacting through dialogue and through an external representation of the model. The approach taken is based on the assumption that students should learn through the adoption of different ways of using dialogue (dialogue roles). We also speculate on what this might mean for supporting people learning to model.

Learning to model involves a large number of activities that are not necessarily directly thought of as "modeling" but are somehow necessary to do! These activities were described by Lave and Wenger (1990) as *legitimate peripheral practices*—from learning how to use a spreadsheet to designing an experiment, from making exploratory observations to producing a formal mathematical model, from checking the fit of a model against the data to discussing the problems of the model with colleagues. Many of these activities require that some external representation is constructed. This may be intended either to personally benefit the representation's constructor or be used to describe/discuss/develop aspects of the model.

If an external representation is used by learners to develop their conceptual understanding of physical phenomena, then we might expect important consequences that relate to the manner in which communication takes place. The understanding of these consequences can be explored in a number of ways. Here we examine what can be learned from modeling the process of describing/discussing/developing a model.

Modeling the modeler is the enterprise of building different kinds of models to explore and describe a variety of modeling activities in a number of different contexts. The resulting models may be descriptive or predictive, may be applicable to individuals with specific experience and knowledge or to groups of individuals with varying backgrounds and levels of achievement indicating some notion of "normal" experience, and to expert modelers or to novice modelers. Some modeling of the modeler is used to develop a better understanding of the cognitive and social processes at work, whereas other modeling may have didactic goals—that is, aimed at changing the world for the people being modeled.

Changing the world for those modeled may involve either the facilitation of current tasks to free up personal (cognitive, social) resources to be able to concentrate on other aspects of the work or the introduction of effectively novel activities that might fundamentally change the way the world is considered.

An example of facilitation might entail modeling students using a pocket calculator with a view to comprehending how to reduce the likelihood of the student making a mistake—either through helping the student to avoid misunderstanding the workings of the calculator or through helping to ease the cognitive load on the student. Work by Harrop and his colleagues at Leeds on ENCAL (Entities, Notation, Calculators) has both these goals (Harrop, 1999). Adding an intermediate representation based on a data flow notation provides the opportunity for calculator users to learn the underlying mechanism by which a four-function calculator works and also to understand the structure of numerical expressions. Currently, this work is only informed by work on modeling, and might well benefit from the process of modeling student's activities with it.

Harrop's ENCAL system, like Ainsworth's COPPERS and CENTS (Ainsworth, 1997), involves multiple linked external representations (MLERs). ENCAL supports children representing word problems in three equivalent ways: concrete (iconic), intermediate (dataflow), and via the use of a calculator. The three representations are maintained by ENCAL as equivalent through all changes to any of the representations (as far as it is possible to do so). In this sense, Harrop is working with multiple equivalent linked representations (MELRs). Ainsworth, Wood, and Bibby studied some of the empirical properties of multiple external representations (MERs) and showed that a mixture of partially redundant pictorial and mathematical representations can have problems for learners (Ainsworth, Wood, & Bibby, 1996, 1997). Their interpretation of their results for CENTS suggested that children were not easily able to map between informationally equivalent pictorial and mathematical representations, partly because of different formats, different operators, and different modalities.

As there is an increasing use of MLERs, there is a corresponding need to understand how these "work" at a cognitive level for both individuals and groups. Zhang and Norman (1994) explored issues in modeling the way in which an individual works with both an external representation and their internal representation. Zhang (1998) sought to extend this work to a context featuring many people working with a distributed representation.

His framework has been empirically tested showing that the way the representation is distributed can make group performance better or worse than any individual's problem-solving performance. He explained the performance in terms of two basic hypotheses: first, the representation-sharing hypothesis, which states that the more a representation is shared, the better the performance of the distributed system in terms of solution steps, and second, the communication hypothesis, which is that the less communication needed, the better the performance of the distributed system in terms of solution times. Zhang simplified the notion of shared representation by considering representation as the rules needed for describing the way a problem is solved, and these might be memorized (internal) or visible (external).

As far as we are aware, no computational model has been produced of Zhang's account of group performance. We argue that the implementation of the model presented in this chapter does generate some of the behavior that is exhibited by (primarily) novice modelers working together. This work points toward the kind of model that could generate collaborative behavior together with human or software agents reasoning with multiple external representations (linked or not, informationally equivalent or not).

ISSUES FOR MODELING MODELERS

Developing models of how people work both with conceptual content of some scientific domain and with each other requires the consideration of issues including:

- how internal and external representations are related and developed,
- how shared artifacts are used (an external representation is an *informational* artifact),
- how a shared artifact is jointly constructed,

- how modelers relate an artifact to both a theory of its functioning and experimental evidence,
- how collaborative dialogue "works" to develop conceptual understanding,
- how people interact in terms of what they know, their social role, and their adopted communicative roles, and
- how people manage the process of coming to a possibly less than perfect agreement.

The model presented here—called *Clarissa* and used as an example in this chapter—is a model of a number of students working on the construction of an external representation of a simple physics experiment. As this representation is a model of the underlying physics of the phenomena being investigated, Clarissa embodies a model of how students work together to develop this model.

The Clarissa model is implemented within a software system that provides a laboratory for the investigation of the implications of different kinds of plausible collaborative behavior. It is built on a model of cognitive behavior that seeks to represent the kinds of reasoning performed by inexperienced students; thus, Clarissa is not a model of optimal novice modeling performance.

In this section some of the work is summarized that has a bearing on modeling modelers, with a special emphasis on how modelers work together using external representations.

Working Together

The enterprise of modeling human participants as always being involved in some carefully coordinated construction of a plan before executing it is somewhat implausible. It may be a good line to explore, but it is not the only interesting line of development possible. Given that we are interested in using modeling to understand modelers, an arguably more promising approach is to adopt a view closer to those held by activity theorists and others, and seek to blur the distinction between planning and acting.

The plan construction approach generally assumes a very rational, "measured" process in which no actions are executed until agreement is reached as to what to do. Furthermore, there may also be an assumption that the meaning of all concepts is shared, or if not shared, debated until their meaning is shared.

Grosz and Sidner and their various colleagues developed an approach to the use of dialogue along these lines (Grosz & Sidner, 1990; Lochbaum, 1994; Sidner, 1994b). Their approach rested on the notion that understanding discourse requires inferring the intentions underlying an utterance, and that this is best done by considering a discourse as constructing plans in a collaborative manner. During discourse, a partial shared plan is augmented so as to construct a full shared plan, at which point the plan is executed and the construction of a new full shared plan begun. This full shared plan is termed a *SharedPlan* and defines a discourse segment.

In educational discourse, however, multiple threads of conversation are maintained. This means that the SharedPlans approach needs to be augmented with some mechanism for deciding which SharedPlan is being referenced by the current utterance (or that a new SharedPlan has begun). A typical solution, used by Rich and Sidner (1997) in COL-LAGEN, is the idea of focus stacks to maintain the status of SharedPlans.

The Clarissa model of the use of dialogue roles can be interpreted in a Vygotskian-like way (Burton, 1998); it can also be seen in terms of distributed cognition. Clark and Chalmers (1998), among others, advocated an externalist view of cognition. Their notion of active externalism involved internal cognitive processes coupled in a two-way interaction with external entities. Clark and Chalmers claimed that the ability to communicate between internal and external processes, extended cognition, "... is a core cognitive process, not an add-on extra" (p. 12). This includes beliefs that are both externally represented and stored by other people.

Modeling Intentions

A closely related issue for the SharedPlans approach is that of the extent to which the participants model the intentions of the other participants. Whether this is necessary or even desirable as a realistic model of collaborative activity is hotly debated. Certainly some position needs to be taken on how far the participants are believed to go in trying to model each other's understanding.

Rich and Sidner (1997), for example, produced a collaborative agent toolkit called COLLAGEN that is also based on the notion of "cooperative dialogues" (though it is usually argued that all dialogues have to be cooperative at some level). Grosz and Kraus (1999) extended and adapted their own formalism of SharedPlans. They make very stringent requirements on a group of agents collaborating together:

> In collaborative activity, plans for subactions also impose some constraints on the group doing the overall activity. In particular, the full group must agree on who will do the subsidiary action, must have confidence that the subgroup can and will do the action, and must be committed to the subgroup's success.

The Clarissa model does not require that the individual needs to believe that some other individual (or subgroup of individuals) can or will do what they say they want to do.

Sidner (1994a) developed a formal language in which to conduct collaborative negotiations that requires the maintenance of such models of the other participants. The basic assumption underlying the work is termed the *mutual belief assumption*. Sidner argued that the mutual belief assumption holds for synchronous communications in contexts in which there is no intent to deceive (i.e., in cooperative dialogues). This does not seem quite right for contexts in which learning might take place for two reasons: first, in the learning situation, the more knowledgeable person (e.g., teacher, or, at least, a person playing the role of teacher) may choose to appear to know less than they do; and second, there may be confusion over beliefs that appear to be identical but mean different things to those that profess these beliefs. Whereas the first state might be termed *knowing deception*, the second term is more accurately termed *unknowing deception*, although in either case the use of "deception" seems unacceptably strong. This suggests that work on the computational modeling of collaborative dialogues for education (both student–student and student–teacher) needs some further attention.

Taylor, Carletta, and Mellish (1996) also formally examined the notion of cooperative dialogues and found that only "doubly nested beliefs" are necessary for plan/goal recognition when dialogue can be guaranteed to be cooperative. Taylor et al. argued that the nesting of beliefs beyond this level is not needed under the assumption that people are not deceptive (intentionally or otherwise).

Given that the strong assumptions of cooperative dialogue just outlined often do not hold in the kinds of dialogues observed in the classroom (or even the laboratory), we are left with the possibility that we have to model complex nested beliefs. There is an unresolved empirical issue here about how much modeling people really do of others, and, if they occasionally do such modeling, whether there is any need to maintain the model over extended periods of time. The indications are that much of the modeling of others by students in educational discourse is partial, governed by the current goals, influenced by stereotypes, and leaps to unwarranted conclusions.

Actions and ER Construction

One of the problems of joint construction is the need to integrate actions into the discourse. Whereas some actions can be regarded as communicative (e.g., pointing), others are usually associated with the execution of mutually agreed plans. In educational contexts, students may choose to force a decision by acting—for example, by grabbing the mouse and making a selection. Most current systems assume willing and effective collaborating agents. Even under this assumption, there are problems. One approach is to regard both actions and speech as examples of communicative acts.

A view that complicates matters can be derived from Vygotsky's observation that when signs/ERs are included in an action, they not only facilitate actions that would otherwise be impossible, they also fundamentally transform the action (Wertsch, 1991; Wertsch & Toma, 1989). This issue is a special focus of activity theory.

Activity theory is derived from the work of Vygotsky and his students, Luria and Leont'ev. Vygotsky is described as having been dissatisfied with behavioral psychology and psychoanalysis. Vygotsky introduced the concepts of artifact-mediated and object-oriented action (Vygotsky, 1978): The relationship between a human and the environment is mediated through cultural and intellectual "tools."

These tools are *mediating artifacts*, and are cultural–psychological in nature. A mediating artifact can lead to the association of meaning and actions. An example is given of a child trying to grab an object. This action is interpreted as pointing by a parent, and, slowly, the child uses the action to point. This action has become a tool to communicate a desire to the parent.

In this way, through the mediation of such tools, the "general law of cultural development" proposes that learning is a two-phase operation: First, a person learns to use words and other signs in a social context and then in an internalized manner.

We might reasonably expect to learn from developing a process-based account of the way in which social interaction can combine with actions on an external representation to generate a new "mental tool." We leave unexplored here how such a process might be directly modeled or whether such behavior could ever emerge from our current models of communicative interaction.

Internal and External Representations

In the last 10 years, cognitive modeling that examines cognition situated in an often uncertain world has become far more common. For example, Altmann examined the role of an external trace of programming behavior in program construction. His model is able to produce an account of behavior associated with episodic memory integrated with search for external information presented on a computer interface (Altmann & John, 1995). Rieman, Young, and Howes (1996) provided a fine-grain model of exploratory learning (IDXL) that depends on scanning both the interface and the available internal comprehension strategies. Kitajima and Polson (1996, 1997) provided a more abstract, comprehension-based model (The LInked model of Comprehension-based Action planning and Instruction taking—LICAI) of exploration of an interface based on Kintsch's ·(1988) construction-integration theory of text comprehension.

These models take some steps that may eventually lead to models of exploration-based reasoning using external representations in unfamiliar domains as the modelers seek to explain exploration-driven behavior by a combination of the situation, prior knowledge, and the task. So far, they generally do not address the issues of:

- using computer applications to learn conceptually difficult material at the same time as learning to use the application's interface,
- how such models are integrated with models of collaboration, or

- how artifact construction is managed by both individuals and the group.

AN APPROACH TO MODELING COLLABORATIVE ER PRODUCTION

A computational model of the collaborative production of an External Representation (ER) would ideally require the modeling of individuals that are capable of engaging in dialogue, of making observations, of acting in the world, of coordinating their construction of the ER as well as reflecting on past experiences and recalling and reasoning with prior knowledge. These issues are illuminated by briefly discussing a computational model of collaboration which has been built (Burton, 1998; Burton, Brna, & Pilkington, 2000; Burton, Brna, & Treasure-Jones, 1997), that allows two or more agents to coconstruct a diagram representing the energy flow in a simple physics experiment. Factors that need to be taken into account are also briefly discussed.

In building such a model, we had to decide on how to tackle a number of difficult questions including: how action, perception, and cognition are integrated; how much planning is necessary to generate coherent dialogue; what social communicative assumptions are held by participants in collaborative dialogue; the extent to which we need to model the participant's models of other participants; the way in which an ER assists in collaborative problem solving; the processes underlying the coconstruction of an ER; and the effect that the roles of the participants have on the modeling process. Finally, we ask whether such a model can be extended to manage multiple ERs utilizing multiple modalities.

Traditional models of single person problem solving made little or no distinction between internal representations of the world and the external world (Agre, 1997). More recently, various computational models have appeared that seek to integrate cognitive aspects of problem solving with aspects of action and perception (e.g., Rieman et al., 1996; Kitajima & Polson, 1996).

In a parallel development, researchers in language generation have developed computational models that allow two or more agents (human or otherwise) to work together. This work has often focused on the production and comprehension of cooperative dialogue, although so far, there is relatively little evidence of making any distinctions between information shared in different modalities, ignoring, for example, the difference between diagrammatic and textual information.

Recently, there has also been an increase in the attention paid to models of the ways in which external representations are utilized in single-agent problem solving (e.g., Zhang & Norman, 1994), and in multiple-agent problem solving (e.g., Rich & Sidner, 1997).

In modeling the collaborative production of an external representation, we choose to distinguish between external and internal representations. In Clarissa, this is done to the extent that agents attempt to convey their own internal representation by updating the external representation. A model of dialogue understanding generation is also needed. Currently, there are systems that seek to model the three-way interaction between the agent and another agent, the agent and itself (i.e., aspects of cognition), and the agent and the context in which the agents find themselves (cf. Rich & Sidner, 1997; Sidner, 1994b).

Taking the notion of artifact construction further, there are very few computational models that consider the four-way interaction of agent with another agent, agent with "itself," agent with artifact being constructed, and agent with physical context. However, Clarissa is an agent that does—very crudely—model such a four-way interaction. The first two of these aspects are, in part, achieved through the underlying simplifying assumption that all conscious thought is essentially internalized speech. The other two aspects are partly dependent on some account of the interaction between the learner's cognitive system and sensorimotor system.

The context of the activity is taken into account within the model in two ways: by explicitly representing the physics equipment including its structure and its effects, and also by modeling the task that has been set to include assertions by the teacher relating to the underlying physics and requirements that should be met, such as that the energy chain should begin and end with a reservoir.

Clarissa is developed for a context in which two (or more) agents collaborate in building a diagram of energy flow for a specific physics experiment involving a light bulb connected to a battery. These agents are initially relatively ignorant of the connection between this setup and the physics of the situation.

The starting point for the model sketched here is ModelCHENE, a previous model of problem solving developed by Bental and Brna (1995) that was itself based on a model, psCHENE, developed by Devi, Tiberghien, Baker, and Brna (1996). ModelCHENE and psCHENE are models of single-agent problem solving (with a limited amount of learning taking place) that take into account interactions between the agent and the physical context as well as between the agent and "itself" and also issues connected with an agent's prior knowledge. They are themselves derived from Tiberghien's (1994) analytic model.

AN OVERVIEW OF CLARISSA

Burton developed Clarissa (Collaborative Learning As Realised In Simple Simulated Agents) to incorporate a model of multiagent collaborative dialogue (Burton & Brna, 1996). A Clarissa agent provides a method for supporting multiple conversational threads related to but different from that of focus stacks. Clarissa was developed in the context described earlier—the collaborative production of an energy flow diagram, an "energy chain." It discriminates explicitly between an individual agent's internalized energy chain and the externalized, diagrammatic energy chain being produced through collaboration (Brna & Burton, 1997; Burton, Brna, & Treasure-Jones, 1997).

Clarissa is primarily a system designed to simulate different ways in which agents collaborate during problem solving and learning. The emphasis is not on cognitive fidelity; rather, it is intended that the discourse generated should be broadly similar to that generated by actual groups of students. It is modeled in part on actual dialogues between pairs of students.

The architecture allows for as many instantiations of a Clarissa agent as are desired. Communication is facilitated by software that (loosely) models the shared environment. This includes a mouse and a chat box in a way that is close to that used by Tiberghien and Baker to gather protocols of pupil behavior using an interface devised by Baker (see Bental & Brna, 1995 for a more detailed description). The interface permits users to draw diagrams representing energy flow. These diagrams are limited: the diagrammatic features are *reservoirs*, *transformers*, and *transfers*. Additionally, these items are expected to be labeled. Figure 8.1 provides an idealized view onto the kind of energy chain produced by students.[1]

Clarissa, Dialogue, and External Representations

The joint construction of an external representation by a group of agents is affected by a combination of the dynamics of the physical context, the task being undertaken constructed, the prior knowledge of the agents, and the social dynamics.

The Role of Dialogue.   Communication and cognition are viewed as intertwined, with neither being in complete control of the agent. Both may initiate and drive the dialogue, cognition, and actions on the world.

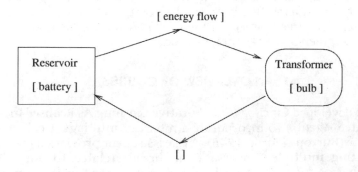

FIG. 8.1. An example energy chain.

---

[1]The system was designed for use by French students.

An interesting set of problems arises from how to represent the internal flow of thought and the external discourse. The design choice made was to regard these as effectively the same. When comparing natural dialogues to those generated by an early version of Clarissa, it was quickly discovered that the system was far too verbose. One view of this is that in a social setting, humans are aware of what is likely to be of interest to those around them, and what is really only of interest to themselves. This is essentially Grice's (1975) maxim of quantity.

Many of a Clarissa agent's utterances are said to the agent itself. These utterances are the cause of the verbosity, and a mechanism was required for preventing these from being said out loud. Like humans, Clarissa attempts to say only things that are of interest to others. Clarissa agents are not able to "learn" this, they merely have a pre-formed notion of what interests others. In terms of studying the nurturing and development of collaboration, it would be important to examine the development of this ability more closely.

How Topics for Discussion Arise.   When the Clarissa system works through the modeling process, potential new topics arise from an individual agent's internal reasoning as well as in connection with:

- the external representation being jointly constructed,
- the shared task description that is found in the physical context,
- the shared experiment, which is also part of the physical context,
- an individual's prior knowledge,
- a change in an agent's understanding of the problem (or of a concept), and
- the computer interface used to construct the desired external representation.

All these do influence problem solving and to a greater or lesser extent contribute to the discourse. The model is not, however, designed to allow discussion about changes in the physical context nor any details of the computer interface (i.e., the interface permits only rudimentary actions on it).

External Representations.   The basic actions on the ER being coconstructed are ADD and DELETE, but these are parametrized to include a type associated with the underlying physics (one of *reservoir*, *transformer*, and *transfer*), its name, its label, and any further information necessary (a transfer requires the definition of its start and finish).

It is also assumed that the external representation of the energy chain is an *acceptable* version of the energy chain for all agents but that it represents a model that is not necessarily believed by any of the agents—that is, we do not assume that any agent's internal version of the energy chain is entirely in agreement with the external version although the agents will have a goal to attempt to achieve this.

Clarissa's Architecture

The architecture includes components that generate and interpret language utterances at a propositional level. For each of these components, the processing is modeled in terms of distinct cognitive and dialogue mechanisms. Figure 8.2 provides an illustration.

For clarification as to how the architecture functions, the flow of information is described starting with (for explanation purposes only) the cognitive system generating a "dialogue goal." As an example, the goal is to get somebody to perform an operation (e.g., "We need to label the reservoir.")

This goal is given to the generator's dialogue system. The dialogue system, eventually but not necessarily immediately, processes this goal. To do so, it first checks with the cognitive system to ensure that the goal is still valid (i.e., that it is still believed that the reservoir is unlabeled and still needs to be labeled). This is the validation process.

The dialogue system then consults a subsystem that deals with language to decide on a reasonable utterance to convey this goal. Presently, this system is very simple indeed—it has a one-to-one mapping between goal and utterance! For our example, it will return "We need to label the reservoir."

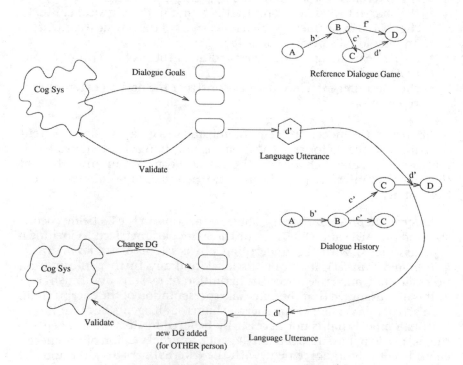

FIG. 8.2. The basic architecture.

The interface here is expected to support some arbitrary form of rhetorical predicate subsystem. This will be needed as, in general, the most appropriate utterance depends on the current state of the conversation—hence the need for the dialogue system to consult the language system.

Having selected an utterance, the dialogue system then evaluates the "relevance" of the chosen utterance. This is done in order to choose one conversational thread to continue among all the other available conversational threads. The utterance is made and placed in the dialogue history (of the speaking agent).

The relevance calculations are complex and are outlined later. They require holding a record of utterances made, and having a notion of what kinds of action/utterance are permissible at any time. The mechanism used is to assign "dialogue roles" to agents.[2]

Turning to the language interpretation mode, this process is reversed, as an utterance (such as "We need to label the reservoir") is received and dealt with. First, it is placed in the dialogue history of the listening agent, utilizing the same basic relevance calculation to determine the conversation for which the utterance is most appropriate.

Then the utterance is examined by the language subsystem, which interprets it as a goal (e.g., "They want me to label the reservoir"). As earlier, this is currently a one-to-one mapping. This goal is then placed into the dialogue system (although it is identified as a goal that has been initiated by somebody else).

Again, when the dialogue system chooses, it will process this goal. In this case the validation process plays a more important role as the cognitive system must decide what to do about this dialogue goal. In general the cognitive system will adopt its own goals, remove the dialogue goal (by saying that it is no longer valid), and presumably some time later set up further dialogue goals. This use of the validation mechanism is the least well implemented within the system.

The Cognitive System.   Although the main interest is in exploring the dialogue mechanisms rather than the cognitive ones, some representation of these cognitive mechanisms is required. Therefore, a very specific domain was selected, along with an available model of problem solving previously developed for the domain—that of building energy chains. The model of problem solving is derived from work by Tiberghien and colleagues (Devi et al., 1996), and implemented in computational form as the ModelCHENE system (Bental & Brna, 1995).

Dialogue Mechanism.   The mechanism chosen is an extension of the dialogue game system outlined in Burton and Brna (1996). There is one (large) dialogue game, which consists of a "state machine" that identi-

---

[2]These include such roles as questioning, modifying the ER, checking the underlying physics.

fies dialogue moves (utterances) that can be made in response to other moves. Notionally, most (although, significantly, not all) dialogue moves can be followed by any number of possible responses, either immediately or later. In other words, people come back to old topics of conversation and start new (parallel) dialogue threads.

To keep track of this, a history of the dialogue is kept. The history mechanism maintains data on which moves were made, the dialogue game states moved from and moved to, and also when the move was made. The dialogue state machine is a separate representation of what the cognitive model could possibly generate. It is not annotated with the conditionals that might be expected because to do so would be an implementation of the cognitive system. Its use is simply to assist the planning/relevance calculations of the dialogue system.

Relevance. Using the dialogue history, it is possible to calculate some notion of relevance. The history is traversed from the most recently active dialogue thread back until a branch is found. Branches are explored (again from the bottom up) before continuing. The first point at which (according to the dialogue game state machine) an utterance is acceptable (i.e., can be made in response to the move that was used to arrive at this state) is the point at which this utterance is most relevant.

In addition to this calculation, some utterances are deemed to be not relevant to anything (and therefore currently un-utterable). There are two main categories of such moves: those that have been made so recently that to say them would be just to repeat oneself, and utterances for which the expected response would be the same as the expected response for utterances that have already been said but not yet been responded to. Human dialogues seem to avoid such ambiguities as well, although people seem to be reasonably tolerant of them. The only reason for putting this category in is to make the output appear more human: The machine could be made to disambiguate these statements in more human-like ways. As well as these two categories, there will be times when it is desirable to limit the moves that an agent can make (to force them into playing a dialogue role). This is done using the same system.

CLARISSA AND EFFECTIVE COLLABORATION

As stated earlier, Clarissa was designed primarily to simulate different ways in which agents collaborate during problem solving and learning. Collaborative activity may help participants learn to collaborate by affording them the opportunity to practice different aspects of collaboration. However, the consequence of stressing the issue of learning to collaborate might reasonably be expected to make the problem-solving process less efficient.

It is also reasonable to expect that students can learn to collaborate through the adoption of one of a number of ways of using dialogue (i.e., dialogue roles). Consequently, different patterns of dialogue role availability and different policies for redistributing these roles during problem solving may lead to different benefits for collaborative learning and an understanding of the predicted relative value of different ways of organizing collaborative activity.

If it is granted that problem solving and learning to collaborate interact in some way, we might ask how this interaction helps or hinders learning to model. In the context in which Clarissa is utilized (i.e., building an energy chain), the students are learning to model through learning to make mappings between the theory/model world and the experimental field (Vince & Tiberghien, chap. 2, this volume). How does the pattern of dialogue roles affect the learning of these mappings?

A metric for collaboration (with respect to Clarissa) was developed. It is a function of the degree to which agents can use all the roles available, and the degree to which they perceive a benefit from the collaboration. The perceived usefulness of the collaboration is measured in terms of the number of utterances received by an individual from a partner that cause that individual to change his or her knowledge base.

Likewise, it is possible to measure the degree to which an individual in a collaboration exercises a wide range of roles in a relatively uniform manner. This relates to the fundamental claim: that the exercising of a range of roles is advantageous. Thus a goal in the kind of collaboration argued for is that all (or most) of the available roles are exercised to a reasonable extent during the collaboration, and that the usage is balanced between the participants—a requirement that reflects a notion that the learning experience is a fair one for all concerned.

The degree to which a role is used is approximated as the number of utterances made by participants while an individual is "playing" that role. This is an approximation in the following respects. The number of moves an individual makes within a role is not considered, inasmuch as to do so would not include information about how long the role was used for, and to what degree the other party was active during that time. The time that the role is used for is not useful because this does not necessarily reflect the amount of activity the participants are engaged in (especially if the implementation is executed on a machine subject to varying loads). Hence the amount of "collaboration time" is approximated by the number of utterances made by either participant. This gives a measure of the length of time a role has been used for, and hence a measure of the degree to which an agent is "using" a role.

Although this measure was designed to examine a quite specific notion of "good collaboration," it is worth reminding ourselves that there is much more to good collaboration than the notion expounded here. The practice of a range of roles has both pedagogical validity and cognitive validity as a means of fostering the forms of long-term learning that are desirable and that take advantage of both relevant domain content and social conditions.

CONSEQUENCES OF THE CLARISSA MODEL

The Clarissa model involves agents adopting and relinquishing dialogue roles. However, the precise set of roles is not determined uniquely, although some constraints do exist. (For example, the "finished" role is necessary to indicate termination of the collaboration.) The current set of experiments with the Clarissa system involves the dialogue roles shown in Table 8.1.

These dialogue roles are subject to some constraints that are related to the policy chosen for the way agents collaborate. Patterns of interaction can then be examined through executing the system with one (or more) agents.

We can also examine the results of the collaboration, which in this case are the coconstructed diagrams representing reservoirs (batteries), energy transformers (bulbs), and energy transfers (often mistakenly identified by the students as wires).

Because the agents operate over a network resulting in some unpredictable computational latencies, each run may be different. To a limited extent, the variability in the model's behavior tests the robustness of the interaction scheme.

The "dialogue" generated by the system, although intelligible, is verbose and is not analyzed here. See Fig. 8.3 for an example dialogue segment and its translation.

The fundamental claim is that the exercising of a range of roles is good for learning to collaborate, and that learning to collaborate effectively may well be best when all (or most) of the available roles are exercised to a reasonable extent during the collaboration and when the usage is balanced between the participants.

TABLE 8.1
Descriptions of Dialogue Roles Used

Dialogue Role	Brief Description
question	raise issues of all kinds
response	seek to satisfy questions
argue	challenge or support statements
generate	examine the current problem in terms of possible approaches
reason	explain chains of reasoning
check	see if the current partial solution is adequate
interface	manage interactions with the external representation of the problem
finished	indicate that there is nothing more that can be done
IWasThinking	bring (possibly old) topics back into consideration

```
Agent1: Somebody should do Theory Model Check on wire2
Agent1: For me, wire2 relates to electrical
Agent2: I agree For me, wire2 relates to electrical
Agent2: I'll update the interface ADD>Transfer:electrical(wire2)/battery1,
bulb1
```

which is roughly equivalent to:

```
Agent1: We should look more closely at wire2 (check the underlying
        physics), as we haven't represented it on our diagram.
Agent1: I think it seems to be the same as the thing on our diagram
        called ''electrical energy''
Agent2: I agree
Agent2: I'll label the transfer as electrical energy
```

FIG. 8.3. An Example Dialogue Segment.

In one set of computational experiments, a form of "normal" collaboration (termed *Free*) was compared with a second form, which is referred to as *MultiSwap*. This MultiSwap collaborative situation is constructed from two separate constraints. Each of these constraints when applied to the Free situation produces a different form of collaboration (Multi and Swap).

First, the social norms are relaxed, producing the Multi form of collaboration. Clarissa normally "expects" only one agent to use any one role at any time. In this environment, different agents are allowed to use the same role at the same time (to do so, the number of roles had to be slightly simplified). The resulting conversations are strange in that the dialogue seems to lose its coherence to some degree as questions are asked together, and agents may "reply" with other questions. But Clarissa agents are blessed with a very good memory, and they return to these questions and answer them more directly when they can. Their memory is a key feature of this collaborative situation.

Second, constraints are included based on observations by Soller (personal communication, 1997) that in successful collaborative groups (in terms of her own metrics), participants tend to swap roles at the beginning of a new episode.

Soller identified a number of dialogue markers to define "episodes," and defined her own set of roles that are similar but not the same as the ones used for Clarissa. The expectation seems to be that, although an episode boundary may be a reasonable place to expect people to drop the roles they are playing, it does not follow that they would choose different ones for the next episode. She found that in the cases where people do choose different roles, collaborative activity is more beneficial (according to her measures).

Swap implements a form of Soller's observation using the opening of a new dialogue game as an indication of a new dialogue episode. These episodes are somewhat smaller than Soller's, but a similar positive effect was obtained. Tests with Clarissa indicate that this form of collaboration is better, both in terms of the way in which roles are distributed between partners, and marginally in terms of the degree of interest found in the dialogue by participants.

MultiSwap, in an educational context, is equivalent to a situation in which collaborators can ask all the questions they have and say everything they can about a problem. They pay careful attention to everything said by their partners. Questions, comments, and suggestions must be noted down. An alternative approach is *Polite* collaboration, which simply involves participants "dropping" their roles at the end of episodes. Rather than swapping roles at the beginning of a new episode, the participant who has led an episode stands back for the next. In other words, and simply put, if you have been taking the lead for a while, stop, and let somebody else take the initiative.

A comparison of Free with Polite indicates the change in the pattern of the collaboration. Figure 8.4 is a single example of the sort of behavior recorded when two Clarissa agents interact using the Free collaboration policy, and shows the final result of this collaboration (the diagram that the agents have constructed). It also shows the roles used by the agents. Notice that agents monopolize a role for long periods of time (although they may not be actively using utterances in this role, they have used some and have not been seen to "drop" the role). For example, the Reason role is used mainly by Agent 2 for the first 90 seconds, and then Agent 3 uses the role sporadically for the remainder of the time. This can be compared to Fig. 8.5 which shows the roles used by two agents in a Polite collaboration. Notice in this case that roles are swapped much more frequently.

Another example occurs in relation to the "interface" role. In each of the examples given in Figs. 8.4 and 8.5, only one agent accesses the interface role. In the Free case, the use of the role is extended, whereas in the Polite case the use is sporadic, as might be expected of a policy in which roles are dropped quite quickly rather than held onto until some event triggers their release.

To give an idea of how MultiSwap relates to Free and some of the other possible situations, Table 8.2 provides a summary of how well each of four policies performs over a range of six dialogue roles. In the table, "X" indicates that the role is badly distributed according the criterion adopted here for even usage. As can be seen, MultiSwap gives distinctly better results relative to the chosen metric than Free, Swap, and Multi (i.e., more "X" entries).

MultiSwap collaboration is much better according to the criteria used here, especially as it seems to encourage the even distribution of all dialogue roles. This implies that all the participants in the collaboration have an opportunity to practice all of the dialogue roles that are avail-

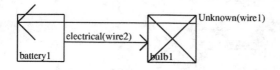

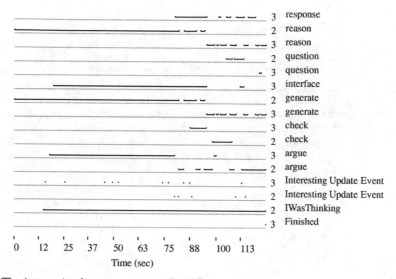

The interaction lasts approximately 120 seconds
The numbers 2 or 3 indicate which agent is using which role
The roles are response, reason, question etc

FIG. 8.4. Example role usage during Free collaboration.

able, and by doing so, the participants should have the opportunity to practice and hopefully improve their ability to execute those underlying processes.

The full results are provided in detail elsewhere (Burton et al., 2000). Further details of the full range of testing carried out, as well as Soller's observations, can be found in Burton's (1998) thesis.

DISCUSSION

We have developed a model that is computational, addresses a wide range of issues, as discussed earlier, but does not cover the detail that more restricted models can manage.

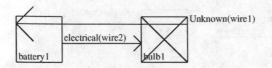

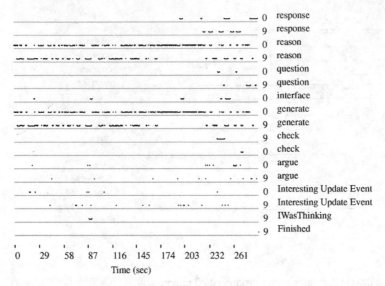

The interaction lasts approximately 270 seconds
The numbers 0 or 9 indicate which agent is using which role
The roles are response, reason, question etc

FIG. 8.5.   Example role usage during Polite collaboration.

Working Together

Fundamentally, a Clarissa agent does very little explicit planning. However, two forms of planning are available. First, it may be necessary for an agent to close a conversational thread in order to make the dialogue move the way he or she wants. So an agent has been given the ability to terminate a dialogue game if doing so frees up another agent to make an anticipated move.

The second type of planning relates to what happens if an agent judges a possible utterance as uninteresting and does not "voice" it. Later, the utterance is judged as interesting by the agent, but now the context within

TABLE 8.2
Summary of Results for Different Policies

	Interesting	Reason	Generate	Response	Interface	Question
Free	X	X	X	X	X	X
Swap	X	X	X	X		
Multi	X	X				
MultiSwap						

Note. X for a given policy indicates the role is badly distributed.

which it makes sense to "speak" has gone. Such situations can be detected by the dialogue system and the agent can "fill in" the relevant previously unspoken moves to make the situation clear for everybody.

In terms of modeling the modelers, the need for this kind of planning is necessary given the extended temporal nature and diversity of the modeling process. The current level of planning can, in principle, handle the need to follow strands of thought for several steps (deciding what data needs to be collected and how, making inferences from the data, considering alternative ways of going about the modeling process), and to pick up strands previously left unfinished.

Moving to the issue of learning to model, this may take place through various peer–peer collaborations and through teacher-supervised activities. Currently, the teacher agent is extremely restricted in terms of its activities. Essentially, it manages the swapping of dialogue roles adopted by the other "student" agents. An extension of the teacher agent's powers could allow the teacher agent to interrogate the student agent to articulate its goals—for example, "What are you trying to do?," "Why are you doing that way?" (The agent ought to be able to do this anyway.)

Modeling Intentions

The importance of generating goals has been reduced and the importance of roles has been emphasized. It is the cognitive processes that individuals learn and use in dialogue that are the important unit of analysis, because these processes are more likely to have been learned by the individual after the collaborative experience.

The emphasis on the dialogue roles that are related to these cognitive processes not only gives us a more convenient unit of analysis, which seems useful from the perspective on teaching and fostering collaboration, but also modeling collaboration. This analysis involves a complex, dialogue-driven interaction between cognitive goals and dialogue goals. As a result, Clarissa manifests behavior that appears to be strongly goal oriented.

So there is no assumption of cooperative dialogues underlying work on Clarissa (other than a very weak notion of willingness to communicate). A Clarissa agent currently does minimal modeling of other participants. All that a Clarissa agent can do is reference the ER being coconstructed and the utterances that have been made. If another agent dissembles, then this may lead to an argument but should still lead to a coconstructed ER—although the quality of the solution may be very poor if one agent decides to be uncooperative.[3]

Note that argumentation is an important aspect of modeling. Explicit argument is present in the empirical data that was used to inform the design of the Clarissa model although it is not usually manifested in a very well articulated way. Although the Clarissa implementation in its current state lacks sophisticated facilities for argumentation, it would not be difficult to handle the necessary extensions.

Actions and ER Construction

Clarissa uses a system of roles to capture notions of permissible activity (both linguistic and "physical"). These roles can be adopted and reallocated at various points in the discourse, allowing different agents to control, for example, the construction of the shared ER.

The coconstruction of an ER is not just about the ways in which people communicate linguistically; it is also about the affordances offered by the context of work as well as about their knowledge and experience of the various tools and facilities that are available. Clarissa's context of work is that of many students each working with his or her own system for communicating and acting on the model being coconstructed. The facilities for changing the model were quite simple, and Clarissa models this reasonably faithfully at the functional level.

For more complex situations—for example, one in which the experimental field also needs describing—there is the possibility that a change in one ER will lead to a change in another, related ER. In some contexts, this change will be managed by the software environment—that is, we have a situation featuring an MLER. In other cases, the link may have to be established by the modeler. In one situation we need to provide affordances for modelers to express the link between one ER and another, and in the other we need to provide affordances to encourage the modeler to reflect on the link between two linked elements of an ER. We can expect some interesting results from an examination of this difference.

Internal and External Representations

Clarissa uses a simple approach to modifying the ER and simulating access via the interface. A Clarissa agent uses the interface to provide it with a persistent diagrammatic representation of the problem-solving

---

[3]This is perfectly possible in the classroom!

state. This means that the simulated students using the interface have effectively externalized some aspects of their beliefs about the nature of the final solution, and these parts will, in general, not be forgotten, as they are evident in the environment.

Indeed, it is assumed that all externalized information will be remembered. On the other hand, the Clarissa implementation is equipped with a very simple way of controlling the extent to which internalized information is forgotten. A model of episodic memory—such as that produced by Altmann—would have benefits for improving the fact validity of the Clarissa model (Altmann & John, 1995).

CONCLUSION

As has so often been the case with computational models, much is currently assumed or simplified, and there is no doubt that a full model of all the factors that might have a bearing on learning would be very difficult to build indeed, let alone describe. However, we sought to indicate some important issues that have emerged from the process of building a model of a group of students learning to model.

More specifically, we introduced Clarissa, a system built to examine the interaction of different role assignment schemes on collaborative behavior during the coconstruction of an ER. There is a long way to go before there is a satisfactory computational model of novices learning to model. However, in the discourse engendered through seeking to model the modelers in the context we have chosen, we can see a number of points that have emerged that we hope will have some value to an audience interested in encouraging the learning of modeling.

The coconstruction of external representations plays a key part in learning to model, but only a part. Likewise, a model of collaborative behavior is also a key part. Clarissa provides a particularly interesting way of thinking about the interaction between the available communicative (dialogue) roles and the (social and physical) constraints of the setting in which collaboration takes place.

Clarissa also raises the issue of the processes by which students learn to collaborate. Burton (1998) argued that learning to collaborate slows down the rate at which students build the external representation of the model of their understanding of physical phenomena. A first interpretation of this is to assume that we should aim either at helping students learn to model or helping students learn to collaborate (but not both). We suggest that during the process of learning to collaborate in the context within which a model has to be produced, students are also learning to model.

A particular result of working with Clarissa is that the adopted role allocation mechanism can have a significant effect on learning in terms of the various processes that are activated during learning.[4] The design-

---

[4]Rather than the actual material learned—Clarissa was not implemented to learn new concepts and procedures

ers of software systems currently being built to support collaborative learning are not always aware of the trade-off between learning and role allocation mechanisms adopted. Developing an understanding of this trade-off from all the research being done in the area of computer supported collaborative learning (CSCL) is really quite hard; Clarissa provides an example of how we might go about evaluating these trade-offs, which might be of value to system designers.

Clarissa does not model the full range of functions that modelers might want to call on. For example, Bouwer, Machado, and Bredeweg (chap. 6, this volume) provide a much more detailed view of what such a modeling environment might look like. Clarissa's implementation suggests ways of organizing small groups of learners and provides a style of informal dialogue that might have value in future support systems where an artificial peer stands in for a student. Although Clarissa lacks the pedagogic reason for interaction found in Luckin and du Boulay's work (chap. 4, this volume), we hope that Clarissa agents will provide a kind of vehicle to study how to deliver effective pedagogic interactions.

ACKNOWLEDGMENTS

Our thanks to Michael Baker, Andrée Tiberghien, and the rest of équipe COAST of UMR-GRIC at the Université Lyon 2 for their help and support.

REFERENCES

Agre, P. (1997). *Computation and human experience.* Cambridge University Press, Cambridge.

Ainsworth, S. (1997). *Designing and evaluating multi-representational learning environments for primary mathematics.* Unpublished PhD thesis, Department of Psychology, University of Nottingham.

Ainsworth, S., Wood, D., & Bibby, P. A. (1996). Coordinating multiple representations in computer based learning environments. In P. Brna, A. Paiva, & J. A. Self (Eds.), *Proceedings of the European conference on artificial intelligence in education* (pp. 336–342). Lisbon: Edições Colibri.

Ainsworth, S. E., Wood, D. J., & Bibby, P. A. (1997). Evaluating principles for multi-representational learning environments. In S. Vosniadou, E. Matsagouras, K. Maridaki-Kassotaki, & S. Kotsanis, (Eds.), Presented at the 7th EARLI conference, Athens, Greece. Retrieved October 18, 2001, from http://www.psychology.nottingham.ac.uk/~sea/EARLI.html

Altmann, E. M., & John, B. E. (1995). *A preliminary model of expert programming.* Technical Report CMU-CS-95-172, School of Computer Science, Carnegie Mellon University, Pittsburgh, PA.

Bental, D., & Brna, P. (1995). Enabling abstraction: Key steps in building physics models. In J. Greer (Ed.), *Proceedings of the world conference on artificial intelligence in education* (pp. 162–169). Charlottesville, VA: Association for the Advancement of Computing in Education.

Brna, P., & Burton, M. (1997). The computer modeling of students collaborating in learning about energy. *Journal of Computer Assisted Learning, 13*(3), 193–204.

Burton, M. (1998). *Computer modeling of dialogue roles in collaborative learning activities*. Unpublished PhD thesis, Computer Based Learning Unit, The University of Leeds.

Burton, M., & Brna, P. (1996). Clarissa: An exploration of collaboration through agent-based dialogue games. In P. Brna, A. Paiva, & J. A. Self (Eds.), *Proceedings of the European conference on artificial intelligence in education* (pp. 393–400). Lisbon: Edições Colibri, Lisbon.

Burton, M., Brna, P., & Pilkington, R. (2000). Clarissa: A laboratory for the modeling of collaboration. *International Journal of Artificial Intelligence in Education, 11*(2), 79–105.

Burton, M., Brna, P., & Treasure-Jones, T. (1997). Splitting the collaborative atom: How to support learning about collaboration. In B. du Boulay & R. Mizoguchi, (Eds.), *Artificial intelligence in education: Knowledge and media in learning systems* (pp. 135–142). Amsterdam: IOS.

Clark, A., & Chalmers, D. (1998). The extended mind. *Analysis, 58*(1), 7–19. Also on-line at http://artsci.wustl.edu/philos/pnp/papers/clarkchalmers.extended.html

Devi, R., Tiberghien, A., Baker, M., & Brna, P. (1996). Modeling students' construction of energy models in physics. *Instructional Science, 24*(4), 259–293.

Grice, H. P. (1975). Logic of conversation. In D. Davidson & G. Harman (Eds.), *The logic of grammar*. Encino, CA: Dickenson.

Grosz, B. J., & Kraus, S. (1999). The evolution of shared plans. In M. Wooldridge & A. Rao (Eds.), *Foundations of rational agency* (Applied Logic Series, Vol. 14, pp. 227–262). Dordrecht: Kluwer.

Grosz, B. J., & Sidner, C. L. (1990). Plans for discourse. In P. Cohen, J. Morgan, & M. Pollack (Eds.), *Intentions in communication*. Cambridge, MA: Bradford Books, MIT Press.

Harrop, A. G. (1999). ENCAL: A prototype computer-based learning environment for teaching calculator representations. In T. R. G. Green, R. Abdullah, & P. Brna (Eds.), *Collected papers of the psychology of programming special interest group* (pp. 58–66). Document available from the authors and online at http://www.ppig.org/papers/11th-harrop.pdf

Kintsch, W. (1988). The role of knowledge in discourse comprehension: A construction-integration model. *Psychological Review, 95*, 163–182.

Kitajima, M., & Polson, P. G. (1996). A comprehension-based model of exploration. In *Human Factors in Computing Systems: CHI'96 Conference Proceedings* (pp. 324–331).

Kitajima, M., & Polson, P. G. (1997). A comprehension-based model of exploration. *Human–Computer Interaction, 12*(4), 345–389.

Lave, J., & Wenger, E. (1990). *Situated learning: Legitimate peripheral participation*. Cambridge, UK: Cambridge University Press.

Lochbaum, K. E. (1994). *Using collaborative plans to model the intentional structure of discourse*. Unpublished PhD thesis, Harvard University.

Rich, C., & Sidner, C. L. (1997). COLLAGEN: When agents collaborate with people. In M. Huhns & M. Singh (Eds.), *Readings on agents* (pp. 117–124). San Francisco: Morgan Kaufmann.

Rieman, J., Young, R. M., & Howes, A. (1996). A dual-space model of iteratively deepening exploratory learning. *International Journal of Human–Computer Studies, 44*, 743–775.

Sidner, C. L. (1994a). An artificial discourse language for collaborative negotiation. In *Proceedings of the national conference on artificial intelligence '94* (pp. 814–819). Cambridge, MA: MIT Press.

Sidner, C. L. (1994b). Negotiation in collaborative activity: A discourse analysis. *Knowledge Based Systems*, 7(4), 265–267.

Taylor, J. A., Carletta, J., & Mellish, C. (1996). Requirements for belief models in cooperative dialogue. *User Modeling and User Adapted Instruction*, 6(1), 23–68.

Tiberghien, A. (1994). Modeling as the basis for analyzing teaching–learning situations. *Learning and Instruction*, 4, 71–87.

Vygotsky, L. (1978). *Mind in society: The development of higher psychological processes*. Cambridge, MA: Harvard University Press.

Wertsch, J. (1991). *Voices of the mind: A sociocultural approach to mediated action*. Cambridge, MA: Harvard University Press.

Wertsch, J., & Toma, C. (1989). Discourse and learning in the classroom. In L. P. Steffe & J. Gale (Eds.), *Constructivism in education*. Hillsdale, NJ: Lawrence Erlbaum Associates.

Zhang, J. (1998). A distributed representation approach to group problem solving. *Journal of American Society of Information Science*, 49(9), 801–809.

Zhang, J., & Norman, D. A. (1994). Representations in distributed cognitive tasks. *Cognitive Science*, 18(1), 87–122.

Chapter 9

Teachers' Explanations of Students' Collaborative Modeling Activities

Kristine Lund

UMR 5612, GRIC, CNRS & Université Lumière Lyon 2

Educational research has examined how students elaborate models in the science classroom (Janvier & Lapointe, 1998; Tiberghien, 1994), as well as the role and function of teachers' tutoring during students' modeling activities (Franceschelli & Weil-Barais, 1998; Janvier & Lapointe, 1998; Larcher & Chomat, 1998). However, relatively little research has been carried out on the processes by which teachers come to understand how students model, or on how teachers can be helped to learn how students model, as part of their training. These questions form an essential initial approach but remain separate from the question involving to what extent teachers actually integrate what they have learned during their training into their professional practice. In a research program that aims to contribute to teaching teachers how students model, such a question should be addressed subsequently in order to evaluate if and how teachers put the information they gain on students' modeling into practice. The assumption here is that teaching teachers about how students model is successful if the teacher-learners can fruitfully bring to bear this new knowledge on their practice.

Although it is recognized that teachers' beliefs about students' knowledge have a direct effect on how they teach (Porlan Ariza, Garcia Garcia, Rivero Garcia, & del Pozo, 1998), the research in the field of teacher education has largely focused on other issues. For example, it has concerned teachers' views of curriculum content (Koliopoulos & Ravanis, 1998), teachers' epistemological views of the domain they teach (Porlan Ariza et al., 1998), teachers' cognitive activities during error diagnosis (de Corte, Verschaffel, & Schrooten, 1991) and teachers' decisionmaking (Shelly & Sibert, 1991). One example of teacher education research that has focused on teachers' beliefs of students knowledge is "Activating Instruction" (Lonka & Ahola, 1995). Its goal is to enhance teachers' understanding of the cognitive processes that underlie students' learning and thereby help teachers design their teaching in order to "activate" their students.

In this chapter, we present a study that addresses the first part of the research program described earlier: What are the tools and methods that may be used to help teachers learn about how students model? As in the Vicarious Learner project (McKendree, Stenning, Mayes, Lee, & Cox, 1998), we see recorded dialogues as a reusable learning resource. We thus also reuse student dialogue, but for a different purpose. Instead of studying the potential benefits of students observing other students' dialogue, we study the potential benefits teachers may gain by observing and explaining students' dialogue taking place within a science lab work session the teachers themselves designed. The teachers' goal during this analysis is to evaluate the design of their science lab work by examining how the teacher and students talked about modeling while going about their lab work activities. This situation occurs within the context of the student teachers' diploma and as part of an action-research group.

Our study, named "Prof-Reflect," takes place within the situation just described. Student teachers and researchers review transcriptions of student dyad and teacher dialogue recorded during a modeling task in the classroom. Our object of study is the action-research group's dialogue during this review. The term *dialogue* is used here to signify a goal-oriented discussion with any number of participants, from two on upward (see also *polylogue*, defined shortly). We examine how the action-research group interprets students' modeling by the analysis of student dialogue and/or teacher interventions (cf. Lund & Baker, 1999).

When Wells (1996) stated that "Teaching and learning are largely conducted through talk, yet the relationship between the talk and the activity goals it is intended to achieve is rarely problematized or treated as a matter for conscious choice" (p. 74), his emphasis lay with the talk and the goals of teachers. He proposed that teachers analyze episodes of talk from their classrooms in order that they become conscious of the options they select. This would allow them to change their discourse if they were so inclined, thus changing the nature of the classroom community. In the research presented here, we provide teachers with a framework used both for designing science lab work on modeling and for interpreting teacher and student dialogue about modeling in science (Buty, Lund, & Chastan, 2000; Tiberghien, Buty, Gaidioz, LeMarèchal, & Vince, 2001). We view their coconstruction of explanations (Chi, Bassok, Lewis, Reimann, & Glaser, 1989; Chi, de Leeuw, Chiu, & LaVancher, 1994; Ploetzner, Dillenbourg, Preier, & Traum, 1999) as a means for student teachers to learn about student conceptions about modeling (as well as their own!) and as a consequence, modify their lab work design as well as the way they themselves talk about modeling.

Proposing reflective situations for teacher education that focus on understanding student dialogue requires that we have gained an understanding of how teachers reflect in such situations. In order to gain such an understanding, we have elaborated an analysis method for describing explicative polylogues. A *polylogue* is a multiparticipant interaction—a communicative situation that gathers together several real live individuals, from four participants on upward (Kerbrat-Orecchioni, in press). According to Kerbrat-Orecchioni, polylogal situations are extremely complex and flexible, having such a mobile and changeable organization that observing them at a particular point in time can never provide a representative picture of the whole. In the sections that follow, we focus on a specific polylogal phenomenon. We describe how explanations are dynamically coconstructed within a specific type of polylogue, thus giving a limited but nevertheless representative picture of that particular phenomenon.

In what follows, we describe our empirical study, briefly present some previous research on explanation and dialogue, propose our analytical model for analyzing explanatory polylogue, and present our illustrative analyses. We describe, from a cognitive and an interactional point of view, the explanatory processes at work during the action-research group's polylogue. The polylogue has five participants, one of whom (the author) is a participant–observer.

We end the chapter with discussion on the possible contributions of our analysis approach for the language and cognitive sciences and for teacher education. Specifically, the contributions concern (a) modeling coconstructed explanatory polylogues and (b) a contribution to the rapidly growing body of research that recognizes the study of teacher and teacher-student dialogue in relation to learning goals as essential in educational interactions.

EMPIRICAL STUDY "PROF-REFLECT"

As we argued in the introduction, we need to find a way to study how teachers understand how students model. Instead of setting up an experiment in the laboratory, which may be more or less difficult for participants to make sense of or get motivated for, we constructed an ecological setting that had meaning for the student teachers' practice. The notion of *meaning* is made more precise in the course of this section. Prof-Reflect, our empirical study, takes place within the context of a real-life situation. It is integrated into the final project work of two student science teachers during the last year of their training. The French teacher training institution requires that students investigate a teaching–learning issue by choosing a theoretical framework, by experimenting with the design of a class session, and by writing a report. Prof-Reflect occurs within the larger context of an action-research project that provides the student teachers with a theoretical framework for the conception and the analysis of teaching situations where students are required to model.[1] The empirical study, although part of a socially recognized institutional process (the student science teachers' final project), is thus influenced by the participants of the action-research project, all of whom have specific goals.

The object of this section is to describe the elements of our situation of study. Such a description subsequently enables us to present a framework in which we can discuss the interactive dynamics of cognition as it emerges within explanatory dialogue.

At the beginning of the student teachers' final project, the action-research group presented the student teachers with a Course Design and Analysis (CDA) tool; in fact, a series of questions. These questions are hereafter referred to as the CDA tool. The CDA tool has six main sections that teachers are asked to complete while designing their course or lab work. In the first section, teachers make explicit the meaning that will be given to the elements of the curriculum that are the object of the teaching and learning situation. In order to do this for their course, the teachers fill out a form (see Table 9.1) that exemplifies a specific way of viewing modeling (Tiberghien, 1994). According to this view (see also Vince & Tiberghien, chap. 2, this volume), elements in a teaching and learning situation can be assigned to the world of theory and model, to the world of objects and events, or to the relation between these two worlds. For example, physics equations are part of theory and model (hereafter T/M), the manipulations of experimental apparatus are part of objects and

TABLE 9.1

The CDA (Course Design and Analysis) Tool's Way of Viewing Modeling for a Specific Teaching Content

A view on modeling	Already known		To be constructed
	Junior high physics	Everyday life	High school physics; second year
Theory and model world (T/M)			
Relation between the two worlds (Link)			
Objets and events world (O/E)			

[1]The COAST and Interaction & Cognition (IC) research teams, both belonging to the GRIC laboratory, funded by the CNRS and the University Lumière Lyon 2, worked together on a 3-year project (1999–2001) with the IUFM (Institut de Formation de Maîtres) of Lyon, a teacher training institution, to experiment with new techniques in science teacher education. This project is part of a larger one, in cooperation with the INRP (Institut National de la Recherche Pédagogique) and other research laboratories where the goal is to design tools for course and lab work design and analysis in the experimental sciences.

events, (hereafter O/E), and using measurements of experimental apparatus in order to construct a valid physics equation is an example of relating the two worlds (hereafter Link; cf. Bécu-Robinault, 1997).

The other questions of the CDA tool are: What information and materials are given to the students? How is the class session organized? What are the teacher's activities apart from summing up? What are the students' activities? And finally, how many conclusions do you ask of the students? How many predictions? How many interpretations?

Keeping the categories in Table 9.1 in mind, the student teachers first studied previous years of the physics curricula of their high school students and categorized the knowledge they found there by filling out the table accordingly—either Theory/Model (T/M), Object/Event (O/E), or Link (between the two). For example, one student teacher classified "We know how to model a force by a vector (vertical/horizontal or combination thereof, direction, intensity and the point of application)" as T/M. Second, the student teachers attempted to ascribe to their high school students, and subsequently categorize (again, either as T/M, O/E, or Link), physics knowledge that could come from everyday life. For example, "I don't perceive a movement in the same way according to where I am, for example in a bus or on the sidewalk" was described as knowledge attributed to high school students and classified as O/E. Finally, student teachers studied the labwork session they themselves constructed and categorized its elements. For example, "In order to get a ball to follow a curved line with a uniform circular movement, one must apply a centrifugal force to the ball" was classified as a Link.

The student teachers were asked to use the CDA tool to construct the experimental lab work session they were to teach. The first questions on the corresponding work sheet are shown in Fig. 9.1. The analyses presented later in the chapter make reference to question II b).

The action-research group's hypothesis is that the view on modeling just described, taken into account during course design and during analysis of student dialogue issued from the class session, helps in two ways. First, teachers better understand their own view of modeling. Second, through the study of student and teacher dialogue, teachers can understand how students model and can begin to see how the different views of modeling (teachers' and students') may affect student learning.

In order for the reader to gain an understanding of the sequencing of activities within our action-research group, we illustrate them in Table 9.2. It describes a selection of activity phases that occurred within the context of the action-research group's work. Their length in time, the participants involved, and the resources present are also shown. In brief, during a first meeting, the student teachers discussed modeling and the CDA tool with their final project director and with the researchers, all participants in the action-research project. During a second meeting, the student teachers presented a proposed lab work session, designed with the CDA tool, to the other participants.

Objective: Show that force plays a fundamental role in the movement of a system.

Materials: A horizontal smooth glass table, a ball, an arc of a circle drawn on the surface of the table with a marker, paper toweling to erase the arc after the experiment.

I) Let's try to get the ball to follow the curve.

a. *Presentation of the experiment* : You have at your disposal a horizontal smooth glass table and a ball. This material has been chosen in order to minimize friction. There is an arc of a circle drawn on the table that looks like the figure below.

b. *The experiment consists* in launching the ball with your hand (making sure the ball stays in contact with the table) and trying, after having let go of the ball, to make it follow the designated trajectory.

Questions: Are you able to succeed? If so, what have you done to do so? What is the position of the ball? What is your position? Describe the method you used. If you are not able to succeed, what do you observe? What does the ball do?

c. *Discussion and conclusion*

< What can you conclude about the phenomenon you observe?

< Discussion on the principle of inertia: explain the following terms: persevere, state of rest, rectilinear uniform movement, the forces that are exerted compensate each other

< What are the forces and what types of forces act on the ball (distance or contact)?

< How did we eliminate a contact force (by the choice of material) that would have hindered the application of the principle of inertia?

II) How can we get the ball to follow the curve?

a. What can you do so that after having thrown the ball, it follows in a circular movement, the designated trajectory on the table? Try to imagine different methods. We will compare them and test together one of the simpler ones.

b. Questions on the principle of inertia: Is the principle of inertia verified? (re-read the principle*), What condition is not verified? What is the difference with the first experiment? What are the characteristics of this force? (Spatial orientation? Direction?)

*A body will maintain its state of rest or its rectilinear uniform movement if the forces that act on the body compensate each other.

FIG. 9.1. The first part of the worksheet given to students during the lab work movement and force.

TABLE 9.2

Description of the Principal Activity Phases of Our Experimental Teacher-Training Project, Their Length in Time, the Participants Involved and the Resources Present

Activity Phase	Time	Participants	Resources Present
Phase 1: discussion on modeling and on the different possibilities of lab work sessions	3 hours	Student Teacher 1 Student Teacher 2 Substitute Teacher Project Director CogSci Researcher PhyDid Researcher	Official curriculum documents describing lab work sessions CDA tool (not filled in) for analysis and conception of teaching sequences
Phase 2: student teacher and substitute teacher present their proposed lab work session to the others	3 hours	Student Teacher 1 Substitute Teacher Project Director CogSci Researcher PhyDid Researcher	Two filled in versions (student teachers 1 and 2) of above-mentioned CDA tool describing the proposed lab work session
Phase 3: proposed lab work session experimented in class with 16–17-year-old high school students	1.5 hours	Student Teacher 1 Substitute Teacher CogSci Researcher Paired students	Teacher and student versions of lab work handouts Experimental apparatus
Phase 4: individual viewing of lab work session video and reading of transcription of filmed student dyad	1.5 hours	Student Teacher 1 Student Teacher 2 Substitute Teacher Project Director CogSci Researcher PhyDid Researcher	Video of lab work session (focused on one student pair) Transcription of student pair's dialogue
Phase 5: Prof-Reflect reflection session on lab work session (focusing on one student pair)	3 hours	Student Teacher 1 Student Teacher 2 Project Director CogSci Researcher PhyDid Researcher	Instructions for reflection session Transcription of student pair 1's dialogue Students' lab reports Two filled in versions (student teachers 1 and 2) of above- mentioned CDA tool regarding taught lab work

Note. Project Director Oversees Student Teachers' Report; Cogsci = Researcher in Cognitive Science (Author); Phydid = Researcher in Physics Didactics

This lab work session was taught in the substitute teacher's[2] classroom as part of the official French national curriculum. Two student dyads and the teacher interventions were audio and video recorded and transcribed by the author. Subsequently, all participants viewed this video and studied audio transcriptions in their own time. Finally, the participants in the action-research project held two reflection sessions (the data examined here is part of the first session, also audio and video recorded and transcribed by the author), where student teachers were asked to study the high school student dyads' dialogue transcriptions and to find justifications therein for any modifications that they would like to propose to two resources. The first resource was the lab work handout for students, composed of questions to answer and procedures to follow (shown in part in Fig. 9.1) . The second resource was the CDA tool itself (Table 9.1 plus associated questions). Figure 9.2 shows the complete instructions for the reflection session. It is the transcription of this reflection session that is the object of analysis for this chapter.

The instructions given to all the participants of the action-research group, but more particularly directed toward the student teachers, dealt with the analysis of transcribed student and teacher dialogue. These instructions were carefully designed (by the two participating research-

---

We ask you to study the students' dialogue and to find justifications therein for any modifications that you would like to propose to the following resources:

< The student and teacher lab worksheets

< The CDA (Course Design and Analysis) tool you filled in

We ask you to explain the reasons behind your proposed modifications. Please consider the following questions when studying the students' dialogue:

1. What are the difficulties that the students experience? Do some of them stem from relating the model to objects and events in the experimental field? **Why?**

2. Do you observe that the students interpret their instructions in a way different than you intended? **Why?**

3. Regarding the knowledge you attribute to the students prior to their participating in the lab work session, do you observe that this knowledge has been utilized? **What is it that makes you say so?** Do you observe that some knowledge has functioned as an obstacle to the learning goals? **What is it that makes you say so?**

4. In the different parts of the lab work session, can you characterize whether or not the students' activity is situated in the "world of theory and model," in the "world of objects and events," or in the relating of the two "worlds?" **What is it that makes you say so?**

FIG. 9.2.   Complete instructions for the reflection sessions (Phase 5).

---

[2]Owing to student teacher 2 going on maternity leave, the substitute teacher replaced her. The substitute teacher participated on an active voluntary basis in the action-research project.

ers) in relation to a number of specific objectives. First, as mentioned previously, the instructions had to generate an activity that had meaning for the student teachers. We define *meaning* in the following way: As the student teachers' objective of their final project was to design (with the CDA tool) a lab work session and experiment it in class, we decided to give them a way for *evaluating* both the design and the actual carrying out of the lab work session. We assumed the student teachers would be motivated to do so considering that they were required to write a report on their final project. Our hypothesis was that lab work design and aspects of teaching modeling could be partially evaluated by studying the dialogue of a student dyad solving the lab work problems in conjunction with the dialogue of a teacher guiding the lab work. Second, the questions were designed to illustrate the effectiveness that viewing modeling in the way already described may have on rendering explicit how the teacher approaches modeling and on pinpointing students' difficulties. Third, explanation production is seen as beneficial for learning (e.g., see Ploetzner et al., 1999), so the questions (note "Why" and "What" in bold in Fig. 9.2) were formulated so as to produce explanatory dialogue (Bruxelles & de Gaulmyn, 2000).

EXISTING RESEARCH ON EXPLANATION AND DIALOGUE

In this section, we review the relevant literature on explanation and dialogue with a view to elaborating a method of analyzing explanatory polylogue. We begin with a question of terminology. The 1996 Oxford English Reference Dictionary defines the verb *explicate* as either (a) to develop the meaning or implication of an idea, principle, etc., or (b) to make clear, explain. The associated adjectives are *explicative* or *explicatory*, whereas *explanatory* is defined as serving or intended to serve to explain. We prefer the adjective explanatory, because as we shall see, the viewpoint we develop differentiates an intended explanation from one that meets the goal of increasing a person's comprehension of something problematic.

The many facets of explanation have been studied using diverse approaches in different domains of research: among them philosophy, psychology, artificial intelligence, linguistics, psycholinguistics, education, and cognitive science. Philosophers who studied explanation have taken a normative approach by concerning themselves with elaborating theories of what does and does not constitute scientific explanation (Apostel et. al., 1970; Hempel & Oppenheim, 1948). Although our approach is a descriptive one, we retain from their work a fundamental distinction that enables us to discuss explanation. According to Hempel & Oppenheim (1948), scientific explanation consists in a description of an empirical phenomenon to be explained (explanandum) and a series of antecedent conditions and general laws that explain it (explanans). Our object of study is not scientific explanation per se; rather, it is the dialogue of people explaining other people's dialogue and actions taking place in the realm of scientific lab work. We thus adapt these terms, defining an *explanandum* to be an object, phenomenon, concept, process, or action; in fact, it is whatever entity is discussed in the Prof-Reflect polylogue as being problematic and needing to be elucidated. An *explanans* is a sequence of utterances (not necessarily the expression of a combination of antecedent conditions and general laws) explaining the explanandum (plural is explananda). We do not describe the nature of an explanans (plural is explanantia) in our case as such. Rather, the focus is on the effect that these phrases-in-dialogue have, namely, on augmenting participants' comprehension of the current explanandum.

We now have a means for discussing what participants in an explanatory dialogue see as problematic (explanandum) and the utterances they propose for explaining it (explanans). But can the phenomenon of explanation be understood with an analysis limited to these two notions? We believe that it cannot be. Following Goodwin and Duranti (1992), we hold that "context and talk [talk being for our purposes, the explananda and explanantia] stand in a mutually reflexive relationship to each other, with talk, and the interpretive work it generates, shaping context as much as context shapes talk" (p. 31). What then, is included in the surrounding context, if the focal point of our analysis is the explanatory talk? As Bateson (1972) suggested, in defining the context it is the perspective of the participant(s) whose behavior is being analyzed that must be taken into account. Such a view is opposed to the view of defining the context as the researcher doing the observing sees it. For Bateson then, context becomes that which is relevant for the participant(s) during the performing of specific activities, as evidenced in their talk or actions. Of course, as an observer, the researcher still *interprets* what is esteemed as relevant (by the participants), through analysis of participants' talk and actions.

At the very least, the context of explanatory dialogue includes different aspects of the people who take part in it (other elements of context are proposed in the next section as part of our proposed analytical model). A first limited definition of explanation could therefore be "a collaborative dialogical process established within an interaction by which a problematic issue is made less so for one or more of the participants." Balacheff (1988) showed in work on mathematics didactics that an intervention during teacher–student dialogue is not inherently explanatory; rather, an intervention becomes explanatory when the knowledge of the person to whom the explanation is directed is taken into account. Baker (2000, 182, translated from the French), working in cognitive science, takes this notion of coconstruction further, defining explanation as "... the set of processes having to do with 1) the structuring of knowledge-in-interaction and 2) the adapting of this knowledge to the goals of the other participants. These two activities are carried out in order to increase the coherence of all participants' mutual representations of the explanation produced." So, not only does the explainer take the person's knowledge to whom he or she is explaining into account, both participants (explainer and explainee) contribute to building a common ground that they may eventually agree on as being the explanation.

Explanation Versus Justification

Now that we have proposed a first definition for explanation, how do we recognize explanatory sequences in dialogue? How can we distinguish between sequences containing justification, analogy, argumentation, and interpretation or even simple information providing? And what signals the beginning and end of an explanatory sequence?

First, explanatory sequences in dialogue cannot always be located with the help of linguistic markers (such as "because," commonly viewed as triggering explanation). In fact, the same response (for example, "He knows because he read it in the newspaper.") can be interpreted as either an explanation or a justification depending on the question preceding it that motivates the response being given. The response is an explanation if the question is "How did he find that out?" and a justification if the question is "Are you sure of what he's telling us?" (Kohler-Chesney, 1983). In the former case, what "he knows" is not disputed; the speaker is questioning the origin of this knowledge: where did he find out what he knows? In the latter case, the response illustrates that the speaker (prompted by the skepticism of her interlocutor; "are you sure?") affirms that the knowledge in question is true and justifies that by saying that it was read in the newspaper. In this example, the surrounding discourse provides us with the necessary context for determining whether or not we are in the presence of an explanation or a justification.

Explanation Versus Analogy

If what looks on the surface (by the presence of linguistic markers such as "because") to be explanation is sometimes *not*, the reverse is also true. A different discursive phenomenon (not containing linguistic markers of an explanatory nature)—an analogy, for example—can under certain circumstances indeed be explanatory. For Plantin (1996), explanation is all speech capable of alleviating uneasiness about an event that does not integrate into the ordinary. He proposed a structure for an explanatory analogy whereby proposition P' *explains* proposition P:

1) Proposition P is not understood.

2) There is no debate about P'. P' is understood.

3) Proposition P is analogous to P'.

4) P is understood. (p. 51)

In this way, explanation can be viewed as an *effect* of discourse rather than as a particular *aspect* of discourse (Kohler–Chesney, 1983). If we adopt this view, we may then characterize explanatory dialogue by the extent to which it contributes to increasing the understanding or alleviating the uneasiness one has in relation to something problematic.

Explanation Versus Argumentation

There are many types of argumentation and ways of arguing that surpass the scope of this chapter; we limit our discussion here to how causality links argumentation with explanation. Plantin (1996) defined the case of argumentation by cause in the following way: A fact or data is accepted and we ask in what way this fact justifies a particular conclusion. Thus, in the relation "fact (data) ← conclusion," the discussion centers on the conclusion. For example, fact = "We don't have any money;" conclusion = "We can't go to the amusement park." In argumentation by cause, one would say, "Yes, we *can* go to the amusement park. We don't need our *own* money, we can *borrow* some." On the other hand, in explanation by cause, the fact is well established and agreed on and we are looking for its cause. In the corresponding relation "cause (fact ← data)," the discussion centers on the cause. For example, fact = "We don't have any money (and we all agree on that)." The cause of having no money is the focus of questioning; why don't we have any? Answers (proposed causes) could be: "You spent it all," "Mother quit her job," or "The conservatives are in power."

These examples distinguish causal argumentation from causal explanation, the former focusing on the pertinence of drawing a particular conclusion, given a certain fact, and the latter focusing on the cause of an agreed-on fact. The causal explanation example illustrates, in addition, that there may be more than one cause for a given fact and that proposed causes can be interpreted as being in the interest of the person proposing them (Plantin, 1996). A particular role a person plays may engender a particular vision of a causal chain, thus enticing the person playing the role to put forth one cause over another as a proposed explanation. We illustrate this with our analyses.

Explanation Versus Interpretation

Now that we have proposed first distinctions between justification and explanation, between analogy and explanation, and between argumentation and explication, let us look at interpretation. Kohler-Chesny (1981) defined three types of interpretation in the context of the paraphrase:

1. Attributed interpretation: "When I say ..., X says (or thinks) that I say ..."
2. Interpretation for which responsibility is taken: "When X says ... , I say that X says ..."
3. Supposed interpretation: "When X says ..., he means ..."

As it is defined here, *interpretation* is a statement divided into two parts, the second of which is somehow different from the first. It is the nature of this difference that forms the interpretation. Alternatively, Kohler-Chesny (1981) defined phrases that *make explicit* to be of the type "When I say …, I mean …" Accordingly, one can explain one's own phrases, but once one proposes alternative phrases for other people's phrases or proposes what others think of one's own phrases, one is interpreting.

Explanation Versus Information Providing or Description

Scriven (1988) put forth that explanations are necessarily descriptive and necessarily provide information. In this light, the question to be asked is not "What is the difference between information providing and explanation?" but rather "How and when do descriptions and information giving count as explanations?"

> Tentatively we can consider the vague hypothesis that the right description is the one which fills in a particular gap in the understanding of the person or people to whom the explanation is directed. That there is a gap in understanding, or a misunderstanding, seems plausible since whatever an explanation *actually* does, in order to be called an explanation at all it must be *capable* of making clear something not previously clear, that is, of increasing or producing understanding of something. The difference between explaining and "merely" informing, like the difference between explaining and describing, does not, I shall argue, consist in explaining being something "more than" or even something intrinsically different from informing or describing, but in its being the appropriate piece of informing or describing, the appropriateness being a matter of its relation to a *particular context*. Thus, what would in one context be "a mere description" can in another be "a full explanation." The distinguishing features will be found, not in the verbal form of the question or answer, but in the known or inferred state of understanding and the proposed explanation's relation to it. (p. 53; italics in original)

Within this view, particular participants' speaking turns that seem to be, for example, on the level of information providing, become explanatory when these speaking turns are understood to be contributing to the building of an explanation's common ground, thus increasing understanding of whatever was not previously clear for one or more of the participants.

Recall our questions. In light of the preceding, how do we recognize explanatory sequences in dialogue? What signals their beginning and end? We propose that explanatory dialogue sequences are excerpts of exchanges between participants that contribute to reaching a common ground on what is to be explained and what is proposed as explanation. Such sequences are delimited by a change in explanatory goal as agreed on by all or most of the participants. Within this collaborative view of explanation, the interaction between participants plays an integral part. Because both explananda and explanantia are coconstructed, the social roles the participants play, as well as their respective goals, need to be taken into account. In the next two sections, we introduce our model and analysis method and present our illustrative analyses.

A METHOD FOR ANALYZING EXPLANATORY POLYLOGUE

Figure 9.3 illustrates our proposed method for analyzing explanatory polylogue; it forms what we have termed our *analytical model*. The elements that we esteem that form the context for explanatory polylogues, whatever their nature, are shown. Each element is discussed in turn for our particular case (The Prof-Reflect reflection session), in light of potential interplay (Goodwin & Duranti, 1992) with the talk (explananda and explanantia) our focal point.

Explananda and Explanantia (Elements 1 and 2)

Let us look at element 1 (the explanandum) or in other words, the entity that is problematic for the participants who are studying student and teacher lab work dialogue. According to our model, an explanandum can either (a) be successively refined and made more specific, in light of proposed explanantia, or (b) change focus entirely. In the former case, as our previous research showed (Lund & Baker, 1999), participants can collaborate on defining what it is that merits explanation, or in other

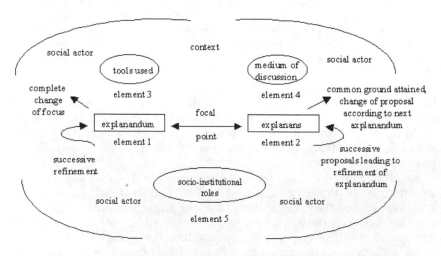

FIG. 9.3. Our view of explanation as a process and a proposed method for analysis.

TABLE 9.3
Examples of Explananda and Explanantia From the Prof-Reflect Polylogue, Beginning at Turn 228

Utterance	Explanatory Phenomenon
228. Jon: at 97 (*intervention number 97 of the transcribed high school student dyad*) what did the girl mean by (*Jon reads*) "so that's it, you can't follow the trajectory, it's a law"	Explanandum: what did the student mean?
229. Connie: I don't know (laughs)	Explanans: a proposition of what the student meant
230. Ginny: uhm, I think what she wanted to say was that it's not possible to follow the trajectory because it's a law. I think that's what she wanted to say. It's a law that we can't follow the trajectory. It's useless to try. There is a law that says so, so obviously	
231. Charlie: do you remember in what kind of tone she said that?	Refinement of the explanandum: can her tone help us understand what she meant?
232. Ginny: I think that's what it was	Reiteration of already proposed explanans; ignores newly refined explanandum
234. Ginny: (inaudible) it meant that there is a law that says that it's absurd to try and get it to follow the trajectory	
235. Charlie: hmmm	Does not ratify explanans

words, which explanandum is worth considering. In the latter case, participants already agree on what is to be explained and are working toward or have reached a common ground on the explanans (element 2) proposed. In both cases, something in the context triggers interest in the current explanandum (Dessalles, 1992; Lund & Baker, 1999). Consider the example extract in Table 9.3 taken from the Prof-Reflect polylogue.

In this example, Jon identifies the explanandum: What did the student mean by what she said? Ginny proposes an explanans of which Charlie is not convinced. He refines what is to be explained by asking about the tone of voice the student used. This new explanandum is not addressed by Ginny, who reiterates her already proposed explanans. Charlie remains unconvinced and common ground is not attained.

In addition to the interplay between the elements of the context—Elements 3 (tools), 4 (medium) and 5 (roles)—and the focal point—Elements 1 (explananda) and 2 (explanantia)—examined later, we postulate that there is interplay between the elements of the focal point themselves; that the nature of the explanandum influences the type of explanans produced.

As previously mentioned, the object to be explained in our study, by the student teachers and researchers, is high school student and teacher *dialogue* during science lab work on modeling. Dialogue was specifically chosen as the general explanandum for our action–research group because we hypothesized that studying dialogue provided a means for accessing the students' conceptual world and our goal was to help teachers produce explanations about students' talk and activities during lab work. It is in this way that the nature of possible explananda influence explanation; producing explanation about dialogue would give different results from producing explanations about students' test results.

Tools (Element 3)

In our view, the nature of the explanada in question is not alone in influencing the production of explanantia. The tools (element 3) used by the participants during their explanation activity also play a role in the kinds of explanations produced. We use the term *tool* here in the Vygotskian sense of *psychological tool* (Vygotsky, 1985)—for example, language, counting systems, algebraic symbol systems, works of art, writing, maps, schemes, diagrams, all types of signs, in fact. As Engeström (1987) pointed out, "Both psychological tools and technical tools mediate activity but only psychological tools imply and require reflective mediation, consciousness of one's (or the other person's) procedures" (p. 60). In the Prof-Reflect polylogal reflection session, the psychological tools available for explanation construction aid in mediating how the different participants view students' modeling activity. They are as follows:

- Language: in other words, the discussion occurring during the reflection session (see Tables 9.3, and 9.4 for example excerpts).
- A printout of 1½ hours of transcribed classroom dialogue centering around one dyad doing lab work and including teacher (the substitute teacher) interventions within that dyad, as well as teacher interventions addressed to the whole class (also working in dyads). See Table 9.5 for an example of high school student dyad discussion.
- The lab worksheet containing instructions for proceeding and given to the students at the beginning of the class (see Fig. 9.1).
- The substitute teacher's copy of the lab work handout—identical to that of the students but with added guiding comments intended only for the teacher.
- The instructions given to the Prof-Reflect reflection session participants (see Fig. 9.2).
- The table (shown in Table 9.1) filled out by the two student teachers, as well as the answers to the associated questions. The table and questions make up the CDA (Course Design and Analysis) tool.

- The dyad's (whose dialogue was partially transcribed in Table 9.5) written responses (in italics) to the lab work questions (see Fig. 9.4).

- The video of the dyad (viewed previously on an individual basis by all the participants in the Prof-Reflect reflection session).

What condition is not verified? *We are not within the conditions of application for the principle of inertia. This is because we are using a string so that the ball follows the trajectory drawn on the table which is not rectilinear.*

What is the difference with the first experiment? *The trajectory is not rectilinear because of the string, the forces are not compensated. The difference is that the ball follows the trajectory drawn on the table because we have added a string. We have added a contact force with the string. There are thus three contact forces: two are contact and one is distance.*

What are the characteristics of this force? (Spatial orientation? Direction?) *With the contact force of the string, the direction of the vector goes from the ball and arrives in the center of the circle that the ball traces. Its spatial orientation is horizontal. Its point of application is the point of contact between the ball and the string.*

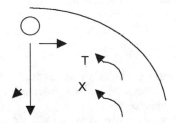

The force exercised by the string on the ball is centripetal. The movement is uniformly circular. Its value and its speed stay constant.

FIG. 9.4. The transcribed dyad's written responses (translated and typed here from the French) to the lab work questions II B.

In our view, these psychological tools facilitate reflective discussion about students' modeling processes and provide a framework (T/M, O/E, and Link) within which to interpret them, thus *shaping* the explanations provided. The section on illustrative analyses shows how one of the participants uses this framework to convince the others that it is useful for interpreting classroom dialogue.

Medium (Element 4)

Element 4 of our proposed model concerns the medium of discussion. In our case, the discussion takes place orally around a table, everyone having his or her own copy of and direct access to the tools described (with the exception of the video, which was not viewed collectively). Past research has shown the influence that structuring the channel of communication can have on the quality of typewritten and graphical interactions produced during computer-mediated problem solving (Baker & Lund, 1997; Tiberghien & de Vries, 1997). Contrary to focusing on the characteristics of the communication channel, the work presented here concentrates on gaining a first understanding of an oral discussion within its context in order to describe the mechanisms at work in elaborating explanations.

Socioinstiutional Roles (Element 5)

The socioinstitutional roles (element 5) that people play during a particular interaction, whether they be permanent professional roles or occasional ones, are part of an *interactive framework* (Vion, 1992, 1999) that allow for an interpretation of participants' utterances. According to Vion, analyzing a verbal interaction consists of apprehending the participants' jointly coordinated and complex activities on two different levels: social and interlocutionary. His interactive framework model defines the following "spaces" of analysis. The first three deal with the interpersonal relationships of the participants (the social level), whereas the last two intervene on the interlocutionary level.

1. Institutional: Participants coordinate activities that permit them to play social roles, be they professional (doctor, patient, teacher, student), otherwise socially recognized (candidate, debater), or occasional (advice-asker, advice-giver).
2. Modular: Within the dominant space that defines the interactive framework, the participants develop diverse types of local interactions called modules. For example, during a medical consultation there will be an interview module, a diagnosis module, a prescription module, and a payment module.
3. Subjective: The subjective space is comprised of self-images that participants display consciously or not, by their behavior (expert vs. non-expert, competent vs. incompetent, courageous vs. cowardly). These self-images are linked to social roles (the doctor plays the expert), but can also be linked to interlocutionary relations.
4. Discursive: The discursive space concerns the management of discursive tasks at the level of the sequence. Discursive tasks include sentence openings, closings, managing misunderstandings, narrating, explaining, arguing, and describing. Their analysis allows the researcher to apprehend how the participants' tasks can signify a particu-

lar role (for example, conversational partner) or a mixture of roles (for example, conversational partner coupled with narrator or listener). It is on this level that we find the cognitive content of explanation.

5. Utterance: The utterance space exemplifies the implication of the participants in regard to their language production. It describes to what extent the participants support the opinions they express. Is what the participant says his or her own personal opinion? The opinion of a group to which the participant belongs?

We can see, for example, how roles influence dialogue through the work of Collins and Stevens (1983). Through the study of transcripts of teachers interacting with students, they identified a set of techniques that has been alternatively called case, inquiry, discovery, or Socratic method. In such a method, where teachers typically lead students through a discussion in order that they notice something relevant to the learning goal, the teachers ask successive questions and the students respond. This is an example of how an assumed role (in this case institutional) can dictate the way in which an interaction plays out and thus influence the way explananda and explanantia are coconstructed.

In summary, with our analytical model as a basis, we further refine our definition of explanation as a collaborative dialogical process carried out between participants in interaction, who choose together what should be explained (explanandum: element 1) and work toward agreeing on what constitutes an explanans (element 2), potentially modifying explananda on the way. Once an explanandum is agreed on, the goal is to agree on an explanans, thus rendering the explanandum less problematic. This process takes place in a particular socioinstitutional situation (element 5) within which there are tools (element 3) used in explaining and a medium (element 4) by which the explaining is expressed, all of which influence what is proposed *for and as* explanation.

Approach for Application of Our Analytical Model

Using our analytical model as a guide, we implement the discourse analysis method following Bergmann in Gülich (1991). Such a method aims to:

1. discover the regularities in the corpus, in other words, the verbal structures that regularly reoccur in certain contexts;
2. reconstruct the problem (and associated goals) that the participants are attempting to resolve with the help of these structures;
3. describe the "method" that permits the participants to solve the problem in question.

As we analyze explanatory dialogue, the first regularities we seek are the verbal structures containing an object, phenomenon, fact, or utterance to be explained (recall our terms: explanandum in the singular, explananda in the plural) and an utterance that proposes an explanation (explanans in the singular, explanantia in the plural) for the given explanandum (Hempel & Oppenheim, 1948). The problem the participants are attempting to resolve can, in fact, be described as a conglomerate of problems, the structure or succession of which become evident with the successive identification of explananda. However, as we argued earlier, simply locating explananda and explanantia in the polylogue is sufficient neither for complete problem reconstruction nor for description of the method the participants use for problem solving. This is why in parallel to this first cognitive analysis of utterance content, we perform Vion's (1992) interaction-based analysis of socioinstitutional roles previously described. This second analysis gives a fuller picture of the conglomerate of problems addressed by the participants in terms of their corresponding goals and social roles and sheds light on the methods they use to solve them.

We propose that through the combination of these two analysis approaches (identification of explanatory phenomena and the examination of the different "spaces" described earlier), we can illustrate how cognition, in terms of utterance content on the discourse level, emerges through the participants' polylogal interaction and in what ways it is explanatory. As a consequence, we can gain a better understanding of how teachers in training solved the problems we set to them and therefore how teachers understand their own view and their students' views on modeling as well as the relation between them.

ILLUSTRATIVE ANALYSES

Remember that our object of analysis is the written transcription of a polylogal explanatory discussion issued from the action-research group's reflection session Prof-Reflect, described earlier and hereafter referred to as the *corpus*. The discussion lasted approximately 3 hours for a total of 1,251 turns. Interruptions were counted as separate turns.

We hypothesize that the analysis of our corpus will aid us in understanding how teachers in training use the view of modeling expressed in the CDA tool to do two things. First, this view of modeling will help them understand how students model, and second, it will illustrate how their own teaching can affect students' understanding of modeling. We also hypothesize that the model we propose in Fig. 9.3 will enable a coherent description of explanatory polylogues and that it can predict how explananda and explanantia evolve within dialogue.

Explananda and Explanantia (Elements 1 and 2)

The corpus was divided into different explanatory sequences, where an explanatory sequence is characterized by the explananda under examination and the explanatory goal they lead to, whether this goal is coelaborated or pursued by one of the participants. Within this definition, a new explanatory sequence begins when the global goal of the explanatory sequence changes. A single explanatory sequence may have a number of different explananda (what is posing a problem) in successive stages of refinement as long as the entire explanatory sequence moves toward a particular goal. Consider Table 9.4 as an illustrative example.

In the extract in Table 9.4, part of a larger explanatory sequence (turns 519–664, only partially shown here), the explanatory goal is established by Charlie, the researcher in physics didactics. What poses a problem for him is the fact that Ginny hesitated during her classroom teaching and had trouble reformulating a question on the students' worksheet (see the next section, Tools, for further detail). Her hesitation becomes his explanandum, but he already has an explanans in mind. In fact, his explanatory goal is to illustrate to Ginny and Connie that the level on which the teacher asks a question influences the level on which the high school students answer. In our example extract, it is Charlie, in his role as teacher-expert and ambassador for the view of modeling as exemplified in the CDA tool, that presents this interpretative framework as being explanatory. What is the method that Charlie uses to reach this goal of explaining to the others? How can we reconstruct the problems he is attempting to resolve?

Recall that in order to begin to answer these questions, we seek for verbal regularities in the form of explananda and explanantia. Table 9.4 shows that questions 1 through 5 are all posed in order to present the elements needed that taken together will produce an explanans that satisfies the explanandum: "Why did Ginny hesitate?" The first question centers on what the student teachers expected as a response from the high school students ("the movement isn't rectilinear"). The second question asks on what level (T/M, O/E, or Link) that response is located (Connie says T/M), and the third calls into question the level she gave. The community-supported answer is O/E, as Ginny proposes. Questions 4 and 5 ask: "What level is the corresponding question on?" The fourth question attempts unsuccessfully to ask what level the question was on that was supposed to elicit the high school students' response, and the fifth reformulates this more explicitly. The question they are discussing (the first in II B) is "Is the principle of inertia verified?" It is on the level of T/M. The production of the explanans (a discrepancy in the levels of Q & A produces problems) is now possible and thus the ultimate explanatory goal is in reach as Charlie has succeeded in showing that the question asked and the desired response are not on the same level.

Figure 9.5 illustrates this same sequence graphically (the lightbulb in answer 5 signifies Ginny's expressed understanding). Charlie breaks down his explanatory goal into reaching common ground on the resolution of two questions. Answer 1 is coelaborated by Ginny and Connie, whereas for questions 2 and 3, even if both Ginny and Connie participate in elaborating a response, Connie's answer dictates the flow of conversation for question 2 and Ginny's answer for question 3. Answer 5 is coelaborated by Charlie and Ginny, who feels she "has understood something." It is precisely this coelaboration that lends credibility to

TABLE 9.4

Extract From the Reflection Session, Beginning at Turn 596

Intervention	Utterance Space	Explanatory Phenomenon
596. Charlie: the, the response that you wanted, remind me, the response that you wanted for the first question, what was it?	Question 1	General Explanandum: What made Ginny hesitate during the reading of question II B? General Explanans: She had problems formulating because the Q and expected A were not on the same level (either T/M or O/E)
597. Ginny: the movement, um, isn't rectilinear	Answer 1	
598. Connie: that's right		
599. Ginny: to the second …		
600. Charlie: um, what's that in? It's in which …?	Question 2	
601. Ginny: with the string, it's when the string is added, (inaudible)	Answer 2	
602. Charlie: ok		
603. Connie: theory/model		
604. Charlie: "the movement isn't rectilinear," that's theory/model?	Question 3	
605. Connie: no	Answer 3	
606. Ginny: no, no, it's object/event		
607. Connie: sorry		

608. Charlie: where is the question?   Question 4

609. Ginny: is the principal of inertia verified?   Answer 4

610. Charlie: the question is at what level?   Question 5

611. Ginny: it's ... principle, so it's model, ok, ah, wow, that's   Answer 5
incredible, I just understood something (laughter)

612. Charlie: a priori, we always said ...

613. Ginny: Oh! So THAT's what was causing the problem!

614. Charlie: What we say is that what is often verified is, if you
ask them something at a certain level, they'll respond to you at
that same level.

615. Ginny: Yeah! That's really cool!

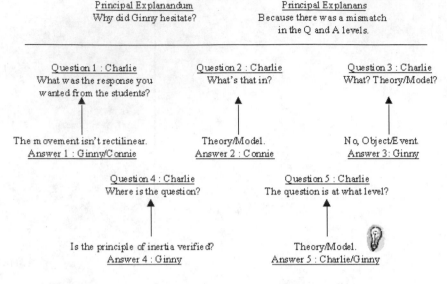

FIG. 9.5. Successive refinement of questions in relation to one explanandum in order to render possible the production of an explanans.

Ginny's understanding; they have both reached a common ground (see Fig. 9.3, our analytical model for explanatory polylogue).

Tools (Element 3)

Let us look now at how this explanatory goal is triggered (Dessalles, 1992; Lund & Baker, 1999). Charlie remembers from his respective reading and viewing of the transcription and video of the high school lab work that Ginny (as substitute teacher) hesitates while reading out the questions on the lab worksheet for the students. This hesitation is shown in Table 9.5, utterance 609, at the end of the extract. She began to read the following:

> II B). Questions on the principle of inertia: Is the principle of inertia veri-
> fied? (re-read the principle), What condition is not verified? What is the
> difference with the first experiment? What are the characteristics of this
> force? (Spatial orientation? Direction?) [from Fig. 9.1, the lab worksheet;
> see also Fig. 9.4].

TABLE 9.5

Extract of Transcribed Classroom Dialogue (Dyad + Occasional Teacher Interventions) That was Analyzed by the Participants in the Prof-Reflect Reflection Session, Beginning at Turn 586.

Utterance	Trigger
586. Ginny: We're talking about the example with the string of course. So "re-read the principle" (teacher reads this from II B). of the handout), there you are, answer the questions, think about it for a while with your partner and then we will answer together as a class.	
587. Sean: principle of inertia	
588. Sean: hmm ?	
589. Kelly: principle of inertia (inaudible) we can't do it by ourselves	
590. Sean: yeah, that's it	
591. Kelly: I dunno	
592. Sean: well, it's not within the conditions of application	
593. Kelly: yes, that's normal	
594. Sean: because the body is not persevering, right? right? (laughs)	
595. Kelly: rectilinear uniform movement	
596. Sean: so, it's not, yeah, yeah, yeah, that's it	
597. Kelly: so, it's not within the conditions of application	
598. Sean: yes	
599. Ginny: try and talk with your partner, discuss amongst yourselves	
600. Ginny: no, because, yes, because (inaudible) Can you yourself verify it?	

continued on next page

TABLE 9.5 (*continued*)

Utterance	Trigger
601. Sean: it's rectilinear	
602. Ginny: the conditions are … , what is not letting the … ?, what is it that … ?	
603. Kelly: the vectorial force	
604. Sean: what?	
605. Kelly: the vectorial force, it's not in there?	
606. Sean: ah no	
607. Kelly: hmm, the ball is (inaudible)	
608. Sean: no, that's not it, in its state of rest, or in its rectilinear uniform movement	
609. Ginny: Hang on a minute, what condition is not verified? It doesn't mean that we have not verified, like for uniformity, we have not verified it, it doesn't mean that. It means which condition does not permit, which condition, wait a minute, how can I say this? Which condition doesn't come into play, you know, let me find a phrase, an explication, ok?	Ginny hesitates: this passage becomes Charlie's explanandum

The fact that Ginny hesitated while reading these questions out loud to her students is what prompted Charlie to lead a type of socratic dialogue (Collins & Stevens, 1983) with the student teachers toward his explanatory goal. This is the method he used to reach his explanatory goal.

In order to understand why Ginny hesitated and why Charlie thought it interesting, remember what the high school students were asked to do (see Fig. 9.1 for the lab worksheet and instructions). In the beginning of the class session, each student dyad had attempted to get a ball to follow a curved line drawn on their table and had discussed why that was not possible in terms of the principle of inertia. They had then discussed the possible methods one could use to get the ball to follow the curve, with Ginny suggesting that they tie the ball to the end of a string and swing the string so that the ball followed the curved line. Ginny explains in turn 542 (not shown) that during her reading aloud of the questions, she had suddenly realized that the students could (although it would not necessarily be entirely correct) give an identical answer to more than just one of the questions. They could answer "The movement is not uniformly rectilinear" to "Is the principle of inertia verified?," to "What condition is not verified?," and to "What is the difference with the first experiment?" (where the students tried to get the ball to follow the curve just by tossing it).

It is this realization of the ambiguity of question meaning as well as Charlie's recognition of the mismatch of question and answer levels that led him to bring Ginny and Connie to examine the nature (what level are they: T/M, O/E, or Link?) of the questions posed to the high school students and the answers (what level are they: T/M, O/E, or Link?) the high school students gave. The assumption here is that if teachers thought about the level on which they posed a question in relation to the level of the answer they wanted, students would be able to answer correctly more easily. Careful reflection on the wording of questions with the CDA framework in mind would also reduce problems of ambiguity.

Medium (Element 4)

The medium we used for discussion was a copresent oral exchange where participants were seated at a table. Because the Prof-Reflect reflection session was filmed for research purposes, participants were asked to all sit along one side of a table so that the camera could film them all simultaneously. This seating arrangement did not necessarily facilitate exchanges.

Socioinstitutional Roles (Element 5)

Consider the interactive framework spaces for this extract (utterances 596–615):

- Institutional: Charlie (the didactics researcher) plays the teacher, while Ginny (the substitute teacher) and Connie (student teacher 1) play the students.
- Modular: goal-oriented pedagogical module stating that levels must match in questions and answers.
- Subjective: Charlie plays the expert while Ginny and Connie are acquiring their expertise in applying this particular view on modeling to dialogue analysis.
- Discursive: Charlie incites explanations by asking particular questions in a particular sequence in order to arrive at a known (for him) result, and Ginny and Connie answer, with Charlie summing up at the end.
- Utterance: At the end, Charlie expresses a community-supported opinion. At the outset, Ginny and Connie coelaborate their answers until Connie makes a mistake. At the end, Ginny stresses her own personal understanding.

The analysis of the interactive framework spaces reinforces the view of Charlie leading a type of Socratic dialogue (as teacher) within a goal-oriented pedagogical module to which Ginny and Connie respond (as students). After leading the student teachers in their responses, Charlie gives an explanation of the phenomena (supported by his research community), an explanation that Ginny coelaborates.

These two types of analyses (explanatory phenomena and framework spaces) enable us to describe the goals associated with the problems the group members attempt to resolve. This sequence is recognized as explanatory because the dialogue shows that Ginny (and maybe, to a lesser extent, Connie) have modified their representation of the importance of "level" in question asking and answering in order to resemble Charlie's.

What is missing from this Socratic dialogue is the "correct" answer. If one ascribes to the CDA tool, it is certainly a beginning that the student teachers realize that the answer (object/event level) expected from the students and the question (theory/model level) posed to the students were not on the same level, but what then? How should the questions in II B be changed? Or should the expected responses be revised?

In fact, looking back to the high school students' answers to the questions in II B (Fig. 9.4), we see that they skip answering altogether "Is the principle of inertia verified?", a problematic question in and of itself because a principle is not verifiable on precisely the grounds that it is a principle. Nor do the students really answer this question orally (see Table 9.5). For this particular question, then, the trigger for our explanatory sequence was not (as one might imagine), the students' different-level answer. Rather it was Ginny's hesitation (as perceived by Charlie) in reading the questions to her class.

Let us examine the other questions and answers in II B in order to see if their levels coincide. The second question: "What condition is not verified?" is on the T/M level. However, as the first question, it is also problematic for other reasons. The Prof–Reflect reflection session participants also discussed this point. What does *verify* mean in this case? In fact, the students' answer is correct: "We are not within the conditions of application for the principle of inertia. This is because we are using a string so that the ball follows the trajectory drawn on the table, which is not rectilinear." Their first sentence is T/M and the second is O/E. The third question: "What is the difference with the first experiment?" is on the O/E level. The students answer here is also mostly correct (with the exception of the last sentence, here deleted): "The trajectory is not rectilinear because of the string, the forces are not compensated. The difference is that the ball follows the trajectory drawn on the table because we have added a string. We have added a contact force with the string." All sentences are O/E. The fourth question: "What are the characteristics of this force? Spatial orientation? Direction?" is T/M. The students also answer on the T/M level: "With the contact force of the string, the direction of the vector goes from the ball and arrives in the center of the circle that the ball traces. Its spatial orientation is horizontal. Its point of application is the point of contact between the ball and the string. The force exercised by the string on the ball is centripetal. The movement is uniformly circular. Its value and its speed stay constant." The students thus seem to be answering in general on the level that the question was asked.

DISCUSSION, CONCLUSIONS, AND FURTHER WORK

There are a number of points to be made considering our analysis of the extracts presented here. This section addresses in different degrees the educational, language, and cognitive sciences.

First, for this example, the CDA tool gives a possible reason for the fact that students do not necessarily respond in the way teachers intend them to. In our case, the students did not respond at all to the first question in II B.

Second, whether they respond unexpectedly or not at all, the reuse of teacher-student and student dialogue in conjunction with the CDA tool as resources for training teachers enables student teachers to evaluate their course and lab work design and the manner in which they present content. This consciousness raising (about the importance of how questions are asked in relation to what is expected of students) that is obviously taking place during the Prof–Reflect reflection session can only be beneficial to the design of classroom activities. We have gained a first understanding of how such a technique can be used in teacher education.

Third, the application of our analytical model permits us to describe in detail (and potentially predict) how a polylogal explanatory sequence of this nature plays out. It also enables us to suggest improvements on facilitating explanatory dialogue:

- Even though it is the student teachers who are asked to do the analyses at the outset of the reflection session, the explanatory sequence is led by Charlie, according to his own institutionalized explanatory goal. His role gives him authority to lead the discussion.

- Proposed explanans are directly related to the interest they represent for the role the person doing the proposing is playing.
- Our identification of successive questions leading toward explanans production serves as a description of how the person leading the discussion attempts to structure the interaction in order to reach his or her explanatory goal.
- If common ground is not reached on the definition of an explanandum, explanantia production is blocked.
- Alternatively, if participants agree to modify and refine the explananda, then there is a possibility for attaining common ground on an explanans.
- There is room for improvement in the way the psychological tools are proposed to the participants. The transcribed classroom dialogue could be organized and integrated with the other tools (for example, labwork sheet and high school students' answers) in a way that facilitates student teachers' analysis.
- The medium for discussion could be slightly restructured so as to better favor exchanges.

In conclusion, we have shown that analyzing the polylogue of an action-research group during a reflection session sheds light on three different issues, the first two relating to education and the third to language and cognitive sciences. First, our analysis illustrates how explaining student and teacher dialogue can help teachers in training come to understand how students model. Second, through such discussion, student teachers become conscious that teachers' ways of posing questions and teachers' use of language may introduce difficulties in students' problem solving concerning modeling. Third, we proposed a method for describing explanatory polylogues, combining the identification of explanatory phenomena with the description of five levels of interactive framework spaces. This approach enabled us to respectively present the cognitive and interactional aspects of explanatory polylogues.

In future work from the educational perspective, we plan to extend our experimental teacher training reflection sessions to a larger public while using communicational technologies to organize tool use. From the language and cognitive sciences' perspective, we plan on pursuing our analysis method with different explanatory corpora.

ACKNOWLEDGMENTS

I would like to thank the student teachers and the high school students for their willingness to be filmed and recorded in the context of this project. I would also like to thank my thesis director, Michael Baker, for guidance in elaborating the ideas presented here, and Christian Buty and Jean-Marie Chastan, without all of whom this work could not have been accomplished.

REFERENCES

Apostel, L., Céllerier, G., Desanti, J. T., Garcia, R., Granger, G. G., Halbwachs, F., Henriques, G. V., Ladière, J., Piaget, J., Sachs, I., & Sinclair de Zwaart, H. (1970). *L'explication dans les sciences [Explanation in the sciences]*. In F. Braudel (Series Ed.), Colloque de l'Académie Internationale de Philosophie des Sciences, nouvelle bibliothèque scientifique, Paris: Flammarion.

Baker, M. (2000). Explication, argumentation et négociation: Analyse d'un corpus de dialogues en langue naturelle écrite, dans le domaine de la médecine [Explanation, argumentation and negotiation: Analysis of dialogue as written natural language, in the medical domain]. In M. Baker, M. Joab, B. Safar, & D. Schlienger (Eds.), Études d'explications dans un corpus de dialogues finalisés. *Psychologie de l'interaction*, 9–10, 179–210.

Baker, M., & Lund, K. (1997). Promoting reflective interactions in a computer-supported collaborative learning environment. *Journal of Computer Assisted Learning. 13*, 175–193.

Balacheff, N. (1988). *Une étude des processus de preuve en mathématique chez des élèves de collège [A study on the processes of proofs in mathematics used by junior high school students]*. Thèse de l'Université Joseph Fourier Grenoble I et de l'Institut National Polytechnique de Grenoble.

Bateson, G. (1972). *Steps to an ecology of mind*. New York: Ballatine Books.

Becu-Robinault, K. (1997). Activités de modélisation des élèves en situation de travaux pratique traditionnels: Introduction expérimentale du concept de puissance [Activities of students doing modeling during traditional experimental labwork: An experimental introduction to the concept of power]. *Didaskalia, 11*, 7–37.

Bruxelles, S., & de Gaulmyn, M.-M. (2000). Explication en interaction: Facteurs déterminants et degré d'efficacité [Explanation in interaction: Determining factors and degree of efficacy]. In M. Baker, M. Joab, B. Safar, & D. Schlienger (Eds.), Études d'explications dans un corpus de dialogues finalisés. *Psychologie de l'interaction*, 9–10, 47–76.

Buty, C., Lund, K., & Chastan, J.-M. (2000). *Rapport intermediare du projet IUFM: Activités d'enseignement et fonctionnement des élèves pour la formation scientifique [Intermediary report of the IUFM project: Teaching activities and student functioning in regard to scientific training]*. Lyon, France: CNRS, University of Lyon 2: GRIC.

Chi, M. T. H., Bassok, M., Lewis, M., Reimann, P., & Glaser, R. (1989). Self-explanations: how students study and use examples in learning to solve problems. *Cognitive Science, 13*, 145–182.

Chi, M. T. H., de Leeuw, N., Chiu, M.-H., & LaVancher, C. (1994). Eliciting self-explanations improves understanding. *Cognitive Science, 18*, 439–477.

Collins, A., & Stevens, A. L. (1983). A cognitive theory of inquiry teaching. In C. M. Reigeluth (Ed.), *Instructional-design theories and models: An overview of the current status* (pp. 247–278). Hillsdale, NJ: Lawrence Erlbaum Associates.

de Corte, E., Verschaffel, L., & Schrooten, H. (1991). Computer simulation as a tool in studying teachers' cognitive activities during error diagnosis in arithmetic. In P. Goodyear (Ed.), *Teaching knowledge and intelligent tutoring* (pp. 367–378). Norwood, NJ: Ablex.

Dessalles, J.-L. (1992). *SAVANT3: Un système EIAO fondé sur l'explication conversationnelle [SAVANT3: An EIAO system based on conversational explanation].* Explication-1992. Actes des deuxièmes Journées Explication du PRC-GDR-IA du CNRS, Sophia-Antipolis: INRIA.

Engeström, Y. (1987). *Learning by expanding, an activity-theoretical approach to developmental research.* Helsinki: Orienta-Konsultit Oy.

Franceschelli, S., & Weil-Barais, A. (1998). La routine conversationnelle comme stratégie de changement conceptuel: Apprendre à modéliser en mécanique [Conversational routines as a strategy for conceptual change: Learning to model in mechanics]. In B. Schneuwly & D. Hameline (Series Eds.) & A. Dumas Carre & A. Weil-Barais (Vol. Eds.), *Cours et contributions pour les sciences de l'éducation, collection exploration: Tutelle et médiation dans l'éducation scientifique* (pp. 211–238). Bern: Peter Lang.

Goodwin, C., & Duranti, A. (1992). Rethinking context: An introduction. In A. Duranti & C. Goodwin (Eds.), *Rethinking context: Language as in interactive phenomenon* (pp. 1–42). New York: Cambridge University Press.

Gülich, E. (1991). Pour une ethnométhodologie linguistique: description de séquences conversationnelles explicatives [Toward ethnomethodological linguistics: a description of conversational explanatory sequences]. In U. Dausendschön-Gay, E. Gülich, & U. Krafft (Eds.), *Linguistische Interaktionanalysen* (pp. 325–372). Tübingen: Niemeyer.

Hempel, C. G., & Oppenheim, P. (1948). Studies in the logic of explanation. In J. C. Pitt (Ed.), *Theories of explanation* (pp. 9–46). New York: Oxford University Press. (Reprinted from *Philosophy of Science, 15,* 567–579, 1948, © by Williams and Wilkins.)

Janvier, C., & Lapointe, Y. (1998). Tutelle dans des activités de modélisation [Tutoring in modeling activities]. In B. Schneuwly & D. Hameline (Series Eds.) & A. Dumas Carre & A. Weil-Barais (Vol. Eds.), *Cours et contributions pour les sciences de l'éducation, collection exploration: Tutelle et médiation dans l'éducation scientifique* (pp. 123–144). Bern: Peter Lang.

Kerbrat-Orecchioni, C. (in press). Introduction. On polylogues [Special Issue]. *Journal of Pragmatics.*

Kohler-Chesny, J. (1981). Aspects explicatifs de l'activité discursive de paraphrasage [Explicative aspects of discursive activity in paraphrasing]. In J.-B. Grize (Ed.), *L'explication: Approche sémiologique Cahiers Vilfredo Pareto, Revue Européenne des Sciences Sociales.* Tome XIX, 56, 95–114.

Kohler-Chesny, J. (1983). Aspects des discours explicatifs [Aspects of explanatory discourse]. In A. Berrendonner & J.-B. Grize (Series Eds.) & P. Bange (Vol. Ed.), *Logique, Argumentation, Conversation, Actes du Colloque de Pragmatique, Fribourg* (pp. 61–78). Bern: Peter Lang.

Koliopoulos, D., & Ravanis, K. (1998). L'enseignement de l'énergie au collège vu par les enseignants: Grille d'analyse de leurs conceptions [Teaching energy in junior high physics class from the teachers' point of view: An analysis grid of their conceptions]. *L'enseignement scientifique vu par les enseignants. ASTER recherches en didactique expérimentales, 26,* 165–182.

Larcher, C., & Chomat, A. (1998). Médiation dans des situations d'entretiens avec des élèves de collège à propos de la modélisation des propriétés thermoélastiques des gaz [Mediation in interview situations with junior high school physics students concerning modeling the thermoelastic properties of gas]. In B. Schneuwly & D. Hameline (Series Eds.) & A. Dumas Carre & A. Weil-Barais (Vol. Eds.), *Cours et contributions pour les sciences de l'éducation, Collection Exploration: Tutelle et médiation dans l'éducation scientifique* (pp. 177–210). Bern: Peter Lang.

Lonka, K., & Ahola, K. (1995). Activating instruction: How to foster study and thinking skills in higher education, *European Journal of Psychology of Education*. Vol. X, 4, 351–368.

Lund, K., & Baker, M. J. (1999). Teachers' collaborative interpretations of students' computer-mediated collaborative problem solving interactions. In S. P. Lajoie & M. Vivet (Eds.), *Proceedings of the International Conference on Artificial Intelligence in Education* (pp. 147–154). Amsterdam: IOS Press.

McKendree, J., Stenning, K., Mayes, T., Lee, J., & Cox, R. (1998). Why observing a dialogue may benefit learning. *Journal of Computer Assisted Learning, 14*, 2, 110–119.

Piaget, J. (1947). *Le jugement et le raisonnement chez l'enfant [Judgement and reasoning in the child]* (3rd ed). Neuchatel: Delachaux et Niestle.

Plantin, C. (1996). L'argumentation [Argumentation]. In J. Généreux & E. Blanc (Series Eds.), *Mémo Collection*. Paris: Seuil.

Ploetzner, R., Dillenbourg, P., Preier, M., & Traum, D. (1999). Learning by explaining to oneself and to others. In N. Bennett, E. de Corte, S. Vosniadou, & H. Mandl (Series Eds.) & P. Dillenbourg (Vol. Ed.), *Advances in learning and instruction: Collaborative learning, cognitive and computational approaches* (pp. 103–121). Amsterdam: Pergamon.

Porlan Ariza, R., Garcia Garcia, E., Rivero Garcia, A., & Martin del Pozo, R. (1998). Les obstacles à la formation professionnelle des professeurs en rapport avec leurs idées sur la science, l'enseignement et l'apprentissage [Obstacles encountered during professional teacher training in relation to their ideas about science]. *L'enseignement scientifique vu par les enseignants. ASTER recherches en didactique des sciences expérimentales, 26*, 207–235.

Scriven, M. (1988). Explanation, predictions, and laws. In J. C. Pitt (Ed.), *Theories of explanation* (pp. 51–74). New York, Oxford: Oxford University Press.

Shelley, A., & Sibert, E. (1991). Computer simulation in teacher education: Enhancing teacher decision making. In P. Goodyear (Ed.), *Teaching knowledge and intelligent tutoring* (pp. 341–365). Norwood, NJ: Ablex.

Tiberghien, A. (1994). Modeling as a basis for analyzing teaching–learning situations. *Learning and Instruction, 4*, 71–87.

Tiberghien, A., Buty, C., Gaidioz, P., Le Maréchal, J.-F., & Vince, J. (2001). Types of tools to design and adapt teaching sequences. In D. Psillos, P. Kariotoglou, V. Tselfes, G. Bisdikian, G. Fassoulopoulos, E. Hatzikraniotis, & M. Kallery (Eds.), *Proceedings of the third international conference of ESERA* (pp. 328–330). Thesseloniki: ESERA.

Tiberghien, A., & de Vries, E. (1997). Relating characteristics of learning situations to learner activities. *Journal of Computer Assisted Learning, 13*, 163–174.

Vion, R. (1999). Une approche du dynamique des interactions verbales et des discours [An approach to the dynamics of verbal interactions and discourse]. In M. Musiol & A. Trognon (Eds.), *Une théorie de la communication est-elle possible? Verbum*, Tome XXI, 2, 243–262.

Vion, R. (1992). *La communication verbale, analyse des interactions [Verbal communication, analysis of interactions]*. In B. Quemada & F. Rastier, (Series Eds.). Paris: Hachette Université Communication.

Vygotsky, L. (1985). La méthode instrumentale en psychologie [The instrumental method in psychology]. (C. Haus, French Trans.) In B. Schneuwly & J. P. Bronckart (Eds.), *Textes de Base en psychologie* (pp. 39–47), Geneva: Delachaux et Niestlé. (Original work from *Istorya razvitya vysshy psykhichesky funktsy*, 1931)

Wells, G. (1996). Using the tool-kit of discourse in the activity of learning and teaching. *Mind, Culture and Activity, 3*(2), 74–101.

Chapter 10

The "Power" of Text Production Activity in Collaborative Modeling: Nine Recommendations to Make a Computer-Supported Situation Work

Denis Alamargot
University of Poitiers

Jerry Andriessen
University of Utrecht

Modeling tasks have as a goal for a student to construct an explicit and runnable model of a domain. To obtain the data needed to construct the model, experimentation may be required. Modeling tasks carried out in collaboration seem to require communication and negotiation at the conceptual level (making explicit and elaborating concepts used), the level of problem solving (goal setting, planning, search for information, steps to take, partial solutions to evaluate), and the level of the collaboration itself (regulation and coordination). In this framework, partners build models of one another, because they have to construct and negotiate a shared task–representation (Erkens & Andriessen, 1994). This is a problem as well as an opportunity for learning.

The exchange of information in such tasks can be mediated by computer systems that transmit and manage communicative actions. The computer interface affords tools and utilities for the exchange of information (chat, e–mail) as well as for problem solving (calculators, simulations, etc.). The study of such affordances is important for understanding facilitation of learning in interactive situations.

The collaborative situation that we describe here permits protagonists engaged in a modeling task to exchange information via a network. In this situation, (short) texts (messages) are produced with different functions, depending on the subtask that is being carried out.

This communicative situation involves, for a given individual, alternating between message comprehension and production phases; learning may result from both the production and the comprehension of text, or from a series of texts. Messages concern the problem at stake, the problem situation, procedures and strategies, partial solutions and goals, conceptual issues, and the collaboration process itself.

The purpose of this chapter is a double one. In the first place, we aim to more precisely define the mechanisms and constraints involved in this passing on of information by participants during Computer Supported Collaborative Learning (CSCL), from the viewpoint of psycholinguistic models of written language comprehension and production. In the second place, and as a result of this psycholinguistic analysis, we propose recommendations for improving computer support for modeling activities by operating on parameters of the exchange of written messages during this process. This is not an empirical text, but it is meant to serve as the starting point of issues to research.

Our exploration is based on the assumption that the communication of knowledge, or more precisely, the activity of passing on knowledge as textual information (i.e., the production of a structured message, comprising at least a written phrase), in an interactive situation, could by itself be important for learning. In the second part of this chapter, we discuss how such learning can be explained. At least, learning by using language for communicating knowledge has two sources: comprehending other people's messages and producing one's own messages. We briefly discuss the current views held about the mechanisms involved in comprehending written information. More important for this chapter, we subsequently proceed to discussing the *epistemic effect* of text production, that is, the hypothesis that the activity of producing written code can bring about learning by the producer of the message. This "auto acquisition" of knowledge through writing is a consequence of using *written* code, and more specifically, the result of the interaction between knowledge and the linguistic processing involved during writing. We discuss two possible explanations of this phenomenon. The first explanation (the *classical* position) supposes that it is the act of writing for somebody, and the involvement in meeting specific communicative constraints, that modifies domain knowledge. The second explanation (the *romantic* position) supposes that, in contrast, free (written) expression of thought on the basis of some theme, *without* the requirement to meet constraints such as dealing with audience, permits the writer to constitute new domain knowledge.

In the third and final part of this chapter, we draw some consequences of this line of thinking to computer-mediated discussion. What general interface characteristics would be required for full text power to be used for conceptual reasoning and problem solving in computer supported collaborative learning (CSCL) situations? This chapter should be taken as an attempt to bring CSCL design experience to bear on issues about how writing affects learning.

THE ROLE OF WRITTEN MESSAGES IN THE COLLABORATIVE MODELING SITUATION

The Notion of Collaborative Modeling

We define a collaborative learning situation as one in which two or more students work together to fulfill an assigned task within a particular domain of learning to achieve a joint product. In ideal cooperation, the collaborating partners (two, at least) must have a common interest in solving the problem at hand. In addition, we suppose that in a learning situation, knowledge of either participant is insufficient to solve the problem. Furthermore, each participant should be mutually dependent on the information and cooperation of the other to reach their (shared) goals. Only when the participants have abilities or information that are complementary can cooperation be fruitful and will it be looked for (Erkens, 1997). As a result, not only may participants share some of each other's knowledge, but also, in principle, new knowledge may be constructed during the activities.

We consider modeling as a problem-solving task, during which (incomplete) knowledge of concepts (called *declarative* or *semantic knowledge*) and knowledge for the application of concepts (often called *procedural knowledge*) are needed for solving the problem. In most educational situations during which modeling tasks are employed, the attainment of more of such knowledge is the main goal. In the collaborative situation, the learning goal is supposed to be served by individuals communicating information. For this communication, both protagonists apply linguistic knowledge, for production and decoding of written messages, and pragmatic knowledge, seen here as knowledge of how to adapt the content and the form of a message to the goals of the situation and its participants. For the regulation of activities, we suppose the existence of metacognitive knowledge, which allows the protagonists to evaluate the implications of different knowledge activities.

Problem solving in individual modeling tasks entails dynamic application of domain knowledge, based on the protagonists' knowledge. Learning is the result of active exploration, applying this knowledge to the problem-solving process. Consequently, learning to model is based on appropriate experiences and reflections by the learner. The learning environment should be specifically tailored to meet these ends. The learner should not only be supported during problem solving, but also, and more importantly, supported in engaging in abstract reflections leading to (declarative) knowledge that would permit new problems to be solved independently of the supporting environment (Salomon, 1993). Many researchers claim this requires extensive use of specific forms of language (Andriessen & Sandberg, 1999; Baker, 1999; Ohlsson, 1993).

A modeling task carried out as joint problem solving with exchange of written messages represents a rich environment. Knowledge acquisition does not merely involve learning by doing, as in the individual case, inasmuch as at least two other modes of learning are possible: learning by observation of the partner's actions, and learning by understanding and producing language through which information is exchanged in relation to the problem-solving situation, between (two) protagonists. Many functions may be served by using language; as stated earlier, we focus on the conceptual aspects—that is, language referring to knowledge of the learning domain.

Concerning the latter mode, learning by using language, comprehension by one protagonist (the receiver) of messages written by another protagonist (the sender) is one of the key activities of learning. As we will see, comprehension activities can take place at many levels of depth and can be very different with respect to their focus of attention, depending on characteristics of the learner, the learning situation, and the type of instruction. Many studies into collaborative learning address these conditions for learning (e.g., O'Donnell & King, 1999). In such studies, the main question often is how instruction can facilitate collaborative learning and to which extent. In other words, receivers' learning is studied in terms of how messages by senders do or do not facilitate learning.

Nevertheless, the comprehension by a protagonist of a message produced by another participant is not the only vector to knowledge acquisition. The companion track of the communication route, that is, the production of the message itself, may also imply or even require, on the part of the writer, a restructuring of his own knowledge. So, even if the activities of language comprehension and production are subordinated to reasoning and problem-solving processes (e.g., Voss, Wiley, & Sandak, 1999), we argue that especially language production activities are not neutral with respect to knowledge construction. The fact that you have to elaborate a message is not a simple translation activity. In point of fact, there is a complex interaction between the process of written language production and the knowledge that is mediated. On the one hand, the nature of the domain knowledge involved may affect the way in which the domain is expressed: What can be thought of clearly is expressed more easily. A domain expert constructs elaborated texts and well-structured written messages with more ease than novices do (Alamargot, 1997; Caccamise, 1987; Kellogg, 1987, etc.). On the other hand, the fact that domain knowledge is expressed, particularly as written text, leads to modification and even growth of that knowledge (Alamargot, Favart, & Galbraith, 2000; Eigler, Jechle, Merziger, & Winter, 1991; Galbraith, 1996, 1999). Seen in this way, the production activity contributes to knowledge construction, in the sense of strengthening existing domain knowledge as well as allowing the generation of new domain knowledge.

In fact, the main point we are trying to make has also been stated elsewhere, by Schwartz (1999): "Language and linguistic representations play a particular role in generating new knowledge and may be a primary mediator of learning effects, whether alone or in combination" (p. 211). Schwartz discussed the process of learning from texts. He started with the observation that the presence of a physical object does not ensure a common ground between two people who both have access to that object. Language may help to construct this common ground, but common meaning and learning between individuals is not assured, either. The point is that (oral) language can serve as a construction tool, perhaps up to the point of what is (socially) accepted as common understanding. Schwartz specifically discussed the power of language with regard to structure—more precisely, as a mediator for restructuring understanding. For example, language may help resolve an ambiguity simply by giving something a name, or calling for an abstract concept that captures or clarifies the meaning of several lower level ones. For social reasons, members of a group move to conceptually safe places to communicate, where interpretation differences do not tend to get in the way. Because of this, group communication tends to move toward abstraction and structure, and this restructuring may be an important effect of language use during collaboration. This helps students to discover specific features that allow differentiating chunks or classes of concepts, much as a botanist can distinguish subspecies of a given flower. In his conception, it is the combination of language comprehension and production activity that fosters learning.

Given the important role of language in learning, in the next sections we discuss the role of the comprehension and production of written language in problem solving. Note that these days, electronic communication essentially is written communication, and even if in the near future audio would become commonplace in such cases, we would still be interested in the specific role of the written communication mode. Our final constraint is that we primarily consider the case of synchronous communication, that is, protagonists act together during the same time slot to solve the problem.

Comprehending Written Messages as a Tool for Modeling Activities

The processes of language comprehension involve the modification (adaptation) of a protagonists' model of the situation, based on external information and feedback from the partner. Partners may jointly explore a problem space, but may also instruct one another during the process. Furthermore, there may be modeling involved in collaborative problem solving, in the sense that partners may capture and copy ways of communication and problem solving from each other.

Within the cognitive perspective we take here, learning is viewed as updating of memory representations by linking new information to information already in memory. If this leads protagonists to apply information to accomplish new things, or to do something in a different way, learning may be said to be successful. The issue of the extent to which a teacher, a learner, or a context decides what is successful or not, is left open here (for a discussion: Andriessen & Sandberg, 1999).

Memory for a particular concept is a function of its individual properties as well as of its relations to other concepts. Current cognitive views on discourse understanding (e.g., Fletcher, 1994, for a review) still rely on the distinction made by van Dijk and Kintsch (1983) between three levels of mental representations. The most superficial and short-lived of these represents the surface form of the discourse. The meaning of the discourse is represented as an interconnected network of ideas called the *propositional text base*, constructed on the basis of syntactic, semantic, and pragmatic interpretation of the sequence of words. The most enduring level of representation is referred to as the *situation model*. This would be similar to the representation that would result from directly experiencing the situation that the discourse describes (Fletcher, 1994). It involves an "integrated structure of episodic information, collecting previous episodic information about some situation as well as instantiated general information from semantic memory" (van Dijk & Kintsch, 1983). Situation models are dynamic and are updated by inferential processes. Conversely, the nature of inferences that are made during interpretation is based on the already constructed situation model. The ease with which a model is constructed depends, among other things, on the coherence of the information; that is, for example, the consistency of the information and of coreferences between information units in a text, all of which supports inference making.

Concerning the nature and amount of inferential processing during comprehension, it seems that this depends on several characteristics of task and comprehender. One of the consequences is that, for some researchers (for a discussion: Garrod & Sanford, 1999), it seems impossible to describe one unique interpretation of the information in a text, because mental representations are the result of an interaction between text and reader. Another consequence is that inferences are an essential aspect of comprehension, because without inferences, no mental models will be constructed. Minimal viewpoints on inferencing stress the economic tendency of readers to infer as little as possible, only to comprehend what is necessary (McKoon & Ratcliff, 1992). Comprehension is seen as an incremental process, in which much processing is shallow, based on perceived semantic relatedness of words in a sentence (van Oostendorp, 1994), or on activated scenarios of real-world knowledge (Garrod & Sanford, 1999). A related proposal by van Dijk (1999) involves the activation of event models, that is, models that represent the subjective interpretation of discourse or text, in which only relevant properties of a situation are represented. The extent to which such properties are shared between participants in a situation is part of the common ground participants develop and extend during joint discursive and other action (Clark & Brennan, 1991). Van Dijk (1999, p. 124) supposed that these subjective representations exert overall and local control over all processes of discourse comprehension and production. This subjective component seems to be very important, and it appears that the effects of collaboration on comprehension depend to a large extent on subjective factors that affect the depth to which a student is engaged in comprehension activities.

Comprehension seen as a learning process is quite sensitive to individual and situational differences and types of knowledge. As a consequence, models of text comprehension do not explain learning. The factors that determine the degree of activation of concepts during comprehension, the amount of related concepts that are activated during reading, and what is learned and to what degree as a result, are to be found outside the model itself, in the attitudes of readers toward the learning situation, and in other characteristics of readers, situations, and instructions (e.g., van den Broek, Young, Tzeng, & Linderholm, 1999). What is learned is determined to a degree by what is useful for the reader, for example, for maintaining comprehension to a degree sufficient to continue a dialogue.

With respect to learning, a minimalist option for comprehension activities is undesirable, as learning requires all kinds of constructive processing activities by the learner, not just the minimal ones (e.g., Goldman, 1996). In addition, it seems not easy to decide what is useful or necessary, neither by a learner (what criterion, where does it come from?) nor by a teacher, because it requires a teacher to decide what is necessary for the learner, leading to problems of responsibility and authenticity (Petraglia, 1998), and, of course, of student modeling.

In addition, it seems that so far nobody has come up with a clear conception about what it means to understand something, nor of the notion of depth of understanding. Here, we suppose that semantic understanding is something gradual that cannot be pinpointed to specific concepts being understood, but more to a sense of easy recognition of something, feeling more familiar, being able to undertake some more or less intelligent action with it, etc. (Bereiter, in press). Understanding is also much related to the situation, that is, the collaborators' local and overall goals (Baker, Hansen, Joiner, & Traum, 1999). It is in this sense too, that groups can understand. This may also be a reason why we often do not observe much explicit understanding or signs of knowledge transformation in electronic discussion groups (cf. Veerman, 2000, p. 159).

To conclude, although it seems obvious that the activity of language *comprehension*, in individual as well as in synchronous collaborative situations, can lead to learning, whatever its nature, a whole series of conditions have to be met before deep learning can be realized. We now turn to the case of (written) language *production*, where we may end up with quite a different conclusion.

Written Message Production as a Tool for Modeling Activities

In this section our aim is to discuss the characteristics and activities of the message producer. This approach is rather unusual, as it supposes that the act of producing a written message for someone else is by itself a situation of implicit (self-) learning. This learning situation rests on the interaction between domain knowledge and the activity of language production, which allows the mediation of this knowledge. In the next section, we briefly discuss the principal dimensions of the activity of text composition. After this discussion, we try to elaborate on the nature of the interaction between domain knowledge and language production. This interaction is discussed from two sides: the effect of domain knowledge on the production of a message, as well as the effect of the production of a message on domain knowledge.

Knowledge Areas and Processes Involved in Text Composition

If domain knowledge (as in long-term memory, in a situation model, a mental model, or an event model) is considered as a source for text production and elaboration, producing a text supposes at least three other kinds of knowledge: (a) linguistic knowledge, for expressing this knowledge; (b) pragmatic knowledge, allowing a writer to elaborate a representation of a potential and missing reader and (c) procedural knowledge, to trigger and to manage processes applied on the three other kinds of knowledge.

More than 20 years ago, Hayes and Flower (1980) proposed a first model (one probably should use the term "blue print") about the nature and the architecture of writing processes and the implied representations underlying text-writing activity. They distinguished three major processes, corresponding to the three main stages of writing: planning, translating, and reviewing. The dynamics of the activity are postulated as sequential, with possible recursion, according to the considered phase of production (implying a process called *monitor*). Within this model, planning serves to establish an outline of the content of the text to be written (things to say, to whom, in what order, how), which implies retrieving content from memory (generating), and organizing this content in function of the instruction and the writer's communicative and processing goals (goal setting). The translating process serves to semantically develop each part of the plan and translation into linguistically elaborated sentences. Reviewing, finally, implies rereading what has been written and eventually modifying (editing) the text content and/or form.

According to this "classic" model, the production of a text is described as a progressive transformation of a multidimensional reserve of domain knowledge into a linear linguistic trace. Obviously, many factors affect this transformation and its efficiency, making it important to be able to handle (in working memory) many constraints and processes at the same time (cf. Flower & Hayes, 1980; Kellogg, 1996), and evoking questions about the effects on the process of the amount and quality of different types of available knowledge. With respect to this last point, a crucial part of written language production is played by the writer's level of expertise of the domain, facilitating not only the production of well-structured text content, but also the planning process as a whole.

The Effect of Domain Expertise on Text Production: "Ce Qui Se Conçoit Bien S'énonce clairement"

Beginners and experts not only differ in the quantity of prior knowledge that they possess, but also in the organization of that knowledge. All knowledge acquisition, and hence the development of expertise in a given domain, requires and depends on a reorganization (restructuring) of existing knowledge, represented (e.g., in long-term memory), or activated (e.g., in working memory), relevant to the domain in question. For example, Egan and Schwartz (1979) compared the recall of diagrams of electronic circuits by novices and experts in the domain. They showed that the content of the products of experts was much more structured, at the semantic level, than that of novices. This phenomenon seemed to be related to a better structure or organization of this knowledge in memory by the experts.

The effect of the development of expertise, which has been examined across a great number of tasks as different as chess playing (Chase & Simon, 1973; De Groot, 1965), playing Go (Reitman, 1976), or computer programming (McKeithen, Reitman, Rueter, & Hirtle, 1981), involves the creation of a great number of semantic relations or associations (chunks—units of knowledge at some higher level of conceptual abstraction; Miller, 1956; Simon, 1974), between the different units of knowledge that characterize the domain in question. The development of expertise can essentially be described in terms of a growth of the number and size of "chunks," which allows an expert to simultaneously access and process a greater number of information units united by a similar conceptual category, and even to create new conceptual categories. This development allows not only the activation of a very elaborated representation in working memory, but also, according to Chi, Glaser, and Farr (1988), the establishment in long-term memory of more and more hierarchically structured knowledge units. In this light, Caillies, Denhiere, and Jhean-Larose (1999) suggested that the knowledge of advanced subjects in a domain is organized in a hierarchical goal–subgoal structure, whereas that of intermediates and beginners is organized in a temporocausal chain. Hence, to be an expert in (or being more familiar with) a domain supposes the existence of a knowledge representation that is denser, in terms of the number of knowledge units, but also contains a greater number of semantic relations between those knowledge units. The hierarchic organization of the units supposes that the lower level units are attached to higher level units, consisting of groups of related concepts that form cohorts of semantic categories (Rosch, 1973; Rosch, Gray, Johnson, & Boyes-Braem, 1976; Rosch & Mervis, 1975).

The question, then, is to explain to what extent richer and denser domain knowledge, which characterizes expertise, can modify the way in which an individual expresses content through language, or more exactly, by means of producing written language. Two complementary processes are considered: the effect of qualitatively structuring text content, and that of facilitating processes subordinated to this structuring process.

Structure of Knowledge and Structuring of Text Content. According to Caccamise (1987), the structure of domain knowledge is more hierarchically organized when the domain is more familiar to the writer (as seen earlier), and this has two effects on the activity of writing a text: the products assembled in working memory will be (a) more extended, because of the greater number of associations between chunks, and (b) already organized in terms of semantic or conceptual relationships. These two characteristics considerably limit the necessity for additional writing processes of organizing knowledge, and they permit to generate text content that is already highly structured and hierarchically organized. From this perspective, Caccamise (1987) had 16 psychology students compose texts on the basis of different topics, manipulating the familiarity and generality of the topics. To find an effect of the topic manipulation on the textual level and the underlying processes, Caccamise analyzed in detail the hierarchical organization of the texts produced in each condition. First, the text content was cut into idea units, and their organization was analyzed in terms of chunks (grouping of units of several related ideas). Chunks could be organized in terms of different hierarchical levels and could eventually be clustered (groups of related chunks). By listing text content in terms of the number of idea units, the number of chunks, the number of idea units per chunk, the hierarchical level of chunks, the number of clusters, etc., the author was able to show that in the case of greater domain expertise, text content can be characterized not only in terms of a greater number of idea units, but also in terms of a stronger hierarchical organization. This organization displayed a greater number of chunks and clusters, related in terms of superordination and subordination. This facilitation was to a great extent due to the structural characteristics of the domain knowledge that could directly furnish the organization of semantic relationships used during text planning and content elaboration (Schneider, Korkel, & Weinert, 1989). More precisely, the hierarchical organization of knowledge by experts allowed them to access greater and more extensive amounts of knowledge, which are already related semantically or conceptually, for further processing by the cognitive system.

In addition to this structural explanation, the effect of greater domain expertise could equally well be related to the facilitation of underlying processes, by reducing their cognitive load.

Accessibility of Knowledge Reduces the Cognitive Load of Writing Processes. The interdependency of higher level processes was investigated particularly well by Kellogg (1987). By starting from the processes distinguished by Hayes and Flower (1980), Kellogg has examined the processing cost of planning, translating, and reviewing as a function of the degree of familiarity of writers with the theme of the (argumentative) text. The degree of familiarity was determined on the basis of a pretest that distinguished two groups of adults, either experts or novices, with respect to the knowledge domain of the text. The specific methodology to appreciate the respective load of each main writing process was inspired by the classical precept, in cognitive psychology, of the secondary task. During text composition, the writer has to react as soon as possible to a beep (regularly sent every 30 s). Reaction time to the beep is assumed to be longer, as processes allocated to text composition are deeper and more costly (see Piolat & Olive, 2000, for an evaluation of Kellogg's paradigm). Moreover, immediately after the reaction to the beep, the writer has to name the process he was involved in (planning, translating, or reviewing). Kellogg's results show that increased degree of familiarity goes along with a significant decrease of the cost of planning. More precisely, domain expertise essentially facilitates generating and organizing of content units, and permits the allocation of more cognitive resources to translating and reviewing. By essentially confirming the results obtained by Schumacher, Klare, Cronin, and Moses (1984), Kellogg showed that if experts and novices produce texts of equal quality, then these texts are the result of different processing loads attributed to generating and organizing: Much more of these are required from a novice than from an expert.

To recap, it seems that domain expertise allows facilitation of generating and organizing processes by (a) imposing hierarchical organization of text content (Caccamise, 1987), and (b) by reducing cognitive load (Kellogg, 1987). This has been shown with adults as well as with 7–14-year-old children, in a series of experiments all concerning the same domain: baseball. These experiments can also be considered as a series of replications of the same paradigm, with different subjects and age groups. The initial experiments were carried out by Voss, Vesonder, and Spilich (1980) with first year students. The authors distinguished experts and novices about baseball on the basis of a knowledge test (37 multiple-choice items), and asked them to explain in writing the rules of the game. When the organization of the texts written by the two groups were compared, it appeared, confirming the expectations of the authors, that the content of the texts produced by experts contained a greater number of idea units (in terms of the number of actions that were described), as well as a greater number of interrelations, allowing the establishment of a hierarchical organization on the basis of the principal theme of the text. This effect of domain knowledge was replicated with younger participants.

McCutchen (1986) was able to show the same phenomenon with 7–10-year-old children, with expository texts (to explain the game of baseball) and with narrative (tell about a game of baseball you saw). Independently of the age, the experts in the domain always produced longer texts that were more coherent in the sense of explicit relations between actions of the game, hierarchical organization of information, etc. These results were again confirmed by De Groff (1987), with 7-year-olds. Finally, Benton, Corkill, Sharp, Downey, and Khramtsova (1995) asked 14-year-olds to revise a narrative containing a scene from a baseball game. The level of knowledge was assessed afterward by the same questionnaire used by Voss et al. (1980). Text content was analyzed in terms of idea units, which were categorized in terms of their level in a hierarchy, which reflected, according to the authors, the functionality of planning processes (generation and organization). The results of this exercise were similar to those of the other studies, in the sense that baseball experts more familiar with the sport produced a greater number of ideas, better organized and more closely linked with the main theme. According to Benton et al., the effect of domain expertise was such that the 14-year-olds could produce texts with the same quality as those by older students. Greater availability of domain knowledge limits the cost associated with planning by facilitating the subprocess of content generation, which helped the subprocess of organization.

Finally, concerning the effect of domain expertise on text production, it seems clear that the way in which text content is generated and organized seems to depend to a large extent on the richness and the existing organization of relevant domain knowledge in memory. This conclusion has been confirmed by experimentation with different age groups and conceptual domains. A writer who is expert in a domain does not produce text in the same way as a novice, independently of age or writing proficiency. This is only one of many aspects of the interaction between domain knowledge and the writing process. In fact, if, as we have just described, domain knowledge affects the way a text is written, then writing a text about a specific domain could also modify domain knowledge. The task of composing a text could be a learning situation by itself. This effect, called epistemic by Eigler, Jechle, Merziger, and Winter (1991), explains the fact that a writer is more expert in a domain after having produced a text about it than before the writing process.

The Effect of the Text on Domain Knowledge: The Epistemic Effect

Different factors contribute to the explanation of the (epistemic) power of the written code for learning. Following Galbraith (1992, 1996), two general conceptions may be distinguished here, with quite different assumptions concerning the interaction between writing and learning. They are called the *classical position* and the *romantic position*, respectively (see also Alamargot & Chanquoy, 2001; Munneke & Andriessen, 2000).

Any writer, as an individual or in a collaborative situation, globally has the choice between two general solutions for composing a text. The first option is composing and adapting a text in order to meet the constraints imposed by potential readers, usually not present except in actual interaction. In this case, depending on the situation of communication, the text genre, and individual writing experience, pragmatic knowledge is used for adjusting and arranging content as well as linguistic form according to the characteristics of the addressee. This strategy might be called the classical way of composing a text. In the second solution, the writer can compose a text by noting down ideas as they come, without explicitly ordering them or reorganizing them in function of some external or internal goal. In this case, which can be called the romantic way of composing a text, a writer does not consider any communicative, pragmatic, or rhetorical constraints, and the resulting text is more like a draft, or a series of notes. It is only in a second phase that the writer considers the constraints of the types mentioned, to be involved in "classical" rhetorical problem solving, eventually leading to the final text.

It is important to note that both positions imply the creation of knowledge through writing, but each of them stresses different processes as being responsible for learning and, possibly different knowledge arising as a result. In the next sections we discuss both explanations for the epistemic effect of text production.

The Epistemic Effect Explained by Rhetorical and Pragmatic Constraints: The Classical Position.   Writing a text always serves some communicative goal, which requires the linguistic realization of the text to respect a number of pragmatic and rhetorical constraints that permit one to reach the envisaged communicative goal. Following Scardamalia and Bereiter (1991), the need for pragmatic knowledge is especially evident in the case of argumentative writing. The function of this type of text is to convince the reader of your point of view, and to reach this communicative goal, the writer needs to adapt, modify, and transform individual domain knowledge. Bereiter and Scardamalia (1987) described this manner of text production as the strategy of knowledge transforming. This writing strategy involves the writer consciously planning the content of the text, while at the same time managing pragmatic and rhetorical constraints (to persuade, explain, reformulate, to more clearly present an argument, to anticipate possible objections, etc.). This mode of planning can be represented as an actual problem-solving situation for the writer, in which the writer is supposed at the same time to deal with constraints concerning the knowledge domain (what do I know?) and pragmatic constraints (how do I say it for this audience?). The activity of adapting text content in function of rhetorical and pragmatic goals and the reverse activity of adapting goals in function of generated text content is supposed to lead to a modification (transformation) of domain knowledge. This "classical" position then maintains that knowledge construction during writing is the consequence of reorganization (transformation) of ideas, a process guided by the rhetorical and pragmatical goals of a text. In this case, planning and conception of a text not only involve the generation and formulation of ideas, but also analyzing the rhetorical problem: writing a coherent text with a specific goal for a specific audience.

In his new model, Hayes (1996) tried to deal with the mental processes that could underlie this modification of domain knowledge during text elaboration. Two processes could be fundamental for this knowledge transformation to occur during writing: reflection and text interpretation.

Reflection allows modification of domain knowledge through the elaboration of text content. The reflection process involves mental operations such as reasoning, inference making, or any problem-solving activity. In this sense it comprises the planning process, as described in the Hayes and Flower (1980) model. More precisely, Hayes and Nash (1996) distinguished three kinds of planning activities: planning by abstraction, planning by analogy, and planning by modeling. Planning by abstraction consists of manipulating and ordering abstract concepts. Planning by analogy allows generalizing knowledge involved in a specific activity, resulting in a similar or familiar activity (for instance, the generic application of a schema to write a new text, in the case of narrative text writing). Finally, planning by modeling, in contrast with planning by abstraction, does not bear on abstract concepts but permits the writer to model, as a systemic representation, the situation and task parameters.

The text interpretation process allows the writer to (re-) read the already written text and to proceed to a comprehension activity with reference to the written text. The process has a double function. On the one hand, at a local level, it allows a writer to read the already written text to continue coherent text production. On the other hand, at a global level, the process allows revision activities of smaller or larger parts of the text, at a conceptual level (coherent content, for example) as well as a linguistic level (appropriateness and accuracy of linguistic forms).

These two processes, reflection and text interpretation, could each play a central role in the modification of knowledge during writing. Reflection supposes that the writer modifies or transforms domain knowledge for incorporation in the text. The three types of planning (by abstraction, analogy, and modeling) could each represent a way of modifying and transforming knowledge. These planning or reasoning modes are not specific for writing, but they are mandatory when a text has to be written.

Similarly, the text interpretation process requires the writer to take the role of the reader of the text. This activity may lead a writer to modify domain knowledge, to create new conceptual relations, to modify a point of view, to change a problem representation, etc. This mode of learning is related to the analysis of the written text. More precisely, according to Scardamalia and Bereiter (1991), the crucial activity for any writer is to ask to what extent and in what way does what has been written (the words, the syntax, implied meaning, etc.) correspond to the initial intentions in writing the text. For example, when the writer detects a mismatch between a piece of text and the initial pragmatic constraints, transformation of knowledge may be necessary to solve this problem and to modify the content and form of the text.

To return to the main issue, in the classical position, it is the presence of rhetorical plans and the constraints imposed by them that oblige the writer to constantly monitor, modify, or create knowledge. In the next section, we present a radically different point of view for explaining the epistemic effect: the "romantic" position.

The Epistemic Effect Explained by Linguistic Constraints: The Romantic Position.   In order to explain the creation of new domain knowledge during text formulation, Galbraith (1992, 1996) contrasted the classical position, described in the previous section, with the "romantic" position. This position claims that the modification of domain knowledge during writing of a text is stronger when pragmatic and rhetorical constraints are weaker. More precisely, according to the romantic conception, the epistemic effect of a text is the result of a dialectic between the writers' disposition and the written text. The "knowledge-constituting" model's (Galbraith, 1999) basic claim is that the knowledge encoded in sentences is represented, implicitly, within a distributed network of conceptual relationships, and ideas are synthesized by constraint satisfaction within this network, rather than being directly retrieved. The main condition for this dialectic to come into play is a writer trying to express his ideas as propositionally correct sentences that follow each other in one way or another. In this way a first rough draft of a text develops, not necessarily very coherent, but also different from a list of notes or an organized outline. Only during rewriting of the first draft in a second phase does the writer try to take into account the rhetorical goals of a text. "Rough drafting and outline planning strategies are not just different ways of reducing cognitive load during writing, but also enable writers to better satisfy different social goals. Thus, outline planning has the advantage that it enables the writer to control the way he presents ideas in public, with the disadvantage that, by prematurely imposing order on thought, it may obscure the writer's emerging conception of the topic; rough drafting has the advantage that it better enables the writer to capture his implicit disposition towards the topic, but the disadvantage that the text has to be revised to conform to external constraints" (Galbraith & Rijlaarsdam, 1999, p. 100).

The writing strategies *outline planning* and *rough drafting* are two different, more or less efficient ways of creating new content during writing. Whereas the classical position supposes that constraints support planning (outline planning), the romantic position stresses free expression of thought (rough drafting). More precisely, it seems that according to the romantic position, the very fact that during rough drafting there are no constraints present for organization, planning, or dealing with an audience, is what allows the activation of the greatest number of ideas. In addition, ideas that are activated and written down give rise to new ideas; in other words, old ideas change because they have been formulated and written down without rhetorical and pragmatic constraints. Only by writing ideas down (as sentences) can new ideas come up. Galbraith (1999) found that individuals that are more sensitive to social constraints, called high self-monitors, according to a test of personality (Snyder, 1986), are less good at this, because these individuals tend to more strongly doubt and ponder about pragmatic constraints of the situation.

To return to the main issue again: In the romantic position, it is the absence of rhetorical and pragmatic constraints that allows a writer to be inventive, because then he or she is not restricted in the elaboration of his or her thought. The motor of content elaboration is to be found in the constraint of having to express complex thought as words.

Conclusion About the Role of Text Production

The effect we are specifically interested in here is the epistemic effect of text composition: the very act of writing as a learning experience. Consciously dealing with the audience seems to divide classical and romantic positions with respect to its role in the interaction between writing and learning.

If learning is conceived as the generation of new knowledge (including transformation of existing knowledge), the classic position proposes that actively considering audience needs during reviewing and rewriting a text creates transformations of ideas. The romantic position favors unconstrained idea generation during the formulation of a rough draft as best for creation of new knowledge.

Another important effect on learning is by the linguistic encoding of a message. In the classical position, working on the language of the message (as opposed to its content) in order to meet pragmatic constraints may have a modifying effect on knowledge. A writer realizes that an idea is different or comes up with a new one when trying to formulate it. The romantic position holds that the process of translating multiple concepts into language (as a sentence) necessarily requires some sort of idea integration. Because one has to formulate a sentence, one's ideas are shaped and restructured.

It may be that the classic and the romantic positions discuss complementary learning processes. The precise differences between the two may involve the nature of knowledge involved, but also task and situational constraints. As a consequence, the implied learning in each case may be different. Instead of elaborating possible differences that have not yet been subjected to experimentation, we would like to discuss the implications of each of these positions for modeling by electronic collaboration. It remains to be seen how the power of text production can modify the parameters of communication and learning during collaboration. This is the learning exercise of the next section.

COLLABORATIVE LEARNING AS TEXT PRODUCTION: PERSPECTIVES ON FACILITATING COMMUNICATION AND MODELING IN CSCL

The situation that we consider in this chapter involves at least two participants engaged in a problem-solving task, communicating via a network. The course of electronic communication can be taken as a writing process, as discussed in the previous sections. The dialogue between participants can be described as a case of synchronous text production, serving to support problem solving and learning. Many chapters in this volume discuss the oral, face-to-face situation. We examine here whether, in order for messages to become tools for modeling, written text production provides added value.

The activities of producing and comprehending written language have been discussed as facilitating learning by:

- Text Comprehension: linking new information to individual domain knowledge;
- Reflection: reflection on knowledge to include in the text by abstraction or analogy, or by modeling parameters of the task situation;
- Text Interpretation: the requirement of interpreting previous text for producing new text, in the light of pragmatic and rhetorical constraints;
- Knowledge Constitution: creating knowledge by writing down ideas.

The question we discuss here is how to arrange a CSCL situation in which these mechanisms are encouraged as much as possible. In fact, given the importance of written text production for sustaining the interaction between writing and knowledge, we see two possible and complementary points of departure for dealing with this question. The first approach is based on the difference between oral and written code. The second approach distinguishes the classical and romantic positions. Altogether, this leads us to a number of recommendations for arranging an electronic collaborative modeling situation.

The Specificity of the Written Code, Compared to the Oral Code

Returning to our main proposition, we have to distinguish between oral and written communication, by discussing whether (or when) the collaborative writing situation may provide extra power over the oral condition. In other words, does written language use foster creation of knowledge during collaboration, because (a) it encourages the author to actively try to understand the partner's knowledge and problem representation, (b) it comprises a productive condition for knowledge constitution, or (c) by some other mechanism? Fayol (1996) discussed four dimensions that characterize writing, compared to speaking or oral conversation. These four dimensions could be used to stage-manage some of the parameters in a collaborative learning situation.

Presence of the Written Trace. The most specific and obvious characteristic of writing is the presence of text. This text is the product of text production, and it is under permanent construction and subjected to additions and changes until the writer decides it is complete. During a composition process, the text can be seen as the trace of its own evolution. For a writer engaged in text production, this implies a double activity: comprehension and production (see Alamargot & Chanquoy, 2001). The text must be read and reread for two reasons: to preserve coherence with what has been written previously, and to be able to access specific parts of the text quickly and effectively for revision.

In the collaborative situation, the texts (messages) that were previously received (by the other) or sent (by the writer) may be available and accessible all the time, depending on the interface. This specific characteristic of written code stresses again the importance of the comprehension activity, discussed earlier. In addition, in the collaborative case, the possibility of feedback may lead to revision of earlier text, to more importance and consideration of the other, in the form of more reflection and text interpretation processes, discussed earlier as two of the learning mechanisms. A first recommendation can be formulated as follows: support comprehension and revision of produced messages.

One of the options here is to think of ways of clearly representing and organizing information used and produced by the participants. It may be informative for the participants to allow easy and visible changes to information already produced. These kinds of activities should be integrated in the problem-solving situation, to make them useful. In other words, rereading and revising earlier messages should be productive for solving the problem in order for learning to occur. The issue of representation calls for thinking about ways of representing ongoing discussion. Some possibilities are outlines, diagrams, links, colors, etc.

The Absence of an Audience. Writing a text normally takes place without the potential reader present, so there is neither interaction nor immediate verbal or nonverbal feedback. Consequently, the individual writing situation requires (depending on the task goal) establishing a mental model of the reader, which requires pragmatic knowledge. We have discussed above the importance of pragmatic knowledge as fundamental for epistemic effects to arise, at least according to the classical position. We return again to this aspect later. Obviously, in the collaborative situation, there is a reader present all the time who needs to be dealt with constantly. Every time the writer produces a message, the reader-model needs to be accessed. In addition, this model is not fixed, but changes as discussion proceeds. Again, rather precise comprehension of the other's messages is crucial here, a least at the level of pragmatics.

For this comprehension (reflection) to take place in collaboration, grounding needs to be fostered. Grounding can be described as the sense of shared understanding of utterances in interaction (Baker et al., 1999). It is the process during which common ground is constructed and maintained. Grounding should be realized with respect to understanding the situation, the other participant, and the problem–solving state. Our second recommendation is based on the conjecture put forward in Baker et al. (1999): "Collaborative learning will be associated with a gradual transition from the use of language as a medium for grounding communication (pragmatic) to grounding on the level of the medium itself (semantic), leading to appropriation of the medium" (p. 46). From the perspective of language production as a learning tool we recommend that the environment support pragmatic grounding, so as to allow a learner to reflect on the semantics of the situation. This could involve access to (multiple) representations of the problem, the colearner(s) and of previous dialogue.

Familiar situations and familiar participants make grounding and communication much easier. Discourse production is easier for more familiar topics, as already discussed. For less familiar cases and participants, some representation of the problem–solving state, a representation of the problem itself, and a representation of the other, in relation to the problem–solving process, should be available, and updateable. In order to monitor ongoing learning, some way of representing what is being learned could help the grounding process. Two recommendations can be put forward here: represent knowledge building activities, to encourage text interpretation processes, and foster reflection by linking conversation to the ongoing problem-solving representation.

Processing Time.   Distribution of processing time is different for written and oral forms. The absence of verbal interaction in the written case allows more time for formulation and reflection. Anyone who has ever experienced or witnessed a chat session, even an educational one, would agree with the observation that it does not permit much room for reflection. Although students may differ greatly with respect to formulation speed and time for reflection, synchronous conversation seems more similar to oral conversation than to writing. This means that the fact that such messages are written may not be enough to benefit from text power. The time allowed for formulating sentences in individual (or asynchronous!) writing is a crucial factor that permits (in principle at least) planning of the content and form of messages at levels other than that of local coherence, allowing reflection on a group of messages to monitor their coherence with respect to a communicative goal (text interpretation).

There is an important role for expertise and preparation here. As we discussed earlier, domain experts need to spend less cognitive resources on planning. For instance, brighter students will be able to more easily communicate their knowledge; the same applies to domain experts. Their messages will be better structured, and because they are more easily produced, domain experts will have more resources left for other tasks. However, research on collaborative learning does not always show positive effects of the presence of domain experts, either students or teachers (Person & Graesser, 1999; van der Linden, Erkens, Schmidt, & Renshaw, 2000), and the reverse case has also been observed: two "wrongs" can make a "right" if they argue together (Schwarz, Neuman, & Biezuner, in press). Although these results are not merely effects of language production, one important point to note is that the fact that text production is easier for an individual does not imply more reflection by default. It may simply mean a faster process, or more resources allocated to things other than learning. On the other hand, the issue of cognitive load may lead students during problem solving to seek "what to do" information rather than "why to do it" information (Katz, Arnois, & Creitz, 1999; Sweller, 1994; Veerman, 2000). Reid and Hards (1998) reported electronic discussion data that suggest that under time scarcity, undergraduates display a greater tendency toward compromise, when this was possible, or a greater frequency of value arguments (i.e., arguments that are not very discussible, such as "Killing animals is cruel") when compromise was not attainable.

Person and Graesser (1999) analyzed tutoring discourse, especially with respect to question asking. Their research showed, among many other things, that this type of teaching seems to be effective, although there is very little understanding between tutors and students. What seems to make this type of discourse effective is tutors employing certain conversational moves (hinting, prompting, splicing, pumping, and summarizing) that do not lead to a tutor's better understanding of the students' conceptions, but nevertheless lead to a student's better understanding of the problem and the concepts involved. One of the general findings in this area is that collaborative learning by instruction requires instruction. That is, without extensive training programs, participants do not learn effectively from each other's feedback. For example, King (1999) elaborated a successful program for teaching fourth-grade pupils to ask thought provoking questions and to understand knowledge construction discourse patterns. Brown and Palincsar (1989) elaborated a program called *reciprocal teaching*, in which young students are guided toward gradually becoming active, self-regulated learners.

Although a slower pace of communication in any type of discourse increases possibilities for reflection, most users tend not to use this opportunity. Among many reasons for this, lack of knowledge about collaboration and lack of motivation for reflection stand out. We would like to put forward two recommendations here: Never stress speed, and encourage (and train students for) using free resources for *collaboration*. Experts should try asking the right questions, and novices should try providing real (partial) answers.

Specificity of Written Forms.   With respect to the language forms used, there are important differences to be observed between written and oral language. For example, written language contains fewer repetitions, and it uses rhetorical forms to replace intonation and prosody (e.g., thematization, perspective, etc.). In terms of coherence, written language is less redundant by default. Processing of written language requires more effort to (re)construct the coherence of a message with respect to previous information. Written language requires more conscious application of cohesive devices, including lexical choices.

However, an important limitation concerning this characteristic of writing is that electronic communication involves short messages, especially if it is synchronous. The focus on coherence, which is important for some of the epistemic effects to take place, has more of a local nature, as it is hard to address all issues at the same time. For example, Veerman, Andriessen, and Kanselaar (2000) found that university students discussing (over a network) a conceptual issue during the task of collaboratively analyzing an educational dialogue had a strong tendency to focus on solving the problem (that is, to select a category from the classification system) instead of trying to find an acceptable answer regarding conceptual issues (e.g., What does this conceptual category mean? What does the speaker really mean? etc.). This tendency was stronger in the case of synchronous discussion than with asynchronous collaboration.

Experienced chatters are quite good at overcoming some of the limitations of electronic communication, but this does not (yet) characterize most of our students. Moreover, the use of new language forms in electronic communication may again advance speed rather than reflection. This leads us to suppose that it may not always be a good idea to use oral communication, even when this becomes a serious possibility in electronic environments. It seems that for learning to take place, production of well-formulated sentences is important, as well as monitoring for organization and coherence.

The Classic or the Romantic Epistemic Effect

The points discussed in the previous section represent general recommendations that involve respecting the written textual format and allowing one to profit from the power of text production activity. Of course, the collaborative situation is more complex than that, and our recommendations should be related to task goals and also to specific phases during the problem-solving process. In addition, most recommendations put forward here may be more appropriate for asynchronous discussions, inasmuch as they assume that participants have time for reflection. This requirement is different in the case of the romantic position. Knowledge construction is a process during sentence formulation and does not call for reflection on the constraints of the situation. It seems that whereas conceptual understanding (learning) takes place at the semantic level, the situations and factors that affect learning are to be found at the pragmatic level. In this way, it may be that the romantic position describes an actual learning mechanism, whereas the classical position describes instructional conditions for learning by reflection. Put differently, the classic conception requires communication to be problematic and the romantic position requires communication to be supported.

The classic position is about learning by knowledge transformation during problem solving. For communication during collaborative problem solving, this implies that conscious reflection should be fostered by allowing revision of produced text and solutions, having access to multiple representations, and participants prompting each others' reflection by posing "why" questions. With respect to the interface, participants need a professional text editor, a text organizer, graphical representations of (partial) task solutions as well as the structure of the dialogue, and perhaps menus for structuring learning dialogues. The instructional situation should incorporate, somewhere at the end, synthesis activities in which communication is summarized, recapitulated, or evaluated.

In contrast, the romantic position is about producing new knowledge during content formulation. The learning situation should encourage unconstrained idea production. Although this could be a characteristic of oral text production, the effort involved in written sentence production is necessary for the effect to take place. In a safe collaborative situation, participants should mutually support each other to produce ideas as much as possible. Maybe the addition of a private notepad for ideas to be shared later could be helpful. We would like to propose two further recommendations: Create a safe social environment that supports knowledge constitution, and encourage new information to be marked as such.

DISCUSSION

The power of text production is only one of the factors important for learning in a collaborative situation. Our recommendations could run counter to other interests in that situation. For example, we do not want to overload problem solvers' views with too many processes to monitor. Computer screens should be customizable in this respect, according to a user's experience and requirements of a specific state of problem solving. This requires great design intelligence, surpassing that of current word processors.

The social dimension, crucial for any collaborative learning situation, is largely ignored in this chapter. It cannot be studied in isolation; neither can any effect of collaborative learning be completely understood without reference to the interaction between individual and situation in terms of the social dimensions. We propose to do that in a later text that focuses more specifically on knowledge constitution, for which the social dimension of collaboration is more important than for the "classic" positions. Hayes' (1996) new model contains a box with a social dimension, including collaboration, but there are few ideas about how and why interactions between social and other dimensions must be incorporated (see Alamargot & Chanquoy, 2001, for a review). Eventually, it can be envisaged on the basis of the knowledge-constituting model by Galbraith (1999), that the acquisition of knowledge in the romantic manner by writing down what comes to mind will be more effective when the writer is less affected by the social context of writing as it is reflected by pragmatic and rhetorical constraints. It may be interesting to find out more about the role of individual differences in this respect, for example, by investigating how these different social sensitivities are reflected in communication and learning by writing. This social perspective on interaction should be more explored.

Similarly, research has provided us many explanations for learning effects of collaboration. It is sometimes hard to distinguish in terminology and explanations between cognitive learning processes and the effects of instructional intervention or training. Conditions under which these mechanisms come into play involve task situations, individual characteristics, and the nature of the domain. All these mechanisms involve verbal interaction. We would like to learn to what extent language use contributes to (or may even explain) the learning effects proposed for collaboration, but that is currently not possible. To illustrate, we list here some possible cognitive learning mechanisms, operating in collaborative learning, as proposed in Dillenbourg (1999):

- Induction: The learner induces new or more abstract information as a result of analysis, for example, by comparing information from different sources or different representational formats. This seems also to be a possible effect of (oral) language use, for example as suggested by Schwartz (1999).
- Cognitive load: As we already discussed for the case of writing, domain experts have more free resources for complex processes because less energy is required for them to generate domain knowledge in a useful format. Expertise (whatever type) present in the collaborative situation could free resources in the same manner. It is up to instruction and the participants to see to fruitful allocation of these free resources.
- Self-explanation: One way of viewing collaborative learning is as a situation in which individuals provide explanations to one another. That self-explanation as constructive cognitive activity can lead to modification of knowledge is an established research finding (Chi, Bassok, Lewis, Reimann, & Glaser, 1989; Chi & VanLehn, 1991). Explaining to others seems to offer even more opportunities for learning when compared to self-explanation, but no substantial significant differences seem to have been observed so far (Ploetzner, Dillenbourg, Preier, & Traum, 1999). Baker (1996b) discussed evidence that one of the main effects of dialogic argumentation is that it makes knowledge explicit, leading participants to reflect on and restructure knowledge.

- Conflict: a discrepancy between knowledge or viewpoints that leads to conflicts, discussion, and eventually, learning. Conflict, in the sense of Piaget (de Lisi & Golbeck, 1999), induces revisions in the cognitive system because an individual may look for alternative arguments or solutions. A collaborative situation may induce discrepancies between individuals, which need to be reset to equilibrium state, a process that may result in revision of knowledge. A change may be behavioral, based on social pressure, but not cognitive at all (e.g., Baker, 1996a; Stein & Miller, 1993).
- Internalization: transfer from the (social) situation to the inner plane, especially examined in the context of child–mother interactions (Wertsch, 1985) where a child becomes able to use new concepts by verbal interaction with a parent, essentially through reflection, it seems.
- Appropriation (Rogoff, 1990): reinterpretation of actions or concepts in the light of what the other says or does. This could be a long-term process, which has properties of socialization, but short-term effects of linguistic production have been reported (Fox, 1987). During interaction, as a result of grounding, learning may take place, by virtue of appropriation of tools (Baker et al., 1999).

We leave the question of the role of language use in these learning mechanisms open here, as there is no experimentation we know of to explain learning by collaboration in terms of effects of message production. This is, for us, a challenge for the near future. In general, this means experimenting with knowledge activation of participants producing written messages in collaborative learning situations. This type of experimentation may clarify some of the complicated results and difficult-to-relate mechanisms that have been proposed to explain collaborative learning.

REFERENCES

Alamargot, D. (1997). *Processus de récupération et d'organisation dans l'activité de rédaction de texte: Effets de l'acquisition de connaissances référentielles [Generating and organizing processes during text production activity: Effects of learning domain knowledge]*. Doctoral dissertation, Poitiers University, France.

Alamargot, D., & Chanquoy, L. (2001). *Through the models of writing*. Boston: Kluwer.

Alamargot, D., Favart, M., & Galbraith, D. (2000, September). *Evolution of idea generation in argumentative writing: Writing as knowledge constituting or knowledge transforming process?* Paper presented at the SIG-Writing Conference, Verona (Italy).

Andriessen, J. E. B., & Sandberg, J. A. C. (1999). Where is education heading and how about AI? *International Journal of Artificial Intelligence in Education, 10*(2), 130–150.

Baker, M. (1996a). *Argumentation and cognitive change in collaborative problem-solving dialogues*. COAST Research Report Number CR-13/96, France.

Baker, M. (1996b). Argumentation et co-construction des connaissances. *Interaction et cognitions, 1*(2–3), 157–191.

Baker, M. (1999). Argumentation and constructive interaction. In J. E. B. Andriessen & P. Coirier (Eds.), *Foundations of argumentative text processing* (pp. 179–202). Amsterdam: Amsterdam University Press.

Baker, M., Hansen, T., Joiner, R., & Traum, D. (1999). The role of grounding in collaborative learning tasks. In P. Dillenbourg (Ed.), *Collaborative learning: Cognitive and computational approaches* (pp. 31–63). Amsterdam: Pergamon.

Benton, S. L., Corkill, A. J., Sharp, J. M., Downey, R. G., & Khramtsova, I. (1995). Knowledge, interest and narrative writing. *Journal of Educational Psychology, 87*(1), 66–79.

Bereiter, C. (in press). *Education and mind in the knowledge age.* Mahwah, NJ: Lawrence Erlbaum Associates.

Bereiter, C., & Scardamalia, M. (1987). *The psychology of written composition.* Hillsdale, NJ: Lawrence Erlbaum Associates.

Brown, A. L., & Palincsar, A. S. (1989) Guided cooperative learning and individual knowledge acquisition. In L. B. Resnick (Ed.), *Knowing, learning and instruction: Essays in the honour of Robert Glaser* (pp. 393–453). Hillsdale, NJ: Lawrence Erlbaum Associates.

Caccamise, D. J. (1987). Idea generation in writing. In A. Matsuhashi (Ed.), *Writing in real time: modeling production processes* (pp. 224–253). Norwood, NJ: Ablex.

Caillies, S., Denhiere, G., & Jhean-Larose, S. (1999). The intermediate effect: Interaction between prior knowledge and text structure. In H. van Oostendorp & S. Goldman (Eds.), *The construction of mental representations during reading* (pp. 151–168). Mahwah, NJ: Lawrence Erlbaum Associates.

Chase, W. G., & Simon, H. A. (1973). The mind's eye in chess. In W. G. Chase (Ed.), *Visual information processing* (pp. 215–281). New York: Academic Press.

Chi, M. T. H., Bassok, M., Lewis, M. W., Reimann, P., & Glaser, R. (1989). Self-explanations: How students study and use examples in learning to solve problems. *Cognitive Science, 13,* 145–182.

Chi, M. T. H., Glaser, R., & Farr, M. (1988). *The nature of expertise.* Hillsdale, NJ: Lawrence Erlbaum Associates.

Chi, M. T. H., & VanLehn, K. A. (1991). The content of physics self-explanations. *Journal of the Learning Sciences, 1*(1), 69–105.

Clark, H. H., & Brennan, S. E. (1991). Grounding in communication. In L. B. Resnick, J. M. Levine, & S. D. Teasley (Eds.), *Perspectives on socially shared cognition* (pp. 127–150). Washington: American Psychological Association.

De Groff, L. C. (1987). The influence of prior knowledge on writing, conferencing and revising. *The Elementary School Journal, 88,* 105–118.

De Groot, A. D. (1965). *Thought and choice in chess.* The Hague: Mouton.

de Lisi, R., & Golbeck, S. L. (1999). Implications of Piagetian theory for peer learning. In A. M. O'Donnell & A. King (Eds.), *Cognitive perspectives on peer learning* (pp. 3–37). Mahwah, NJ: Lawrence Erlbaum Associates.

Dillenbourg, P. (1999). Introduction: What do you mean by "collaborative learning?" In P. Dillenbourg (Ed.), *Collaborative learning: Cognitive and computational approaches* (pp. 1–19). Amsterdam: Pergamon.

Egan, D. E., & Schwartz, B. J. (1979). Chunking in recall of symbolic drawings. *Memory and Cognition, 7*(2), 149–158.

Eigler, G., Jechle, T., Merziger, G., & Winter, A. (1991). Writing and knowledge: Effects and re-effects. *European Journal of Psychology of Education, 4*(2), 225–232.

Erkens, G. (1997). *Cooperatief probleemoplossen met computers in het onderwijs: Het modellerenvan cooperatieve dialogen voor de otwikkeling van intelligente onderwijssystemen [Cooperative problem solving with computers in education: Modeling of cooperative dialogues for the design of intelligent educational systems]*. Doctoral dissertation, Utrecht University, The Netherlands.

Erkens, G., & Andriessen, J. E. B. (1994). Cooperation in problem–solving and educational computer programs. *Computers in Human Behavior, 10*, 107–125.

Fayol, M. (1996). Le production du langage écrit [written language production]. In J. David & S. Plane (Eds.), *L'apprentissage de l'écriture de l'école au collège* (pp. 9–36). Paris: Presses Universitaires de France.

Fletcher, C. R. (1994). Levels of representation in memory for discourse. In M. A. Gernsbacher (Ed.), *Handbook of psycholinguistics* (pp. 589–607). New York: Academic Press.

Flower, L. S., & Hayes, J. R. (1980). The dynamic of composing: Making plans and juggling constraints. In L. W. Gregg & E. R. Steinberg (Eds.), *Cognitive processes in writing* (pp. 31–50). Hillsdale, NJ: Lawrence Erlbaum Associates.

Fox, B. (1987). Interactional reconstruction in real-time language processing. *Cognitive Science, 11*(3), 365–387.

Galbraith, D. (1992). Conditions for discovery through writing. *Instructional Science, 21*, 45–72.

Galbraith, D. (1996). Self-monitoring, discovery through writing and individual differences in drafting strategy. In G. Rijlaarsdam, H. van den Bergh, & M. Couzijn (Eds.), *Theories, models and methodology in writing research* (pp. 121–144). Amsterdam: Amsterdam University Press.

Galbraith, D. (1999). Writing as a knowledge-constituting process. In M. Torrance & D. Galbraith (Eds.), *Knowing what to write: Conceptual processes in text production* (pp.139–159). Amsterdam: Amsterdam University Press.

Galbraith, D., & Rijlaarsdam, G. (1999). Effective strategies for the teaching and learning of writing. *Learning and instruction, 9*(2), 93–108.

Garrod, S., & Sanford, A. J. (1999). Incrementality in discourse understanding. In H. van Oostendorp & S. Goldman (Eds.), *The construction of mental representations during reading* (pp. 1–27). Mahwah, NJ: Lawrence Erlbaum Associates.

Goldman, S. (1996). Reading, writing, and learning in hypermedia environments. In H. van Oostendorp & S. de Mul (Eds.), *Cognitive aspects of electronic text processing* (pp. 7–42). Norwood, NJ: Ablex

Hayes, J. R. (1996). A new framework for understanding cognition and affect in writing. In C. M. Levy & S. Ransdell (Eds.), *The science of writing* (pp. 1–27). Mahwah, NJ: Lawrence Erlbaum Associates.

Hayes, J. R., & Flower, L. S. (1980). Identifying the organization of writing processes. In L. W. Gregg & E. R. Steinberg (Eds.), *Cognitive process in writing*. Hillsdale, NJ: Lawrence Erlbaum Associates.

Hayes, J. R., & Nash, J. G. (1996). On the nature of planning in writing. In C. M. Levy & S. Ransdell (Eds.), *The science of writing* (pp. 29–55). Mahwah, NJ: Lawrence Erlbaum Associates.

Katz, S., Arnois, J., & Creitz, C. (1999). Modeling pedagogical interactions with machine learning. In S. P. Lajoie & M. Vivet (Eds.), *Artificial intelligence in education* (pp. 543–550). Amsterdam: IOS Press.

Kellogg, R. T. (1987). Effects of topic knowledge on the allocation of processing time and cognitive effort to writing processes. *Memory and Cognition, 15*(3), 256–266.

Kellogg, R. T. (1996). A model of working memory in writing. In C. M. Levy & S. Ransdell (Eds.), *The science of writing: Theories, methods, and applications* (pp. 57–72). Mahwah, NJ: Lawrence Erlbaum Associates.

King, A. (1999). Discourse patterns for mediating peer learning. In A. M. O'Donnell & A. King (Eds.), *Cognitive perspectives on peer learning* (pp. 87–115). Mahwah, NJ: Lawrence Erlbaum Associates.

Mc Cutchen, D. (1986). Domain knowledge and linguistic knowledge in the development of writing ability. *Journal of Memory and Language, 25,*431–444.

Mc Keithen, K. B., Reitman, J. S., Rueter, H. H., & Hirtle, S. C. (1981). Knowledge organization and skill differences in computer progammers. *Cognitive Psychology, 13,* 307–325.

McKoon, G., & Ratcliff, R. (1992). Inference during reading. *Psychological Review, 99,* 440–446.

Miller, G. A. (1956). The magical number seven, plus or minus two: Some limits on our capacity for processing information. *Psychological Review, 63,* 81–97.

Munneke, L., & Andriessen, J. E. B. (2000, September). *Learning through collaboratively writing an argumentative text.* Paper presented at the Third International Workshop on Argumentative Text Production, Verona.

O'Donnell, A. M., & King, A. (Eds.). (1999). *Cognitive perspectives on peer learning.* Mahwah, NJ: Lawrence Erlbaum Associates.

Ohlsson, S. (1993). Learning to do and learning to understand: A lesson and a challenge for cognitive modeling. In P. Reimann & H. Spada (Eds.), *Learning in humans and machines* (pp. 37–62). Oxford: Pergamon Press.

Person, N. K., & Graesser, A. G. (1999). Evolution of discourse during cross-age tutoring. In A. M. O'Donnell & A. King (Eds.), *Cognitive perspectives on peer learning* (pp. 69–86). Mahwah, NJ: Lawrence Erlbaum Associates.

Petraglia, J. (1998). *Reality by design: The rhetoric and technology of authenticity in education.* Mahwah, NJ: Lawrence Erlbaum Associates.

Piolat, A., & Olive, T. (2000). Comment étudier le coût et le déroulement de la rédaction de textes. La méthode de triple tâche: Bilan méthodologique (How to study the cost and the course of text production activity. The triple task method: A methodological review). *L'Année Psychologique, 465,* 465–202.

Ploetzner, R., Dillenbourg, P., Preier, M., & Traum, D. (1999). Learning by explaining to oneself and to others. In P. Dillenbourg (Ed.), *Collaborative learning: Cognitive and computational approaches* (pp. 103–121). Amsterdam: Pergamon.

Reid, F. J. M., & Hards, R. (1998). The effects of time scarcity on conflict and compromise in computer conferencing. *Computers in Human Behavior, 14*(4), 637–656.

Reitman, J. (1976). Skilled perception in GO: Deducing memory structures from interresponse times. *Cognitive Psychology, 8,* 336–356.

Rogoff, B. (1990). *Apprenticeship in thinking.* New York: Oxford University Press.

Rosch, E. (1973). On the internal structure of perceptual and semantics categories. In T. E. Moore (Ed.), *Cognitive development and the acquisition of language* (pp. 111–114). New York: Academic Press.

Rosch, E., Gray, W. D., Johnson, D. M., & Boyes-Braem, P. (1976). Basic objects in natural categories. *Cognitive Psychology, 8,* 382–439.

Rosch, E., & Mervis, C. (1975). Family resemblance in internal structure of categories. *Cognitive Psychology, 7,* 573–605.

Salomon, G. (1993). On the nature of pedagogic computer tools: The case of the writing partner. In S. P. Lajoie & S. J. Derry (Eds.), *Computers as cognitive tools* (pp. 289–317). Hillsdale, NJ: Lawrence Erlbaum Associates.

Scardamalia, M., & Bereiter, C. (1991). Litterate expertise. In K. A. Ericsson & J. Smith (Eds.), *Toward a general theory of expertise: Prospect and limits* (pp. 172–194). Cambridge, UK: Cambridge University Press.

Schneider, W., Korkel, J., & Weinert, F. E. (1989). Domain specific knowledge and memory performance: A comparison of high and low aptitude children. *Journal of Educational Psychology, 81*, 306–312.

Schumacher, G. M., Klare, G. R., Cronin, F. C., & Moses, J. D. (1984). Cognitive activities of beginning and advanced college writers: A pausal analysis. *Research in the Teaching of English, 18*, 169–187.

Schwarz, B. B., Neuman, Y., & Biezuner, S. (in press). Two wrongs may make a right ... If they argue together! *Cognition and Instruction.*

Schwartz, D. L. (1999). The productive agency that drives collaborative learning. In P. Dillenbourg (Ed.). *Collaborative learning: Cognitive and computational approaches* (pp.197–218). Oxford: Pergamon.

Simon, H. A. (1974). How big is a chunk? *Science, 183*, 482–488.

Snyder, M. (1986). *Public appearances, private realities: The psychology of self-monitoring.* New York: W. H. Freeman.

Stein, N., & Miller, C. A. (1993). A theory of argumentative understanding: Relationships among position preference, judgements of goodness, memory, and reasoning. *Argumentation, 7*, 183–204.

Sweller, J. (1994). Cognitive load theory, learning difficulty and instructional design. *Learning and Instruction, 4*, 295–312.

van den Broek, P. W., Young, M., Tzeng, Y., & Linderholm, T. (1999). The landscape model of reading: Inferences and the online construction of a memory representation. In H. van Oostendorp & S. Goldman (Eds.), *The construction of mental representations during reading* (pp. 71–98). Mahwah, NJ: Lawrence Erlbaum Associates.

van der Linden, J., Erkens, G., Schmidt, H., & Renshaw, P. (2000). Collaborative learning. In R. J. Simons, J. L. van der Linden, & T. Duffy (Eds.), *New learning* (pp. 37–54). Dordrecht: Kluwer.

van Dijk, T. A. (1999). Context models in discourse processing. In H. van Oostendorp & S. Goldman (Eds.), *The construction of mental representations during reading* (pp. 123–148). Mahwah, NJ: Lawrence Erlbaum Associates.

van Dijk, T. A., & Kintsch, W. (1983). *Strategies of discourse comprehension.* New York: Academic Press.

van Oostendorp, H. (1994). Text processing in terms of semantic cohesion monitoring. In H. van Oostendorp & R. A. Zwaan (Eds.), *Naturalistic text comprehension* (pp. 35–55). Norwood, NJ: Ablex.

Veerman, A. L. (2000). *Computer-supported collaborative learning through argumentation.* PhD Thesis, Utrecht University, The Netherlands.

Veerman, A. L., Andriessen, J. E. B., & Kanselaar, G. (2000). Learning through synchronous electronic discussion. *Computers and Education, 34*(2–3), 1–22.

Voss, J., Vesonder, G. T., & Spilich, G. J. (1980). Text generation and recall by high knowledge and low knowledge individuals. *Journal of Verbal Learning and Verbal Behavior, 6*, 651–667.

Voss, J., Wiley, J., & Sandak, R. (1999). Reasoning in the construction of argumentative texts. In J. Andriessen & P. Coirier (Eds.), *Foundations of argumentative text processing* (pp. 29–41). Amsterdam: Amsterdam University Press.

Wertsch, J. V. (1985). Adult–child interaction as a source of self-regulation in children. In S. R. Yussen (Ed.), *The growth of reflection in children* (pp. 69–97). Madison, WI: Academic Press.

Chapter 11

Argumentative Interactions, Discursive Operations, and Learning to Model in Science

Michael Baker
CNRS & Université Lumière Lyon 2

Doing science is essentially a group activity, and the same is often true of learning to do science. Given that the activity of any group usually relies on communicative exchanges using language in its various linguistic, symbolic, and pictorial forms, then language is necessarily involved in doing science and in learning to do it. But linguistic exchanges are not just means of coordinating activities (cf. Clark, 1996, 1999). Considered as a system of signs (Saussure, 1915/1972), language is also a cultural repository of concepts; and considered in its primary manifestation, as social interaction (Bahktine, 1929/1977), language is the means by which concepts are engendered. In the continuation of Vygotsky's work, social interactions are considered to be the primary means by which scientific notions are coelaborated, building on their everyday correlates, with the scaffolding of a more capable person such as a teacher.

In this chapter we argue that one particular type of social interaction—*argumentative interaction*—plays a specific and important role in one aspect of learning science: learning to model. In order to support this claim, we first describe epistemic, cognitive, and linguistic dimensions of modeling in science, and of argumentative interactions, and then propose general relations between them. These general claims are then illustrated by analysis of three specific interaction sequences, drawn from corpora collected in situations that were designed for learning to model. We conclude that argumentative interactions embody discursive operations by which different types of concepts and knowledge are dissociated from each other, this being a necessary precursor to establishing complex relations between models and their associated experimental fields, that is, to modeling itself.

LEARNING TO MODEL: EPISTEMIC, COGNITIVE, AND LINGUISTIC DIMENSIONS

Modeling in science involves trying to establish complex relations between elements of a model (with its attendant syntax, and in relation to a theory) and objects and events in an experimental field (Tiberghien, 1994, 1996). Two aspects of the modeling process are important to remember in this context, since they are the ones that usually pose problems for students who are learning to model.

Firstly, it is not the case that every element of the model must have a correlate in the experimental field: There exist model elements, such as "the environment," that do not correspond to determinate tangible objects.

Secondly, it is not the case that every object or event in the experimental field must be taken into account (or represented) by the model. An obvious example would be that in modeling a simple electrical circuit, the color of the wrapping of the battery should not normally to be taken into account. Apart from such simple examples, what is at stake here is the way in which the experimental field is to be represented, or conceptualized, and this is not all obvious for students. For example, suppose the students are asked to model energy in a simple electrical circuit involving a battery linked to a bulb by two wires. It may appear obvious that there are four elements in the experimental field to be taken into account: the battery, the first wire, the second wire, and the bulb. However, the two wires should correspond to a single model element: a transfer of energy from the battery to the bulb, in terms of electrical work. Furthermore, students do not always even isolate precisely these four entities to be modeled: Rather than selecting the battery as a whole, they may decide that it is its internal chemical structure or the terminals that are to be selected, and similarly with the bulb (the whole bulb or just the filament?)

This process of selecting objects and events reveals the first way in which language enters into the picture. Modeling involves selecting elements in the material world, a way of conceptualizing or representing them that will be specific to each spoken language; and such languages embody, amongst other things, ways of seeing, thinking, dividing up the world.

Modeling itself involves a complex process of matching between model and experimental field that implies adjusting representations, or "levels" of description, of each in order to get a "fit" that satisfies all constraints in the problem-situation. Tiberghien (1994, 1996) termed this process one of creating a *semantics* or *meaning* for the model and the experimental field. How is this done, inasmuch as neither the model itself nor the experimental situation provides the answer directly? In addition to obeying model constraints, the student-modelers have to draw on additional sources of knowledge—from what they have learned in other areas of science, and from what they know about the material world from their everyday experience. For example, in modeling energy in electrical circuits, knowledge about electricity learned in school comes into play, if only to understand that this is just one type of energy (electrical work); knowledge from everyday life (such as the fact that if a wire is not connected, then the bulb will not light up) can be drawn upon, possibly in order to eliminate inadequate models.

This necessity to introduce new sources of knowledge reveals a second way in which language relates to modeling in science. Any scientific practice is, of course, carried out using different aspects of language—formal and "natural"—and there is a continuum between the language that students use in their everyday life and the language they use in the science classroom. In some cases, clear lexical distinctions exist—such as the everyday word "weight" in comparison with the scientific term "mass"—but in others, a single word such as "energy" can occur in its (school or other) scientific context, as well as being able to participate in everyday language structures that can also be used with respect to tangible objects (e.g., "She's got a lot of energy!" vs. "She's got a lot of apples!"). When students use such apparently scientific terms, therefore, the *sense* in which they are using them is not always clear (perhaps to them, and certainly not to the researcher).

If, therefore, being able to model involves to be able to elaborate relations between model and experimental field, using different types of knowledge, a necessary condition for modeling is to be able to distinguish or dissociate these types of knowledge and levels of description in the first place. An example of dissociating different types of school-learned knowledge would be understanding that energy is not the same as electricity, or, more generally, that the way in which things are described outside school is not the same as the way they should be described in school. An example of dissociating levels of description would be understanding that "lighting up [of a bulb]" is an event to be modeled in the experimental field, whereas "light rays" is a model-level term, used to describe a particular mode of energy transfer.

Thus, several years ago in (unreported) work carried out with Tiberghien, and as part of a teaching sequence on energy, we first asked students to write a textual description of an electrical circuit, then to classify parts of their texts (words or clauses) into three categories: electricity, objects and events, and "other" (i.e., what could not be in the other categories, in fact corresponding to energy). The idea was to help students to distinguish different levels of description as part of modeling, and for them to have an intellectual need to learn about energy.

In summary, modeling and learning to model can be seen as involving three types of dimensions. The *epistemic* dimension concerns the different types of knowledge that must be brought to bear on the problem at hand, relating to different social practices and areas of experience. The *cognitive* dimension concerns conceptualizing or representing different areas of knowledge and perception—models and experimental fields, different sources of knowledge—and making adjustments to each of these representations so that a satisfactory matching can be made between them. The *linguistic* aspect involves using different types of sign systems and language registers in modeling, in producing written solutions, and/or in communicative interaction with other people.

In distinguishing these three aspects, we do not wish to suggest that they correspond to different mental, social, or other faculties; for our purposes here, they can be viewed as aspects of a single human and social reality. In fact, modeling as we described it involves doing cognitive work on and in language in relation to different areas of understanding and experience.

We next discuss how specific discursive processes at work in argumentative interactions can be closely linked to these dimensions of modeling.

ARGUMENTATIVE INTERACTIONS: EPISTEMIC, COGNITIVE, AND LINGUISTIC DIMENSIONS

In order to understand the specific role that argumentative interactions can play with respect to learning modeling, we need to understand what argumentative interactions are, how they function with respect to cooperative problem solving, and to describe the discursive processes at work in them.

Argumentative Interactions

We consider the situation in which a group of people (interlocutors, L1, L2, ...) cooperate in solving a particular problem, *P.*

The first condition for argumentative interaction is that there should exist, in the interactive context, a *diversity of proposals* concerning *P* (for example, solutions to it, or methods for obtaining such solutions) that we shall term $s_1, s_2, ... s_n$.

Secondly, $s_1, s_2, ... s_n$ can be differently distributed across interlocutors. For example, L1 could propose s_1, and L2 s_2; or else, L1 could propose s_1, then s_2, and, realizing that both cannot be accepted, engage L2 in finding arguments in order to determine which of s_1 or s_2 is more plausible.

Thirdly, from the points of view of the interlocutors, $s_1, s_2, ... s_n$ have *different epistemic statuses*—more or less plausible, true, believable, acceptable, etc.

Fourthly, the interlocutors feel obliged to *choose* between $s_1, s_2, ... s_n$, for different possible reasons inherent in the cooperative problem-solving situation—the proposals are seen as mutually contradictory, only a single solution is possible, etc. We describe this "problem of choice" as an *interlocutionary* problem, *I.*

Finally, in order to resolve the *interlocutionary problem*—which proposal(s) should be accepted?—the interlocutors establish links between them and other proposals called arguments or counterarguments, the creation of which potentially modifies the epistemic statuses of the initial proposals; for example, one is now seen as false, less plausible, obviously better, etc. There is also a second way in which the epistemic statuses of proposals can be modified, which is to transform their meaning using what we term *discursive operations*, to be described later. The idea is quite a simple one: The plausibility of a proposal depends on what is meant by it.

This point of view on argumentative interactions in cooperative problem-solving situations (developed in Baker, 1996, 1999) has several implications. Firstly, such interactions are not primarily, or only, attempts to convince (a rhetorical point of view), but are more generally oriented toward choosing what should be accepted or not. Secondly, argumentative interactions are not always purely adversarial, in which interlocutors attempt to impose their proposals (a dialectical point of view); they can also take the form of *cooperative explorations of a dialogical space* of solutions (cf. Nonnon, 1996; Walton, 1989). This is, in fact, the form that most argumentative interactions take in situations where students are trying to coconstruct new knowledge.

We now describe three dimensions of argumentative interactions, corresponding to those described for modeling:

- The *cognitive* dimension of argumentative interaction relates to types of reasoning used (e.g., quasilogical, inductive) and the generation and expression of arguments. One possible cooperative learning mechanism associated with argumentative interactions is thus that the necessity to express justifications or explanations as arguments causes knowledge restructuring (cf. the "self-explanation effect," Chi, Bassock, Lewis, Reimann, & Glaser, 1989; Chi & VanLehn, 1991).
- The *epistemic* dimension of argumentative interaction relates on one hand to the intrinsic nature of what is being discussed: some topics are more debatable by their nature than others (Golder, 1996). On the other hand, it relates to the diversity of types of knowledge that can be appealed to as arguments, each of which can have more or less "weight." For example, an argument that appeals to simple facts of everyday experience (e.g., "When you're standing on the earth and you drop something, it falls down.") is likely to carry more weight than an argument that appeals to more or less complex reasoning. Furthermore, with respect to the capacity of argumentative interactions to trigger changes in epistemic statuses (e.g., "belief"), it is clear that certain types of knowledge or belief are more resistant to change (diSessa, 1982) or "epistemically entrenched" (Gardenförs, 1992) than others.
- The *linguistic* dimension of argumentative interactions concerns the choice of linguistic expressions, oriented toward certain points of view (e.g., describing a person as a "freedom fighter" or as a "terrorist"), the use of connectors (e.g., "therefore," "since") to structure discourse, and linguistic registers (e.g., formal, informal) relating to social situations in which language is used.

Discursive Operations

We mentioned earlier that one way of choosing what proposal(s) to accept is to weigh arguments in the balance, and that another—that we now discuss—was to transform, explore, or *negotiate* the meaning of those proposals.

For our purposes here, it is useful to consider processes that work along all three of the dimensions already discussed: epistemic, cognitive, and linguistic. These are processes whereby language is used to do cognitive work on knowledge or understanding. We term these processes *discursive operations*. Similarly, Vignaux (1988, 1990) termed them *linguistic-cognitive operations*: they are "the means by which discourse performs ... cognitive work on representations" (p. 307). The idea is again quite simple: In producing discourse about some aspect of experience, we do not simply "describe" it, but rather (re-)present it in a certain way; and in successively elaborating our discourse, especially in collaboration with other people, we elaborate or transform our way of (re-)presenting that experience (cf. Edwards, 1993; Edwards & Potter, 1992; Harré & Gillet, 1994).

Argumentative interactions are, we claim, contexts in which the use of such discursive operations is particularly intense because the precise meaning of proposals is especially at stake. An argumentative interaction involving particular topics (or theses) is not simply a matter of exchanging (counter-)arguments in order to win a dialectical game. Most often, the topics debated are not fixed, but undergo shifts in meaning and topic as a result of the interaction. This is part of common experience; common rejoinders are often "If by x you mean y, then I don't agree" or, "That's not what I meant." Thus, the result of a constructive debate (Baker, 1999) is not so much determining who has won, but rather a deepened understanding of the topic under debate, and the different possible points of view about it. Naess (1966) termed this *precization* (the process of making more precise). Debates often begin with a "surface" difference of opinion, and then shift toward more general or fundamental oppositions of underlying points of view. Thus Walton (1992) described the example of a debate on the desirability of the institution of tipping in the United States, that gradually transforms itself into a debate on the more fundamental issue of what should be the role of the state in regulating work practices.

In the rest of this chapter we discuss and illustrate three principal discursive operations at work in argumentative interactions: *negotiation of meaning, conceptual dissociation,* and *conceptual association.*

By *negotiation of meaning,* we mean what is perhaps the most general(ized) type of discursive operation, by which different or alternate meanings of linguistic expressions are compared and successively refined in verbal interactions. Take the example of a debate where one person claims that "It is always wrong to take life away from a person" and another claims that it is not always wrong. Then it is clear that the debate can turn around what is meant by "wrong" (subjective, intersubjective, or objective?), by "life" (Is a plant alive in the way in which a mammal is?), and by "person" (Is a fœtus a person?; Is an insane person to be considered as a person in the same sense?). Arguments and counterarguments are then produced under certain meanings of what they are intended to attack or defend. This is what we mean by the discursive operation of negotiation of meaning.

Secondly, and more specifically, a claim or thesis can be made more precise by *dissociating* the concepts that underlie or relate to it. This corresponds to what Perelman and Olbrechts-Tyteca (1958/1988) termed *argument by dissociation*. For example, Grootendorst (1999) analyzed the (highly contentious) case where, in a papal declaration, in order to defend the Catholic church against possible accusations of anti-Semitism during World War II, the writer of the declaration dissociates the concept of "anti-Semitism" from that of "anti-Judaism," denying the former and partially conceding the latter. Of course, such conceptual dissociations could be performed in any type of interactive context, but the point is that in this case they perform a specific function in a (written) debate: defense against an attack by partial concession. This is what we mean by the discursive operation of *conceptual dissociation*.

Thirdly, conceptual dissociation has a counterpart in the form of *conceptual association*. This involves attempting to subsume different proposals under a single, usually more general, concept so as to "dissolve" the opposition between them. Suppose that one person claims that "It is better to eat animals rather than plants," whereas another claims that "It is better to eat plants rather than animals." Either could attempt to dissolve the verbal conflict by associating both plants and animals under the same category of "living things": "They're the same!—plants and animals are both living things, so neither is better than the other." (Of course, the debate could continue with a new attempt at conceptual differentiation: They're both living things, but they get their energy in different ways, one from digestion and the other from photosynthesis).

All three of these discursive operations can fulfil different functions in argumentative interactions: defending or attacking a thesis, or negotiating a compromise outcome in which each participant can be "right," within specific meanings of what they are saying. We now discuss how they relate to modeling.

RELATIONS BETWEEN ARGUMENTATIVE INTERACTIONS AND MODELING

From the previous two sections, the special relations between modeling in science and argumentative interactions should now be evident. Modeling involves establishing complex relations between different levels of description (model and experimental field), which in turn requires adjusting representations or descriptions on these two levels, and bringing new sources of knowledge to bear on the problem. Doing modeling effectively presupposes that such levels of description and types of knowledge can be effectively distinguished from each other on a conceptual plane.

When modeling is carried out in predominantly languaged-based interaction—and in argumentative interactions in particular—then specific discursive operations may be put into play that work precisely on the level of transforming representations and descriptions of concepts and knowledge. Thus, argumentative interactions can play an integral role in cooperatively learning to model, to the extent that they can oblige students to work on scientific conceptualizations of the material world.

Clearly, all of these discursive operations just described can occur outside argumentative interactions, but we claim that, when there is no manifest interpersonal problem or disagreement, nothing compels the interactants to perform these operations. Once such a disagreement arises, however, and argumentative interaction ensues, then the interactants are under a special *interactional pressure* to defend their views and themselves (their self-images), in a sense relating to their interpersonal relationship (see Muntig & Turnbull, 1998). This pressure forces meanings to undergo transformations by the use of discursive operations.

In the next three sections of this chapter, we discuss three examples of argumentative interaction sequences taken from corpora collected in situations in which students carried out modeling problems in science. The examples illustrate the different discursive operations carried out in argumentative interactions, in close relation to modeling.

FIRST EXAMPLE: CONCEPTUAL DISSOCIATION AND ASSOCIATION AS ARGUMENTATIVE DEFENSES

This example of argumentative interaction (extracts of which are shown in Tables 11.1 and 11.2) is taken from a corpus collected in a classroom situation (Langlois & Tiberghien, 1990). The students' task was to define a property of balls of different substances that can explain their different rebound behaviors (in fact, the coefficient of restitution) by carrying out experiments (dropping the balls from different heights).

Just prior to the sequence shown in Table 11.1, the students had performed an experiment where they dropped two balls of the same size from the same height, one made of rubber and the other of steel.

In line 86, Laurent observes that the rubber ball rebounded to a slightly lower height than the steel one. Hortense then produces an utterance that is interpreted by Laurent as saying that the observation can be explained by the differences in mass of the two balls, which is what Laurent then denies (line 88). Inasmuch as the students' task is to pro-

TABLE 11.1
Corpus Example 1, Extract 1

N	Loc	Dialogue
86	Laurent	it [the ball] rebounds all the same a bit lower, that's normal, but after all ...
87	Hortense	yes but look, with respect to the masses, look, one can see that the steel one is ... is heavier
88	Laurent	yes, but it's not a matter of mass
89	Hortense	well, all the same there's the potential energy involved, I'm sorry! < 3 sec>
90	Laurent	... ok, but if you had ...
91	Hortense	if we had ...?
92	Laurent	if you had a big steel ball ... it would rebound
93	Hortense	and if we release them at the same height, so that one has a greater mass than the other, the one with the greater mass would have a higher potential energy ...
94	Laurent	yes but
95	Hortense	so there would be more
96	Laurent	do you think that if ... if you had an enormous rubber ball like that, that's a kilogramme, do you think it would rebound a lot?
97	**Hortense**	**yes, but that's only valid in the case of an elastic impact**
98	Laurent	well
99	Hortense	in fact I think ...
100	Laurent	we'd be better off thinking about that since, theoretically, it's more simple, given that it's a soft impact
101	Hortense	well yes, there is precisely ... <laughs>
102	Laurent	so what can we say if there is a soft impact? < 2 sec>

Note. In this table, as in other similar ones later, the column labeled "N" corresponds to the numbering of the intervention, "Loc" is a name identifying the locutor (the students' names have been changed, while preserving gender, for confidentiality), and "Dialogue" reproduces a transcription of the students' verbal interaction. As with all other extracts from interactions shown in this chapter, this extract has been translated by the author from the original French.

duce a general expression for explaining rebound behavior, any proposal about a particular experiment can be interpreted as such a potentially general statement. We can therefore reconstruct the initial verbal conflict that initiates the argumentation sequence as follows:

Hortense: (The "mass explains rebound" thesis). The rubber ball rebounded less than the steel one because the rubber ball is less heavier than the steel one: difference in rebound behavior is due to difference in mass.

Laurent: No: difference in rebound behavior is not due to difference in mass.

Here we have a single thesis that is proposed, with respect to which the students attribute different epistemic statuses.

Throughout the sequence 89 to 96, the students develop their own arguments (in the case of Hortense) and counterarguments (in the case of Laurent), with respect to the "mass explains rebound thesis," neither really attending to the other. Hortense's argument in favor of her thesis is basically that because "mass" is a term in the potential energy equation, then mass must be involved in the situation; because the steel ball has a higher mass, it has more potential energy, and so will rebound higher (and so the rubber ball lower). With respect to our remarks on the epistemic dimensions of modeling and of argumentative interactions, this is an argument that appeals to school science knowledge. Laurent's counterargument appeals to a different type of knowledge, derived from everyday intuition: What would happen with a very big rubber ball? Surely it would not rebound much? So it is not mass that explains rebound behavior, but the substance.

What is interesting for our discussion here, is how Hortense defends her thesis against this counterargument (line 97 in Table 11.1): "Yes, but that's only valid in the case of an elastic impact." This is a case of *conceptual dissociation* in argumentative interaction, during a modeling problem. The students were discussing "impacts" in general, and Hortense introduces a conceptual distinction: "[perfectly] elastic impact"/"soft [inelastic] impact." Furthermore, this discursive operation fulfils a specific function in the argumentative interaction: It is a specific type of defense of a thesis against an attack, that partitions the universe of discourse into two domains, within each of which both interlocutors can be "right" (or at least not clearly wrong). The verbal conflict is thus "dissolved," or redefined, so that it no longer obtains; and in fact, the defense is successful to the extent that Laurent concedes indirectly by taking up the topic of "soft" impacts.

The students therefore decide to discuss the case of "soft" impacts and the additional factors that would need to be taken into account in explaining the experimental result, as shown in Table 11.2.

At first, the students engage in a comparative discussion about energy and momentum in the two types of impact introduced previously. The students disagree with respect to Hortense's claim (that becomes a thesis to be defended) that air friction should be taken into account because (she argues, in line 116) "otherwise it [the ball] would rebound to the same height." This defense (rebounding to the same height) then introduces a subsidiary verbal conflict because Laurent disagrees with it, and introduces a counterthesis: "loss at the moment of impact" is the factor to be taken into account, rather than air friction.

TABLE 11.2

Corpus Example 1, Extract 2

N	Loc	Dialogue
111	Laurent	wait ... soft impact, well, you've got conservation of momentum but ... the kinetic energy isn't conserved! I think that that's what we've seen ... by contrast, in an elastic impact, both are conserved ...
112	Hortense	yes, elastic impact, there is the total energy that's conserved
113	Laurent	yes
114	Hortense	yes, but there is the friction ... of the air!
115	Laurent	oh, I don't think that that's especially the air friction that enters into it!
116	Hortense	but yes it is, otherwise, it would rebound to the same height
117	Laurent	no [it wouldn't]
118	Hortense	yes [it would]
119	Laurent	it's the loss at the moment of impact
120	**Hortense**	**it's the same, it's also a sort of friction! it's a sort of friction either with the ground or with the air**
121	Laurent	yes but, after all, air friction in comparison with friction ... if if you call that friction with the ground, it's rather negligible
122	Hortense	ah well yes

As with the previous extract, it is Hortense who performs a specific discursive operation in the attempt to dissolve the conflict between the two theses (air friction/loss at impact), that this time corresponds to *conceptual association*, that is, the inverse of conceptual dissociation: "It's [loss at impact] the same, it's also a sort of friction! it's a sort of friction either with the ground or with the air." Because, as Hortense claims, air friction and loss at impact are both types of friction, there is no fundamental conflict, and thus nothing to argue about. This time, however, her argumentative move is not successful, inasmuch as she has to concede that loss at impact viewed as "friction with the ground" is negligible.

In our analyses of two extracts of an argumentation sequence in a physics modeling situation, we illustrated two discursive operations—conceptual dissociation and association—that reconceptualize the universe of discourse and function as argumentative defenses (successful or not). It is clear that such operations are potential mechanisms of conceptual change, given that they work on a conceptual plane (whether or not, in a given case, the change is normatively positive or not).

SECOND EXAMPLE: NEGOTIATION OF MEANING AND GRADUAL DISSOCIATION OF TYPES OF KNOWLEDGE

The corpus, from which the sequence analyzed in this section was taken, was collected in a physics class of a secondary school (students aged 16–17 years) in the Lyon area of France. The class was experimental to the extent that a new teaching sequence (Tiberghien, 1996) on the theory and model of energy in physics was being tried out on the students. The students' task was designed for learning about modeling in physics, and the theory/model of energy in particular (Devi, Tiberghien, Baker, & Brna, 1996; Tiberghien, 1994, 1996). In the part of the energy modeling teaching sequence discussed here, students are asked to produce a qualitative model (diagram) called an *energy chain* in order to represent energy storage, transfer, and transformation in a simple experimental situation involving a bulb connected to a battery by two wires. They do this on pencil and paper, sitting side by side in the classroom.

Table 11.3 shows the first extract from an argumentation sequence involving two students. Their common solution up to this point is quite usual for this task: They have understood that the battery is a reservoir of energy and that the bulb is a transformer of energy. Their problem now is to determine the nature of the transfer(s) of energy between the battery and the bulb, and it is on this point that they disagree and engage in argumentative interaction.

In the first part of the sequence (lines 181 to 191), Fiona proposes and elaborates a quite common (and doubly erroneous) solution to the question of the transfers, that is represented in Fig. 11.1.

The first error with this solution is that it is not necessarily the case that a model element must correspond to every object in the experimental field: It is not because there are two wires that there must be two transfers. Secondly, this solution confounds two bodies of (school physics) knowledge: concerning electricity and concerning energy. Fiona proposes that the transfers go round in a circle because she is thinking of electrical current in the circuit. In fact, there should be just one energy transfer, from battery to bulb, called *electrical work*.

During this sequence, it is clear that Gordon does not fully follow Fiona's reasoning (as shown by "wait" in line 185 and the "Mm!" in line 189); he is concentrating on his own line of thinking, as shown by his repeated insistence on determining the "mode" of transfer.

It is only when Fiona makes explicit what she is going to draw (line 192: "there, we'll do another one in the other direction") that Gordon realizes that he disagrees (line 193: "Ah, no, no, no, no!"). Fiona's defense in line 194 reveals the electrical model with which she had been thinking: "But yes it is, but the circuit, it's obviously got to be closed." However, she quickly rectifies her error, on the basis of everyday knowledge—bulbs don't store or produce energy—and retracts her thesis. In so doing (line 196; see also the later line 206), she negotiates a

TABLE 11.3

Corpus Example 2, Extract 1

N	Loc	Dialogue
		(Common solution up to this point:)

reservoir   transformer

| battery | (bulb) |

N	Loc	Dialogue
181	Gordon	So, right, now the transfers. So, the transfer
182	Fiona	The transfer, there are two
183	Gordon	The transfers. So, modes of transfer
184	Fiona	In fact we have to do an arrow in each direction. Transfer 1, transfer 2. We do a transfer like that and a transfer like that, that we'll name afterwards
185	Gordon	Then, wait, euh, so from the battery there's a transfer
186	Fiona	We've got a transfer that is uhh
187	Gordon	So that is ((inaudible)) by two conducting wires. So the first conducting wire
188	Fiona	So uhh I do an arrow like that, I put, one, transfer one, like that, Gordon?
189	Gordon	Mm!
190	Fiona	And uhh I put wire, first conducting wire? … Transfer 1, first conducting wire? … And after I put transfer 2, second conducting wire
191	Gordon	Therefore, mode of transfer. So first wire, conducting wire, you put it underneath
192	Fiona	We'll put transfer. And there, we'll do another one in the other direction, it's the second
193	Gordon	Ah, no, no, no, no!
194	Fiona	But yes it is, but the circuit, it's obviously got to be closed
195	Gordon	Yeah, but the battery
196	Fiona	Ah yes, but there isn't any energy, there isn't the case where, in fact, the bulb doesn't produce energy, so the wire that goes back to the battery, it's just for closing the circuit, it's not a transfer

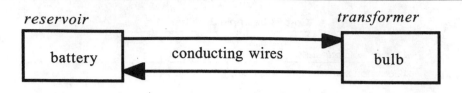

FIG. 11.1. The solution initially proposed by Fiona.

more refined meaning of the term *transfer*—the wire is not a transfer, it is just for closing the circuit—by (the beginnings of) *conceptual dissociation* (/energy/electricity/).

However, Gordon has not yet understood this conceptual difference. The continuation of their interaction is shown in Table 11.4.

From lines 197 to 209, roles in the argumentation now switch round: Gordon now defends Fiona's thesis that he had previously rejected (!) and that she has now retracted. This illustrates clearly the fact that in argumentative interactions in such problem-solving situations, students' thinking is highly volatile. We can thus not expect firm commitments to theses and strictly adversarial argumentation. Gordon is now fixed on the idea that there must be two "transfers," otherwise the circuit would not be closed, and it would not "work." In countering this view, Fiona further refines what is meant by *transfer* and the dissociation between energy and electricity (see line 206). It is only when Gordon establishes the link between what Fiona is saying and his previous insistence on the idea of "mode" that his view wavers: (line 215) "Ah yes, in fact there's only one mode of transfer, it's true." Fiona sums up their discussion in line 221: "The issue is, I really agree with you that there is a second wire that closes the circuit, but the question is whether it's a transfer or not." Gordon now understands, so concedes (line 223): "No but ok. No, it's not a transfer."

In summary, this sequence of argumentative interaction provides a clear example of negotiation of meaning, turning around the terms and notions *transfer* and *mode*, that is associated with a *gradual* dissociation of concepts and types of knowledge relating to energy and electricity. It is important to note that both students do not achieve these dissociations at the same time; in fact, their intersubjective differences in points of view create a tension that drives these discursive operations. Within the argumentative interaction, the function of these discursive operations is firstly for one student to retract his or her initial point of view, and then, when it is adopted by the interlocutor, to provide a counterargument against it. Conceptual dissociation, therefore, has a critical or counterattacking function in this example, whereas in the previous one, it had a basically defensive function.

TABLE 11.4

Corpus Example 2, Extract 2

N	Loc	Dialogue
197	Gordon	Yeah but hang on, ok but wait, there's a negative pole. So, it goes from the negative pole to the negative pole? And from the positive pole to the positive pole?
198	Fiona	No, from the positive pole to the negative pole
199	Gordon	That's exactly what I thought!
200	Fiona	((laughs))
	<...>	
206	Fiona	No but look, there really is a second transfer for closing the circuit. But in fact, it's not a transfer, it's just for closing the circuit, so that the energy can go through.
207	Gordon	Hang on, the current circulates from the positive pole of the battery to the negative pole of the bulb, but from that thing there, on the stand ...
208	Fiona	And then after, it comes back from the positive to the negative or from the negative to the positive. Mmm.
209	Gordon	plus, minus and plus to minus ... Well then yes it is, that's right, there are two transfers!
210	Fiona	But no, there aren't two transfers.
211	Gordon	But yes there are!
212	Fiona	But no, because look, you can't ... or else ...
213	Gordon	But in any case, if there's only one, it won't work, I'm sorry
214	Fiona	Well yes, but that's all you keep on saying
215	Gordon	Ah yes, in fact there's only one mode of transfer, it's true
216	Fiona	No, there's only one transfer because
217	Gordon	The mode of transfer it's ...
218	Fiona	Look, you go from the plus to the minus
219	Gordon	Yes, yes no but
220	Fiona	After that it goes from the plus to the minus, minus plus. Yes, no but what I mean to say is ...
221	Gordon	There's only one mode of transfer that ...
222	Fiona	The issue is, I really agree with you that there is a second wire that closes the circuit, but the question is whether it's a transfer or not
223	Gordon	No but ok. No, it's not a transfer
224	Fiona	Because she says clearly that a transfer is the thing that
225	Gordon	It's a sort of, it's a mode
226	Fiona	It's a system ... a transfer

THIRD EXAMPLE: CONCEPTUAL DISSOCIATION
AS AN ARGUMENTATIVE OUTCOME

The third and final example that we discuss is taken from a corpus of computer-mediated interactions produced by students using the CONNECT Computer-Supported Collaborative Learning environment (Baker, de Vries, & Lund, 1999; de Vries, Lund, & Baker, 2002). Although such typewritten and synchronous interactions, carried out via the Internet, are different in many significant respects from spoken face-to-face interactions (Clark & Brennan, 1991), our example shows that discursive operations can occur in them similar to those already discussed. In fact, CONNECT was specifically designed to favor the production of argumentative and explanatory interactions, bearing on scientific notions.

CONNECT comprises two interfaces, on the first of which two students compare their individual texts, written to solve a specific problem, and engage in a typewritten discussion whilst so doing. On the second interface, the students can write a common text on the basis of their individual texts. We carried out a study with secondary school students (aged 16–17 years) performing a task that involves modeling sound in physics, using a molecular model. The students are asked to write a text that explains sound in terms of movements of molecules, for the following experimental situation:

> Two tambourines, T1 and T2, are hanging from a support, a small ball suspended from support touches skin of T2. When the skin of T1 is struck, the small ball resting on the skin of T2 moves. Consider three zones of molecules, from left to right, between T1 and T2: A (against T1), B (in between A and C), C (against T2).
>
> Question: What happens to the molecules near tambourine 1, the molecules in between the two tambourines, and the molecules near tambourine 2 (A, B, and C in the figure)? What changes in the behavior of the little ball when tambourine is hit harder with the stick? Using two tambourines with a lower sound having a skin that is much less tight, what changes in the behavior of the skin of the second tambourine when hitting the first?

From the point of view of studying argumentation about scientific notions, this task is interesting because students typically have a range of different conceptions with respect to it—sound as a type of wind, left to right displacement of molecules, and so on (Linder & Erickson, 1989; Maurines, 1998)—that create a wide potential space of debate.

In the extract analyzed next, the students discuss two segments of their individual texts. On the first interface of CONNECT, the students are invited to express their attitudes (using check boxes) with respect to all segments of their own and their partners' texts, in terms of either "YES," "NO," or "?". We required them to do this so that they would read the texts attentively, and so that combinations of attitudes could focus their discussion. In Table 11.5, the two text segments are shown, together with the students' expressed attitudes. It is interesting to remark, from the point of view of social dimensions of argumentation, that Andrew does not express a direct "NO" with respect to Boris' sentence, but rather an ambiguous and noncommittal "?".

Table 11.6 shows an extract from the student's computer-mediated interaction that is initiated by the apparently paradoxical nature of Boris' statement that the tambourine skin can be more easily moved, yet the ball moves less. In fact, the meaning of the verb "to move" will be an object of negotiation in the ensuing debate, because one conceptual difficulty associated with sound is that it is a type of *movement (propagation) of a movement (vibration)* of molecules. The students will thus have to dissociate these two specific types of movement.

It appears that what Boris initially means by "move" is amplitude, that is, the extent to which the skin of the tambourine will stretch outwards, as shown by his defense of his claim (Table 11.6, line 44), according to which the slack skin will "move more" (i.e., a long way outwards), but will wrap around the little ball, thus making it "move less."

Andrew's attack, in line 45, reveals that he is working with a different meaning of "move," as *vibration*, a specific type of movement. In fact, in the original French of this transcription, the students both use, up to this point, a verb from everyday language (*bouger*, to move) to describe movement, a more scientific term that also exists in French in the form of a noun (*mouvement* = movement). The negotiation of meaning of "movement" and "to move" is therefore carried out in a situation where the following intersubjective difference obtains:

Boris: "to move" (bouger) = amplitude.

Andrew: "to move" (bouger) = vibration.

In line 46, Boris appeals to an everyday analogy (with a piece of cloth) in an attempt to defend his point of view, in fact, trying to relativize the question: "difficult to know ..." In his reply (line 47), Andrew, in fact, explicitly dissociates "vibration" and "movement," and Boris takes up this proposal (line 48), agreeing that although "vibration" and "move-

TABLE 11.5

Text Segments Discussion and Attitudes Expressed by the Students

Student	Sentence discussed (text)	Attitudes expressed	
		Andrew	*Boris*
Andrew	7. The less tight skin of tambourine 2 absorbs vibrations more, and so vibrates less itself	**YES**	**YES**
Boris	7. The less tight skin can be more easily moved by the molecules, but the ball moves less	**?**	**YES**

TABLE 11.6

Corpus Extract (Two Tambourines Problem)

N	T (m:s)	Loc	Dialogue / actions on the interface
43	16:19	Andrew	If the skin moves more, why does the ball move less?
44	19:15	Boris	the skin moves more because it is less tight, but the air pressure exerted is the same. This skin therefore "wraps around" the form of the ball.
45	21:24	Andrew	Don't agree. In my opinion, the skin of T2 moves less (see my phrase 7).
46	27:20	Boris	difficult to know once one looks at the skin, one sees it move more that the one with the tighter skin when you hit something hard, which is stable in space, it won't move, whilst a piece of cloth that's not under tension, for example, yes [it will move]
47	33:14	Andrew	Another explanation: take a string that's not under tension. If you touch it, it's going to move a lot but it won't vibrate much. By contrast, a string under tension, like a guitar one, it will move little but vibrate a lot.
48	36:37	Boris	i agree with your 7 but at one point I thought that you didn't agree with mine. For me the two phrases are right, it's just that simply they don't explain the same thing (vibrations and movements)
49	39:23	Andrew	NO. If a less tense skin vibrates less, itm movesss more, therefore the ball must move more as well.
50	40:34	Andrew	pardon, have you understood?
51	43:29	Boris	Hypothesis: with the same air force exerted on T2: a tight skin will vibrate more than a less tight skin but will move less than the latter
52	43:37	Andrew	[attitude "YES" expressed with respect to sentence 1 of Boris: ìlt perturbs the air molecules contained between t1 and t2. They move further away from each other.ì]
53	43:44	Andrew	Yes
54	43:47	Andrew	Yes
55	47:55	Boris	as for the ball, I think that it would move less with the less tight skin since the skin would vibrate less so it would "transmit" a lot less vibrations.
56	0:01	—	[change to phase 3—cooperative writing task interface]
57	0:33	Boris	Agreed?
58	1:17	Andrew	Maybe

Note. In this table, the "dialogue" column is a direct translation from the original French that was typed by the students themselves on the chat interface. In translation we have attempted ment" (now the scientific form of the noun, in French) are not the same (conceptual dissociation), both of the students' claims can be "right." In his reply (line 49), Andrew rejects this attempt to dissolve the verbal conflict, and, in fact, further refines the difference between vibration and movement: *if something vibrates less, it moves more.* This is a third proposed interpretation for "movement," as *frequency* (the number of times the string moves back and forth in a certain time). The argumentation sequence ends with no clear agreement: "Agreed?" "Maybe."

In summary, in this argumentation sequence, we can see the students attempting to negotiate shared meanings for the terms *vibration* and *movement* (in its everyday and scientific terminologies), and thus to dissociate the related concepts. This is, in fact, a crucial distinction to be made in order that sound can be understood as a movement (displacement) of a vibration of molecules, not successfully achieved in this case.

SYNTHESIS AND CONCLUSIONS

In this chapter, we argued that argumentative interactions put special sociointeractional pressure on people who engage in them to define what they mean, and thus to perform certain discursive operations: negotiation of meaning, conceptual dissociation, and conceptual association. In order to defend or attack a view or thesis, its meaning must be more precisely defined; an attack or defense may be effective under one interpretation of a thesis but not under another. A discursive operation is a transformation of meaning, understanding, or concepts, viewed as indistinguishable wholes with their linguistic counterparts, that is accomplished in and by discourse. It is a means by which discourse does work on meanings. Negotiation of meaning involves adjusting meanings in order to attain mutual understanding, conceptual dissociation involves distinguishing concepts from each other, and conceptual association involves subsuming concepts under more general ones.

Modeling involves adjusting different levels of description (model, experimental field) in order that a match can be found between them. In order to do this, different types of (school-learned and everyday) knowledge need to be brought to bear on the question. A prerequisite for modeling is to be able to clearly distinguish these different types of description and knowledge in the first place, and in cooperative modeling situations, language necessarily plays an important role in these processes.

We conclude that the discursive operations described here, at work in argumentative interactions, can precisely play an important role in learning to model because they can enable types of descriptions and knowledge to be differentiated from each other, and more clearly understood, this being a prerequisite for modeling.

Analysis of three extracts from interaction corpora collected in cooperative modeling situations revealed that the discursive operations described here function essentially as means of defense against argumentative attacks, or as attempts to "dissolve" verbal conflicts. In the first extract, one student dissociated elastic and inelastic impacts as a means of enabling each student to be "right," then associated air friction with "loss at impact," claiming that both were types of "friction." In the second extract, the students negotiated the meaning of the term *transfer*—of energy or of electricity?—in order to gradually dissociate these two types of knowledge. In the third extract, the students attempted to untangle complex semantic relations between the concepts of "vibration" and of "movement," with the latter appearing in everyday and technical language forms.

It was clear that the discursive operations carried out in these argumentative contexts did not necessarily lead to elaboration of more refined, or normatively preferred, meanings of concepts underlying modeling tasks. Thus, in analogy with the title of Toulmin's (1958) classic work, *The Uses of Argument*, we should perhaps speak here of *The Uses and Abuses of Argumentation*, inasmuch as students can use it to attempt to avoid or else to address complex conceptual issues. However, because it is well known that students often solve problems without genuine understanding of underlying notions (Driver, Guesne, & Tiberghien, 1985), we can at least say that the interactive processes and discursive operations we described are potentially constructive, given that they do, in fact, work on a conceptual-linguistic (i.e., discursive) plane.

Argumentative interactions are therefore to be seen as embodying interactive and discursive processes that create potential opportunities for conceptual learning, rather than as cooperative learning mechanisms *per se*. The most important question for further research, therefore, is to understand how to create situations, involving direct teacher intervention and/or specially adapted pedagogical materials, in which this potential can be realized.

ACKNOWLEDGMENTS

I would like to thank Andrée Tiberghien for teaching me the little I know about modeling, Andrée Tiberghien and Françoise Langlois for allowing me to use the first corpus analyzed in this chapter, Andrée Tiberghien and Jean Gréa for their collaboration in collecting the second corpus, and Kristine Lund and Erica de Vries for collaboration in collecting the third corpus analyzed here. Many thanks to Paul Brna for organizing the workshop that stimulated me to write this chapter in the first place, and for his tireless encouragement and patience. This research is financed by the CNRS and Université Lumière Lyon 2.

REFERENCES

Baker, M. J. (1996). Argumentation et co-construction des connaissances [Argumentation and co-construction of knowledge]. *Interaction et Cognitions, 2*(3), 157–191.

Baker, M. J. (1999). Argumentation and constructive interaction. In P. Coirier & J. Andriessen (Eds.), *Foundations of argumentative text processing* (pp. 179–202). Amsterdam: University of Amsterdam Press.

Baker, M. J., de Vries, E., & Lund, K. (1999). Designing computer-mediated epistemic interactions. In S. P. Lajoie & M. Vivet (Eds.), *Artificial intelligence in education* (pp. 139–146). Amsterdam: IOS Press.

Bakhtine, M. (1977). *Le Marxisme et la Philosophie du Langage* [Marxism and philosophy of language]. (Original work first published in 1929 under the name of V. N. Volochinov). Paris: Les Editions de Minuit.

Chi, M. T. H., Bassok, M., Lewis, M. W., Reimann, P., & Glaser, R. (1989). Self-explanations: how students study and use examples in learning to solve problems. *Cognitive Science, 13*(2), 145–182.

Chi, M. T. H., & VanLehn, K. A. (1991). The content of physics self-explanations. *Journal of the Learning Sciences, 1*(1), 69–105.

Clark, H. H. (1996). *Using language.* Cambridge: Cambridge University Press.

Clark, H. H. (1999). On the origins of conversation. *Verbum, XXI*(2), 147–161.

Clark, H. H., & Brennan, S. E. (1991). Grounding in communication. In L. B. Resnick, J. M. Levine, & S. D. Teasley (Eds.), *Perspectives on socially shared cognition* (pp. 127–149). Washington DC: American Psychological Association.

Devi, R., Tiberghien, A., Baker, M. J., & Brna, P. (1996). Modeling students' construction of energy models in physics. *Instructional Science, 24,* 259–293.

de Vries, E., Lund, K., & Baker, M. J. (2002). Computer-mediated epistemic dialogue: Explanation and argumentation as vehicles for understanding scientific notions. *Journal of the Learning Sciences, 11*(1), 63–103.

diSessa, A. (1982). Unlearning Aristotelian physics: A study of knowledge-based learning. *Cognitive Science, 6*(1), 37–75.

Driver, R., Guesne, E., & Tiberghien, A. (Eds.) (1985). *Children's ideas in science.* Milton Keynes, England: Open University Press.

Edwards, D. (1993). But what do children really think?: Discourse analysis and conceptual content in children's talk. *Cognition and Instruction, 11*(3 & 4), 207–225.

Edwards, D., & Potter, J. (1992). *Discursive psychology.* London: Sage.

Gardenförs, P. (Ed.). (1992). *Belief revision.* Cambridge: Cambridge University Press.

Golder, C. (1996). *Le développement des discours argumentatifs* [The development of argumentative discourse]. Lausanne: Delachaux & Niestlé.

Grootendorst, R. (1999). Innocence by dissociation. A pragma-dialectical analysis of the fallacy of incorrect dissociation in the Vatican document "We remember: A reflection on the Shoah." In F. H. van Eemeren, R. Grootendorst, J. A. Blair, & C. A. Willard (Eds.), *Proceedings of the Fourth International Conference of the International Society for the Study of Argumentation* (pp. 286–289). Amsterdam: SIC SAT.

Harré, R., & Gillet, G. (1994). *The discursive mind.* London: Sage.

Langlois, F., & Tiberghien, A. (1990). Résolution de Problèmes de Physique par des Elèves des Lycées. *Rapport Interne, LIRDIS* [Resolution of physics problems by secondary school children. LIRDIS Internal Report]. (Université Lyon-I) et Laboratoire CNRS-IRPEACS.

Linder, C. J., & Erickson, G. L. (1989). A study of tertiary physics students' conceptualizations of sound. *International Journal of Science Education, 11,* 491–501.

Maurines, L. (1998, January). Les élèves et la propagation des signaux sonores [Students and the propogation of sound signals]. *Bulletin de l'Union des Physiciens, 92,* 1–22.

Muntig, P., & Turnbull, W. *(1998).* Conversational structure and facework in arguing. *Journal of Pragmatics, 29,* 225–256.

Naess, A. (1966). *Communication and argument: Elements of applied semantics*. London: Allen & Unwin.

Nonnon, E. (1996). Activités argumentatives et élaboration de connaissances nouvelles: le dialogue comme espace d'exploration [Argumentative activities and elaboration of new knowledge]. *Langue Française, 112*, 67–87.

Perelman, C., & Olbrechts-Tyteca, L. (1988). *Traité de l'argumentation. La nouvelle rhétorique* [Treatise on argumentation: The new rhetoric]. Bruxelles: Editions de l'Université de Bruxelles. (Original work published 1958.)

Saussure, F. de (1972). *Cours de Linguistique Générale* [Course on general linguistics]. Paris: Payot. (Original work published 1915.)

Tiberghien, A. (1994). Modeling as a basis for analyzing teaching–learning situations. *Learning and Instruction, 4*, 71–87.

Tiberghien, A. (1996). Construction of prototypical situations in teaching the concept of energy. In G. Welford, J. Osborne, & P. Scott (Eds.), *Research in science education in Europe* (pp. 100–114). London: Falmer Press.

Toulmin, S. E. (1958). *The uses of argument*. Cambridge: Cambridge University Press.

Vignaux, G. (1988). *Le discours acteur du monde: Enonciation, argumentation et cognition* [Discourse as an actor in the world: Utterance, argumentation and cognition]. Paris: Ophrys.

Vignaux, G. (1990). A cognitive model of argumentation. In F. H. van Eemeren, R. Grootendorst, J. A. Blair, & C. A. Willard (Eds.), *Proceedings of the second international conference on argumentation* (pp. 303–310). Amsterdam: SIC SAT.

Walton, D. N. (1989). *Informal logic*. Cambridge: Cambridge University Press.

Walton, D. N. (1992). *Plausible argument in everyday conversation*. New York: State University of New York Press.

Author Index

Subject Index